MW00390769

ELEONORA'S FALCON

WILDLIFE BEHAVIOR AND ECOLOGY
George B. Schaller, Editor

ELEONORA'S FALCON

Adaptations to Prey and Habitat in a Social Raptor

Hartmut Walter

THE UNIVERSITY OF CHICAGO PRESS
Chicago and London

HARTMUT WALTER is associate professor in the Department of Geography at the University of California, Los Angeles. The author of numerous scholarly papers, Walter has been invited by the sheikhs of Oman and Abu Dhabi to study their private falcon collections.

The University of Chicago Press, Chicago 60637
The University of Chicago Press, Ltd., London

Printed in the United States of America
83 82 81 80 79   54321

Library of Congress Cataloging in Publication Data

Walter, Hartmut, 1940–
  Eleonora's falcon.

  (Wildlife behavior and ecology)
  Bibliography: p.
  Includes index.
  1. Eleonora's falcon.   2. Birds of prey—
Behavior.   3. Birds—Behavior.   I. Title.
QL696.F34W34   598.9'1   78–14933
ISBN 0–226–87229–7

For my parents

Contents

ACKNOWLEDGMENTS xi

1 STUDYING FALCONS 1
   Background 2
   Study Aims 3
   Itinerary and Study Plan 4
   Field Identification 5

2 GEOGRAPHY 12
   Distribution 12
   Breeding Habitats 13
   Population Status 23

3 POPULATION ECOLOGY 32
   Colony Size and Structure 32
   Clutch Size and Breeding Success 51
   Egg-laying, Incubation, and Hatching Time 59
   Growth Rates of the Young 67
   Mortality and Its Causes 77

4 THE HUNTING OF MIGRANT BIRDS DURING
THE BREEDING SEASON 84
   Division of Labor 84
   Hunting Area, Period, and Techniques 85

5 BIRD MIGRATION IN THE FALCON'S BREEDING AREAS 113
   Structure of Bird Migration 115
   Eleonora's Falcon and the Migration Pulse 122
   Conclusions 130

6 A FURTHER ANALYSIS OF RAPTOR/PREY INTERACTIONS 134
   Hunting Success 134
   Selective Hunting 138

Killing the Prey 141
Antiraptor Behavior of Prey Species 143
Hunting Behavior from April to July 143
Switch from Insect-Hawking to Bird-Hunting 149

7 THE FALCON'S PREY   159
Methodology   159
Nature of Prey Remains 161
Insects and Other Nonbird Food 163
Analysis of Bird Remains 165
Prey Remains at Paximada and Mogador 168
Prey Biomass and Falcon Energetics 177
Impact of Eleonora's Falcon on Bird Migration 184
Are Prey Remains a Mirror of Migration Density? 188
Analysis of Prey Migration Patterns 189
Summary and General Conclusions 200

8 PATTERNS OF FALCON BEHAVIOR 203
Study Methods 203
Sexual Behavior 205
Territorial Behavior 218
Agonistic Behavior 237
Acoustic Behavior of Eleonora's Falcon 254
Behavioral Development of Young Falcons 262
General Discussion 266

9 THE NONBREEDING SEASON 270
Departure from Breeding Areas 270
Fall Migration 272
Geography of the Winter Range 277
Falcon Ecology and Behavior 280
Spring Migration and Return to the Mediterranean
Region 285
Geographical Dispersion of Juveniles and Subadults during
Spring and Summer Months 288
Discussion 290

10 EVOLUTIONARY ECOLOGY 295
Comparing Atlantic and Aegean Populations 295

"Absent" Caribbean Niche 299
Origin of Eleonora's Falcon 303

11 HUMAN IMPACT 310
Discovery of Eleonora's Falcon 310
Princess Eleonora of Arborea 312
Medieval Falconry in Sardinia 313
Fishermen and Other Predators 314
Indirect Effects of Human Endeavor 316
Future of Eleonora's Falcon 321

12 ELEONORA'S FALCON AND OTHER BIRDS OF PREY:
A COMPARATIVE ANALYSIS 323
Adaptive Value and Function of Morphological
Characters 324
Dispersion, Territoriality, and Sociability 330
Selection and Occupancy of Nest Sites 341
Breeding Behavior 343
Predator/Prey Relationships 345
Reversed Sexual Dimorphism in Raptors 347
Raptor Research 360

APPENDIXES 363
A Tables 25–38 364
B Hunting, Feeding, and Food-caching Behavior 382
C Records of *Falco eleonorae* from Madagascar, Réunion,
and Mauritius 383
D Genetic Base of Color Dimorphism 384

REFERENCES 385

INDEX 401

Plates follow page 114

Acknowledgments

My falcon studies have brought me into contact with interested and generous people in many countries over some twelve years. It is a particular pleasure to thank all of them for their great hospitality and their involvement and support before, during, and after my field projects.

Most of all, I have to thank Dr. Dietrich Ristow (Munich), who dared to accompany me on my first island stay in the Aegean Sea; I will remember his courage and dedication with deep appreciation. I am also greatly indebted to my wife Geraldine and my brother Ernst Christian for their participation in the Moroccan field studies.

In Germany I was greatly assisted by Dr. K. H. Buchholz, who provided the initial spark for the whole study by telling me of "a small cliff in the blue sea inhabited by scores of dark falcons." The Ornithological Department of the Museum Alexander Koenig in Bonn, under the direction of Prof. Dr. G. Niethammer and Dr. H. E. Wolters, with the assistance of Mrs. Adam, offered me work space and valuable aid on taxonomic questions. Of particular importance were the friendship and support offered by Helmut and Cilly Linke and by Hans Deetjen (Bonn).

In Greece I am indebted to B. Antipas of the Hellenic Society for the Protection of Nature, to Max E. Hodge, FSO (now in Arizona), to former mayor Dr. G. Katapotis, and to fisherman Karalambos and his friends in eastern Crete, who provided the vital food and water supplies to the falcon islands under often adverse weather conditions; today they are the trusted and enthusiastic guardians of several falcon colonies.

In Sardinia, I am grateful for the long-standing collaboration with Prof. R. Stefani and Helmar Schenk in Cagliari, and for my close friendship with Franco Ruggieri and Marcella and Gabriele Severino.

On Madagascar, Ambassador A. B. Vestring, J. R. Challinor, R. J. Russell, and Mr. Pieninck were not only extraordinarily hospitable but also so helpful that I managed to find "my" falcons on this vast minicontinent within a short period of time.

In the gulf region, I am greatly indebted to Dr. J. B. Platt of the Sulman Falcon Center in Bahrain, to Ralph H. Daly, OBE, and his assistant M. D. Gallagher in Muscat (Oman) for their encouragement and enthusiasm regarding the breeding of the sooty falcon in the gulf, to His Highness Shaikh Zayed bin Sultan al Nahayan, president of the United Arab Emirates, and to Abdul Rahman Khaleq, Abdul Khader, and Dr. M. Morsy Abdullah in Abu Dhabi for the promotion of my research. Very helpful also was the assistance of Ambassador H. Neumann, Dr. P. Schmidt, W. Grohs, and R. Behrendt (now in Bonn).

On Cyprus, I received truly outstanding support at the Royal Air Force base at Akrotiri through the kind and highly efficient support of Air Vice-Marshal R. D. Austen-Smith, CB, DFC, RAF, of Group Captain D. Cook, OBE, RAF, of the commander of the Eighty-fourth Squadron (Helicopters), of Squadron Leader S. Collins, of my pilots, flight lieutenants J. Plumley and A. Campbell, and of the commander of the Port Squadron RCT, Major S. Birch. Special thanks go to Squadron Leader Richard Foers, RAF, who organized my stay at Cape Gata and was a seasoned and enthusiastic guide to the most interesting avifauna of Cyprus.

Among the ornithologists who have contributed comments or information to this study, I would like to express my thanks to D. W. Anderson (Davis, California), F. Bernis (Madrid), G. Bologna (Rome), G. Cant (New York), K. Curry-Lindahl (Nairobi), A. Forbes-Watson (Nairobi), F. Goethe (Wilhelmshaven), T. Howell (Los Angeles), V. Jovanović (Belgrade), E. Moltoni (Milan), J. Steinbacher (Frankfurt a.M.), E. Stresemann (Berlin), R. Vaughan (formerly Hull, England), and G. Watson (Washington, D. C.).

In the United States, my friend Dr. Luis Baptista from the Moore Laboratory of Ornithology at Occidental College (Los Angeles) has helped in many ways since we first met at Berkeley in 1967. His laboratory greatly assisted with the analysis of falcon vocalizations. Curator Lloyd Kiff of the Western Foundation of Vertebrate Zoology (Brentwood, Los Angeles) assisted with raptor literature and the measurement of eggshell thickness. Finally, I greatly appreciate the research and technical support offered to me at the University of California at Los Angeles (UCLA) over the past six years. In particular, my colleagues and students at the Department of Geography have not only tolerated but actively supported my bird studies at all times. Special thanks go to the departmental secretaries, Carol, Barbara, Evelyn, and Cynthia, for not giving up on my handwriting. This book owes a great deal to the graphic arts specialist of this department, Noel L. Diaz, who prepared the drawings and most of the figures with his usual expertise, artistic style, and enthusiasm. I am very grateful indeed for his collaboration.

The various parts of this study on falcon ecology and behavior were sponsored and financed by the Committee for Research and Exploration of the National Geographic Society (Washington, D.C.), by two research grants from UCLA, and by the "Studienstiftung des Deutschen Volkes" and the "Deutsche Forschungsgemeinschaft" during the initial stages in 1965–69. I deeply appreciate this assistance and the personal interest shown by the officers of these institutions and foundations.

Through Eleonora's falcon I have found a number of dear friends. Some of them will be happy to learn that this book finally exists. I hope its content—for which I take full responsibility—will reward them for their patience and generosity and will foster new friendships among those who share the love of birds and the never-ending curiosity that underlies all scientific endeavor.

1 Studying Falcons

Birds have aroused the curiosity and admiration of countless generations since the ancient civilizations of Egypt and Greece. The fascination of observing and studying birds is well known. It is not merely their ability to fly and the ease with which they move about that attracts us; we are drawn by the beauty of their flight, by their colors and sounds, and by the grace and harmony of their movements. We encounter birds nearly everywhere on earth, and they seem easy to understand and to identify with. Unlike the mammals, for instance, which rely heavily on their acute sense of smell for orientation and social communication, birds perceive their surroundings visually and acoustically—much the same as humans do. I feel that this relationship has greatly helped us to learn about avian ecology and behavior. As we attempt to understand human dependence on the terrestrial ecosphere, birds are prime targets of comparative research on interactions between populations and their environments.

This book deals with a species of raptor that has adapted to a rather unusual constellation of environmental factors, including kind of prey, physical habitat, breeding period, hunting strategy, and coexistence in a colony. More than in many other bird species, the key factors of survival—the vital threads tying a species to its physical and organic environment—are laid out with a clarity that proves this little-known falcon occupies a unique ecological niche.

This book therefore should interest not only the bird enthusiast and friend of the raptors but, even more, the ecologist and anyone else interested in the many ways this bird has adapted to prey and habitat. Rather than taking a piecemeal approach to the intricate web uniting this bird and its complex environment, I have attempted to produce a modern version of the classic natural-

1

history study. This, I believe, is the perspective that will best promote an understanding of this falcon's role in its environment.

BACKGROUND

Falcons have fascinated kings, poets, hunters, and others for thousands of years. Their power, their aesthetic appeal, their apparent speed, and their control of energy and movement have contributed to this interest and love. For many years, falcons have been man's companions in the more sophisticated forms of hunting, just as have horses and dogs.

More recently, falcons have achieved a new importance in the search for a better life for human beings, serving as indicators of environmental quality. Occupying a prominent position at the top of various ecological food chains, they depend on the many organisms at the lower ecological levels. The well-being of falcons thus reflects the health of those lower levels.

Many raptor species have declined over the past thirty years. Several falcon species, particularly the peregrine falcon (*Falco peregrinus*), have become prominent research targets for students of pesticide residues and for ecologists interested in wildlife conservation. In spite of this, we still know little about the ecology and behavior of most falcons in their natural surroundings.

This book attempts to portray one of the least-known European species, Eleonora's falcon (*Falco eleonorae*). This raptor has the distinction of being one of the last bird species discovered by science in Europe, and it is noted for its late mating season and unusual prey.

Eleonora's falcon was first described from Sardinia in 1839; it was named after a Sardinian princess of the Middle Ages. It occurs in two quite different phases. The species breeds in colonies of from two to two hundred pairs across the Mediterranean and parts of the adjacent Atlantic Ocean, and the breeding season occurs later in the year than in almost any other European or North American bird species. Falcon chicks normally hatch in the middle or at the end of August and are fed with small forest and scrub birds flying across the sea on their annual migration from Europe to Africa. Most breeding colonies of Eleonora's falcon lie on rather isolated and inaccessible cliffs, often in rough and dangerous waters. From December to March the species is absent from its breeding areas; it appears to migrate to southeast Africa, where it has been found on Madagascar and the Mascarene Islands. These restricted winter quarters are another unusual factor, since even the populations of Atlantic colonies in the Canaries and Morocco appear to migrate to and from Madagascar not by crossing the entire African continent but by flying along its northern and eastern coastlines.

STUDY AIMS

This study was initially undertaken simply to throw light on the breeding biology of this gregarious falcon and to define accurately the synchronization of its breeding cycle with Mediterranean bird migration. In the end it became a work of much wider scope: it aimed to assess the ecological and behavioral characteristics of various breeding colonies of the species, to study the falcon in its winter quarters in Madagascar, to see how such an aggressive bird exists in a high-density environment, and so forth. This led to the search for the nature of the adaptive mechanisms and the evolution of the unique ecological niche of Eleonora's falcon since the polar ice cap began to retreat about 18,000 B.C.

The specific objectives were to study (1) the reproductive cycle and breeding success; (2) hunting strategies and prey composition; (3) social behavior within a falcon population; (4) the comparative ecological and behavioral characteristics of two major colonies; (5) the role of local terrain and of continentwide ecological dynamics in influencing falcon ecology and behavior; and (6) the evolutionary pathway and ecological niche of this species through a comparative analysis of other raptors, particularly other falcons.

In the beginning I was particularly interested in predator/prey relationships. Many authors had found the remains of migrant birds at the falcons' nesting sites, but nobody could explain how, when, and where they had been captured. Later I began to investigate social organization, particularly the question of intraspecific coexistence. This book is a report of my research into these questions of adaptation to prey, habitat, and social life and attempts to describe and explain the major ecological and behavioral patterns that have created and helped to maintain Eleonora's falcon and its niche.

ITINERARY AND STUDY PLAN

Field observations were primarily collected in two of the colonies of Eleonora's falcon that are known to be the largest during the reproductive season. Smaller colonies were studied for short periods only, to arrive at some comparative data on falcon behavior. Nine expeditions and research trips were undertaken between 1965 and 1977, to several colonies in the Aegean Sea, on Cyprus, Sardinia, Mallorca, and two colonies along the Atlantic coast of Morocco.

I visited the island of Paximada near Crete in 1965 and 1966. During the late summer of 1965, I was able to study the breeding cycle and the feeding and development of falcon chicks in detail from day to day (10 August to 23 September, and 5–10 October); I also observed hunting behavior and bird migration and collected the prey remains at most nests, with some regularity at twenty-two "study nests." I made behavioral observations by monitoring a "study population" on the "upper slope" of Paximada, and a small blind I built some 6 m in front of a nest site (no. 8) made it possible to monitor parental behavior both by sight and by sound. I visited Paximada again in January 1966 (no falcons were present) and in July 1966 before the beginning of the egg-laying period.

In August and September 1966 I studied a colony at the western end of this species' world distribution. Here, on the Isles of Mogador, I collected prey remains and relevant breeding and hunting data in order to compare the Paximada colony with this Moroccan one. In September 1966 my friend H. Deetjen and I discovered a new falcon colony north of Mogador, and in October of the same year I paid a brief visit to Mallorca's breeding sites.

Mogador became the focus of more research on Eleonora's falcon in the summer of 1969; although I was severely handicapped by a boat accident and other misfortunes, I collected a large amount of data on social interaction, agonistic behavior, and communication among Eleonora's falcons. In recent years I have concentrated on the hunting strategies of different falcon populations. In 1974 I monitored a colony near Sardinia; in 1977 I was able to observe some of the colonies of Eleonora's falcon on Mallorca and on Cyprus. In December 1973 I flew to Madagascar to find the answer to some of the questions surrounding the species' winter habitat.

Most of the time, a good pair of binoculars, a pencil, and a notebook were all I required for my study. Occasionally, particularly on Paximada and in Mogador, I used tape recorders and walkie-talkies to store or follow up sudden and complex happenings in the sky or on the ground. I spent two winters and one fall working with the collections of the Museum Alexander Koenig in Bonn, identifying the mass of collected feathers and preparing my dissertation and related articles on Eleonora's falcon.

Particular study methods used will be described in the appropriate chapters. One of the guiding principles was to disturb the breeding populations as little as possible and to interfere with the falcons' activities only when no harm could be anticipated.

FIELD IDENTIFICATION

Eleonora's falcon is similar in length to the peregrine falcon (*F. peregrinus*) because of its long wings and tail, but it is much more slender in build and weighs less than half as much as a female peregrine. When it perches, the tips of its wings and tail are level. Eleonora's falcon is dichromatic, with a light and a dark color phase occurring in both sexes. There is only a slight difference in size between males and females.

Adult, Dark Phase

Entire plumage dark brown to slate black; often looks black from a distance. On the upper side the primaries show the darkest plumage, while the feathers of the lower back and tail have a lighter, ashy brown tinge. In flight, the underside of the wing shows a contrast between the lighter primaries and the very dark lesser wing coverts. In good light, the fanned tails of some birds show ten to twelve washed-out gray to buff tail bars.

Adult, Light Phase

Upper parts uniformly dark brown to slate black and ashy brown. White or cream-colored cheeks and throat with dark brown mustached stripe. From lower throat to breast, belly and undertail feathers increasingly buff to rufous, with many dark brown dots and stripes. The degree of spotting and the shading from cream to buff and rufous varies considerably from bird to bird and allows the observer to recognize individual falcons among a group of 10 to 20 birds.

A few Eleonora's falcons have been observed by Vaughan
(1961a) and myself that appeared to be intermediary to the
phases described above. Either they possess a nearly uniformly dark
underside but still show a whitish throat and cheek plus the mustached stripe, or they are uniformly dark with a lighter and
somewhat striped breast and belly.

The differentiation into two phases is a convenient and useful
morphological tool. But among the total world population of
Eleonora's falcon there appears to be a gradient from the few very
dark birds at one end of the continuum to the very light birds at
the other end, with whitish undersides and few stripes. Most falcons lie somewhere between, with light cheeks and throat; they
count as light-phased birds, although some have rather dark
breasts or bellies.

Adult, Both Phases

Characteristic are yellow greenish to bright golden talons. It has
been my experience that males' talons are always more golden
than their mates'. Similarly, the cere at the base of the beak and
the ring around the eye appeared whitish-gray and bluish in
females and lemon-tinged to golden in males. I suggest using this
coloration of the featherless body parts to determine the sex of
adult falcons during the reproductive season. Also, "at close range
the female's more powerful build, especially about the head and
bill, is noticeable" (Vaughan 1961b).

In flight, Eleonora's falcon exhibits long wings, broad at the
base, and an equally long tail. From below, perhaps the most
distinctive characters are the markedly dark underwing coverts
(fig. 1). Although this bird often assumes a typical falcon silhouette, as it glides it sometimes looks more like a small hawk,
owing to its broad, long wings.

It is usually easy to distinguish individual falcons within a small
breeding population, for there are at least twelve major variable
characters. Each falcon is likely to possess a different combination
of these characters from its mate and neighbors. Here is a list of
the twelve characters, with examples of how each may vary among
a falcon population:

1. Head (example: all dark, white spot near ear, extra-large
white cheek).

2. Beak (base grayish, bluish, or yellowish).

Fig. 1. Eleonora's falcon (*Falco eleonorae*). Adult female of the light color phase. Twelve characters are listed that may help in identifying individual falcons in a breeding colony. Adults of the light and dark color phases as well as juvenile and immature Eleonora's falcons are shown in flight.

3. Voice (vocalizations are important only if different from the average).

4. Throat (large white, lower edge dark, very dark).

5. Breast (black stripes, brown yellow ground color, much reddish).

6. Belly (light brown, strongly rufous with dark stripes, lighter than usual, without stripes).

7. Flank (reddish, buff, with or without contrasting stripes).

8. Flag (feathers all buff or rufous or with dark stripes).

9. Tarsus (color greenish or golden yellow).

10. Tail (molting?).

11. Wing (molting feathers in both wings or one wing only).

12. Posture (perches normally or lies down on breast and belly when resting).

Juvenile Characters

More than 99 percent of the fledged young resemble the light rather than the dark phase. How the molt proceeds over a period of two to three years to result in a much larger percentage of dark-phased birds has still to be established. The certitude that one can distinguish birds of light and dark phase while they are still in the nest (Stresemann 1943) has recently been confirmed: only dark-phased fledglings possess barred undertail coverts.

Almost uniformly dark fledglings are rare: apart from a few rufous spots and feather edges on back and belly, they look just like adults in the dark phase. D. Ristow has found some on Paximada, and R. Foers and I saw one such fledgling on Cyprus in September 1977.

The lightest fledglings have creamy throats, cheeks, and undersides, distinct dark head caps, creamy necks and napes, light stripes over the eyes, and dark mustaches. All feathers on the backs and shoulders have light-colored margins. Tail feathers have a dozen distinct bars. In flight, wing and tail bars are clearly visible from below.

The darkest fledglings have a buff to rufous ground color on throat, breast, and belly. Their head caps are rufous brown with many thin black streaks, and the cheeks are also streaked black. Tails, wings, and upper parts are as above, but the light parts of the feathers are more rufous. Some of those fledglings will turn into dark-phased adults. Others turn into rather rufous and dark-masked light-phased Eleonora's falcons.

Immature Plumage

The year-old falcons have already molted their primaries, which in flight still show some four to six light bars from below. The tail is already like that in adult birds or still barred like the juvenile bird. Some birds possess slightly elongated central tail feathers. There is some buff on the front and between beak and eye. From above, the shoulder and back are much lighter than the rest of the body (even buff, owing to light feather margins; fig. 1).

General Remarks

Eleonora's falcon cannot be confused with any other European bird of prey. The closest in appearance to the juvenile and immature Eleonora's falcon is the juvenile peregrine of the Mediterranean form *F. peregrinus brookei*. Its general color is very similar indeed, but its mustache is wider and its tail is shorter, displaying six light bars at the most (plate 4).

On migration in the African and Arabian region, our species can be confused with its nearest relative, the sooty falcon (*F. concolor*). In Madagascar I found it impossible to distinguish a dark-phased Eleonora's falcon in flight from the many uniformly gray and dark-colored sooty falcons. The light phase could be confused with the light plumage of juvenile sooty falcons, which resemble the hobby. It seems, however, that in good light the dark underwing coverts of dark-phased Eleonora's falcons should allow identification, since they are darker than those of sooty falcons and other African falcon species.

The juveniles and immatures of both species are very similar except that the sooty falcon is a bit smaller than Eleonora's falcon.

Reversed Sexual Size Dimorphism

In most bird species the male is larger than or the same size as the female. Among birds of prey (including owls) the reverse is found: females are usually larger and heavier. In extreme cases (certain large hawks and falcons) a male may weigh one-third to one-half less than its mate.

Eleonora's falcon belongs to a group of falcons that exhibit little sexual dimorphism in size. In the field, size differences should not be taken as reliable indicators of sex. As the following data summaries indicate, there is a considerable individual variation and overlap between the sexes.

Weight

Eleven females out of twenty-three adult Eleonora's falcons that were trapped or caught by D. Ristow and myself between 18 August and 15 September 1965 (Paximada colony, Greece) weighed (in grams) 340 (2), 365 (2), 370, 400, 403, 405, 410, 419, and 450. The average weight was 388 g. I shall use 390 g as the mean weight of adult females in later sections of this book. We were not able to weigh any adult males at this colony. Data from the literature are unavailable. I estimate that males weigh about 10% less than females, that is, 350 g on the average. A young male I raised in 1965 weighed 440 g on its 32d day in October, only 310 g the following January, and 330 g in March, exactly six months after hatching.

Since I was not able to tell whether a falcon had been fasting or feeding before it was weighed, some of these data may be on the high side, including some hardly digested prey items.

Measurements

To illustrate the degree of reversed sexual size dimorphism in Eleonora's falcon I have summarized Reiser's data on 41 adult falcons (19 males, 22 females) from the Aegean Islands, listed in his *Ornis Balcanica* (1905; see accompanying table).

Sizes of Eleonora's Falcons

Length of Body Parts	Average Value	Range
Total Length		
Male	41.2 cm	37.0–43.0 cm
Female	42.6 cm	38.5–45-5 cm
Tail		
Male	19.0 cm	17.5–21.0 cm
Female	19.5 cm	17.5–21.0 cm
Wing		
Male	31.6 cm	30.0–33-5 cm
Female	32.7 cm	31.0–36.6 cm
Bill		
Male	22.5 mm	21.0–25.0 mm
Female	23.5 mm	22.0–25.0 mm

There is a large overlap in all these measurements. Even the total range is very similar between the sexes. The average values of female Eleonora's falcons exceed those of the males by less than 5%. The species exhibits only a slight degree of reversed sexual size dimorphism, a remarkable trait since several of its congeneric relatives exhibit a pronounced difference in size between female and male.

In recent years the question of the adaptive value of this dimorphism in raptors has generated a series of hotly debated hypotheses. I will examine this issue in more detail toward the end of this study after introducing all those factors that might have played a role in the selective process.

Color and Size of Falcon Eggs

The eggs of Eleonora's falcon resemble those of the European hobby falcon (*F. subbuteo*). The ground color is usually a reddish brown, but some eggs are more yellowish or whitish. Most eggs are dotted with a rather dense pattern of small spots of a darker color, and some large spots may be concentrated at the poles as well as around the center. Eggs belonging to the same clutch often display their relationship by nearly identical patterns. A beautiful color plate of a dozen eggs of different shapes and colors (natural size) can be found in Reiser's *Ornis Balcanica* (1905).

The average size of 143 eggs was 42.1 × 33.2 mm (Reiser 1905; Makatsch 1958; and data from table 36 in Appendix A). The eggshell weighs about 2 g. The weight of live eggs changes over the incubation period. I weighed some 54 eggs toward the end of their incubation time (19 and 20 August 1965, Paximada colony). The mean was 24.2 g, the range 19.5–29.5 g. The heaviest egg was also the largest one, measuring 45.0 × 36.0 mm.

The quality of falcon eggs has become crucially important in recent years. Eggshell-thinning has been observed in many species on several continents, accompanied by reduced breeding success (Ratcliffe 1967; Anderson and Hickey 1972, 1974; Peakall 1976). This can be correlated with human-generated pollutants that concentrate in the falcon's prey species. The quality of certain falcon eggs can be used as a bioindicator of the pollution status of an area where falcons live. Eggshell-thinning in Eleonora's falcon and its value in identifying pollution will be discussed in conjunction with other threats to the survival of this species (chapter 11).

2 Geography

DISTRIBUTION

Eleonora's falcon is a characteristic inhabitant of the seashores of the Mediterranean basin. Only in the western part of its range does this raptor extend into the cooler Atlantic habitats of northwest Morocco and the Canary Islands. All the currently or formerly known breeding colonies lie between long. 14°W to 33°E and lat. 43°N to 28°N, along the entire Europe-Africa boundary from the Canaries in the west to Cyprus in the east. As far as is known, there are no breeding records of this species in the Black Sea or the Caspian Sea.

Immature and other nonbreeding falcons can be found considerable distances from the seashore and from their native colony. Members of this raptor species have been shot, observed, or studied in all countries bordering the Mediterranean Sea, but not north of the Alps; I have also been unable to find any records of Eleonora's falcon in the standard ornithological reference books of Bulgaria and Rumania. The record farthest away from a known breeding colony has come from the Turkish city of Ordu (41°N, 37°52′E) on the southeast shore of the Black Sea (Ristow 1975).

Eleonora's falcon is not evenly distributed throughout its breeding range (fig. 2). This gregarious raptor occurs in a rather irregular geographical pattern. Some of its breeding colonies are within sight of neighboring ones, but some are hundreds of miles away from any other colony. This irregular dispersion is the result of two geographic phenomena. First, the many islets and islands of the Mediterranean are unevenly distributed over the basin; they cluster in large groups in the Aegean Sea, but only a few exist in the western part. Second, Eleonora's falcon breeds only on high cliffs or on top of a rocky isle's substrate. Such habitats do not occur on many miles of coastline around the Mediterranean and

12

adjacent Atlantic. They are most common on small islands. Given fifty more rocky isles in the western Mediterranean between Spain and Algeria, one could certainly expect many more breeding colonies of Eleonora's falcon in this area than there are today. Most breeding locations are either rather inaccessible to humans or in remote corners.

BREEDING HABITATS

I have yet to see a breeding habitat of Eleonora's falcon that would not be worthy of a picture postcard—towering cliffs on jewellike islands in the blue or green Mediterranean. Mallorca is typical. While tourists hastily take snapshots of the jagged rock formations at the Punta de la Troneta, beneath the vantage points of Cape Formentor (plate 8) several Eleonora's falcons are likely to chase each other up and down the pale limestone cliffs in a fantastic display of aerial acrobatics. Because of the height of the cliffs, however, they can hardly be seen without good binoculars, and their characteristic calls mingle unnoticed with the crashing of the surf and the exclamations of the tourist groups.

Other colonies lie on small offshore isles. The two classic breeding spots of this species, discovered by Alberto della Marmora, are the small rocks of Vacca and Toro off the coast of Sardinia, scarcely visible from this large island's beach in the haze and glare of the Mediterranean summer. Many Aegean colonies have been reported from similar offshore rocks that hardly classify as isles; rather, they constitute a hazard to navigation and more often than not offer only dangerous landings. On such islets Eleonora's falcon does not necessarily prefer to breed on the steepest cliffs. Krüper noted this as early as 1864, and I have found it to be true in my study colonies. The vertical cliffs, or "falaises," offer few nesting spots and are generally exposed to the prevailing winds. Eleonora's falcon prefers somewhat protected and sheltered breeding habitats, but continued harassment and predation seem to force the species from such preferred sites to safer habitats on steep cliffs.

Since the members of a colony commonly utilize an area of 20 to 50 km around breeding sites during some part of the summer and fall months, a description follows of the general character and environment of the falcon colonies I have studied.

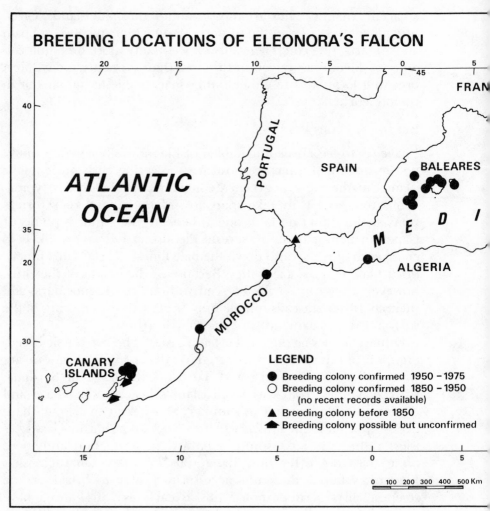

Fig. 2. World distribution of Eleonora's falcon.

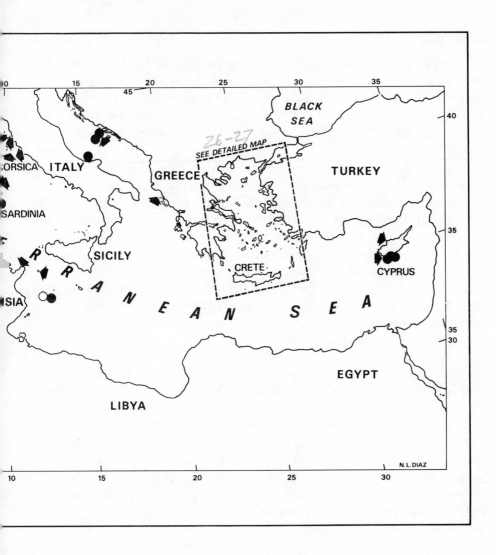

BLACK SEA

26-27

SEE DETAILED MAP

ITALY

CORSICA

SARDINIA

GREECE

TURKEY

SICILY

CRETE

CYPRUS

RRANEAN SEA

SIA

LIBYA

EGYPT

N.L. DIAZ

45

40

35

35
30

15 20 25 30 35

10 15 20 25 30

Paximada Colony

Of the many Greek isles with the name Paximada, Paximadi, or Paximadia, this is the one belonging to the group of the Dionysian Islands off the northeast part of Crete in the southern Aegean Sea. Paximada (35°23′N, 26°11′E) lies some 16 km northwest of Cape Sideros. The Greek capital city of Athens lies about 360 km to the northwest.

The island is only 1,000 × 600 m and rises 120 m. It consists of crystalline calcareous rocks of the Permian or Carboniferous epoch. Its shoreline is deeply dissected by numerous ravines (plate 10). The upper edge of the steep, high west coast also forms the ridge of the island. From here the surface slopes gently to the east, where there are only a few precipitous cliffs. Compared with its island neighbors, which appear to have been affected by rather simple sedimentation and faulting processes in their geologic history, Paximada is older and more complex. The surface consists in many spots of loosely piled small and large rocks, often sharp-edged, resembling a large heap of rubble. According to my Greek friends, the word *paximada* is used for the dry bread eaten by Crete's peasants. You have to break it up into pieces then soak them in water; otherwise it is as hard as stone. Either this island looked to the Greeks like their dried-up pieces of bread or the bread looked like the rocky rubble of some of the Greek islands.

The vegetation of Paximada consisted in 1965–66 of a low, open type of Greek chaparral (*Phrygana*); except for a few evergreen shrubs about 2 m high, the largely sclerophyllous, thorny vegetation was not higher than 50–100 cm. Many areas were almost free of shrubs owing to the rocky substrate (plate 11).

There was no freshwater spring or pool on Paximada. The nearest river was on Crete, where there were also a few fertile valleys planted with olives, oranges, and other fruit trees.

Physical Factors

The island environment mirrors the general ecosystem of the eastern Mediterranean coast. Mild winters with rain and warm to hot and dry summers characterize the annual cycle.

There was a strong contrast in temperature and humidity between the wind-exposed and sheltered and the sunny and shaded areas of Paximada. This was apparent at once to the human attempting to live for some time on this heap of rock rubble. The physical environment was affected by two main factors: The incident solar radiation and the force of the wind. The wind blew relentlessly during the 1965 study period; there were only five calm days among fifty. The sky was often clouded, and the wind generally came from the northwest (rarely north or southwest) as part of the *meltemi* storm system that has a strong cooling effect on the Aegean coasts. The force of the wind at sea level varied between 4 and 7 on stormy days. A bit of rain fell over Paximada from a passing thundercloud on 28 August.

The water temperatures at the southeast shore of Paximada were measured on three occasions at a depth of 1 m below the surface. They varied from 24°C (20 August) to 22.5°C (20 September and 7 October).

The air temperatures varied with the microhabitats of the island, but the daily range was small. On 10/11 September I measured the air temperature in the shade at 1 m above ground level some 50 m above the sea near our cave residence. The minimum temperature was 23°C, the maximum value 29°C. In August it was hotter at the same location (32.5°C at noon on 27 August, but later in the falcon's reproductive season it was much cooler (26°C on 20 September and 23.5°C on 7 October at noon). The air temperature around a falcon's nest scrape was recorded on 27 August at 11:00 A.M. Holding the thermometer under the boulder of nest 16 and 52, some 10 cm above ground level, I recorded temperatures of 32.5°C and 31.5°C. The nearby nest 15, situated under a rather leafless *Euphorbia* shrub, also was at 32.5°C. At the same time the temperature in the sun at 1 m above ground level was 36°C.

It was generally rather humid in wind-exposed and shaded areas. On the hot and wind-sheltered slopes, however, it appeared to be rather dry, owing to the strong radiation and heat reflection of the rocks. Salt spray from the surf pounding the west coast of Paximada was of no importance to the falcons, since most of them nested high up on slopes and cliffs facing south and east.

Biotic Factors

In 1965/66 the flora consisted of at least nine different shrubs, the most conspicuous of which was the tree spurge (*Euphorbia dendroides*). Late summer was the worst period for plant collecting (no blossoms), and so my botanist friends were not able to identify the other shrubs present. In January 1966 the island was covered with lush annual grasses and various herbs.

Of the fauna we need mention only a few relevant forms. There were many small snails; though they were hidden because of the summer heat, their empty shells lay all over the island. There were many resident and visiting arthropods; among them were ants, moths, butterflies, grasshoppers, beetles, flies, spiders, scorpions, bees, and ectoparasites like fleas and lice. The ecosystem of Paximada itself could not support its invertebrate fauna. Highly nutritive materials were brought to the island from the surrounding sea and airspace. A relatively small colony (ca. 30 pairs) of Mediterranean herring gulls (*Larus argentatus*) carried in fishes and organic debris from Crete's shores; in January I found many olive stones that the gulls spit up on Paximada after raiding the olive groves of eastern Crete during periods of bad weather. The gulls had already finished their breeding season on 1 July 1966 but were still holding on to their territories at dusk, night, and dawn. They had abandoned the main part of the island from August to October 1965 except for some outlying rocks near the water surface.

More important to the falcons was a large colony of Cory's shearwaters (*Calonectris diomedea*). This albatrosslike bird has an unusually long breeding season. Its single young were rather small during the middle of August and still not fully fledged in early October. I estimated there were some 400 pairs over the entire island in 1965, breeding in caves and holes under rocks, sometimes in direct contact with a falcon pair living under the same boulder. The shearwaters fed themselves and their young with squid and other marine organisms.

A dozen or so rock pigeons (*Columba livia*) frequented the island and may have been breeding there. Other birds observed included a few Audouin's gulls (*Larus audouinii*), shags (*Phalacrocorax aristotelis*), dozens of Manx shearwaters (*Puffinus puffinus*), and some thirty-four other bird species passing over or resting on Paximada during their seasonal migration (table 32).

The organic materials carried onto Paximada by many of these birds, including the falcon itself, nourished a sizable population of black rats (*Rattus rattus alexandrinus*) and a common small lizard (*Lacerta erhardii*). This omnivorous lizard fed on almost any kind of vegetable or animal matter. The eastern slope of Paximada had a lizard specimen for every 20 square meters. I estimated the total population of this quite distinct island form as 10,000 to 50,000 individuals in the late summer of 1965. Although small (a large specimen caught had a total length of 19.7 cm), these lizards were fearless and ready to exploit every opportunity. They were true commensals of Eleonora's falcon (Walter 1967).

It was difficult to estimate the population of black rats. They disturbed us a great deal during the 1965 season but have subsequently become less bothersome to overnight campers. D. Ristow and I caught several; the largest had a total length of 44.3 cm, and its tail was 23.3 cm long. The rats seemed to live mostly on vegetable matter, but they may have played a part in egg predation of falcons (and gulls?).

The other mammals on Paximada were three goats and a hare, which had been introduced by local people and were the remainder of much larger groups. The goats were shy and wild. How these mammals managed to survive on this island rock remains a question.

Mogador Colony

The Isles of Mogador lie less than a mile off the Atlantic coast of central Morocco, about 600 km south of Tangier. The African mainland opposite the island consists of an extensive area of large sand dunes, covered here and there with some dense scrub or a few cultivated vegetable fields. A few kilometers inland, the land rises onto a small plateau that supports some coniferous vegetation, apparently the result of afforestation programs. A small river widens at its mouth, forming an attractive little lake right across from the isles, frequented by waterfowl, herons, and migrating birds of many families. Unfortunately, this was eliminated during massive earthworks in the summer of 1969.

The Isles of Mogador consist of one main island and several small cliffs surrounding it on the western and northern sides. They reflect the power of the waves and wind that gradually wear down the soft limestone and sandstone of this island group.

The main island (often called Ziron by local informants) is about 800 × 300 m and not higher than 30 m. Precipitous cliffs line the northern and western coasts. The isle is covered with a dense type of maquis. A few dilapidated houses and the grim walls of a former open-air prison dot the "scenery" of this island.

Only about 60 m north of the main isle lies the 150 × 150 m, 25 m high "atoll" isle (plate 13). It can be reached on foot from the main isle at low tide. It looks somewhat circular and has steep cliff walls not only on the north and south, but also in the center. The latter has collapsed and been replaced by an oval basin about 40 m in diameter, filled with seawater, with access to the ocean by two large portals on the northern and southern sides (fig. 4). The surface consists of sand dunes and some shrubs up to 1 m in height.

Adjacent to atoll isle lies a smaller cliff, "Smea" (70 × 30 m, 15 m high), a massive calcareous rock that harbored only two or three shrubs on a sheltered spot, since the remainder of this cliff is fully exposed to the surf and salt of the Atlantic during winter storms. In September 1966 half of it was flooded again and again by heavy breakers (plates 14, 15).

To the west of the main isle, protecting it from the impact of the sea, lie several small cliffs. Next to its northwest point, some 35 m away, a yellowish cliff rests in the foaming white surf, resembling the towers of a submarine. This tiny cliff (12 m high, 20 m long, and about 12 m wide) became one of my main study areas. I named it the "submarine" cliff (plate 16).

Physical Factors

Characteristic of all rock surfaces in the Isles of Mogador is extreme weathering, which is particularly obvious on Smea isle and the submarine rock. The microrelief is often bizarre. There are holes up to 7 ft deep; there are crevices, potholes, and pigeon-holes all over the surface. This creates a highly irregular texture that easily surpasses in complexity even the uneven surface of Paximada island.

The cool Canary current causes dense layers of fog almost daily during the breeding period of Eleonora's falcon. The fog mass is 50 to 150 m high and may engulf the island and its cliffs at any time of day. Wind is normal, and stormy conditions are not rare on late summer days. The wind blows mostly from the north, sometimes from northeast and west.

The climate is very maritime, showing only small daily fluctuations in temperature and humidity. The water temperature measured 17°C at 1 m depth on 20 August 1966 at 19:00 local time. The corresponding air temperature on the atoll isle at 1 m above

the ground was 19°C. On 25 August I measured the air temperatures at the same place at 13:00: 22°C in the shade, 31°C in the
sun; the sandy surface about 20 m above sea level registered 55°C
in the sun. A weather station in the small coastal township opposite the isles (31°30′N, 9°36′W) registered temperature maxi-
mums of 23°C and minimums of 17°C during August and
September. The relative humidity was usually above 90°C. Occasionally, however, this uniform weather pattern is interrupted. In
July 1969, several times we had easterly winds from the arid high
plateau of the Atlas Mountains. It became very hot and dry indeed, and the temperature registered up to 42°C (24 July at
10:00). Then the wind shifted to the north and the rather cool
"normal" weather pattern returned.

The pounding surf and its salt spray posed a certain threat to
the falcon population. The isles are very low, and some falcon
nests were less than 8 m above normal sea level. A few of those
were washed out after a few days of heavy surf during the 1966
season.

Biotic Factors

The cliffs and sand dunes of the Isles of Mogador were inhabited
by a small number of invertebrates. Certain moths (Micro-
Lepidoptera) and beetles (Coleoptera) lived among the feathers
found in falcon nests. A few skinks (*Chalcides* sp.) and geckos were
the only reptiles I found. Some rabbits lived on the atoll and the
main isle in 1969.

The relatively large colony of Eleonora's falcon was dwarfed by
those of other bird species. In July 1969 there were still hundreds
of swifts (*Apus* sp.) around, and several of the 1,000 to 2,000 pairs
of herring gulls (*Larus argentatus*) had not yet raised their young
by 11 July. Gulls remained on or returned daily to their small
breeding territories well into August. In addition, there were
perhaps 1,000 rock pigeons (*Columba livia*), some of which had
eggs or young in the middle of July.

An occasional peregrine falcon, a shag, and several other sea-
and shorebirds were observed on the islands. Passerines were,
however, uncommon. I observed some ninety-four species of
birds from 20 August to 22 September 1966 on the isles and the
adjacent mainland.

Other Colonies
Salé Colony

Near the Moroccan capital city of Rabat the shoreline rises to form a cliff habitat extending about 12 km to the north. The brown reddish sandstone of the rocks has been under permanent assault by the sea, creating dozens of coves and bays surrounded by cliffs 10 to 50 m high (plate 12).

This is the African mainland; during the spring, wheat fields seemed to extend right up to the edge of the cliffs where Eleonora's falcon would breed a few months later. Some people lived and moved within 100 m of the cliffs all the time. Trucks unloaded garbage and rubbish at the edge of the cliffs. Looking down, one could see scores of rusty cans and other solid waste littering the rock ledges. The worst I ever saw in connection with a breeding habitat was a dead mule, its tongue and intestines protruding, some 40 m beneath the cliff top in a typical falcon breeding cove.

The Salé colony was rather deserted by humans during the breeding season of Eleonora's falcon. Herring gulls and some shag and raven (*Corvus corax*) shared this cliff habitat.

San Pietro Colony

A spectacular coastal landscape of high cliffs formed by trachytic rocks is the site of another breeding colony of Eleonora's falcon. Here at the western end of a large isle off Sardinia, protected from human disturbance by government regulations restricting access to an aeronautical facility in this area, falcons breed in high cliffs facing the open sea (plate 9). This makes it difficult to study them at close range. Some rusty car wrecks and other rubbish near falcon nesting sites defaced this aesthetic habitat in July 1974, indicating occasional disturbance owing to human activities. The falcons shared their breeding area with herring gulls and rock pigeons. A detailed description of this colony including some climatic data can be found elsewhere (Mocci Demartis 1973).

Most, if not all, of this raptor's breeding habitats resemble one or another of the foregoing descriptions. The Canaries, the Tremiti Isles, and the large number of Aegean islands harboring Eleonora's falcon may be more distant from a large isle or the mainland, and may be higher or as low as the Modagor Isles, but they all serve as relatively secure breeding areas. This raptor's general tameness and disregard for human activity that does not pose a direct threat indicate that it might well be able to breed in many other places around the Mediterranean. It probably did so in the past, but persistent persecution and other human influences caused it to desert many locations; the rocks of Gibraltar and of the Iles d'Hyères near Marseilles (France) were apparently inhabited by Eleonora's falcon before the nineteenth century but have not seen a breeding attempt since.

POPULATION STATUS

It is difficult to estimate the total population of any animal species except when only a few dozen are left. Eleonora's falcon is easier to estimate than other raptors because the bulk of its population is concentrated in a few regions. Most of its breeding colonies lie on barely accessible cliffs in the Atlantic or Mediterranean. Although the Mediterranean has achieved fame for its color and gentle nature, its waters can in fact be exceedingly rough during any part of the year. The Aegean Sea is particularly rough from August to October. Fishermen have always been reluctant to visit the falcon's breeding cliffs even on calm days owing to the unpredictable weather patterns. Several ornithologists, among them J. Steinbacher, have repeatedly risked their lives in the rough waters near falcon colonies. F. P. W. Wyer apparently lost his life while climbing the cliffs of a falcon colony (L. Kiff, pers. comm.). No wonder, then, that few ornithologists have managed to estimate falcon numbers with any accuracy.

Because of the difficulty of the terrain and the discreet behavior of the falcons when disturbed by humans, I have postulated that even a skilled observer will see no more than a third of all breeding pairs in a colony of 50 to 150 pairs during a brief day-long visit (Walter 1968a). It may take several days of systematic search to discover some 90 percent of the nest sites. This phenomenon can be appreciated only by those who have spent weeks and months studying this species. Vaughan (1961a), the first to estimate the world population of Eleonora's falcon, had to deal with antiquated and often incomplete or general data ("large colony"). Through careful guessing and appropriate interpretation, which illustrate his expertise, he arrived at a grand total of 1,550 to 2,000 breeding pairs, concluding: "I would suggest that the total world population of Eleonora's falcons is under 4,000 birds, about half of which breed in the Aegean and Crete."

Subsequently, Vaughan was criticized for this estimate by Warncke and Wittenberg (1961), who scolded him for his acceptance of some colony sites where falcons have been observed only before the breeding season. They contended that Vaughan's somewhat "generous" interpretation of the literature might create the impression that Eleonora's falcon is more numerous than it actually appears to be. They concede, however, that several more colonies exist in the Northern Sporades area than were mentioned in Vaughan's article. Subsequently, Makatsch (1969) visited the northern Aegean islands in spring and summer. Referring to the May and June data by Reiser (1905) and Banzhaf (1937), he concluded: "In my opinion, the proof of breeding is not necessary because the expert knows that the Eleonora's falcons will then begin to deposit their eggs on the very same islands a few weeks later."

In the past fifteen years, several old colonies have been surveyed. Some were found to be as large as or larger than they were fifty to one hundred years earlier. A few others have declined in importance. At the same time a large number of previously unknown colonies were discovered. Thus, there is a need for another population survey.

Several years ago I started out to develop a directory containing all previous and current information on the many breeding locations of Eleonora's falcon. This directory was to become part of this book. But in the meantime I have become convinced that the scientific merits of publishing exact breeding locations, population numbers, informants, and so forth, might be outweighed by the potential harm to the falcon colonies discussed. The eagerness of nature-film producers, commercial tourist operators, and lines of bird watchers, has already caused some disturbance in at least one of the larger colonies. I have therefore decided to publish the directory separately in a restricted edition (Walter 1978b), available only upon request.

In the following, I present only a summary of this status report, which has been updated to contain all information available to me until December 1977.

A colony of Eleonora's falcon can be defined as a breeding location within which falcons are in nearly continuous contact with other members of the breeding population. Some 148 different breeding locations have been identified, including 40 as yet unconfirmed locations that have been mentioned in the literature. Of the 108 confirmed colony sites, 2 became extinct before the species had been scientifically described (Gibraltar and Iles d'Hyères), 11 colonies were discovered between 1850 and 1950 but have since ceased to exist or have not been surveyed, and 95 have been positively confirmed since 1950 to contain nests, eggs, or young of Eleonora's falcon (figs. 2 and 3).

There are twelve major breeding regions (A–L). The largest are the Cyclades and the Dodecanese islands in the Aegean Sea between Greece and Turkey (regions I and J), and the smallest lie in the Adriatic Sea and the Ionian Sea (F and G). More colonies will undoubtedly be discovered in the near future; in my estimate, they could add up to fifteen to twenty locations, mostly in the Aegean and in northwest Africa.

To gain the perspective needed to assess this falcon's need for conservation measures, its impact on prey species, and its potential response to human activities, I have estimated the minimum, mean, and maximum number of breeding pairs.

The *minimum estimate* refers to the number of breeding pairs confirmed since 1950. Where an author has provided no data other than "colony exists," I have generally allocated some 15 breeding pairs; this may be too high in some cases but should be considered a conservative estimate on the whole. Recently unconfirmed and questionable locations have received zero breeding pairs in this minimum estimate. Since many authors report only the number of nests, eggs, or young they actually saw in a part of the breeding habitat, it is clear that this estimate must be well below the true population level of Eleonora's falcon. It has the distinction, however, of a solid and relatively up-to-date data base. Adding up the minimum estimates of each region (table 1), we arrive at a grand total of some 1,930 breeding pairs of Eleonora's falcon.

The *mean estimate* of the total breeding population in 1977 is much higher, totaling some 4,400 pairs. This figure was arrived at by (*a*) using census data, (*b*) doubling or tripling the number of nests or pairs seen during short visits wherever this seemed warranted, (*c*) assuming a stable or slightly decreased population for those colonies for which no recent data exist, (*d*) guessing the population number of a few probable but still unproven locations,

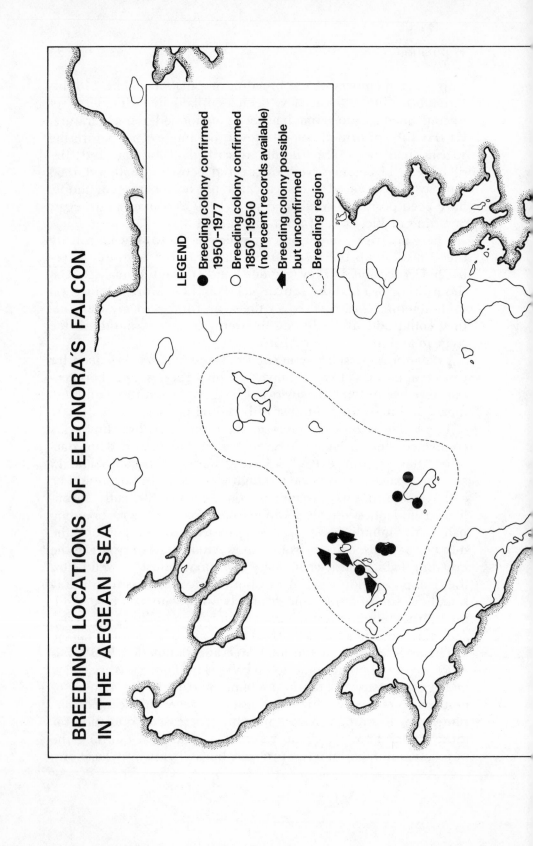

BREEDING LOCATIONS OF ELEONORA'S FALCON IN THE AEGEAN SEA

LEGEND

● Breeding colony confirmed 1950–1977

○ Breeding colony confirmed 1850–1950 (no recent records available)

◄ Breeding colony possible but unconfirmed

▱ Breeding region

Fig. 3. Confirmed and potential breeding locations in the Aegean Sea.

N.L. DIAZ

(e) considering 2 to 30 pairs a "small" colony, 31 to 70 pairs a "medium-sized" colony, and 71 to 200 pairs a "large" colony. This is the estimate that in my judgment comes closest to reality. It was not conceived in an optimistic mood; it simply reflects the experiences I have had and read about regarding the survey of entire breeding populations. Annual fluctuations will obviously occur, and some of the old records may in the next couple of years be totally invalidated. On the whole, however, this is unlikely.

The *maximum estimate* of breeding pairs is supposed to provide an upper ceiling of falcon numbers. It is based on our current knowledge of colony sites and population numbers and means that under better-than-average breeding conditions, this estimate will come closer to the real number of breeding pairs than the mean estimate. Included also is a guess at the maximum number of breeding pairs in still-undiscovered locations. I think there is an overall probability of about 30% that each colony will come close to its maximum estimate. On the whole, however, we should not expect the world population of Eleonora's falcon to reach the grand total of some 7,000 pairs (table 1).

TABLE 1
Breeding Colonies and Population Estimates

Region[a]	Number of Locations	Colonies Confirmed since 1950	Former Colonies Not Confirmed since 1950	Suggested but Unconfirmed Colony Sites	Breeding Pairs		
					Minimum Estimate	Mean Estimate	Maximum Estimate
A	7	4	0	3	16	43	97
B	4	2	2	0	180	350	450
C	18	18	0	0	235	371	533
D	5	2	0	3	70	160	350
E	13	6	1	6	175	315	495
F	5	3	0	2	25	100	175
G	4	1	1	2	40	100	170
H	13	8	1	4	135	330	480
I	32	16	6	10	200	968	1,675
J	27	22	0	5	323	720	1,170
K	15	10	2	3	461	855	1,230
L	5	3	0	2	70	88	175
Total	148	95	13	40	1,930	4,400	7,000

[a]*Regions are*: A—Canary Islands, B—Atlantic coast, C—Balearics and Columbretes, D—North African coast, E—Islands of the Ligurian and Tyrrhenian seas, F—Adriatic and Ionian seas, G—Channel of Sicily, H—Northern Aegean Sea, I—Cyclades, J—Dodecanese Islands, K—Southern Aegean Sea, L—Cyprus. See also figs. 2 and 3.

Conclusions

This status report shows clearly that Vaughan's estimate of "under 4,000 birds" (Vaughan 1961a) is too low. The minimum estimate comes very close to his population level, even though it includes only those Eleonora's falcons that are breeding in colonies confirmed since 1950. There are undoubtedly hundreds of falcons breeding in locations that have not been surveyed for more than seventy-five years. In addition, there must exist a sizable number of nonbreeding immature and perhaps even adult Eleonora's falcons. While the first group has been censused in my mean and maximum estimates, the latter two are difficult to assess because of the almost complete lack of data.

Breeding statistics and the discussion on the mortality rate (chap. 3) of Eleonora's falcon indicate that the average mortality during the first year might reach 50%, as has been reported for hobby and peregrine falcons (Hickey 1969). If each pair has one or two fledglings each year, there should be about 50% of this first-year population left at the beginning of the second year; that is, 0.5 to 1.0 nonbreeding falcons for every breeding pair. This would add at least 965 to 1,930 falcons to the minimum estimate of 3,860 individual birds (total: 4,825 to 5,790 falcons) or 2,200 to 4,400 falcons to the mean estimate of some 8,800 birds (total: 11,000 to 13,200), and 3,500 to 7,000 falcons to the maximum estimate of 14,000 breeding specimens (total: 17,500 to 21,000). This last and most optimistic estimate of the world population of Eleonora's falcon is about five times as high as Vaughan's. The most realistic figure in my opinion is 12,000 falcons, 9,000 of which breed, while the remaining 3,000 make up a pool of nonbreeding immature and adult falcons.

Some readers may be surprised by the relatively "high" number of Eleonora's falcons. Is this not the age where we have seen a massive decrease of raptor populations in many parts of the world? I am well aware of this and have been concerned about raptor conservation at least since 1955. But here we are after the facts, and they show what I consider a rather healthy population size of Eleonora's falcon, even at the minimum estimate level. It is, by the way, not uncommon (as one referee of this manuscript reminded me) to find that a raptor population presumed to be small turns out upon close investigation to be much larger.

Table 1 deserves to be analyzed in more detail. The four

regions of the Aegean Sea area (H–K) contain between 57 and 65% of the world population of this species at each of the three estimate levels. The Aegean Sea must therefore be considered the distribution center of Eleonora's falcon. Here we have some fifty-six recently confirmed locations and probably an additional twenty or so breeding spots all in relative proximity to other colonies. The remaining 35 to 43% of the world population breeds in a rather discontinuous (disjunct) fashion in clusters of a few or even in isolated colonies (figs. 2 and 3). Another aspect of the status data concerns the size distribution of the various breeding colonies (table 2). I have established eight size classes beginning with 2–4 pairs as class no. 1. The upper limit of each of the other classes is twice as much as the preceding one (8, 16, 32, etc.). Using the figures from the mean estimate as a data base, most colonies fall into the third and fourth size classes; that is, some 62% of all colonies consist of 9 to 32 breeding pairs. Only four colonies fall into the seventh size class (129 to 256 pairs), and at present no colony appears to belong in size class 8, with 257 to 514 breeding pairs. Most of the larger colonies (classes 6 and 7) are in the Aegean Sea, but isolated large colonies occur also in Morocco, Mallorca, and Sardinia.

TABLE 2
Size Distribution of Breeding Colonies

Size Class	Number of Breeding Pairs in Each Colony	Number of Colonies per Size Class
1	2–4	4
2	5–8	9
3	9–16	28
4	17–32	31
5	33–64	12
6	65–128	7
7	129–256	4
8	257–514	0

SOURCE: Data taken from the mean estimate value of breeding pairs (Walter 1978b).

The colony directory (Walter 1978b) contains few clues for predicting future population fluctuations in Eleonora's falcon. It has not been possible to survey more than a few of the ninety-five colonies in any given year. It may well be that a slight decline of some regional breeding populations has occurred over the past twenty-five years. The discoveries of new colonies in all regions during this time period tends to mask any absolute decline in numbers, since we do not know whether the new colonies have merely been overlooked by previous researchers or whether they represent newly settled sites.

In 1977 I was able to survey more than a dozen colonies on Mallorca, on Cyprus, and near Crete. The results indicate unchanged if not slightly higher breeding populations compared with previous detailed surveys conducted in 1956/57 on Cyprus, in 1965 near Crete, and in 1966 on Mallorca. At least in these breeding areas, Eleonora's falcon has been able to maintain its population numbers. Whether this raptor can continue to remain unaffected by the many human-induced factors that have contributed to the decline of other raptor species since 1945 remains to be seen. An analysis of the actual and potential magnitude of these factors will be carried out in chapter 11.

3 Population Ecology

Colony size and composition, clutch size, and breeding success are standard criteria of a species' ecological relationship to its prey, its enemies, and its physical environment. A comprehensive ecological analysis of Eleonora's falcon has to include quantitative observations on breeding density and reproductive success. This is an arduous and complex task; owing to other equally important parts of my study I could not devote nearly as much time to gathering data on population ecology as I had wished. But, limited as these data are, they permit cautious generalizations and may, I hope, serve as a foundation for monitoring this raptor.

COLONY SIZE AND STRUCTURE
Population Census

The number of breeding pairs cannot be estimated from a distance. For instance, approaching the Mogador Isles in a boat usually yielded the observation of not more than 10 to twenty-five falcons circling or hunting right above and near their breeding grounds; that is, less than 10% of the adult population even at the height of the season in September.

A census taken in the breeding habitat before the middle of July is probably of little value, since most falcons either have not yet arrived or are hunting insects on a nearby inland habitat. Between 25 July and 5 September one parent falcon will generally be at the nest site at all times and often will not abandon it even if a human observer is only 10 to 15 m away. In September and October, nest sites become more visible than before, since the young falcons often stand in front of them, and also because of the large amount of feather remains filling and surrounding them. As a rule, however, even a skilled observer will see at most one-third of the nest sites or breeding pairs in a large colony during a visit lasting just a few hours. The best strategy for censusing the population is to systematically search under boulders and in crevices and holes for nest sites in every suitable (and even seemingly unsuitable) part of the breeding habitat. We conducted such a search during the first days after arrival in the easily accessible areas and continued it later in the remaining ones.

On Paximada, we found 70 nests between 10 and 25 August 1965, but we still discovered more even on 9 October, one day before my departure. At Mogador, nests were more concentrated and more easily visible. Thus it took just two days to locate 75 nests. But here again, additional nest sites were found, particularly in the central basin of the atoll isle, until the very last day. Nest sites were classified according to substrate and microhabitat. Wherever possible, the phase of the breeding birds was determined. In addition, we took notes on nonbreeding immature and adult falcons.

Population Size
Paximada

In 1965 the breeding population was about 150 pairs. A total of 142 nests were found spread out over the entire island from the highest point down to the edge of the spray zone of the surf (fig. 4). Not more than 5 to 10 immature falcons and possibly a few single adults made up the nonbreeding part of the population.

At the beginning of the following season it was too early for an adequate census. The breeding population was large, however, and appeared to be roughly of similar size. Detailed observation of a small section in the "upper slope" area revealed the same number of pairs as had been found during the preceding season.

In 1969 and 1971 the colony had approximately the same size. The population had certainly not increased by any substantial amount (Ristow, unpublished). In 1976, J. R. Parrott conducted a partial survey of this colony from 5 to 9 September. This census is not representative of the whole colony, since cliffs and gullies were not well censused, but Parrott's data indicate a definite decline of pairs with young on the easy slopes of the island. This trend has persisted during the 1977 season. No explanation has so far been found for this development. The total breeding population has maintained itself very well, however. First, Ristow was able to band as many falcon chicks as ever in 1977; second, I observed a surprising number of falcons during a survey con-

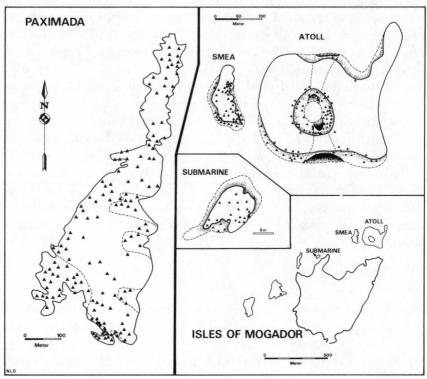

Fig. 4. Distribution of nest sites on Paximada (1965) and on the Isles of Mogador (1966). Maps are based on field sketches and do not accurately reflect the distances between nest sites. A few nest sites from the main island of the Isles of Mogador are omitted on this map.

ducted from a boat on 15 October 1977. About 220 falcons were dispersed in the air over the whole island. Most were adults; at most 20% were juveniles. I was surprised at the large number of falcons perched on the steep cliffs along the southern and western coasts of the island. It looked as if there were more pairs in these steep sections of the colony than in 1965. I estimated the total breeding population of Paximada in 1977 at between 150 and 200 pairs. Thus the population has certainly not declined over the past twelve years.

Some fifty years earlier, Meinertzhagen (1921) had already classified this colony as a "large" one. Local fishermen, who seemed very knowledgeable about the population of Eleonora's falcons in the southern Aegean Sea, told Ristow that there had been more falcons on Paximada before the 1940s. One of them, Mr. Karalambos, remembered that as a youth he and his uncle had repeatedly visited the island in September and had returned with some sixty young falcons hanging over their shoulders. Ristow got the impression that there had been five or ten times as many pairs then as during the 1960s and early 1970s.

Mogador

In 1966 the resident population consisted of about 175 pairs. No immature Eleonora's falcons were regularly present. We located 168 nest sites; one lay in a sand dune near a cliff, and all the others were situated on rocky substrate, distributed over a few cliffs of the main island and five of its offshore cliffs to the west and north (fig. 4). In 1969 no detailed census could be made because of the human-caused disturbances of that season. The entire breeding population consisted of more than 150 pairs—quite possibly up to 200 pairs, since there were more breeding pairs in the walls of the atoll inner basin than there had been in 1966. Vaucher estimated the size of this colony in 1905 as "hundreds" (after Heim de Balsac and Mayaud (1962), Contant and de Naurois (1958) estimated about 200 pairs, Vaughan counted 100 ± 10 pairs in 1959 (Vaughan 1961a), and Etchécopar and Hüe (1964) estimated a population of 200 individuals in about 1961. Thus, the breeding population may have fluctuated considerably; considering the difficult census work in this species, however, it is more likely that some observers underestimated the size of the colony, which may have exhibited only minor fluctuations since the beginning of this century. Between 1966 and 1969 I noticed a shift of nest sites away from easily detectable locations on ledges and cliff rims and an increased use of dark caves and pigeonholes. This might well be a response to increased human predation of eggs and young. This trend might even have existed before 1966, since Vaughan's data on nest site location (see below) of the 1959 season show a relatively higher use of ledges and rims as nest sites than do my 1966 and 1969 data. Such a shift could cautiously be interpreted as a first indication of suboptimal breeding conditions.

Other Colonies

The falcon colonies near Salé (Morocco), on Mallorca, and on the

San Pietro isle (near Sardinia) belong to a different type of breeding habitat. Nearly vertical "falaises," rather precipitous-looking
cliffs, extend for many miles along the coast of the mainland or a
large island. Eleonora's falcon breeds along such habitats in clusters ranging from a few to more than 30 pairs that are separated
from each other by hundreds or thousands of meters, creating a
number of subcolonies.

In 1966 we found 30 breeding pairs along 5 km of rocky
coastline near Salé, but 10 to 20 more were probably located farther north in another series of cliffs. About 8 nonbreeding, immature falcons were resident in this colony (Walter and Deetjen
1967).

During the same season, Thiollay (1967) censused some 132
breeding pairs on the magnificent limestone cliffs of northwestern
Mallorca, spread out over more than 50 km of up to 300 m high
coastal cliffs. In October 1966 I also visited Mallorca and observed
a number of falcons at their breeding sites, but I did not attempt
to make a census of the entire population. I returned in September 1977 and found at least 11 colonies between Soller and
Formentor, totaling between 105 and 192 pairs.

The San Pietro colony extends over some 6.6 km of cliffs on the
northwestern coast of San Pietro island. Mocci Demartis (1973)
censused it in its entirety in 1972 and found 52 resident pairs and
perhaps some additional nonbreeding birds. Again, without attempting to census it, I made some ecological and behavioral observations there during the 1974 breeding season. Concentrating
on only one of the four breeding zones mapped out by Mocci
Demartis, I found a small cluster of 5 pairs where there had been
only 2 in 1972. This colony should be censused annually in order
to arrive at some meaningful data on population dynamics.

Discussion

Paximada and Mogador have always harbored "large" colonies of
Eleonora's falcon. That they still do so and that there has been no
rapid decline comparable to that of the peregrine falcon (Hickey
1969) is the first and most noteworthy result of comparing data
from different years and authors. It is likely, however, that both
colonies were larger in the past. Apart from Vaughan and Carruthers in 1959, nobody seems to have spent nearly as much time

and effort on locating and examining nesting sites and their contents as we have done. Since there were always more nests than we expected to find, I have come to the conclusion that estimates derived from brief and cursory studies and explorations during the August/September period are invariably too low.

The other colonies mentioned can be classified as "falaise-type" breeding areas where high, precipitous cliffs provide only limited nesting opportunities. The preference for shelter and visual protection (see chap. 8) makes many cliff surfaces unsuitable or suboptimal to this falcon. As a result, clusters or "visual neighborhoods" develop along such a coastal habitat.

Ratio of Color Phase

The existence of two phases and of mixed-phase pair bonds in Eleonora's falcon facilitates the fieldwork in a colony. Social interaction can be monitored in an instant once you know that pair x is composed of two dark-phased birds while neighboring pair y has a light-phased male and a dark-phased female. But the phase ratio is of interest for other reasons as well, raising several issues that still await resolution:

1. There have always been more light-phased than dark-phased falcons in any colony known so far.

2. The phase ratio may be linked to physiological and behavioral factors like reproductive performance and dominance.

3. Do different colonies exhibit consistently similar or different phase ratios over the years? Can the phase ratio be used as an indicator of the genetic exchange between different populations?

4. Do falcons prefer to mate with their own color phase, with the other one, or do they select their partners at random?

Paximada

In 1965 about a third of the breeding adults belonged to the dark phase (46, or 32% of 146 individuals). Males were more often dark colored than females, and there were more pairs with light- and dark-phased partners (57% of 58 pairs) than those in which both partners belonged to the light (38%) or the dark phase (5%).

The lower sample size in 1966 and 1969 does not allow a good comparison, but it is safe to say that there was no major difference in the phase ratio.

The data have been tabulated (table 25) and can be summarized: between 21 and 34% of different sample sizes of
Paximada falcons belong to the dark color phase; the remaining
66 to 79% were light-phased falcons.

The Paximada colony appeared to have more mixed-phase
pairs than uniform-phase pairs. We collected data on 58 pairs; 33
of them (57%) consisted of a light- and a dark-phased partner.
Both falcons belonged to the dark phase in only three cases, while
22 pairs consisted of light males and females. This seems to indicate some preference for mixed-phased pairs. A statistical
analysis, however, clearly demonstrates that the observed values
(lower portion of table 25: 22 light–light, 21 light female–dark
male, 12 dark female–light male, and 3 dark–dark combinations)
do not significantly differ (chi-square test) from the expected values (26, 17, 9, and 6, respectively) obtained through the random
selection of mates. In other words, the phase ratios of males and
females for the whole population sufficiently explain the observed
distribution of phases in a sample population of 58 pairs; preference for any particular phase combination in the pair formation
does not appear to exist in this colony.

Mogador

The phase ratio of the Mogador colony was different in the two
years of our study. In 1966 fewer than 20% of the falcons we were
able to check belonged to the dark phase. In 1969, more dark
falcons were found (41%). In both years, dark-phased females
outnumbered the males of the same color phase (table 24). Characteristic for Mogador were a few dark-breasted individuals that
should be considered an intermediate phase; they were also
noticed by Vaughan (1961*a*). He made several counts of perched
and sitting birds and found a ratio of 4:1 or 5:1 in favor of the
light phase (table 25). The phase ratio of 25 pairs from 1959
(28% dark phase) is nearly equal to that of 31 pairs from 1969
(29%), but different in 37 pairs from 1966 (only 15% dark phase).

The phase contribution among 37 pairs during the 1966 season
(27 light–light, 6 light female–dark male, 3 dark female–light
male, and 1 dark–dark pair) does not significantly differ from the
expected values obtained through random pair formation (23, 9,
4, and 1, respectively).

Other Colonies

My data are too limited for any meaningful comparison with respect to the San Pietro, Mallorca, and even the Salé colonies. In
the last, the light-phased falcons appeared to heavily outnumber
the dark-phased adults; only 1 of 23 birds belonged to the dark
phase.

Discussion

A comparison of the data assembled (table 25) yields some interesting perspectives. First, only the two large samples exhibit a
pronounced difference in the phase ratio. Paximada had almost
one-third dark-phased birds, while Mogador had less than one-
fifth of these. Smaller sample sizes, however, show a nearly identical phase ratio during other breeding seasons within and between
these colonies. Thus, no clear-cut differences seem to exist with
respect to their phase ratios. Second, our data together with those
of Vaughan (1961*a*) from a few other colonies add up to a ratio of
133 dark- to 376 light-phased falcons, which equals 26% dark-
versus 74% light-phased individuals. Such a ratio looks like a simple Mendelian genetic system of a dominant light-phase factor
gene and a corresponding recessive dark-phase factor gene. In
reality, however, we find a continuum of color variation from very
light to very dark. There can be little doubt that several different
genetic factors contribute to the coloration of a falcon. Most
dark-phased adults acquire their plumage gradually over a period
of at least two years following their rather brown yellowish fledgling pattern.

    Another factor complicating the genetic pattern is the dissimilar
phase ratio among male and female falcons. The scarcity of uniformly dark pairs appears to be a result of random selection of
mates. If the total pool of female falcons contains only 10 to 20%
dark-phased individuals, even fewer uniformly dark pairs will
exist in the colony, since some of the dark females will pair up
with light-phased males.

    The offspring of a uniformly dark pair cannot always be ex-
pected to be dark-phased, since most dark-phased birds will also
contain some light-phase genes in their genotypes; likewise the
offspring of uniformly light pairs may be light- or dark-phased,

since many light-phased birds also possess genes for dark-phase
coloration (see Appendix D for data received in 1978).

In summary, the ratios of color phase do not differ much in
these two colonies or in others studied by various authors. A certain uniformity therefore seems to exist throughout the falcon's
range. This might indicate a considerable genetic exchange between different colonies. The underlying causes of the near 1:4
ratio in favor of the light phase cannot be established through a
simple data comparison. They will be further discussed with respect to breeding success by phase and pair combination.

Dispersion: Spacing and Density

Much attention has recently been devoted to the dispersion of
animals in space. It may be accidental; if it is not, what factors
determine dispersion patterns? In social birds like gulls, a considerable amount of information has been gathered by Tinbergen
(1957), Patterson (1965), Bongiorno (1970), and others illustrat-
ing the nonrandom type dispersion of nest sites, even though
these birds do not possess individually "owned" feeding grounds.

In Eleonora's falcon we also have a social species with communal feeding areas; the falcon is more heavily armed than the
gull and is prepared to prey on and to kill other birds. Thus we
can expect that the dispersion of the breeding population reflects
in some way the antagonistic disposition of this raptor and the
behavioral mechanisms that enable it to coexist with its conspecifics or prevent it from doing so.

Paximada

The distance between nest sites varied from 6.5 m to about 50 m
and averaged 20 to 30 m. The overall density of the colony was
about 2.5 pairs/ha on the plane of the island's map but much less
considering also the many oblique and vertical surface areas. The
densest concentration occurred in the upper part of the southeast
slope. This "upper slope" area contained 11 nest sites in an area of
2,300 m² (density almost 48 pairs/ha or 210 m²/pair).

A rather similar pattern prevailed during the 1966, 1969, and
1971 seasons. We can conclude that a population of some 150
pairs can be expected to distribute itself on Paximada island in the
manner described above.

Mogador

In 1966 the breeding density on the Mogador Isles was about 5.6 pairs/ha even though the main island (with 90% of the total surface area), possessed less than 10% of the breeding population (11 nest sites). The rather low "long cliff" had two pairs, and the "outer cliff" had only one. On the three other islets falcons were breeding much more densely than in any area of Paximada. The nearest distance to a neighboring nest site varied from 2 to 70 m (average ca. 10 m).

At least 84 pairs were breeding on the atoll island; 55 of them had chosen nesting sites in the weathered cliffs of the central basin. Its cliffs are about 20 m high and about 200 m long and— taking into account the two rock portals—offer about 3,800 m² of vertical surface area, which corresponds to a density of 145 pairs/ha or 70 m²/pair. The distances between 10 nest sites at nearly equal heights around the upper rim of the central basin were 2.7 to 15 m (average 10 m).

The south walls of the atoll contained 25 nest sites on a surface area of 3,500 m² (length 180 m, height about 20 m except for the rock portal), corresponding to 68 pairs/ha and 140 m²/pair. The remaining five pairs had nest sites on the north side (3) and on top of the atoll (2).

The entire surface of Smea isle above the high-tide line was used for nesting by at least 48 pairs of Eleonora's falcons. Its total surface area, including the vertical walls of the west, south, and east sides, amounts to about 3,300 m²; the breeding density was therefore 145 pairs/ha or 69 m²/pair. Several falcon clutches in the southeast corner of Smea were less than 2 m apart.

All 23 pairs of falcons on the submarine rock were distributed over the entire surface area of about 1,000 m², which corresponds to 230 pairs/ha and 43 m²/pair. Three years later, in 1969, submarine, Smea, and atoll were once again heavily settled. Because my notebook was lost, I cannot provide an exact listing of my findings except for certain sections. The submarine population, which will be described in great detail below (chap. 8), had slightly declined (to 18 pairs and a single adult male) compared with 1966.

Other Colonies

Salé. The breeding density of about 6 pairs per km of rocky coastline cannot be compared with that of the two large colonies. Relating it once again to the vertical rock surface in the five bays used by the falcons, the average density reached 7.5 pairs/ha; in the most populated bay it amounted to 10 pairs/ha or 1,000 m^2/pair. Thus, the breeding density, measured in relation to rocky surface used, was about five times lower than on the "upper slope" of Paximada and ten to twenty times lower than in the main parts of the Mogador colony. Distances between nest sites were larger than in the colonies already described. They varied between 15 and 70 m (average ca. 30 m).

San Pietro. Census data assembled by Mocci Demartis (1973) equal a density of 7.9 pairs per km of rocky coastline. I observed a cluster of 5 nest sites; the nearest nest of another cluster was at least 120 m away. Nearest-neighbor distances varied between 4 and 16 m (average 7 m). The density in relation to the vertical rock surface could not be estimated, since there was too much unoccupied cliff surrounding this cluster.

Discussion

The falcon populations studied exhibited a wide range of density levels. Eleonora's falcon seems always to occur in at least two interacting pairs (although I am expecting the day when somebody will discover a truly solitary nest site). In large colonies the spacing-out of nest sites is generally much wider than in comparable colonies of seabirds. Cormorants, boobies, and others breed at such a high density that only one or two meters separate adjoining nests. In gulls, however, there is also some variation in density levels. Though their nests can still be found closer together on the average, I have seen clusters similar to that of the Mogador and Paximada colonies of Eleonora's falcon in the herring gull (*Larus argentatus*) as well as in a colony of the western gull (*Larus occidentalis*) on the Farallon Islands off San Francisco. While distances between nests are little more than an individual's body length in cormorants and boobies, those gulls, like the falcons, had spaced out their nest sites with some 10 to 50 times their body length in between. This dispersion pattern creates a considerable area around the nest site. We shall see later that this space plays a vital role in the social organization of Eleonora's falcon.

The density per unit area of a breeding population of Eleonora's falcons appears to vary in a predictable manner depending on: (a) the macro- and microstructure of the physical landscape (terrain, relief, substrate); (b) the number and density of available nest sites; (c) the size of the falcon population; (d) the behavior of the falcon; and (e) the effect of factors limiting population growth and survival (e.g., human predation and disturbance).

In general, a nearly inaccessible island with a rugged and dis-sected surface is likely to harbor more falcon pairs per unit area than an island with relatively even terrain and easy access for predators. We may also postulate (analogous to the findings of students of gull behavior) that high fledgling rates and low predation rates are likely to increase the local population density, since falcons can be expected to return to the places where they were born or have successfully completed a breeding cycle. Being a gregarious species, Eleonora's falcon may also be attracted to already densely populated areas; such a factor has been detected in the highly gregarious black-headed gull (*Larus ridibundus*) by Patterson (1965).

The "falaise-type" colonies seem to be affected by factor *b*. This generates the above-noted pattern of breeding clusters in "sub-colonies" where the generally sheer cliffs are lined with ledges and perforated with holes and caves.

The two large colonies showed various degrees of dispersion, particularly within the same colony, that cannot be explained by the scarcity or abundance of nest sites. In both countless suitable nest sites were available near and between the occupied ones. Also, this dispersion cannot be explained by territorial behavior, since territories are initially small and expand gradually *after* the nest site has been selected. The falcon population living in the most complex and dissected terrain (the submarine) had the highest density and the smallest average distance between neighbors, while those settling in simpler and more even terrain had a low density and large distances between neighbors.

If we consider four of the above-mentioned dispersion factors equal (*b, c, d,* and *e*), which is reasonable considering the more densely settled areas of the two large colonies in 1965 and 1966, then we find that terrain complexity is inversely related to nest-spacing. The underlying mechanism that appears to guide the

spacing of nest sites cannot be explored without first including
nest-site type and selection in our analysis.

Characters and Selection of Nest Site
Paximada

Nests were rather evenly distributed over steep and easy slopes
and represented types A and B (fig. 5). The high, vertical west
cliff of Paximada was not used as a nesting area. At first sight it
seemed to be the perfect falcon sanctuary, but it is fully exposed to
the strong northwest winds (the *meltemi*) that are common during
the late summer months in the southern Aegean Sea. The falcons
preferred the hottest and least windy parts of the island and
selected their nest sites for sun exposure and wind shelter. The
nest exits (a few nests had more than one) led toward the north
(16), northeast (14), east (37), southeast (29), south (36), southwest
(9), west (5), and northwest (2). Of the 142 nest sites, 120 were
situated in shady, sheltered holes and caves under projecting
boulders, 13 were under shrubs (particularly *Euphorbia dendroides*), and only 9 were unsheltered in the open. In all cases the
rocky substrate was covered with sand and plant debris.

The nest scrape proper measured about 25 cm in diameter. It
was usually close to the entrace (or exit) of a sheltered nest site;
the latter varied in size but showed some common features. The
detailed measuring of 16 nest sites (table 26) revealed a maximum
entrance height of 15 to 45 cm (mean: 24 cm), entrance width of
25 to 135 cm (mean: 51 cm), and depth of 24 to 100 cm (mean: 47
cm). Figure 6 illustrates ground plans of and entrances to six
falcon nest sites. It appears that falcons typically used holes and
caves that they could enter in an upright position (20 to 25 cm)
and in which they could turn around without hitting the walls with
their wing and tail feathers, but which were generally not wider
and deeper than two nest scrape diameters (50 cm).

Mogador

In 1966, 67 pairs were nesting on nearly horizontal surfaces and
the upper rim of cliffs, and 101 pairs had selected sites somewhere in the nearly vertical cliffs. A few were breeding so low in
the cliff that their young were later washed away by a rough sea.

The leeward and otherwise wind-sheltered nesting sites were

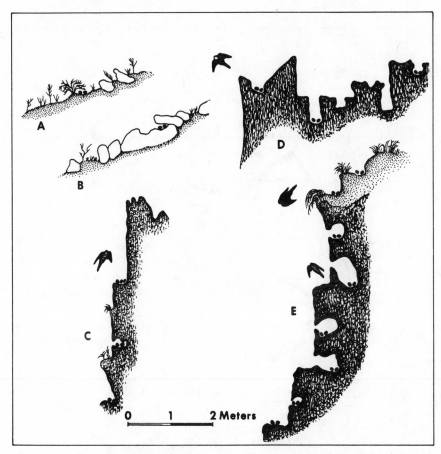

Fig. 5. Typical nest sites of Eleonora's falcon. *A*, under bush (Paximada); *B*, under boulder (Paximada); *C*, on ledge and in small caves of high cliffs (Salé, San Pietro); *D*, in potholes and cliffs (Mogador); *E*, clifftops and caves, ledges, and pigeonholes of highly weathered cliff (Mogador).

the rule. Only 15 nests lay on wind-exposed cliffs facing north and northwest. The large majority (143) were in potholes, pigeon-holes, caves, and under boulders; the rest (25) were relatively unprotected—placed on ledges and along the rims of cliffs or rocks. Vaughan (1961a) provides good photographs of the Mogador nest sites and also gives the following description of 84 nest sites:

at one large colony [from the context it is evident that he refers to the Mogador Isles] (*a*) open cliff ledges, 36; (*b*) under large rocks on a steep

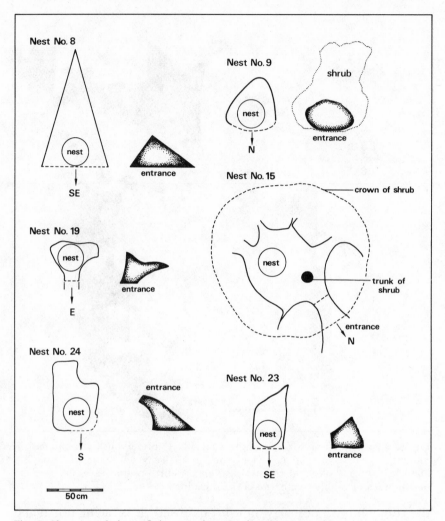

Fig. 6. Shapes and sizes of six nest sites (Paximada 1965). Dimensions are indicated by ground plan and frontal view of entrance opening.

sandy slope above the cliffs, 18; (*c*) on ledges or in cavities within a yard or two of the cliff top, 14; (*d*) in the open or partly under low bushes above the cliffs, 9; (*e*) in vertical potholes about 18 inches deep in large rocks about 20 feet above high water, 7.

In general, the nesting sites represented types *C, D,* and *E* (fig. 5). Their dimensions varied more than on Paximada, owing to the variety of surface texture. Potholes, crevices, and caves were at least deep enough to completely conceal a falcon from any nearby surface; some were 25 cm deep, others more than 2 m. The nest entrance was generally large (compared with the Paximada data), so that a falcon did not have to squeeze himself through it (plates 17 and 20).

Other Colonies

Salé. Sites were relatively evenly distributed on northwest, west, and southwest—facing cliffs, that is in places relatively exposed to wind and weather. More sheltered ones were unavailable.

One pair had used the abandoned nest of a shag (*Phalacrocorax aristotelis*) as their nest site, 8 pairs had found holes or caves in the cliff, and the rest had deposited the clutches in relatively unsheltered depressions and niches. In general, this colony represents type *C* of the nesting sites (fig. 5).

San Pietro. In 1974 five pairs occupied nest sites in sheltered holes and small caves facing west and northwest. Thus they conformed to the general pattern of this colony as described by Mocci Demartis (1973) for the 1972 breeding season. The nesting sites can therefore also be classified as type *C* localities (fig. 5).

Discussion

The preferred and typical dimensions of nesting sites may help explain why this species does not breed in certain cliffs that seem ideally suited. Too small a ledge, too small an entrance or volume of a pigeonhole will not attract a breeding pair. The texture of Paximada and Mogador rock surfaces, on the other hand, offered many more adequate and typical nesting sites than were actually used. Similar observations were made along the Colville River in Alaska by White and Cade (1971). Where there were no cliffs, there were no raptors. But not all the cliffs were inhabited by raptors (peregrines, gyrfalcons, rough-legged hawks) and ravens.

In the small as well as in the large colonies most nesting sites are sheltered from the elements and protected from view. The noticeable exception to this pattern were some ledge-breeding pairs in Paximada and on the atoll of the Mogador Isles. That most falcons in San Pietro and also along the coast of Mallorca (Thiollay 1967) nest on north- to northwest-facing cliffs does not mean that the falcons attempt to avoid hot temperatures.

Paximada offers a good example for a preference for wind-sheltered, sunny slopes where they are available. Many colony sites simply consist only of west- to north-facing cliffs, or suitable nest sites tend to be found there more often because other sites have higher wind and surf exposure.

American studies of golden eagle nests indicate regional preferences for certain directional orientations. In Montana, "almost half the cliff nests faced south, only about one-tenth faced north" (McGahan 1968). A comparative analysis of northern and southern eagle populations has shown that "differences in directional orientation of golden eagle nests are explainable on the basis of temperature-dependent nest-site selection" (Mosher and White 1976). Alaskan data show a "significant directional preference to the southeast, while the Utah population shows an equal preference to the northwest." The authors hypothesize that developing eagle chicks "may be quite sensitive to thermal stress."

The existence of two color phases in Eleonora's falcon raises the question of physiological differences between phases. Such a difference has been demonstrated by Mosher and Henny (1976) in the screech owl (*Asio otus*), where there was a significant difference in oxygen uptake between the red and gray color phases. Is the dark phase of Eleonora's falcon perhaps better adapted to the stress of extreme heat or cold? Nest-site selection in this raptor might be affected by the thermal adaptiveness of its two color phases.

The data on nest exit directions from Paximada were separated by sex and phase. A statistical test (chi-squared) showed no significant difference between the observed and the expected values (i.e., the null hypothesis was confirmed). This means that the light- and dark-phased adult falcons had the same preferences for sheltered and warm nest exits facing east, southeast, and south. But if it is the falcon chicks that are susceptible to thermal stress, we cannot expect any directional difference between the two phases. All falcon chicks have white down feathers and are probably sensitive to microclimatic conditions until about thirty days after hatching regardless of phase.

A detailed analysis of the position of nesting sites reveals that most falcons can see little or nothing from their nest scrapes except a patch of blue sky or a shrub or boulders. This means that they themselves cannot be seen. Indeed, all nests in my study areas were positioned in such a way that *no visual control* could be exerted from one nest entrance over any other in the immediate neighborhood. This suggests that the selection of the nest site is related to a "security factor" rooted in a visual perception of the environment.

A falcon may feel comfortable only where it enjoys a certain degree of *privacy* from its nest site. A complex terrain with many visual obstacles increases this privacy and reduces the importance of spacing out nest sites. We may postulate the existence of a visual prerequisite for a suitable nest site in Eleonora's falcon. The visual information received from an actual rocky substrate would be considered (perhaps influenced by interaction with already-settled neighbors) and translated into distance required for this particular terrain. Such a visual mechanism would result in nest spacing related to terrain complexity and could well explain the dispersion patterns of Eleonora's falcon that we have already discussed. Figure 7 illustrates by a schematic model how the surface texture of a cliff relates to visual privacy. The more broken up or complex it is, the smaller becomes the angle of its visibility sector. Even at high breeding density, visual privacy needs could be satisfied in the highly structured cliff environment (*B*), while a contrasting evenly textured cliff (*A*) would require larger distances between nest sites and a resulting lower density in order to adequately provide for visual privacy.

The existence of the perception or image of a species' structural and spatial environment has recently been pointed out in several species of songbirds by Berndt and Winkel (1974), who have termed it the *Ökoschema* (ecoscheme). Bongiorno (1970) has shown that laughing gulls (*Larus atricilla*) select their nest sites more in response to substrate and landscape structure than to distance and other factors in their colonies. Visual barriers like hedges between fields have been shown to increase breeding density in British partridges (*Perdix perdix*), according to Jenkins (1961).

Newton (1976*b*) has summarized comparable observations for various raptor species in his essay "Population Limitation in Diurnal Raptors":

in seacliff nesting falcons, territory expressed by aggression takes the

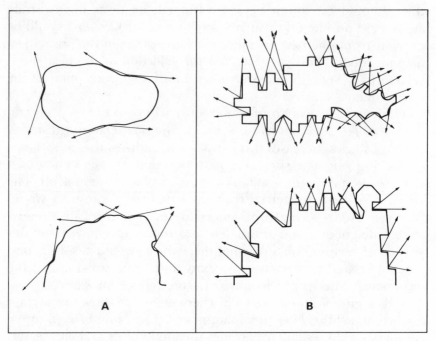

Fig. 7. Schematic illustration of the suggested relationship between terrain structure, nest-site selection, and "visual privacy." Ground plan above, cross section below.

form of a quarter sphere in front of and below the eyrie but extends little above it, and not at all behind (Beebe 1960). Pairs thus nest closer if their eyries do not face one another than if they do. Likewise, pairs of tree-nesting species are often closer together on a slope, where they occupy different levels, than on the flat (Craighead and Craighead 1956), and ground nesters are often closer when they are separated by a ridge than when they are in the same valley (Balfour 1962).

An innate or acquired image of visual privacy needs in Eleo-nora's falcon might thus be used in assisting with the selection of an individual's *structural niche* during the breeding season. Probably most vertebrates need to satisfy such structural niche require-ments, but in only a few cases has it so far been possible to sepa-rate the selection and properties of the usual ecological (resource) niche from that of the structural niche. Eleonora's falcon appears to serve as an excellent example of the important function of terrain complexity and structure in the social organization of birds; at this stage we have examined only its density, spacing, and nest-site patterns and dimensions, but we will return to the functional structural niche when we discuss territoriality and agonistic behaviors.

CLUTCH SIZE AND BREEDING SUCCESS

How many eggs make up the clutch of a bird species is a matter of considerable interest from the standpoint of ecology and evolution. The survival rate of the young may be directly correlated with the seasonal food supply but may also be related to competition from siblings. Eleonora's falcon lays fewer eggs than almost any other European falcon. Only the hobby (*Falco subbuteo*) comes close, with a clutch of two to four eggs, while the other species generally lay more than three eggs—in the case of *Falco tinnunculus* and *Falco naumanni* up to six eggs (Glutz, Bauer, and Bezzel 1971).

The specific questions asked regarding clutch size and breeding success were: Is there a general difference between the Paximada and Mogador colonies? Within the same colony, are there larger clutches in specific areas? Which pairs breed earlier than others? What factors diminish the reproductive success?

Paximada

In 1965, 234 eggs were found in 111 nest sites (average of 2.11 per nest). However, since some of these clutches were discovered only in late August and the beginning of September, we cannot rule out the possibility that some of them had suffered egg losses before they were found. For instance, Erwin Stresemann, editor of the *Journal für Ornithologie*, advised me (Walter 1968a, p. 333) to assume the robbery of at least one egg if a clutch consists of only one egg. Seventeen of the 111 nests contained only one egg. Out of these, only 7 eggs hatched, the others were abandoned, destroyed, or such, underlining the existence of predation and other disturbance factors at nest sites concerned. Some of the single-egg clutches might also have been second clutches of the same season. Only 153 (65%) of the 234 eggs hatched and yielded 140 fledglings (60%); this would equal 1.38 chicks and 1.26 fledglings per pair (table 27).

To establish data on clutch size and breeding success that are as free of interference factors as possible, I have computed the breeding data separately for all clutches showing no sign of disturbance or predation. Eighty-five clutches with a total of 190 eggs fulfilled this condition. Thirty-seven eggs were addled or the embryos died before or during the hatching process (19%), giving a fertility rate of 81%. Thirteen young died before fledging (7%), and 140 fledged. Thus, 74% of all eggs deposited yielded fledglings. We arrive then at the following corrected breeding statistics for undisturbed falcon pairs of the 1965 breeding season: 2.24 eggs, 1.80 young, and 1.65 fledglings per pair (table 3).

TABLE 3
Breeding Success (Summary)

Colony	Number of Clutches	Clutch Size/ Pair	Young Hatched/ Pair	Young Fledged/ Pair
Paximada 1965	85	2.24	1.80	1.65
Paximada 1969[a]	79	2.01	1.82	1.73
Mogador 1959[b]	20	3.15	2.85	2.60
Mogador 1966	31	2.97	2.74	2.65

NOTE: Only seemingly undisturbed pairs are included.
[a]Data from Ristow (pers. comm.).
[b]Data from Vaughan (1961a).

In 1969, data collection began when most eggs had already hatched. This fact and additional observations on the destructive impact of shearwater families (*Calonectris diomedea*) on clutches and young of this falcon population demand caution in the interpretation. It seems quite possible that some eggs had disappeared before the first visit to a nest site. That would affect the breeding statistics by lowering the average clutch size and raising the average breeding success, since the unknown number of lost eggs (and clutches) cannot be accounted for.

Ristow's data (pers. comm.) concern 82 nest sites; 21 had contained one egg, 41 two eggs, and 20 three eggs each, giving a total of at least 163 eggs (table 27). Three clutches with a total of four eggs had been destroyed or abandoned. One hundred and forty-four falcon chicks were born (88%) and 137 fledged (84%).

If we consider once again only the nest sites with no evidence of disturbance or predation, we have to compute the data of 79 pairs, 19 of which had only one egg, representing an astonishing 24% of all clutches compared with only 9% for the 1965 season. This again raises the possibility of two- or three-egg clutches and their decimation before observation.

Fifteen eggs (9%) failed to produce live falcon chicks (fertility rate 91%), and seven young died before fledging time (4%); 86% of the eggs yielded fledged young. The corrected values of reproductive success are 2.01 eggs, 1.82 young, and 1.73 fledglings per pair during the 1969 season (table 3).

Since the dark color phase is less common than the light one in Paximada and all other colonies as well, it is worthwhile to examine whether this scarcity might be related to the breeding success rate of each phase. The data for the 1965 season show that on the average dark-phased females laid as many eggs as light-phased ones but hatched out fewer young and produced fewer fledglings (tables 29 and 30). The differences are not statistically significant but show up in undisturbed as well as in potentially disturbed sample populations. Further data are needed to clarify this result. Should they confirm a trend indicated by the Paximada data, we would have identified an important cause of the scarcity of the dark phase, since even minor differences in breeding success will alter the phase ratio within a few generations.

Mogador

In 1966, 55 clutches contained 168 eggs, or 3.05 eggs per pair. Fortunately, other students of our species have collected relevant data during the 1958, 1959, and 1963 seasons (table 4). In 1969, I was able to collect breeding data for only 13 pairs. It appears that the average clutch size (2.98 per pair) is very high indeed compared with that on Paximada. A consistent and typical feature is the occurrence of clutches of four eggs and the accompanying

TABLE 4
Clutch Size (Mogador Colony)

Year	Number of Nest Sites	Clutch Size				Average per Pair
		1	2	3	4	
1958[a]	21	0	3	16	2	2.95
1959[b]	59	3	7	39	10	2.95
1966[c]	55	0	8	36	11	3.05
1969[d]	13	0	2	7	3	3.15
Total	148	3	20	98	26	2.98

[a] Contant and de Naurois (1958).
[b] Vaughan (1961a).
[c] Walter (1968a).
[d] Walter (unpublished).

absence of single-egg clutches. Vaughan (1961a) writes, however, that "genuine clutches of one seem to occur, for we found three birds incubating single eggs, two of which hatched, and no evidence to suggest that they had lost eggs."

Clark and Peakall (1977) report that in 1972 9 out of 179 clutches from the Mogador and Salé colonies were single-egg clutches. They especially affirm that these clutches were not the result of egg breakage: "In Eleonora's Falcon we are certain that only a single egg was laid."

Different parts of the Mogador colony may show slightly different clutch sizes. According to Vaughan (1961a), the colony consisted "of a nucleus of birds on one small islet and some scattered outlying groups." He found 136 eggs in 45 clutches (average 3.0/pair) in this "nucleus," which refers either to the atoll island or to Smea isle, but only 27 eggs in 10 clutches of the "outlying groups" (average 2.7/pair; did these contain the single-egg clutches?). Wyer (unpublished ms) also distinguished a "main colony" of 42 nests with 123 eggs (2.92/clutch) from eight "outlying nests" with 22 eggs (2.75/clutch) during the 1963 season. In 1966 and 1969, the "nucleus" clearly lay on the atoll island (at least 84 pairs in 1966), where most nest sites were inaccessible. The 28 accessible ones had an average of 2.87 eggs each in 1966 (see above). On Smea isle, however, there were relatively more four-egg clutches during the same season: 19 nest sites had 1 clutch of two, 10 clutches of three, and 8 clutches of four eggs each (average 3.37 eggs/pair). Further observations could yield useful information on this difference between sections within the same colony.

Turning now to the hatching and fledging success of the Mogador population, I can report these data for the 1966 season: 85 (88%) of 97 eggs from 33 clutches hatched; 7 (7%) eggs were addled or failed to hatch viable chicks, and two clutches with 5 eggs were destroyed or abandoned. Eighty-two chicks would most likely have fledged had they not been taken by human predators. Thus, 85% of the eggs would have yielded fledglings. This equals 2.94 eggs, 2.58 young, and 2.48 fledglings per pair (table 28).

If we compute the same excluding the two lost or abandoned clutches, we arrive at these corrected figures: 31 clutches with 92 eggs, 85 chicks, and 82 fledglings, equaling 2.97 eggs, 2.74 young, and 2.65 fledglings per pair (table 3).

In 1959, Vaughan and Carruthers had 20 nests containing 63 eggs under observation. "Out of these 63 eggs, 6 were either addled or found to contain dead chicks. Out of the 57 chicks which hatched from those eggs 5 were found dead near or in the nests when several days old, and 7 more were taken by Arabs for food" (Vaughan 1961a). This equals 3.15 eggs, 2.85 young, and a maximum of 2.60 fledglings without human interference.

The breeding success data collected in 1972 by Clark and Peakall (1977) for both the Mogador and the Salé colonies corroborate the findings so far. The hatching success of 131 eggs was 87%; recognizable embryos were contained in 14 (44%) of 32 failed eggs. Mortality "among c. 150 nestlings from 0–2 weeks of age was about 4% and from 2 weeks about 6%."

Other Colonies

Regarding the clutch size, Vaughan (1961a) computed an average of 2.5 eggs for 40 clutches from various Mediterranean colonies. An island of the Northern Sporades group in the Aegean Sea had 10 nest sites, half of which contained two or three eggs each (Warncke and Wittenberg 1961).

In the Salé colony, we observed the nest sites at the end of September; the number of falcon chicks, some of them already on the wing, may provide a minimum estimate of clutch size and hatching success. Seventeen nest sites contained 48 young (2.82/ pair): 4 had two, 12 had three, and one nest site had four young each. Taking into account a 10% infertility and a 5% mortality factor, we would arrive at an estimated 3.29 eggs, 3.00 young, and 2.82 fledglings per pair.

In remarkable contrast to the foregoing data, the 1977 breeding census of the Cape Gata colony on Cyprus produced an extremely low rate of reproductive success. This colony was surveyed on foot from the clifftop and from a helicopter flying along the cliffs toward the end of the nestling season in the last days of September. The colony consisted of 25 resident pairs, of which only 13 were found with a total of 20 nestlings between three and six weeks of age. Seven of the 13 pairs had only one nestling each. At most, three additional eyries with about 5 nestlings may have been overlooked during the survey. Thus the nestling rate of this colony was only 0.8–1.0/pair, considerably below the values so far reported from any other colony of this raptor. It should be added that this colony is practically free of human interference except for some exposure to aircraft noise (Walter and Foers, in prep.).

Discussion
Clutch Size

1. Clutches of Eleonora's falcon contain one to four eggs; the average does not seem to differ in small and large populations. A significant difference exists between two Atlantic colonies on the one hand (2.95 to 3.29 eggs/pair) and all known Mediterranean colonies on the other hand (2.0 to 2.5 eggs/pair). More data from other Atlantic colonies (Canaries) and also from some western Mediterranean breeding places are needed in order to evaluate this geographic difference. The clutch size of Paximada is typical for the eastern breeding range of Eleonora's falcon. Clutches with four or more eggs have never so far been found in any Mediterranean colony except for a freak clutch of seven eggs mentioned by Giglioli (1907).

2. The constancy of the clutch size over a number of years (table 4) must be expected in a species where diets differ before and during the breeding season and where the young are fed with prey that is usually not available to the adults while the eggs are developing in the ovary.

3. The clutch size not only was constant but appeared to be of normal size wherever controlled in the 1950s and 1960s, compared with Krüper's and Reiser's data from the last century and early in this one (Krüper 1864; Reiser 1905). The only disturbing factor appears to be the increasing occurrence of single-egg clutches in Mogador, Paximada, and probably also in the Cape Gata colony on Cyprus. This trend needs to be monitored with great urgency, since it could mark the onset of a general shift to smaller clutches in Eleonora's falcon.

The Paximada population suffered much more from disturbance and interference owing to natural factors than did the falcons of Mogador. This resulted in the loss of 19% of the falcon eggs and could be responsible for the low hatching rate (19% of all eggs in undisturbed nest sites did not hatch) during the 1965 breeding season.

I have no evidence that Eleonora's falcon would destroy or eat its own eggs, though such behavior has been reported for the peregrine falcon (Herbert and Herbert 1965; Hickey 1969) and accounts there for the otherwise unexplainable disappearance of eggs.

A comparison with other species shows rather high ratios of destroyed and abandoned clutches: Red-footed falcons lost or abandoned 16.1% of their eggs; hobbies suffer a sometimes enormous predation by natural enemies, particularly crows: 15 (46.8%) of 32 clutches were destroyed by hooded crows (*Corvus corone cornix*) in a central European breeding area near Berlin. Dutch kestrels abandoned 16.7% of 413 clutches; Austrian lesser kestrels lost 46 (14.07%) of 327 clutches (from data summaries in Glutz, Bauer, and Bezzel 1971). We may conclude that the percentage of deserted, destroyed, and lost clutches and eggs is low to normal in Eleonora's falcon. The location of this species' breeding colonies on small rocky islands or precipitous cliffs undoubtedly lessens the impact of natural predators on this falcon.

Fertility

Eggs that were infertile or contained dead embryos accounted for 8 to 19% (average 11.5%) of all eggs. Other falcon species in Europe show a similar percentage of eggs that fail to hatch. In the kestrel, Cavé (1968) found a 6% infertility, while an additional 0.8% contained dead embryos. In the red-footed falcon, 16.2% of 105 eggs from 30 nests were addled or contained dead chicks (Horváth 1955, 1956). We may conclude that the populations under study produced highly fertile clutches well within the range of other falcon species.

Chick Mortality

From 3 to 7% of all eggs (from undisturbed pairs) hatched chicks that did not survive to the fledgling age. This equals fewer than 10% of all chicks born (N = 439). Most of these chicks died within their first week after hatching. Clark and Peakall (1977) report, however, that "mortality among c. 150 nestlings from 0–2 weeks of age was 4% and from 2 weeks to departure was about 6%." Data from other European falcons show a higher degree of chick mortality. Cavé (1968) found that 242, or 16.6%, of 1,457 chicks of a Dutch kestrel population died; 199, or 27.6%, of 721 chicks hatched out by lesser kestrels in Austria died before fledging time (Bernhauer, after Glutz, Bauer, and Bezzel 1971). Of the young of a red-footed falcon population in Hungary, 32.4% did not fledge (Horváth 1955). With the exception of Cavé's data, such high mortality rates were generally caused by natural predation (hawks, owls, snakes, etc.). In colonies of Eleonora's falcon this factor is nearly nonexistent. Here, chick mortality is usually related to the rather scarce impact of disease, accidents, and parasites and to the failure of last-hatched chicks to put on weight at a normal rate.

There was no appreciable difference in chick mortality in the Mogador colony between nests with two, three, and four young. In Paximada, however, the combined values of the 1966 and 1969 seasons (table 27) show that 172 (96.6%) of chicks born in 116 nests containing one or two eggs each were reared to fledgling stage; 119 chicks from 48 nests of three eggs each resulted only in 105 fledged falcons (88.2%). Chick mortality was only 3.4% among the former, but 11.8%, or three times higher, among the latter group.

Productivity

The net productivity of the Paximada population was only 1.26 fledglings per pair in 1965; 150 pairs produced 189 young. The 1969 value of 1.67 fledglings equals the raising of 250 fledglings by 150 pairs and comes very close to the corrected figures for undisturbed pairs in 1965. By contrast, the Mogador colony—if protected from human predation—showed fledgling rates of 2.48 (1966) and 2.60 (1959); that is, each pair produced one more falcon than did those at Paximada. This means that 150 Mogador falcons would raise a corresponding number of 372 to 390 chicks to fledging stage, which is 97 to 106% more than the Paximada falcons accomplished in 1965, and 49 to 56% more than in 1969 at this Aegean colony.

At the eastern end of the range, Eleonora's falcon does not do so well. The data from Cape Gata on Cyprus of 0.8 to 1.0 nestlings/pair are extremely low for this species. Unfortunately, these are the first detailed breeding data from any of the Cyprus colonies (Walter and Foers, in prep.). It is therefore not known whether the productivity of the Cyprus population has always been on the low side or whether it was higher in the past.

In the peregrine falcon 1.5 young were reared per occupied site for 67 British and American sites (Hickey and Anderson, in Hickey 1969). This includes nonbreeding and unsuccessful adults. The number of young per successful pair of a stable population varied from 2.37 (British Columbia) to 2.5 (Britain), according to the same authors. Other studies report a productivity of 1.91 to 3.4 for the kestrel; 2.08 for the lesser kestrel; 1.6 to 1.83 for the red-footed falcon, and 1.1 to 2.36 for the hobby (Blutz, Bauer, and Bezzel 1971).

The net productivity of Eleonora's falcon is normal to high (with the single exception of the Cape Gata colony on Cyprus in 1977) compared with that of other congeneric raptors. The losses from predators and other natural factors are lower in this raptor than in the other species. This seems to offset the relatively small clutch size, resulting in a high percentage of fledged young. Were it not for human interference (see chap. 11), populations like the one in Mogador that suffer almost no natural disturbance or predation losses would be very successful indeed: only about 15 to 17% of the eggs would fail to produce reared young.

EGG-LAYING, INCUBATION, AND HATCHING TIME

Eleonora's falcon is the latest breeder of European birds that raise only one brood a year. Although some urban birds and a few other species may breed in late fall and winter, they are known to breed during the other seasons of the year also.

Direct information on the exact timing of the falcon's breeding cycle has been difficult to come by. Most data refer to the hatching period. It therefore seems advisable to treat egg-laying, incubation, and hatching periods together. Vaughan (1961a) has summarized the available information as follows: Egg-laying of our species occurs "from 15–20 July onwards into early August. There is no evidence that it ever lays much earlier than this." Eggs are laid "at intervals of a day or more." Incubation "starts with the first or second egg" and lasted in one case (Cyprus colony) for 28 days. The first chicks hatched on 14 or 15 August (Mogador), 21 August (Aegean Islands) and 22 August (Cyprus).

Egg-laying

I visited Paximada island on 1/2 July 1966; only about 10% of the breeding population was present, and I found no eggs anywhere on the island. By the time of the next visit (20/21 July), the entire breeding population had apparently arrived; a thorough search yielded only two nest sites containing single eggs, one of which still contained only one egg 24 hr later.

In 1969 we visited the Mogador isles first on 11 July. Territorial and courtship behaviors of the falcons suggested that the breeding season was about to progress to the egg-laying stage. A single egg was found in a nest site on atoll island (no. 51). The nest contained two eggs on 14 July and four eggs on 20 July. On 20 July, out of 11 nest sites on atoll island, 4 contained a full clutch (3 with 3 eggs, 1 with 4 eggs), and 4 were still without any eggs. All of them had full clutches during the next week, on 31 July.

On 19/20 July 1974, five falcon pairs on the Isola di San Pietro were getting ready for egg-laying. No pair was incubating, and probably no eggs had been deposited. Thus the timing appeared typical and resembled my Paximada observations of 1966.

In conclusion, the breeding season of Eleonora's falcon began about a week earlier in the 1969 season of the Mogador colony than in the 1966 season of the Paximada falcons. Hatching data (see below) confirm that the Mogador falcons generally begin to breed a few days ahead of any other known colony.

Incubation

On Paximada, the eggs of the same clutch usually hatched on different days in 1965; incubation therefore must have begun before the full clutch had been laid. The hatching intervals of 60 eggs were recorded: It was one day in two-thirds, and 2 to 4 days in one-third of all cases. Incubation began, therefore, at least 24 hr before the laying of the second egg and might indeed have begun as soon as the first egg was laid. No data on the length of the incubation period were collected.

On the Isles of Mogador, falcon chicks from the same clutch generally hatched out on different days. In 1969, the length of the incubation period was approximately determined in three cases (table 5). The first egg of pair 51 had been laid at least 33 days before hatching occurred, and the second egg was not yet ready to hatch at least thirty-one days after its deposition. The first egg of pair 11 took 33 days to hatch, the second one at least 33 days. The second egg of pair 45 took 30 to 32 days to hatch, and the third one 31 days or less.

Eleonora's falcon seems to incubate its clutch a bit longer than

TABLE 5
Length of Incubation Stage

Date	Pair No. 51	Pair No. 11	Pair No. 45
11 July	1 egg	0 egg	0 egg
14 July	2 eggs	0 egg	0 egg
20 July	4 eggs	0 egg	1 egg
22 July	4 eggs	2 eggs	2 eggs
13 August	4 eggs, (one cracked)	2 eggs	3 eggs
19 August	4 chicks	2 eggs	3 eggs
22 August	4 chicks	2 eggs	1 egg, 2 chicks
23 August	4 chicks	1 egg, 1 chick	3 chicks

its nearest European relatives: hobby (28 days), kestrel (27 to 31, mostly 29 days), lesser kestrel (28 to 29 days), and red-footed falcon (27 days?) (Glutz, Bauer, and Bezzel 1971).

Vaughan's (1961a) statement is not detailed enough to support a 28-day incubation period of Eleonora's falcon: "in a Cyprus colony a clutch of three was completed on 29 July, and the first chick hatched on 25 August, giving a period of 28 days." When were the first and second eggs laid, and when did the last chick hatch? A cautious interpretation of the Mogador data shows a 30- to 33-day incubation period for that colony, perhaps with an average of 31 days (or one full summer month).

Hatching
Paximada

One day in August or September a falcon's egg will develop a small crack near its equator or central part. Usually the chick hatches within the next 24 hr, but occasionally it takes 2 to 4 days.

During the 1965 season, the first egg hatched about 15 August then one in each of two clutches hatched on 19 August. The most common hatching dates of first chicks were 25 and 26 August; the average of 70 nests was 26 August (table 6 and fig. 8). Second and third eggs of a clutch hatched 1 to 5 days after the first one. Eighty-two (76%) of 108 Paximada falcon chicks hatched on or before 31 August, 56 of them between 24 and 27 August. Half of the 26 September hatchings occurred in 7 of 21 clutches from the northern part of Paximada, where nest sites are less sheltered and therefore more exposed to wind and weather.

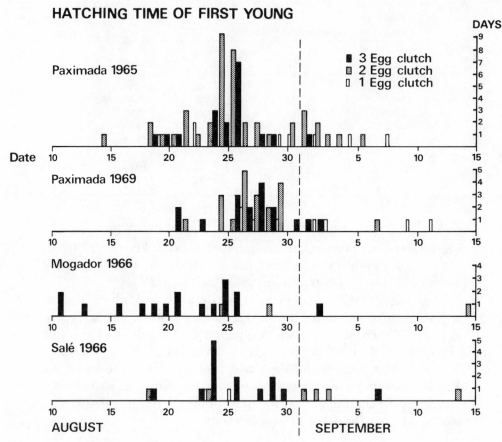

Fig. 8. Number of clutches hatching per day between 10 August and 15 September in three different colonies. See also table 6.

In 1969, D. Ristow (pers. comm.) observed the hatching process in about a dozen late clutches and estimated the hatching date of falcon chicks in other nests from their weight and plumage development. Most first chicks hatched between 26 and 29 August; the mean value for 45 first chicks was 27 August (table 6 and fig. 8).

A separation of the 1965 and 1969 data on clutch size reveals that the first egg in a three-egg clutch hatches 1 to 2 days earlier on the average than the first egg of a two-egg clutch. Compared with single clutches, the differences are 4 and 7 days respectively. The standard deviation of the hatching time was smaller in three- and two-egg clutches than in single clutches (table 6).

TABLE 6
Summary of Hatching Dates of First Chicks

Colony	Clutch Size	Number of Nest Sites	Mean ($\overline{X}$) Hatching Time	Standard Deviation (σ)
Paximada	3	18	25 Aug.	± 2.99 days
(1965)	2	44	26 Aug.	± 4.46 days
	1	8	29 Aug.	± 6.34 days
Total		70	26 Aug.	
Paximada	3	17	25 Aug.	± 3.59 days
(1969)	2	20	27 Aug.	± 3.08 days
	1	8	1 Sept.	± 5.82 days
Total		45	27 Aug.	
Mogador	4 + 3	17	20 Aug.	± 5.47 days
(1966)	2	3	2 Sept.	± 8.65 days
Total		20	22 Aug.	
Salé[a]	3	13	26 Aug.	± 4.79 days
(1966)	2	6	30 Aug.	± 8.59 days
	1 (at least)	2	24 Aug.	——
Total		21	27 Aug.	

[a] No weights taken. Rough estimate only.

Mogador

During the 1966 breeding season, a number of pairs had chicks during our first visit on 23 August. The first were hatched on approximately 11 and 12 August. The majority of first chicks hatched between 18 and 26 August (average of 20 pairs: 22 August), but in three clutches the first eggs did not hatch until 29 August, and 2 and 15 September (fig. 8).

Of a total of 67 falcon chicks, 65 (97%) had hatched by 31 August. Unlike Paximada, hatching of more than 50% of the chicks spread out over a period of 8 days (18–25 August).

It is questionable, however, whether these data are representative of the 1966 Mogador season. It is so difficult to monitor many nest sites that one is happy to have a large number of data even if they come from only a limited area of the whole colony. For instance, almost no data were available from the large number of falcon pairs breeding in the deep, dark, and moist pigeonholes of the central basin on atoll island. I tend to believe that their eggs hatched later than the ones reported above because the nest sites were presumably less desirable than those in drier and warmer locations and would therefore have been occupied later.

Vaughan (1961a), who probably had no access to this pigeon-hole area of the central basin, reports from the 1959 breeding season: "the first chick hatched on 14 or 15 August; about five hatched on each of the succeeding days; and by the time we left on 27 August just over half the 155 eggs under observation had hatched." In 1959, therefore, the hatching period seemed to spread generally over a longer time than in 1966. In both seasons, however, more than just a few chicks hatched before 20 August. The latter observation was confirmed in 1969, when 5 out of 9 pairs already had at least one chick (20 eggs, 10 chicks) on 19 August.

A statistical analysis of the 1966 data gives a mean value of 20 August for 17 clutches containing three or four eggs each and of 2 September for three clutches containing two eggs each (table 6).

Other Colonies

Salé. In 1966 I estimated the age of falcon chicks from their size, feather development, and behavior on 28 September: in 18 of 23 nest sites the young were between 30 and 40 days old. The rest contained chicks of 14, 20, 25, 26, and 28 days. The first egg must have hatched in this colony about 18 August, and the average hatching date of the first chicks in 21 clutches was about 27 August (table 6), 5 days later than in the nearest colony during the same season (Mogador) and nearly equal to the Paximada averages. In 1969, I observed one pair with small chicks and saw five adult falcons sitting on their eggs or chicks on 26 August. Had the latter had chicks older than a week, they could not have covered them so well. Thus, this brief observation seems to confirm the relatively late hatching time of Salé falcon clutches compared with the much larger Mogador colony farther south on Morocco's Atlantic coast.

Conclusions

The large majority of falcon chicks hatch out within a period of 8 to 10 days. The closest synchronization of hatching dates in a colony occurred on Paximada in 1965 among 18 three-egg clutches. The Mogador colony appears to hatch out more chicks before 20 August than the other ones. The second Moroccan colony (Salé) does not follow the Mogador pattern. My earlier suggestion that it does (Walter 1968a, p. 335) must therefore be corrected. The high degree of synchronization between different pairs of Eleonora's falcons within each colony is remarkable. What is the adaptive significance of this trait found in this and in many other gregarious species? Emlen and Demong (1975) have analyzed the reproductive statistics of 15 colonies of bank swallows (*Riparia riparia*) in New York State. These authors hypothesize that there are "at least two advantages of synchronous breeding for bank swallows: (1) it reduces losses to predation by minimizing the time over which colony members are vulnerable and (2) it maximizes the potential for group localization of food through social foraging." The latter point is backed up with data showing that retarded individuals and probable starvation losses occur "much more frequently among late nesters than among any other category." Both advantages (less time for predation and social foraging) can be used to explain the synchrony within a colony of Eleonora's falcon. Falcons nesting extremely late would be virtually alone, faced with climatic conditions that must be suboptimal for hunting migrant birds. Falcons breeding too early would also be disadvantaged because they could not procure enough bird prey for their nestlings.

A comparison of hatch dates (table 6) reveals an interesting point. The mean hatch dates of the largest clutches were earlier than those of the other clutches. In general, it seems that a high percentage of females that are going to lay three to four eggs each deposit their first egg several days ahead of females with smaller clutches. A comparison of the pooled breeding data from Paximada and Mogador (tables 27 and 28) indicates that the number of fledglings per nest was higher in those pairs that had larger clutches:

Clutch Size	Number of Nests	Number of Fledglings/Nest
4 eggs	3	3.67
3 eggs	74	2.27
2 eggs	111	1.41
1 egg	38	0.61

This means that an early breeder contributes more to the colony-wide reproductive success because it is likely to produce more eggs and a larger number of fledglings than normal and late breeders. The lack of banding data does not permit any deeper probing into the significance of this pattern. Thus, we can only ask: Who are the early breeders among Eleonora's falcons (senior, dominant colony members?), and What factors enable them to lay their clutches ahead of the majority and produce an above-average clutch size?

Another point of interest is the unusually late breeding season of our raptor species. Eleonora's falcon is a bird of temperate latitudes breeding after the summer solstice, some two to three months after its return from its winter quarters south of the Sahara. Lofts and Murton (1968) have stated, "Generally, the ultimate control of avian breeding seasons can be accounted for in terms of the available food supply and egg laying is usually confined to a period which anticipates the season when food for young is most readily available." Clearly, the huge biomass of fall migrants is the *ultimate* factor determining the late breeding season of Eleonora's falcon. This species provides, at least among European birds, a spectacular exception to the usual breeding season (spring) as a result of natural selection favoring the onset of the reproductive season after 1 July. Less evident are the *proximate* factors Eleonora's falcon uses to determine the proper timing of courtship and egg-laying. It has been shown that "seasonal daylength changes provide the most reliable environmental information" about the optimal timing of breeding in north-temperate birds (Lofts and Murton 1968). Other environmental stimuli, such as temperature, can by contrast be "hopelessly variable and uncertain."

The Mogador data indicate a remarkable constancy of the breeding season over many years. The same can be said for the colonies in the Aegean Sea. Since practically all other variables I can think of (wind direction, precipitation, humidity, abundance of arthropods or migrant birds in June and July) fluctuate considerably from year to year, it is highly probable that changing day length is the major proximate factor determining the surprisingly constant timing of this raptor's breeding season. In this particular case, egg-laying begins within 20 to 40 days after the summer solstice.

The cause and significance of Mogador's distinctly earlier breeding season cannot be fully explained at this time. More data, particularly from the Canaries, as the most westerly breeding region, and from the Balearic colonies are needed for comparative studies. Here we can say only that the prey species most important for raising the brood are available earlier at Mogador than in the Paximada area north of Crete. However, though Salé should enjoy the same advantage as Mogador, it does not in fact seem to possess a parallel timing. Thus we might look at the unusual breeding density of the Mogador colony. The courtship behaviors of one male will be seen by 20 to 50 others in the atoll central basin, on Smea, and on the submarine rock. That could not only stimulate but accelerate the behavioral and physiological cycles of a number of pairs and perhaps the entire population.

There can be little doubt that bird migration is not a food source for adult Eleonora's falcons at Paximada (or probably at most Aegean colonies) until *after* the clutch has been laid. Indeed, the *hatching* of falcon chicks in this colony appears to be closely synchronized with the onset of bird migration (see chap. 5).

GROWTH RATES OF THE YOUNG

The growth and development of falcon chicks depends on the hunting ability and social behavior of their parents. The weight curves of falcon chicks are a barometer of their health and their potential to grow up to fledging age. The daily or weekly weight increase also tells us when falcon chicks require larger or smaller quantities of food. Another question should draw our attention: In many raptor species the later-hatched young regularly die as a result of food competition with the elder sibling(s). Does this occur in Eleonora's falcons?

I shall concentrate here on growth rates; later I shall discuss the behavioral development of the falcon chick. On Paximada, I weighed the chicks of 21 study pairs during my regular monitoring and prey collection days (about every five days). Chicks were placed in a small bag and weighed on two sensitive spring scales (100 g and 500 g range, error factor about 1%). I repeated this with a smaller number of Mogador chicks.

General Observations

The analysis of the Paximada growth curve (fig. 9) yields the following observations:

1. Falcon chicks grow very little in their first 5 days of life or after they have passed the 30- to 35-day mark. They grow most between the 10th and 15th days: net weight increases about 25 g/day (table 7).

2. There is a considerable range of data points for the same age level. This is partly the result of individual variation and also

reflects the generally slower growth rate of the third-hatched young in the Paximada colony. However, even among first chicks there may be a large difference in weights of chicks of the same age. This may be a function of the parents' ability to provide an abundance of prey items to the young; diseased chicks were rare in both colonies. In addition, weights may be dependent on the sex of the chick, even at this age level. One chick that later turned out to be a female already weighed 475 g on its 26th day, whereas a male from the same colony (both were single chicks) needed three more days to attain that weight.

3. Falcon chicks usually weigh more between their 30th and 55th days than any time before or after. This maximum weight (much fatty tissue) is about 40 to 100 g above that of the adult bird. The fledglings become airborne at about 37 days, with a weight of 470 to 510 g, but some need a few more days because of overweight. The heaviest Eleonora's falcon I have ever found weighed 540 g at an age of 36 to 37 days. That is 90 to 175 g (20 to 48 percent) more than the live weight of adult females in the same colony (Paximada).

4. The weights of second-hatched chicks appear to be generally within the range of first-hatched young. This would mean that they generally manage well in getting a sufficient share of the food offered by the parent falcons. The data from last-hatched chicks (runts) from three-egg clutches, however, show a definite retardation of weight increase for those that managed to fledge. Thus, those chicks were affected by competing for food with their two elder siblings. A lower growth rate coupled with younger age (1 to 5 days) means that a decidedly smaller chick will be found in a nest scrape with two larger chicks. Five pairs lost their third-hatched chick; two chicks starved, the other three disappeared with no trace. This happened within their first 10 days. Older retarded chicks eventually will catch up with their elder siblings during the long period between a chick's 35th and 55th days of life when the normal young continue to grow their wings and tail feathers but receive and eat little food; though their weight does not increase, the retarded young continue to gain weight. In 1969 D. Ristow (pers. comm.) found that in 4 of 16 nests containing three chicks each, one chick, presumably the runt, died before fledging time. A fifth nest contained two normal chicks and one retarded chick. In two nests containing two chicks each, one chick

also perished. In both cases, starvation had probably caused the death.

The small falcon chicks of the Mogador colony appeared to put on weight at a slightly faster rate than their Paximada equivalents, but the data on the larger chicks lie within the Paximada range. The third- and fourth-hatched chicks grew considerably faster than their Paximada counterparts. To illustrate this point, I have added some Mogador data on third-hatched chicks to the curve of Paximada mean weights of first- and second-hatched chicks (fig. 9). They lie below the curve, whereas the corresponding data points of third-hatched Paximada young lie above it. This suggests that the falcon population of Mogador carries more prey to the young, enabling all three or four of them to develop at a normal pace.

TABLE 7
Development of Young

Age in Days	Average Weight (in g)[a]	Average Change in Weight over Last 5 Days (in g)
0	20–25 (egg)	—
1	15–22	—
5	42	4–6
10	140	20
15	265	25
20	372	22
25	432	10
30	450–90	4–12
35	470–510	ca. 4
40	470–510	ca. 0
45	425–500	ca. − 9 to − 2

[a] Data on first- and second-hatched chicks (Paximada 1965).

Specific Growth Histories

Let us now compare the growth histories of the chicks of 9 Paximada and 6 Mogador falcon pairs (figs. 10 and 11).

Paximada Colony

The single chick "Sokrates" of pair 16 from Paximada's upper slope (a second egg did not hatch) was one of the first to hatch in this colony, on 19 August. I weighed and observed it almost daily. Its growth rate was rather low compared with that of three other single chicks from the same colony. After about 25 days, however,

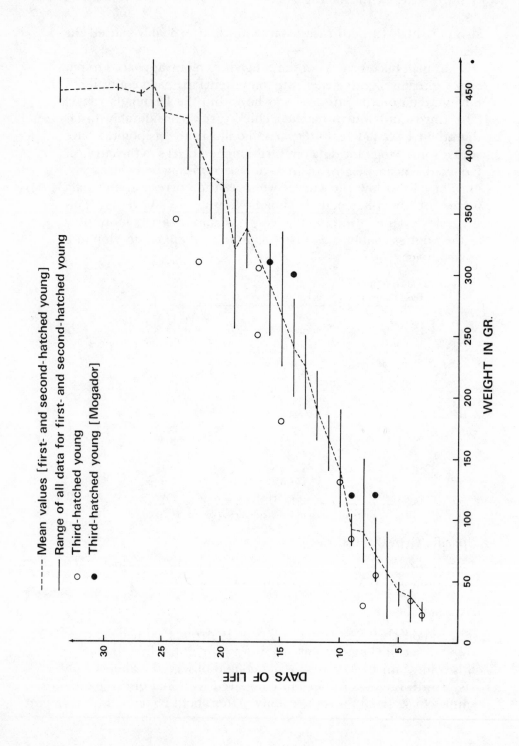

Mean values [first- and second-hatched young]

Range of all data for first- and second-hatched young

○ Third-hatched young

● Third-hatched young [Mogador]

WEIGHT IN GR.

DAYS OF LIFE

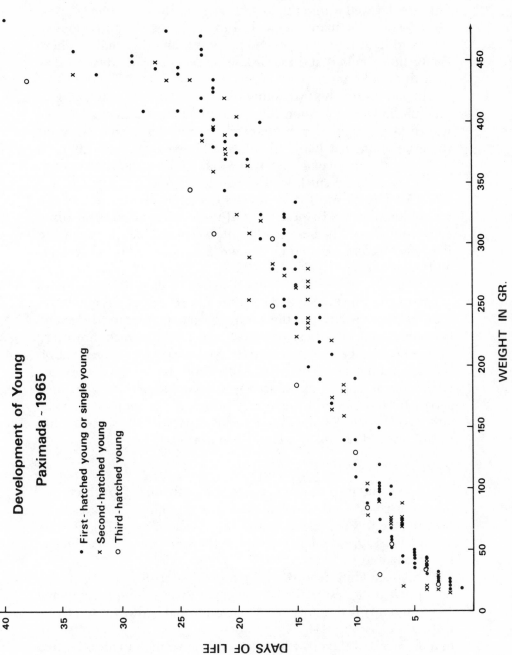

Fig. 9. General growth band of young Eleonora's falcons from the Paximada colony (1965). *Below:* Individual data points for first-, second-, and last-hatched falcon chicks. *Above:* Mean growth curve. Four data points from the Mogador colony have been added for comparative reasons (see text).

Sokrates lay well within the weight range of the other chicks. Male 16 was not a dominant member of the upper-slope study population, and he carried less prey to his nest than other males. There can be little doubt that these circumstances contributed to the slow growth of Sokrates.

The curves for the two young of pair 23 and the two young of pair 25 lie close together. The second-hatched appears to have grown as much as or only slightly less, and definitely not faster, than the sibling hatched 1 (pair 23) or 2 days earlier (pair 25).

Two out of three pairs that successfully raised three chicks each had a last-hatched chick with a retarded growth pattern (pairs 8 and 15). The curve of the runt lies definitely above those of the two older siblings. In nest 8 the three young hatched on three consecutive days; in nest 15 the interval was 1 day between the first- and second-hatched chicks and 2 days between the second- and third-hatched chicks (fig. 10).

In nest 24, the second chick hatched 1 day after the first-hatched, the third chick 4 days after the second. One might assume that this would put the youngest one at a greater disadvantage compared with those of nests 8 and 15. This chick, however, overcame this age problem, and its growth curve matches that of the second-hatched (fig. 10). This case is an exception on Paximada; it can be explained by the particularly diligent and successful hunting and feeding efforts of the parents. It may be added that male 24 was dominant compared with some of his neighbors and occupied a larger ground territory.

Mogador Colony

There exist no differences between the individual growth curves of single chicks and those of young with siblings. The slowest growth rate was registered by the two young of pair 17. Here the second chick grew relatively slower than Sokrates of Paximada (fig. 10, pair 16).

The outstanding feature of the individual growth curves from one four-young nest (pair 20) and three three-young nests (pairs 7, 13, and 14) is the normal to above-normal growth rate of the youngest chick (fig. 11). The competition for food does not seem to have affected the growth pattern of the youngest chicks in any negative way. In fact, the first-hatched chick seems to grow no faster than at least one of its siblings. This suggests that there is an

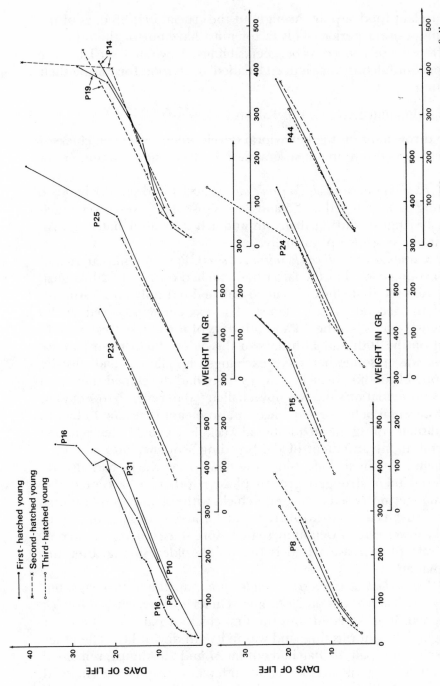

Fig. 10. Growth histories of individual falcon chicks from Paximada (1965). The curves illustrate the development of single chicks and of two and three siblings. P 16 refers to the single chick ("Sokrates") of pair 16. P 6, P10, and P 31 are curves of other single chicks. The chicks of pairs 14 and 19—although of different ages—were successfully exchanged by the author. The first-hatched chick of pair 44 was transferred to nest 9 by the author (with a slightly older single chick) during its fourth day. It was then successfully raised by pair 9.

abundant food supply throughout the crucial first 35 days of the young-raising period. This factor must have outweighed the age difference of 1 to 5 days between siblings. As we shall see later, the Mogador falcons were indeed "loaded" with food for raising their young.

Experimental Exchange of Falcon Chicks

To throw light on the behavioral development of falcon chicks, I exchanged the young of several nests on Paximada in a number of ways.

1. *Exchange of small chicks (same age)*. Pair 21 and pair 52 had two young each, hatched on 25 and 26 August. They were exchanged on 29 August, during their 5th and 4th days after hatching. All four chicks grew up normally.

2. *Exchange of small chicks (different ages)*. Pair 14 and pair 19 had two young each, but the latter had hatched on 19 and 20 August, whereas the first chick of pair 14 hatched out only on 25 August, and the second on 27 August. The exchange occurred on 29 August, that is, on the 3d and 5th days of the chicks from pair 14 and on the 10th and 11th days of the older chicks from pair 19. This was a somewhat risky exchange: female 19 had already stopped brooding over her chicks (they had developed their own thermoregulation) and was now challenged to revert 5 to 7 days in her parental behavior sequence. It also meant that pair 19 had to feed their young for an additional week. For pair 14 the exchange meant an advancement of the breeding sequence and a sudden demand for much food, since the new foster chicks had already entered their strongest growth phase. Both pairs accepted this exchange and raised their foster chicks without any complications. The growth curves (fig. 10) are normal; the second chick of pair 19 had a lower rate of weight increase before the exchange occurred. Its rate of increase parallels that of its older sibling after the exchange.

3. *Small chick added to small single chick*. Pair 9 had two eggs, but only one hatched out on 25 August. On its 6th day, when the chick weighed 38 g, I added to it the first chick of pair 44. The latter weighed 36 g at this time and was in its 4th day of life. The other two chicks of pair 44, hatched out on 27 and 29 August, remained with their original parents. Again both pairs accepted the changed number of chicks. The foster chick of pair 9, now like a second-

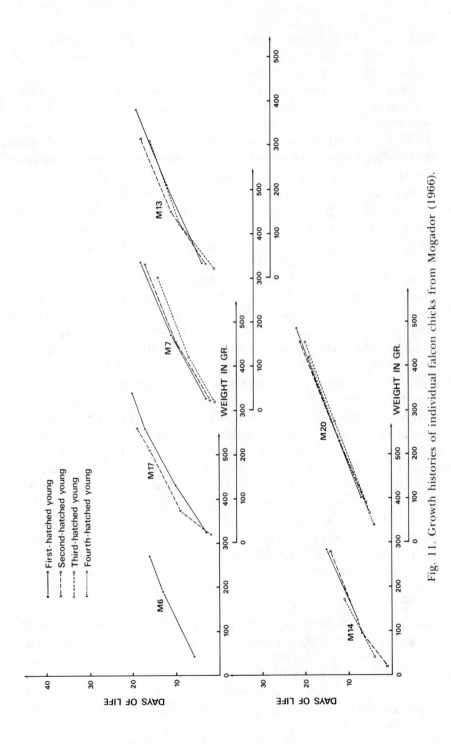

Fig. 11. Growth histories of individual falcon chicks from Mogador (1966).

hatched to the originally single chick in nest 9, grew up normally, but its younger sibling—now the oldest one in nest 44—grew up with a slight weight advantage (fig. 10).

4. *Exchange of large young.* On 22 September 1965 I exchanged the single young Sokrates (nest 16) for the oldest foster chick in nest 14 (born to pair 19). Both were 35 days old, but female 16 was dark phased and female 14 was light phased. Males 14 and 16 were both light phased. The oldest foster chick in nest 14 had therefore not seen a dark-phased falcon except in its first 11 days of life before the initial exchange (male 19 was dark phased, female 19 was light phased). The following morning, both young were being fed repeatedly by their new foster parents; surprisingly, therefore, parents and young had accepted each other. But when I returned to the isle about two weeks later, a puzzling change had occurred: pair 14 had only one fledgling but pair 16 had two. Since all three took to the air on my approach, it was impossible to check their identities on their aluminum bands. The circumstances and the comparison with other parent/young groups indicate, however, that Sokrates must have returned to his proper parents (pair 16), while the young taken out of nest 14 remained in the territory of pair 16. No young were missing from any other nest of the upper-slope area. The distance between nest sites 14 and 16 was about 25 m. This result can be interpreted to show that we can successfully exchange the young of Eleonora's falcon almost up to the time they become airborne. They apparently will not be rejected and will not reject their foster parents. Sokrates probably returned to his original parents and their territory because of the exact knowledge of his home area that is characteristic of all young falcons. Why the other fledgling did not do the same remains unclear. Does the fact that it had already been moved into another nest once before (from 19 to 14 at the age of 11 days) play a role in this?

Conclusions

The analysis of the growth rates of young Eleonora's falcons adds some important insights into the ecological fitness of the two large colonies under investigation.

1. The Mogador population managed to raise three and even four young per nest at normal growth rates in spite of age differences between siblings. Although I collected relatively few

weight data, they may well stand for the many other young I inspected in 1966 but had no time to weigh.

2. The Paximada population appeared to be controlled by a definite limiting factor: food supply. Last-hatched chicks of pairs with three and sometimes even two young had a better than even chance in this colony either to grow up in a slightly retarded fashion or to starve within the first ten days.

3. The general growth curve of our Paximada sample population, as well as the individual growth histories, demonstrates a considerable variability in weight data. Single chicks do not automatically grow faster than those with siblings. Parental hunting behavior and success certainly will affect the chick's growth rates. Pair 16's relatively poor feeding performance, evidenced by Sokrates' slow growth and this pair's subordinate social status, contrasted with pair 24's excellent feeding record coupled with a more dominant social rank. The question arises whether dominance and hunting success (plus parental care) are positively correlated in some way.

4. The development of the young falcons did not appear to suffer from the experimental transfer into other nest scrapes at ages between 3 and 11 days. The adults did not harm the foster young placed into their nests. They accepted each one and even tolerated the addition of one young to a single-chick family. Even the transfer of 35-day-old young was initially accepted by the foster parents. This is somewhat reassuring should it ever become necessary (I sincerely hope not!) to transfer or exchange young Eleonora's falcons as a last resort in falcon management and conservation.

MORTALITY AND ITS CAUSES

Raptors in general are afflicted with few diseases. Since many of them must feed on diseased or decaying animals, they have to be resistant against a large number of disease organisms. Eleonora's falcon is no exception to this rule. Less danger comes from pathogens than from natural hazards and the falcon's enemies, particularly man himself.

Disease

In the outdoors, most animals that die are never found and reported. Many pathogens do not themselves cause death but weaken the infected individual and possibly have a synergistic effect with other pathogens or parasites.

A dead Eleonora's falcon found on Paximada in 1965 had a blind eye. The same fate fell on the smaller of the two chicks of pair 60. The cornea of the left eye was whitish and swollen on 22 September 1965. On 8 October both young had become airborne and were gliding in the updraft. In what way the young falcon overcame his disability could not be determined.

The single chick of pair 51 was hatched out on Paximada on 25 August 1965. It looked normal on 5 September but appeared to be retarded by about five days (weight: 296 g; mean weight on 21st day, 380 g [range 355 to 420 g]). The chick had weak or paralyzed talons and could not stand up properly. Six days later it was still alive but looked emaciated and was lying on its back. Its remains were still in the nest area on 8 October.

Competition among siblings and the resulting starvation have already been mentioned. It was certainly the most common cause of death in the Paximada falcon population, both in 1965 and in 1969.

Parasites

All falcons of the colonies studied probably harbor a number of endo- and ectoparasites. I have noticed only ectoparasites: ticks, feather lice, and louse flies.

The single chick of pair 48 was covered with hundreds of pinhead-sized, blackish ticks (Paximada 1965). It looked skinny and died a few days later. This is the only case I have seen where an ectoparasite may have played an important role in the death of a falcon. Ristow (pers. comm.) noticed many ticks on the heads of two siblings in 1969. Thus, in general, fewer than 0.5% of the falcon chicks were afflicted with large numbers of these small blackish ticks.

The Paximada falcons, adults and large young alike, were also the hosts of some large species of feather lice (*Mallophaga*) whose identity has still to be determined by specialists. Similarly, some louse flies (*Hippoboscidae*) were running up our arms (and difficult to catch) during the regular weight controls of the study nests on Paximada. There were always just one or a few of these parasites per bird.

Accidents

The dashing and beautiful courtship and display flights around cliffs and ravines can be assumed to result sometimes in a broken wing, a fatal accident in this species. On 21 September 1965 I found a healthy adult male on Paximada with a broken left wing. Some of the intraspecific fights between falcons may cause severe injuries and perhaps even death. However, this appears to be mostly accidental rather than intentional. There is a photograph in a popular British *Birds of the World* encyclopedia that shows an adult Eleonora's falcon standing on a freshly killed juvenile fledgling. This photograph seems to depict a rather unnatural or rare event. For instance, the young falcon might have been shot; an adult falcon may then have taken possession of it since it had lost the image of a live bird.

Cannibalism

I have never observed a case of cannibalism in this species. But, once a chick is weak and does not respond to parental stimuli, I believe there are occasions when it would be eaten by the adult falcon. By eating an apparently diseased young, the parent falcon can reduce the chance that disease will spread among the remaining siblings. As in other falcon species (Brosset 1973), the young did not attempt any serious attacks on their siblings.

Enemies
Man

There can be little doubt that man—in the form of local fishermen and young boys, sport hunters, international egg collectors and a newer breed of bird photographers, falconers, and tourists—constitutes the only real enemy of Eleonora's falcon today. Fishermen have probably preyed on the eggs and young of this species for hundreds, perhaps thousands, of years: the young falcons are still famous for their delicate meat and fatty tissues among all the fishing circles in the Mediterranean island world. There is no reason why men should not have lived on the Isles of Mogador when the latter served as an important commercial center producing purple dyes for Juba II, king of Mauretania (65 B.C.–23 A.D.). If they did, the people probably persecuted the falcon the same way the Moroccans did in 1966. This would still allow the species to raise a good number of young in inaccessible nest sites. However, modern hunters, egg collectors, and some irresponsible "falconers" now appear to take a large toll of these formerly secure populations.

Fortunately, Eleonora's falcon is not yet on the brink of extinction; many of its colonies will remain remote and difficult of access for decades. Natural circumstances also help protect the falcons during the reproductive season: the *meltemi* winds often blow so violently in the Aegean Sea during September that they have been hailed by Reiser (1905) as an "excellent protection for the brood"—few would dare to land a boat in rough seas at the steep cliffs protecting a colony.

Mammals

Among the "natural" enemies of Eleonora's falcon, the greatest impact probably has been caused by rat populations inhabiting many of the Mediterranean islets. On Paximada there has been a sizable population of black rats (*Rattus rattus alexandrinus*) for many years. They appear to subsist mainly on a vegetarian diet but will apparently readily feed on falcon eggs. A freshly broken clutch showing the tracks of a rat in the soft sand of the nest scrape was brought to my attention in 1965 by an alarmed and visibly distressed adult female falcon. Even some small falcon chicks may fall prey to the rats. As a whole, however, falcons carefully guard their clutches and small young day and night; rats can become predators only when no adult is at the nest site. Human disturbance increases a rat's chances of nest predation.

Another, and somewhat unlikely, falcon enemy is the domestic goat (*Capra hircus*). Shepherds sometimes bring herds of goats and sheep to the offshore islands during the winter months. Some of these are not ferried back and become feral. In 1965 we shared Paximada not only with the rats and the falcons but also with three wild-looking and exceedingly shy goats. They were the last survivors of a larger herd (many skeletons lay around) on this rock without any freshwater source. We found more destroyed clutches near favorite goat haunts than elsewhere. On several occasions I witnessed falcon pairs trying to evict a goat from their ground territory by dive attacks. A goat may quite accidentally step on a falcon clutch.

No feral goats were present on Paximada during the following seasons. On Mogador, rabbits populated the dense parts of the isles, but their impact on falcon survival was probably negligible. Most of the breeding places of Eleonora's falcon are too small to harbor any mammal predator like foxes or weasels, which affords much security to any colonial bird breeding on islands.

Birds

Eleonora's falcon has to fear certain larger raptors, possibly peregrine and lanner falcons, and the eagle owl (*Bubo bubo*). In 1965 we found on Paximada the remains of ten adult falcons, six of which had been plucked in such a way that only another bird was likely to have been responsible for it. Falcons, eagles, and owls probably migrate over or live temporarily on Paximada in spring and early summer months. Repeatedly, I saw peregrines fly through the Mogador colony in 1966 and 1969; they were mildly harassed and left quickly. Kestrels and migrating hawks and eagles prompted instant communal alarm and defense of the airspace over Paximada.

The greatest danger from a bird predator so far witnessed was the sudden appearance of an immature parasitic jaeger (*Stercorarius parasiticus*) over the Mogador colony on 23 August 1966. When spotted, this predator of the food, the eggs, and young of other birds was immediately and vigorously pursued and attacked by four falcons; it defended itself elegantly and stooped down on the falcons before leaving the area.

The bird species most harmful to the Paximada falcons was the rather harmless-looking Cory's shearwater (*Calonectris diomedea*). Some of the hundreds of pairs used nesting holes under boulders and in crevices that were also holding the nest scrapes of pairs of Eleonora's falcons. Some of the falcon chicks of those pairs, even older ones, mysteriously disappeared in 1965 and 1969; the only explanation we can provide is that a falcon chick might lie in the way of a shearwater trying to reach its single young in the almost total darkness of the night. The sharp beak of a shearwater is a powerful weapon; once picked up by it the falcon chick would probably be swallowed or carried deeper into the hole.

Gulls, ravens, and other birds do not normally affect the falcon's survival in any way.

Mortality Rate

Banding recoveries are still too scarce to indicate the mortality during the first, second, and following years. Undoubtedly, a high percentage of the fledged young will perish during the first two years. The adult falcon has relatively little to fear compared with other animals and should therefore reach a considerable age.

Comparative data from the peregrine and the hobby indicate that 55 to 60% of the recovered banded falcons died within their first year of life; 16 to 18% of banded peregrines recovered in Sweden and Germany died within their second year. A few banded peregrines reached an age of over fifteen years. Hickey and Anderson (in Hickey 1969) state: "As a general rule in avian population dynamics, it can be said that the low productivity of birds that do not breed at 1 year of age is offset by low adult mortality rates." These authors "regard [mortality rates] as probably approximating those that should characterize stable populations of the peregrine": 56% for the first year, 22% for yearlings, and averaging 19% per year for adults.

If we apply the same rates to the Mogador and Paximada colonies about 57 new breeders would be required each year to offset the adult mortality of a stable population of about 150 pairs each. Since about 78% of the fledglings will die before reaching maturity during their third year, each colony would have to produce on the average between 260 and 300 fledglings a year in order to maintain itself. This equals 2.00 fledglings per pair. Without human interference the Mogador population would have exceeded this value by a large margin (2.48 to 2.65; see table 28), while Paximada fell short of it (1.26 to 1.73; see table 27). If the mortality rates gained from the rather extensive collection of data on peregrines approximate those of Eleonora's falcon, we may conclude that any of its colonies can maintain itself only if each pair rears about 2 young each year. When we consider the relatively low clutch size in all Mediterranean colonies (2.00 to 2.50) and subtract 15 to 25% as losses of eggs and young, we see that most of those colonies would hardly be able to maintain stable populations. A stable population with a net productivity of only 1.0 to 1.5 fledged young per year could exist only if one or more of three conditions are met: (1) the population possesses a much lower mortality rate than found in the peregrine falcon; (2) the colony receives a continuous influx of surplus adults from other colonies; or (3) subadult falcons in their second year join the breeding ranks.

Conclusions

Man is the greatest enemy of Eleonora's falcon. The abandoning of traditional breeding islets like Vacca (Sardinia) and the shift to more inaccessible nesting areas within the last decade amply prove this statement.

Diseases, accidents, intraspecific aggression, and the impact of mammal and bird enemies result in the loss of only a small percentage of clutches, young, and adults. Occasionally, however, such impacts become more pronounced: the large number of destroyed and abandoned clutches as well as the numerous one-egg clutches on Paximada appear to reflect the combined effects of rats, goats, and shearwaters. Since the Isles of Mogador did not possess either goats or shearwaters, its falcon population had another advantage over Paximada in the quest for survival.

The rather speculative discussion of mortality rates and survivorship indicates the danger this species faces in the last decades of this century. Its natural mortality rate has probably been somewhat lower than that of other raptors owing to its secluded breeding areas. Migration and winter range (see chap. 9) lie in sparsely populated regions of the world. Though the species has been able to cope with the more traditional impact of man, we must seriously question whether its mortality and fledgling rate can counteract the drastic effects of today's human-caused disturbance and extermination of its colonies.

4 The Hunting of Migrant Birds during the Breeding Season

Knowledge of hunting behavior and ecology provides the main key to understanding a raptor's ecological niche. Like all organisms, Eleonora's falcon must maintain a balance of energy expended and energy taken in. During the reproductive season, additional energy is required for the development of eggs and young. The ratio of hunting success is critical for the survival of the species. If it is very low, the species risks expending more energy than it can gain. We can expect selective processes affecting body shape and weight, physiology, timing of the breeding season, and development and number of young to influence and be influenced by hunting efficiency and choice of prey items.

We begin with a description and interpretation of hunting behavior from about the middle of August to the middle of October, that is, during the young-raising period when the demand for food is highest in all colonies and *migrant* bird species make up the staple diet of this species.

DIVISION OF LABOR

As with other falcons, there is a division of labor between male and female during the breeding season. The latter guards the young and the ground territory very carefully almost twenty-four hours a day. It also plucks the prey and feeds small pieces of it to the chicks until they can do it themselves. The male is the hunter who supplies food to the whole family. In families with chicks of two weeks and older, both parents may hunt, even simultaneously. My observations at various nest sites lead me to believe that females hunt the same type and variety of bird migrants as males do. Following are three diary excerpts with examples of sexual role reversal: females returning from a chase and males transferring prey directly to their nestlings.

23 September 1965 (Paximada)
  6:15   Female 24 returns from hunting with a bird, hides it.
  6:25   Only 4 of 10 females of the upper slope are present. The rest
           must be hunting simultaneously with their mates.
  6:37   Female 19 lands with a bird prey.
  6:42   Female 23 arrives at its nest site with a bird prey.
  6:47   Female and male 23 land, each with a bird prey.
  6:49   Male 24 lands with a bird prey.
  6:55   Female 24 lands with another bird prey.
1 September 1966 (Mogador)
  7:00   Female 35 has arrived with a live, wing-beating warbler (*Sylvia
           hortensis*). She remains calm and standing for about 2 min, then
           flies to young.
  7:20   Female 34 arrives at nest with a bird prey from which the male
           rises and moves to the side.
17 September 1966 (Mogador)
  15:50 Male 302 has landed with a whitethroat (*Sylvia communis*) in his
           talons. Female is absent. Male has apparently been waiting for
           the female to arrive. At 16:05 he walks over to the young, who
           take the prey out of their father's bill and busy themselves with
           plucking it.

HUNTING AREA, PERIOD, AND TECHNIQUES
Introduction

Migrating passerine birds are usually hunted in the airspace over
the open waters and near the shores of the Mediterranean Sea
and the Atlantic Ocean. This characteristic seems to be shared by
every colony. Eleonora's falcon also hunts right above its colonies
on small offshore islets. From the standpoint of the migrants
those islets appear as useless as the sea itself: there is no food,
water, or shelter, and they are filled with raptors.

The only known exception might be the colony reported on the
Djebel Acbkel mountain near Bizerta in Tunisia (Gouttenoire
1955, after Vaughan 1961*a*), which—if confirmed—would lie
some 20 km inland from the sea, right next to a large lake. Here,
then, the lake surface might well play the same role for the hunting ecology of the falcon as the surface of the sea usually does.
This deviation from the rule is therefore not important. Eleonora's falcons normally do not hunt birds over any large island or
continental area.

Farther south—but at the same time of the year—another falcon, the sooty falcon (*Falco concolor*), breeds right in the middle of
the Libyan sand desert, also feeding its young with migrants. This
falcon makes use of the barrenness of the sand desert as Eleonora's falcon exploits the inhospitality of the saltwater desert.

We need not make direct hunting observations to determine the
daily hunting period. It is enough to check a number of nest sites
and time the arrival of one or both adults with fresh prey. On
Paximada our routine observations of the upper-slope population
as well as the close-up watch of pair 8 and its young from a blind
gave us ample opportunity to collect data on hunting and on the
arrival of adults with fresh prey.

In Mogador I watched some parts of the colony during selected
time periods in 1966; three years later—but earlier in the season
(before egg hatching)—the submarine rock population yielded
additional information.

In Salé, we had only several mornings and afternoons to look
out for any hunting behavior and its timing. Even less time was
available at the Mallorca and Sardinia colonies, but Thiollay
(1967) and Steinbacher (1971) monitored these colonies at other
times.

Compared with other birds of prey, this species is particularly
active at dawn, during the morning hours, and at dusk.

The Hunting of Migrants at Paximada

We had been on the island two weeks before we found time to
tackle seriously the question of when, where, and how the falcons
captured their prey. We had to devote time to getting installed
and organized on the isle, to surveying the colony, and to general
ecological observations of the falcon colony. Fresh remains of migrants were already dotting the neighborhood of nest sites. It
turned out that the easiest way to watch a "kill" was to lie flat on top
of Paximada staring at the cloudless sky.

Area. During windy or stormy weather (prevalent on 45 of 50 late
summer days in 1965), most migrants were caught directly above
Paximada or in front of it. The flight time between nest site and
hunting area was at the most a few minutes. Owing to the size of
the colony, we regularly spotted several to many falcons above
Paximada during the main hunting period. The hunting area

extended about 1,500 m to the northeast and southwest, 1,000 m to the northwest and southeast, and was at least 1,000 m high measured from sea level. Its broadest part (northwest–southwest) was parallel to the steep west coast of Paximada and nearly perpendicular to the prevailing wind direction (from northwest). The falcons used the strong updraft of the cliff to carry them quickly several hundred meters above Paximada (fig. 12).

We believe some hunting even took place above 1,000 m. Up to about 1,000 m we could follow a falcon without using our binoculars; beyond that height falcons were quickly lost even with good field glasses. We estimated flight levels utilizing the experience of a Herr V. Lucanus (1913), who had carried out some "aeronautical experiments" during the First World War. He determined that the European rook (*Corvus frugilegus*), a black crow similar in size to Eleonora's falcon, was visible up to 1,000 m above the observer's position on clear days without the help of any optical instrument.

During the few days without winds the three-dimensional hunting space described above was much less frequented. Instead, falcons were circling over a wider area of the sea perhaps up to 5,000 m away from the breeding grounds. Some went even farther and covered some 20 to 30 km in flying to Crete.

Period. Falcon chicks slept at night; their mothers rested with them; the males were positioned nearby on one of their lookout and resting posts. Throughout the night, one heard the flight calls of single falcons every 10 to 40 min (sometimes the falcon colony was perfectly quiet for several hours). After 3:00 the flight calls became more frequent. About an hour before sunrise (5:30–6:05 local time), nearly all the males of the colony disappeared from the island. Some feedings had already occurred at this time, but most prey items were brought to the nest sites within the first hour after sunrise. Hunting activities decreased rapidly within the second hour, and little prey was caught after 8:00.

Figure 13*A* illustrates the daily hunting period of pair 8. It was observed for 77 hr and 50 min between 15 August and 20 September 1965. The early-morning peak and the fast decline of hunting activity during the following hours are evident. There is a curious gap in the arrival of prey between 6:30 and 7:00. I can only suggest that it might indicate a short resting and feeding period (a "break") of the male falcon during his hunting period.

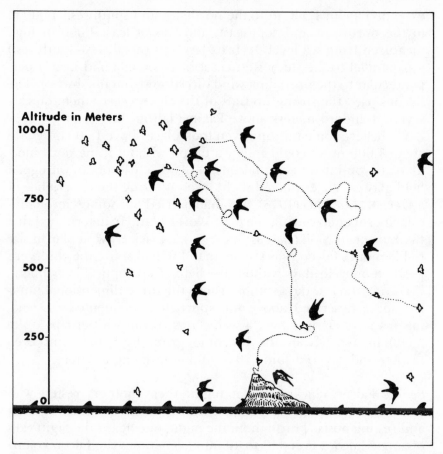

Fig. 12. Generalized cross section through the airspace of the Paximada colony on a windy September morning. Many of the resident Eleonora's falcons are hunting high above the colony.

The female contributed 2 of the 33 birds captured by the pair. Figure 13*B* summarizes the prey arrival data from seven pairs of the upper-slope population (pair 8 was not a part of it). Once again, a histogram shows two peaks in the early morning. Most males of the upper slope had returned to their resting and lookout posts by 8:00, where they remained nearly all day.

Few chases and prey arrivals were observed after 11:00. Shortly before and after dusk the colony was much alive, and some hunting took place. The targets were the migrants that had rested on Paximada during the previous daylight hours.

Techniques. This colony practiced the *standing flight* in large numbers over the breeding island, the typical hunting technique of Eleonora's falcon at Paximada. The falcon flies head-on into the wind but does not move relative to the ground. Its tail is not fanned and its wings are mildly bent, making 160 to 200 wingbeats a minute. In spite of this nearly normal forward flight behavior, the falcon effectively does not move because the forward-propelling force of his movements is equal to the backward-driving force of the air current; the two forces neutralize each other so that the falcon literally remains ("hanging up there") in the same position relative to the ground. Falcons can maintain standing flight for at least 10 to 15 minutes. It should be noted that the well-known "hovering" of American and European kestrels (widely fanned tail) is quite a different thing although its effect is the same: a fairly constant field of vision is generated that enables the raptor to detect the movements of potential prey items more easily.

The standing flight is a waiting and lookout position during the hunt. Since the falcon's prey is flying from Europe to Africa—that is, more or less from a northern to a southern point—it is usually aided by the strong winds with which it is drifting toward the falcon colonies. The falcons simply wait somewhere in the airspace until a prey object approaches. As soon as a falcon recognizes a migrating bird of suitable size in its field of vision, it abandons the standing flight and tries to reach the migrant as quickly as possible. There were more falcons standing above 800 m than at lower altitudes of 600, 500, or 300 m. From every point of the island we could see about 25 falcons in the sky (more or less above us). Each falcon kept a distance of about 100 to 200 m from all its neighbors practicing standing flight. Thus, during the early morning, when nearly all of the 150 males were hunting simultaneously, there was a broad, high barrier to bird migration in the air north of Crete; from sea level to 1,000 m above it, several km wide and deep, there existed a unique live bird trap, the "Paximada falcon wall." It is the extreme form of gregarious hunting in this species (fig. 12).

A good way to detect bird chases over Paximada was to watch for sudden zigzag flights and clusters of falcons going through loops, stoops, and so on. Migrants were generally not visible above

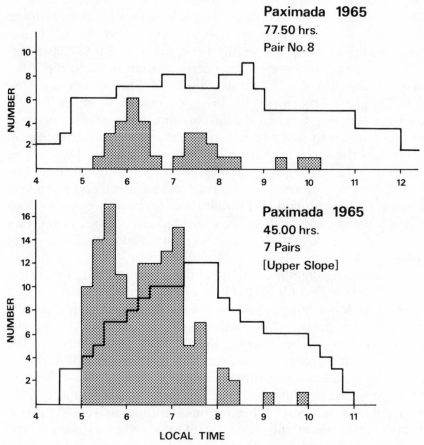

Fig. 13. Falcons arriving at their nest sites with fresh kills of migrant birds at different hours of the day. *Shaded*: Number of times prey arrivals were recorded

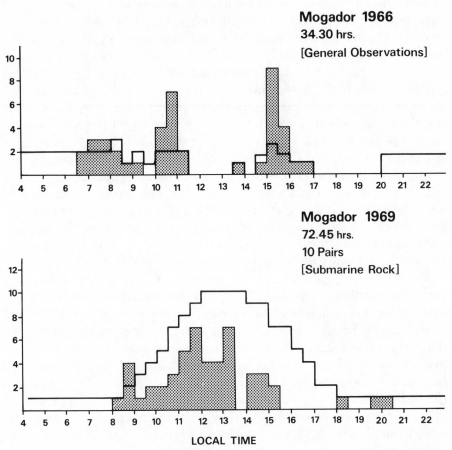

during each time section. *Unshaded*: Number of days falcon pair or population was observed throughout each time section.

several hundred m, but when they were chased, tiny white flashes beamed from the sky every second or two because their often light-colored undersides reflected the sunlight during evasive maneuvers. What interactions occurred between prey and predator along this "falcon wall"?

The first falcon to attack usually attempted to fall upon the migrant from high above, thus increasing its speed and impact. Most migrants responded by quickly dropping down a bit, arresting their flight, or flying an irregular zigzag pattern (fig. 14). As more falcons attacked from the sides and from behind, the migrant lost even more of its flight altitude. It tried, however, to continue its flight, since it could not seek shelter in the rough sea below. The more attacks a migrant had to repel, the lower was its flight level; finally, though it had escaped all its pursuers so far, a new attack would make it accidentally touch the water. Apparently shocked by the whole experience, it would begin to lose control and it was usually caught only seconds later.

Should the migrant escape the first attack, the falcon would turn around and try its luck again; in the meantime, however, other falcons that had been on nearby lookout positions and had observed the first chase might approach and join in the hunt. Thus the same migrant might be pursued and attacked by 3, 5, even 10 to 20 falcons in short sequence. The victim of this combined hunt would gradually wear out and slow down, and it might finally be captured by a falcon that was attacking for the first time. A falcon that was not accompanied by other members of its colony would usually give up a chase after 3 to 8 unsuccessful attacks.

The group hunting was not an organized event but was more accidental in nature; each falcon hunted only for its own and its family's needs. If other falcons saw each other's potential prey, they simply converged upon the migrant as each falcon tried to grab it.

If the attacked migrant found itself traveling high in the air directly over Paximada during the chase, its escape attempt was likely to be different:

4 September 1965 (Paximada)
6:15   Again a small migrant that succeeds in the escape method of
        simply dropping like a stone in absolute vertical flight. It acceler-
        ates to a terrific speed that I have never before seen in a small

HUNTING CASE STUDIES

ELEVATION IN METERS

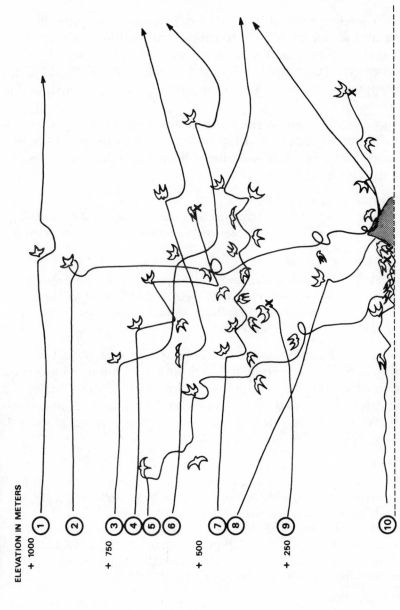

Fig. 14. Pursuit and attack of migrating birds by Eleonora's falcons near Paximada isle. Flight paths of 10 migrants are indicated. In this simplified pattern, 5 are captured (x). See text for details.

bird. The pursuing falcons do not follow that quickly, perhaps owing to their greater wing surfaces and air resistance. The migrant stops its downward race only ca. 3 m above the ground with spread wings and fanned tail, then disappears into a bush.

Such an escape had its hazards too. Falcons on standing flight at lower altitudinal levels tried to capture the falling "stone." I have also seen a falcon that was flying low along the island's slope succeed in picking up a migrant just when it was braking for landing. Some of the observed hunting episodes are illustrated in figure 14.

Migrants were safe in the midst of the falcon colony as long as they did not attempt to fly from bush to bush or to take off before darkness had set in. Occasionally a falcon swept down on a resting bird without catching it.

20 August 1965 (Paximada)
A small warbler was harassed by a falcon that was dive-bombing a bush in which the warbler had sought shelter. The migrant did not move.

4 September 1965 (Paximada)
Suddenly a willow warbler (*Phylloscopus trochilus*) flies from bush to bush in front of nest site 23. Female 23 takes off and attempts in an awkward-looking low flight to follow and capture the migrant, but she has no success.

A successful hunter returned at once to the nest site. It usually tried to avoid being seen by its neighbors, which might have tried to seize the prey. Having delivered his prey to the female, the male carefully cleaned claws, talons, and beak and scratched his head. Within minutes he might take off again and reach a standing flight position in the "falcon wall."

16 September 1965 (Paximada)
6:36   Male 19 calls "hay-kack" high in the air. Female 19 takes off to meet her mate; male has landed, female has followed; male delivers prey accompanied by the usual call notes.
6:46   Male 19 takes off, circles quickly a few times over the peak of Paximada, then "climbs" gradually up to ca. 250 m right above my observation post, where it assumes the standing flight position about 3 to 4 minutes after takeoff.

Considering the time the falcons need to fly to and from their lookout positions, it is truly amazing that they often catch more than one bird per hour during the early morning peak hunting period. I often saw a falcon male carry three prey items—all migrating birds—to his family within 60 min. The Paximada record observation was made on 8 September 1965, when male 8 caught five birds between 5:37 and 6:12. The same male captured seven more birds within the following four hours (Walter 1968a). At least twice, four bird captures per hour were recorded (male 24 on 4 September from 5:12 to 5:59, and male 23 on 30 August from 5:09 to 6:05). These observations mean that some falcons can hardly have been in the air for more than a few minutes when capturing a migrant.

It is difficult to describe the atmosphere on the upper slope during the morning hours. Above us was the flying wall of falcons, all facing the northwest wind, some visible in their plumage details, others so high that we were unable to say whether they belonged to the light or dark phase, the rest at an altitude that strained the eyes trying not to lose them in the wide blue sky. Some falcons were circling low over the slope while others arrived with prey or took off for a new hunting flight. A female took off from her nest for a short round of low circling flight, perhaps to inspect the immediate surroundings, or out of boredom, or trying to spot the male somewhere in the air. At least one falcon family was noisily telling everyone else that prey had been delivered and now was being plucked and fed to the young.

Hunting can also succeed without the standing flight technique. Undoubtedly some hunting took place at wave level. Other hunting techniques might have been employed but escaped our attention because of their infrequency. Some migrants approached or left the island during times when most falcons had already completed their daily hunting "work load." They were discovered by perching falcons or by those that had been gliding about the cliffs. A number of these raptors immediately set out in hot pursuit. Some migrants were also quite accidentally met by falcons returning from insect-hunting over Crete or perhaps simply from an unsuccessful hunting period.

27 August 1965 (Paximada)
17:00   Three yellow wagtails (*Motacilla flava*) attempt—one after the other—to reach Paximada, flying 0.3 to 2 m above the waves.

Each time, 5 to 8 falcons chase them, flying either behind or above the wagtails and trying to grab the slow-flying migrants when passing over them. Each wagtail escapes at least five attacks by moving suddenly in a lateral direction. Finally all three are captured before they can reach the safety-promising rocks of Paximada. One wagtail is pressed so hard by the attackers that it falls into the sea four times; once it plainly sits in the water without beating its wings for ca. 5 sec; when it has raised itself out of the water, a falcon captures it right away. It is noteworthy that the falcons avoid touching the salt water.

3 September 1965 (Paximada)

12:00   A male oriole (*Oriolus oriolus*) takes off from Paximada. He has already reached the airspace above the sea when he is spotted by two falcons. The oriole goes higher; one falcon attacks but is hindered by the second one. Both become entangled. A third falcon now pursues the fast-disappearing bird and grabs him at once with apparent ease. The first two falcons now begin to chase the third, successful one, but it converges with a fourth falcon (its mate) that receives the prey and races to the ground with it, landing in front of its nest.

It remains for me to describe the hunting behavior on Paximada during the few (10%) calm days. The standing flight was not practiced then, probably because it requires too much expenditure of energy without the assistance of the wind. Instead, falcons were seen gliding high and low over wide areas of the sea, probably distributed over an area of at least 5 km radius from Paximada. Theoretically, it is possible that some falcons also hunted above 1,000 m, using the standing flight technique in high-altitude winds. But it would have meant hard work for the falcons to arrive at such altitude through a calm lower air mass. In any case, prey was captured and the chicks received some fresh food, although it appeared to be a very small quantity.

On calm and windy days alike, Eleonora's falcons on Paximada also captured flying insects like dragonflies (Odonata), large butterflies and moths (Lepidoptera), and locusts (Orthoptera) that flew through the Paximada airspace. Some falcons continued to visit Crete even after their chicks had hatched (or were these the falcons that had lost clutch and family?). There they hunted flying insects low and high over the olive and orange groves. Their numbers, however, were rather low compared with the weeks before 20 August (see chap. 6).

The Hunting of Migrants at Mogador

One of the main reasons for selecting the Mogador colony as a sample population from the western range of the species was its unknown and somewhat mysterious hunting behavior; a two-week stay on the isles in 1959 did not provide much information to Vaughan and Carruthers. Their remarks (Vaughan 1961a) suggest a hunting behavior quite different from that of the Paximada colony: "birds were seen to leave the colony for the mainland in a continuous stream from shortly before dusk onwards. Even more striking evidence of the concentration of feeding at or near dusk (and perhaps dawn at Mogador) in August was the fact that we never saw a bird make a kill nor even a bird carrying prey during a fortnight's stay on the breeding islands. On one occasion two Swifts and two Nightingales were brought to one nest between 6:30 P.M. and 8:30 A.M." This leads one to hypothesize that the Mogador falcons prefer to hunt over the mainland at dusk (and perhaps throughout the night and at dawn?) rather than over the sea in the early morning like those on Paximada.

Area. Birds were hunted directly over the Isles of Mogador and above the adjacent sea. The hunting area was, however, larger than at Paximada, even during stormy weather. It extended for 3 to 5 km from the west to the northeast of the colony; falcons commonly disappeared after 3 to 5 min of flight in the misty air over the Atlantic, returning with bird prey in their talons. Hunting also took place up to at least 1,000 m above the colony and perhaps also above the distant hunting places just described (fig. 15).

We observed a regular movement of falcons to and from the mainland. It took place all day, particularly between the isles and the small lake south of the town that was later drained (in 1969). Occasionally, we also saw falcons on a hunting flight at dusk:

21 August 1966 (Mogador)
19:00   A falcon flies east from the isles until it reaches the shore; flies low over the town (70 to 15 m altitude), and finally drops down 2 km distant over the scrub forest.

Contrary to Vaughan's (1961a) observation, however, we never noticed a "general exodus" from the colony to the mainland be-

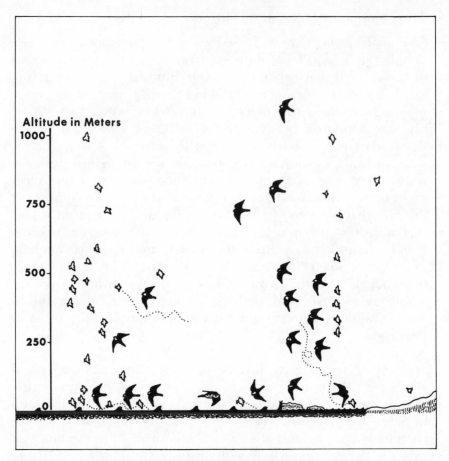

Fig. 15. Generalized cross section through the airspace near the Isles of Mogador off the Moroccan coastline on a windy September day. Falcons can be found hunting low above the waves and at varying altitudes up to 1,000 m.

fore and at dusk, although we especially watched for such a phenomenon. Since we observed the falcon population later in the season than Vaughan, it is possible that an exodus at dusk occurs more often at an early stage of the breeding season.

Period. During the night the falcons rested on the isles; the females stayed with the chicks and the males were perched only meters away from their families.

The falcon population hunted throughout the entire day; at any daylight hour some falcons were on a hunting mission. Most falcon males but also some females were observed hunting during the early morning hours. However, the morning does not appear to be the only or peak hunting time during the day. More chases were observed during the late morning and early afternoon hours during the 1966 season. Figure 13 is a histogram assembled from the data on observed chases and prey arrivals during 34 hr and 30 min specially devoted to studying hunting and feeding behavior (23 August to 17 September). In addition, hunting activities were followed but only summarily recorded in our diaries while we were weighing the falcon chicks, collecting feather pluckings, climbing the cliffs, and so forth. They provided further evidence for the difference in daily hunting periods between Mogador and Paximada.

In 1969, the submarine rock population was monitored from 30 July to 22 August for a total of 72 hr and 45 min, mostly between 10:00 and 16:00 (fig. 13d). More prey was captured during the late morning hours than in the afternoon. Only once, on 12/13 August, did we find the opportunity to observe this population during the late evening, night, and early morning. Three prey items were brought back to the submarine rock between 18:00 and 20:30, but none were brought the following morning before 8:00, although the falcons became active around 5:00 and 6 to 8 falcons were already in hunting position above the rock at 5:25. On the whole, relatively few prey arrivals took place; however, the falcons were regularly seen feeding on bird remains. They had probably captured the birds and hidden them during the morning hours before our arrival. The total food demand was certainly much smaller than in 1966. The eggs had not yet hatched, and some pairs had no eggs at all.

Techniques. The differences in hunting behavior between Mogador and the Paximada colony were relative. What was seldom practiced in Paximada was in common use here and vice versa. Although the standing flight was a regular feature of the Mogador falcons, no falcon wall was created in the airspace near the colony site. As a whole, there were rarely more than 20 to 30 falcons in the air above the entire colony. Very rarely did I see falcons in a hunting position above the narrow straits between the isles and the harbor of the town. Rather, a cluster of "pirates" waited for their victims directly above the isles (fig. 15).

23 August 1966 (Mogador)

During the early afternoon a few falcons stand high in the air. Seven to 15 falcons are gliding low above the colony (atoll island); there have constantly been 3 to 4 falcons at at least 300 m altitude.

15:00   First chase: a small bird is chased by 4 falcons beginning at an altitude of ca. 350 m; I see at least eleven misses; by then the migrant has been forced down so low that I lose sight of it and its pursuers behind the cliffs.

15:15   One chase at ca. 400 m altitude; migrant escapes.

15:30   Another chase, altitude ca. 300 m; migrant escapes. In the meantime, I have seen several falcons "climbing" much higher into the air; one individual finally disappears into the sky.

15:50–   Continuous observation of one Eleonora's falcon (fig. 16): It
16:04   rises gradually but vertically from the atoll island until it has reached ca. 500 m altitude. Here it practices standing flight, looking out for prey. After 3 to 5 min it encounters its first migrant. The falcon gives chase, misses four times, and gives up. It now assumes a new lookout post farther south and immediately spots another migrant. The falcon misses three times, gives up, and flies northwest, where two other falcons are on a lookout post in the air. Without success it stoops three times on the third migrant. The falcon now flies east, practices the standing flight once again, detects the fourth migrant, and captures it with its second attack. It returns in a fast, straight flight to atoll island, the bird prey in its talons.

25 August 1966 (Mogador)

8:00   Falcons are standing in hunting position above the isles. Some must be higher than 700 m.

16:00   Many falcons standing in the sky during the afternoon hours, all headed into the fresh wind from the north.

1 September 1966 (Mogador)

The females are alone at the nest sites during the early morning hours while their mates are hunting. Some of the latter stand very high in the sky (at the limit of visibility), but they do not form a closed phalanx or falcon wall as over Paximada. Only 2 to 8 falcons are that high; the rest fly at 50 to 150 m altitude or chase birds directly above the waves.

In addition to the standing flight above the colony, the Mogador falcons regularly used at least two other hunting methods to capture migrants on windy days. As the above observation shows, hunting low above the waves was practiced more often than in

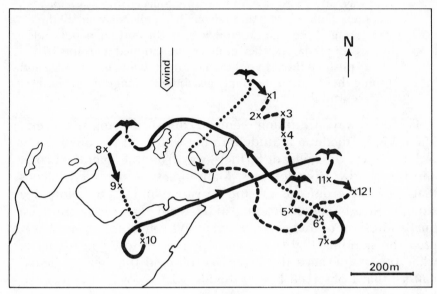

Fig. 16. Hunting flight of an Eleonora's falcon over the Isles of Mogador (23 August 1966). The falcon chased 3 migrants and attacked 11 times before capturing the third migrant some 14 min after takeoff. Steep climb in altitude (.....), steep descent in altitude (-----), attack (x), capture (x!).

Paximada. Approximately one-third of all pursuits occurred at this lowest possible altitude. A falcon would leave the breeding cliff and head straight into the often misty areas to the north and west of the isles, flying low; that is, generally below 50 m altitude.

Should it spot a migrant flying even lower, the chase would begin. As has been illustrated for the Paximada colony, such a chase gives the falcon a great advantage over the free air battle between prey and predator: the chased bird can seek escape only in a lateral direction.

23 August 1966 (Mogador)
15:10   A falcon zigzags low over the sea. At its third attempt it catches a small bird that has flown upward again to ca. 40 m altitude. The falcon, male 52, returns to the colony. His prey is a juvenile woodchat (*Lanius senator*).

1 September 1966 (Mogador)
         During the morning I observed a number of chases directly above the rough sea. Twice I saw a falcon pursuing a migrant

that way, and I also saw four herring gulls (*Larus argentatus*) pursuing both migrant and falcon. The gulls followed all the zigzagging of the first two and were in the end the better and successful predators: they grabbed the fatigued migrants by either pushing them into the water, then diving into the sea and fishing them out, or by simply grabbing the migrants from the surface with their bills.

The third way of hunting seems to consist of flying for several km at low or medium altitude into the wind and the open sea in order to meet the migrant farther away from the mainland coast and the nearby Mogador isles. Many times we observed falcons that took off from the ground territory and then followed a straight, steady course leading away from the colony until we finally lost sight of them several km away. Some of them probably used the standing flight over the open sea 3 to 7 km offshore, while others (perhaps the majority) followed the "search flight" pattern that I observed best at the San Pietro colony (see below): flying into the wind, turning and gliding once in a while as well as changing altitude, thus covering a large area while always on the lookout for some migrant passing by. Thiollay (1967) has called this the "technique of exploration."

During two rare calm days (14 and 21 September 1966), the Mogador falcon population followed the Paximada pattern: hardly any falcon was seen high up in the air on a standing flight lookout position. The falcons were either resting or gliding around the periphery of the colony. But some must have left and found their prey, since I observed several prey arrivals.

During both windy and calm days, some Eleonora's falcons were hunting insects throughout the day over the coastal region with its wadi, dune, and scrub vegetation. Of particular interest to us, because of Vaughan's (1961a) remarks, were those falcons that left the isles shortly before dusk heading for the mainland. I am certain they were catching insects over the mainland, but it is possible that they might encounter small birds that were just beginning to fly up to continue their nocturnal migration for Africa south of the Sahara. We never saw as many as Vaughan did, and we never saw a "stream of falcons" leaving at that time of the day. But we noticed that some falcons left and others brought prey back to their families shortly before nightfall (hunting location undetermined).

The Hunting of Migrants in Other Colonies
Salé Colony

This colony offered an ideal chance to test the hypothesis, developed after the completion of my Paximada and Mogador studies, that Eleonora's falcon is a "sea bird" or at least a *bird of the sea* during its breeding season (Walter 1968*a*).

Area. No bird-hunting took place over the mainland, nor did falcons remain in hunting position right above the falaises of the mainland shore:

1 October 1966 (Salé)

10:30– Eight falcons take off from the cliffs at a 90° angle to the
12:30 coastline, heading straight into the steady northwest wind. During this period only two or three falcons return with prey (always birds) from the open sea to bay no. 7. In spite of a careful watch and a telescope (20×), it is impossible to follow the departing falcons to their proper flight destination. Six falcons leave the isle flying low above the waves. At about 700 m distance from the coast, 3 of them gradually rise to ca. 150 to 300 m altitude and are soon out of sight. The others follow the air currents above the waves as shearwaters do, gliding and beating the wings alternately and progressing in a zigzag pattern until what must be well over 3 km offshore. Two other falcons of that group of 8 climb to 200 and 400 m altitude respectively right above the colony; then they suddenly take off in a horizontal direction, flying northwest in a straight line out over the sea.

Similar observations were made during the other days at this colony. It seems, therefore, that the airspace several km offshore and parallel to the Moroccan coastline constitutes an important hunting area for this colony. Since the surveyed part of the Salé habitat was more than 5 km long, its respective hunting area is probably even longer and may well be as wide, extending right up to the shore, where some minor hunting took place.

Period. The daily hunting period probably extends over most daylight hours, with a peak in the morning. During our short visits we observed 1 chase, 4 prey arrivals and feedings, and 14 departures for the open sea. They occurred between 9:00 and 12:30, with a peak around 11:00, but one falcon left the colony in straight flight northwest in the late afternoon (16:45). We did not observe this population during the early morning hours.

Techniques. The hunting techniques used by the Salé population differ from those of the two larger colonies. The standing flight was rarely practiced above the colony. Hunting low above the waves and the "search flight" technique far from the shore appear to have been the preferred ways of hunting.

The only chase observed concerned a migrant that had almost reached the shore:

28 September 1966 (Salé)
9:00   At 200 m from the shore a black-phased falcon chases a small
         bird at ca. 50 m above sea level. After the first attack the migrant
         drops down to wave level; it is still 10 m away from the cliff
         when the falcon misses in its third attack. The migrant reaches
         the shore and is safe.

Although more observations from this colony would be desirable, we may postulate from the available evidence the normal hunting behavior of this population. Hunting generally took place from sea level to above 500 m altitude and far from the shore, mostly out of the range of vision. Because of the large dispersion of the colony, most migrants were probably chased by only one or two falcons (note the "teaming up" of falcons). Since there were few or no other falcons around, the hunting birds were gliding, circling, rising, and falling in the airspace ("search flight") above the sea until they spotted a migrant.

The closer a migrant was to the African coast, the lower would generally be its flight level, since it was likely to prepare for landing and resting. We can therefore expect that the hunting level at Salé was low close to shore and higher farther away from the African coastline.

Mallorca Colonies

On 10 October 1966 I watched the Dragonera falcons from the shore of the main island in the hope of seeing a falcon wall or some other hunting formation. But between 6:30 and 9:30 I saw falcons only three times gliding up to 300 to 400 m altitude, where they practiced the standing flight for a short while. They then returned to a lower altitude and engaged in flight displays like other falcons there (up to 11 individuals observed simultaneously).

The geographical position of the falcon colony on Cape Formentor seems ideal for the capture of migrants arriving from the west, north, and east. During my brief visit in the early afternoon hours of 9 October 1966, I witnessed truly astonishing flight displays but no hunting behavior except the return of one falcon from the open sea at 15:00. Fortunately, this population had been studied by J. M. Thiollay and J. Trotignon earlier during the same season. The following is but a pale summary and translation (from French) of the most pertinent information contained in Thiollay's (1967) well-written paper.

Area. "Almost all of them leave [the breeding cliff] over the sea, either toward the northeast, where there is no land, northeast or southeast in the direction of Menorca, which is too distant (50 km) for them to return from there so quickly [within less than two hours]" (p. 33). This statement resulted from observations on 25 August. The following day, several hundred migrants passed by the cape, and the falcons hunted extensively so that "the attacks followed each other almost without interruption." This time the falcons remained close to the shore, circling above the water between 20 and 1,000 m from the shore. Migrants were closely pursued as long as they flew above the water, but they were immediately abandoned over land. Here some peregrine falcons were observed hunting and capturing the same migrants that Eleonora's falcons had been chasing over the sea—a striking example of "ecological separation" of raptors (Thiollay 1967). A few falcons climbed so high above the colony that they became practically invisible in the blue sky.

This colony, therefore, hunted migrants at the end of August close to the shore, apparently frequently at wave level and probably less than 100 or 200 m above the sea. Other falcons took off from the cliff for long flights several km offshore, climbing to 300 m altitude (24 August). Thiollay even postulates that this raptor is capable of making up for the absence of migrants near its colonies through hunting flights (often in groups) of "several tens of kilometers" (p. 37). At dusk, frequent departures and arrivals suggest to Thiollay an evening hunting area with a radius of 20 km around the colony.

Period. Thiollay describes Eleonora's falcon as "the most nocturnal of the European falconiformes with respect to the beginning and the end of the day. The two first hours of the day are the crucial moments of the hunting activity." The hunting success during the early morning bird migration determines the falcon's activities later in the day.

On 25 August a falcon that did not spend the night at the colony site returned a few minutes before sunrise, followed by another one some 11 min later. The following day, the first falcons were circling in front of the cliffs some 30 min before sunrise. Soon afterward the first migrants arrived. The falcons were more numerous and excited than the day before, but they did not commence hunting until after sunrise. Few migrants arrived after 7:30, and shortly thereafter the falcons returned to their respective breeding cliffs, the majority arriving from the northeast.

On other days (fewer migrants at the Cape, less wind?) the falcons appeared to hunt until 9:00 or 10:00 and had returned to the breeding location before noon. Not much happened until after 17:00, when sizable numbers of falcons left for the east (open sea and Menorca) or the west and southwest (inland area of Mallorca). These observations resemble the "exodus" of the Mogador population described by Vaughan (1961a), since many falcons apparently spent the night away from the nest site. Thiollay was not able to establish the final destination of these falcons. Did they hunt birds leaving Menorca after dusk, did they hunt insects (and bats?), or did they do both? Since they did not return and since they cannot hold more than one bird at a time, I consider this "exodus" at dusk to be a rather unimportant affair that can at the most supply additional food for the hunting falcon itself but not for its mate and small chicks.

In conclusion, the hunting period strongly resembled the Paximada pattern except for the dusk and overnight "excursions" of a number of falcons.

Techniques. Thiollay (1967) does not describe the standing flight, although he observed some falcons that became "presque invisibles dans l'azur du ciel." These specimens almost certainly practiced the *standing flight* hunting technique. More common and characteristic, however, was the *search flight technique*, which Thiollay was able to observe again and again. He describes it as repeated circling above the ocean at a height of 20 to 150 m altitude; the falcon then glides down to wave level for 200–300 m before rising for another round of circles. This pattern changes instantly if a potential victim is spotted. The bird reaches an "extraordinary acceleration" through a slightly changed wing position and quick, strong wingbeats. The prey is reached in no time at all and will be followed closely, attacked from above and the side. I studied the hunting behavior of Eleonora's falcons on Mallorca in some detail from 12 to 15 September 1977. My observations confirm most of Thiollay's (1967) data; in addition, I monitored frequent standing flight techniques. Many hunting flights in front of the magnificent cliffs resembled those that will be described from the San Pietro colony (chap. 6).

San Pietro and Toro Colonies

Both locations lie close to the southwest tip of Sardinia. They appear to be the ideal base for a raptor preying on spring migrants returning from Africa. Instead, a sizable falcon population has continued to exist in this area at least since the visit by Alberto della Marmora in the 1830s that led to the scientific discovery of Eleonora's falcon.

My observations of the hunting behavior in the San Pietro colony date from the beginning of the breeding season and will be discussed in detail later (see chap. 6). The observed pattern indicates, however, the hunting area and technique used during the nestling stage. Essentially, this is a Salé type of hunting behavior, with no or little standing flight but much search flight. As soon as migrating passerines become predominant in their diet, the falcons can be expected to hunt several miles over the sea as well as close to the shores of the large San Pietro island. The colony site is directed west and northwest and can therefore receive a large group of migrants that have crossed a large distance of the open western Mediterranean. I would guess that most hunting takes place in the morning hours; some hunting activity should be noticeable through the early afternoon.

The Toro colony was observed by J. Steinbacher for a few days and nights during the 1968 and 1969 seasons (Steinbacher 1971). Toro is a colossal mass of rock southeast of San Pietro and southwest of Sardinia itself. In September, Steinbacher writes, "they mostly stood 100–200 m high in the air, several 300–400 m high, in a long chain over the W and S walls of the island which lies opposite Sardinia." This is where they held their "characteristic hunting position" (he refers here to the standing flight of the Paximada falcons). The migrants "can't go a long way near Toro, the falcons fall down on them like stones, primarily at dawn and dusk, but also at night during full moon. Then we often heard their calls, when they—as happened frequently—attempted to steal each other's prey."

The only other reference to nocturnal hunting comes from Krüper (1864), who was told by a Greek monk that "these falcons hunt at night." Steinbacher refers to nights when the moon is full; still, I doubt that the falcons really captured significant numbers of migrants during such nights.

On Paximada, Mogador, Salé, and San Pietro I have heard falcons in the air at night; they were few, however, and seemed simply to fly around for a while or to arrive and depart. Some may also have been disturbed by shearwaters and other organisms on the ground.

The young falcons slept more or less soundly during the night hours at Paximada and also in captivity. Krüper (1864) also reports that the chicks "sleep calmly through the night." At least in the Aegean Sea area this species therefore seems physiologically adapted to an active diurnal period and a restful nocturnal period.

These comments, however, do not rule out successful nocturnal hunting. Steinbacher's observations should be followed up with a detailed analysis of prey arrival times at falcon nest sites. Any such arrival between 22:00 (10 P.M.) and 3:00 (3 A.M.) local time should be considered true evidence of nocturnal hunting.

Discussion

Eleonora's falcon becomes a bird of the sea when raising its brood because the unlimited airspace over the sea allows this predator to maximize its hunting success. If the reported colonies of the falcon all were to lie in some inland areas of Spain, Greece, and North Africa, Eleonora's falcon would utterly fail in its hunting style, since small birds attacked above land would immediately try to reach cover. That is, indeed, what some migrants accomplished directly over Paximada Island.

We can assume that the different hunting areas, time periods, and techniques are not a result of random trials but an optimum response to the bird migration patterns in geographic space. So many falcons with several family members to feed cannot be expected to hunt miles away from the colony or high up above the sea unless they have been successful there in the past. The hunting observations alone therefore suggest different bird migration patterns: migrants appeared to fly very high and to pass only during the morning hours through the Paximada airspace but to fly lower (even very low) and pass throughout the entire day near the Mogador colony. A study of bird migration utilizing visual and radar observations will be needed to show whether this assumption is justified—whether Eleonora's falcons, in fact, exhibit hunting behaviors that promise maximum success ratios as predators of small migrants (see chaps. 5 and 6).

The *standing flight* technique was regularly or predominantly used only in the two large colonies. After my observations at the San Pietro colony it occurred to me that the standing flight might be a response to crowding in large colonies. At the Sardinia colony I several times saw falcons switch from gliding into a fast wingbeat shortly before hunting and grabbing an insect. Quite clearly, the falcons gave up the gliding flight in order to achieve greater maneuverability within an instant of time through a "staccato" wingbeat, which could propel them immediately in nearly any direction. As long as there are no or few other falcons hunting in the same air zone, the search flight seems to be energy-saving and more efficient than the "standing flight," since it explores more hunting space; with many other falcons in the air, however, a split second will decide which falcon will attack first. Here those falcons that constantly look ahead (where the prey comes from) while beating their wings have an advantage over those that glide to the side, the back, and so forth, since the former can switch from standing flight to chase with no time lag. The standing flight is practiced where there are large groups of falcons hunting within the same few hundred meters of horizontal and vertical airspace.

The Mogador pattern is interesting because it demonstrates that three different styles can be practiced, implying the utilization of three different food resources concentrated in different parts of the three-dimensional hunting zone. If Mogador falcons used only the standing flight technique, they would miss most of the migrants that approach the North African coast at wave level as well as those that fly at various altitudes far away from the colony.

The hunting behavior of Eleonora's falcons at Mogador and the Sardinian colonies resembles that of peregrine falcons wintering along the Texas coast, which took land birds small enough to be prey for Eleonora's falcon by coursing into the wind, chasing them out over the sea, and forcing or dropping them into the surf (Hunt, Rogers, and Slowe 1975).

Figure 17 summarizes the hunting strategies of the five colonies. Because standing flight predominated among the Paximada falcons, that population exploited the horizontal space least and the vertical space most. The other four colonies exploited the horizontal space below 150 m altitude more than the high-altitude areas. The search flight technique appears to be the most widely used way of hunting bird migrants above the sea.

Eleonora's falcon is not as powerful as the peregrine falcon, nor is it as swift as the hobby or merlin. All its hunting techniques are known from some other aerial bird of prey except the unique standing flight. Naturally it cannot perform all of them to perfection. I would say it is an all-round hunter of small flying animals. But its treasure box of tricks, combined with its sharp eye and strong wings, make it dangerous enough to meet high in the air above the sea or far from the shore of the nearest isle or mainland.

This social raptor does not appear to carry out an organized and structured form of hunting in a group. An exception might be the joint hunting excursions of the two partners of a pair that I was able to document at the San Pietro colony (chap. 6). Thiollay (1967) observed groups of falcons passing by Formentor on their way out over the sea. There is definitely a strong gregarious component in all the behaviors and activities of this species. Hunting pairs and groups appear to be deliberate rather than accidental formations leading to higher hunting success (chap. 6). When confronting a migrant bird, each falcon acts in a "selfish" way. If falcons see each other's potential prey, they simply converge upon the migrant, since each falcon would like to grab it. This is strongly reminiscent of the food piracy of laughing gulls (*Larus atricilla*), which force other birds (terns) to give up their fish when they fly near a gull colony. The gulls belong to the "selfish group," since each gull that joins a chase appears to be interested only in its own advantage (Hatch 1975).

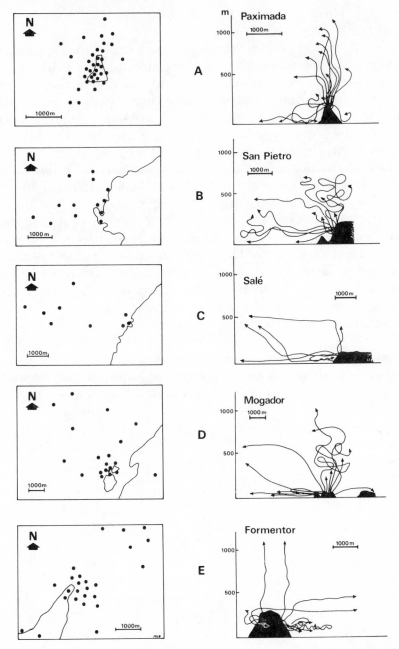

Fig. 17. Schematic view of hunting strategies at five colonies. Each colony differs in its utilization of the three-dimensional airspace *Left*: Typical horizontal dispersion of hunting falcons. *Right*: Characteristic vertical dispersal pattern of falcons leaving the colony site. Formentor scheme developed after description by Thiollay (1967). San Pietro scheme represents strategy before bird migration season; all others are typical during heavy bird migration.

As to the timing of daily hunting, there can be little doubt that the Paximada population spent the least amount of time for hunting activities. Owing to frequent fog and low clouds, there must have been less hunting at Mogador during the early hours of the day. But, on the average, Mogador falcons hunted more hours per day, since they were active then and also had many prey arrivals in later morning and afternoon hours (fig. 13).

The other Mediterranean colonies appear to follow the Paximada pattern except that Toro and Mallorca report much more hunting or absence from the colonies during the night hours than the Aegean island. This difference may be due to the large distance between Paximada and the nearest large isle. The dusk and night activities of Eleonora's falcon will probably remain shrouded in mystery until somebody manages to put tiny radio transmitters on several breeding adult falcon males. Whatever it is that the falcons are doing, it does not appear to have a significant impact on the food supply of the falcon chicks.

To evaluate each colony's adaptation to the spatial and resource factors of its macroenvironment, we must now investigate the structure and dynamics of the annual migration of millions and millions of birds attempting to cross the Mediterranean (or east Atlantic) and the extensive desert areas to the south.

5 Bird Migration in the Falcon's Breeding Areas

The seasonal departure and arrival of millions of birds in northern latitudes has fascinated curious minds for thousands of years. Aristotle speculated on the disappearance of swallows, cuckoos, and cranes from Europe. More recently, we must thank R. E. Moreau for his most illuminating contributions to the study of "Palearctic-African bird migration systems" (Moreau 1961, 1972).

As soon as winter cold, ice, and snow recede farther north, Europe is invaded each year by millions of small passerine birds belonging to some one hundred different species. Most of them are insectivorous birds that use the long summer days and the abundant insect food supplies of central and northern European habitats (from city and field to forest and tundra) to raise one or two broods before leaving Europe again at the end of the summer. Moreau (1972) "made the guess that, on the average, from every five acres of Europe one trans-Sahara migrant set out for Africa." This figure means that some 5,000 million will attempt to cross the Mediterranean/Atlantic and the adjacent Saharan desert barriers. In other words, these birds will have crossed the 4,000 km area between Portugal and Lebanon within roughly 100 days. If such a migration were spaced out evenly along this distance and distributed evenly over the entire period, we could expect 10 million birds to cross this line each day, at a density of 12,500 birds per kilometer. On an hourly basis, each kilometer of the 4,000 km line would see 520 migrants passing through on the way to Africa.

Another wave of migrants, the millions of birds that will spend the winter months in the Mediterranean/North African areas, crosses over parts of the Mediterannean/Atlantic later in fall. There is some overlap of these two groups of migrants, however, and Eleonora's falcon captures some passerines of the second group, although its bird quarry consists principally of trans-Saharan migrants.

Depending on their points of departure and flight direction, these warblers, orioles, shrikes, and so forth, face a grueling journey. The Mediterranean Sea is up to 1,000 km wide (Ionian Sea). Narrow sea-crossings can be made near the Straits of Gibraltar, the Channel of Sicily, and the Bosphorus, but, except for diurnal migrants such as raptors and storks, few migrants appear to take advantage of such favorable factors of Mediterranean geography. The average migrant crosses several hundred kilometers of sea. When it arrives in North Africa, few food resources await it in late summer and fall. This may partly explain why some migrants appear to fly not only across the sea but also across the subsequent 1,500 to 2,200 km of the Sahara in one nonstop crossing. Depending on the force and direction of the wind, the average passerine migrant will need 40 to 60 hr of flight time for such a journey.

Visual observations, bird-banding records, and trapping have yielded much information on the Mediterranean portion of the Palearctic-African migration systems. The speed, height, and direction of the trans-Saharan migrants is relevant to our inquiry, since they directly affect the hunting behavior and the reproductive success of Eleonora's falcon. New observation techniques have greatly increased man's ability to monitor bird migration since about 1946. One simple technique uses the disk of the full moon (Lowery 1951). The observer registers the number and direction of nocturnal migrants that fly in front of it during clear nights. The exact knowledge of the coordinates of the moon's position permits a relatively precise computation of the migration course and density. But this method offers no insight into the vertical component of bird migration, and it can be used only a few nights of a month.

Radar techniques cover a much wider horizontal space and can provide accurate data on the altitude of migrating birds. The radar scope registers small echoes of small passerine migrants and larger ones of waders, raptors, and cranes, or any other large birds. To determine the direction and velocity of migrants, films or repeated photographic exposures of the radar screen must be made. If the radar antenna is on a mobile base (ship), the radar data must be corrected to account for the movements of the base during the monitoring period.

PLATES

Plate 1. Male Eleonora's falcon (light color phase) in front of its nesting site.

Plate 2. Male Eleonora's falcon (dark color phase).

Plate 3. Falcon pair on its perch. The female belongs to the dark color phase and the male represents the light phase. Photo by D. Ristow.

Plate 4. Museum specimens of Eleonora's falcon and other falcon species found in the Mediterranean region. *From right to left*: (1) European hobby falcon, female, adult, Germany; (2) peregrine, male, juvenile (November), Sardinia; (3) Eleonora's falcon, female, immature (September), Greece; (4) peregrine, female, juvenile (June), Mallorca; (5) Eleonora's falcon, female, adult, light phase, Mallorca; (6) Eleonora's falcon, immature, dark phase (July), Turkey; (7) Eleonora's falcon, male, adult, dark phase, Mallorca. Note the similarity between the immature peregrine and the light-phased Eleonora's falcon.

Plate 5. The long wings of Eleonora's falcon are often held in this fashion, creating an unusually elongated body shape.

Plate 6. Same bird as in plate 5 (an adult female) assuming an eaglelike posture.

Plate 7. A light-phased falcon flying over the atoll isle (Mogador). The bird's underside appears dark except for its cheek.

Plate 8. Spectacular Mediterranean cliffs like this one at Mallorca's Cape Formentor are the haunts and breeding habitats of Eleonora's falcon.

Plate 9. Heavy surf batters the cliffs of the San Pietro isle near Sardinia. Eleonora's falcon breeds high in the cliff and hunts small migrant birds over the sea.

Plate 10. Paximada. Typical breeding site along the south-facing slope with peninsula marking the southwest tip of this island.

Plate 11. Paximada. Rugged topography of the "upper slope" study area.

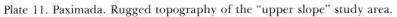

Plate 12. African mainland coast near Salé in western Morocco, site of a sizable colony of Eleonora's falcon. Note the proximity of cultivated fields behind the coastal bluffs.

Plate 13. The Isles of Mogador. View from the top of the submarine cliff toward the atoll isle and the African mainland.

Plate 14. Mogador. Smea Isle. Some 48 falcon pairs were breeding on this small cliff (70 m long, 30 m wide). View from atoll isle.

Plate 15. Mogador. Smea Isle photographed from a small boat.

Plate 16. Mogador. Submarine cliff from the southeast. A substantial falcon population inhabited this tiny cliff.

Plate 17. Clutch of three eggs in a narrow crater hole. Note the feather remains in the foreground, indicating that the falcons hunted migrant birds before hatching time (Mogador).

Plate 18. Incubating the clutch (Paximada).

Plate 19. Falcon chick less than a day after hatching.

Plate 20. Four falcon chicks perched on a thick cushion of bird feathers (Mogador).

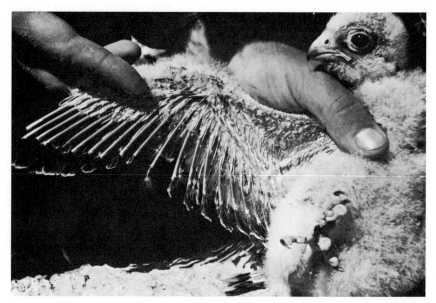

Plate 21. Nestlings at the age of 22 days. Note the contrast between the fully developed foot and the sparsely feathered wing.

Plate 22. A very light-colored fledgling.

Plate 23. Male falcon with a captured bird. It has already transferred the prey from its talons into its beak for delivery to the mate. The latter can be seen in the background demanding the prey with intense screams.

Plate 24. The female has grabbed the prey and the male falcon takes off.

Plate 25. Female feeding a nestling.

Plate 26. Female and her three young at the end of a feeding period. A small feather from the dismembered prey adheres to the female's right front and remains there for several hours.

Plate 27. The elder nestling has begun to pick up prey remains while both adults are absent from the nesting site.

Plate 28. Falcon pair resting. Photo by D. Ristow.

Plate 29. A collection of passerine bird corpses found within one ground territory of the atoll isle (Mogador) on 23 August 1969. Most of these corpses were grasshopper warblers (*Locustella naevia*).

Plate 30. Insect-hawking Eleonora's falcons over oak woodland in Sardinia (May 1974).

Plate 31. Falcon pair perched on the edge of the precipitious central bluff of the atoll isle (Mogador). Prey remains were frequently found here, although the nest scrape lay some 90 cm below the edge.

Plate 32. Pair from the atoll central bluff population (Mogador). The nesting site lies at the left edge of the photo. The entire ground territory of this pair consisted of the small ledge and the platform in front of it.

Plate 33. Madagascar winter habitat of Eleonora's falcon in the open secondary woodland near Morondava. The large trees are baobabs, used as roosts by the wintering falcons.

Plate 34. Pair of Madagascar kestrels (*Falco newtoni*).

Plate 35. Sooty falcon (*Falco concolor*) in Madagascar. This species shares its winter habitats with Eleonora's falcon.

Plate 36. The Sardinian princess Eleonora of Arborea, after whom the new species of falcon was named by zoologist Gené in 1839. In this painting Eleonora is holding up her famous book of laws, the "Carta de Logu" of 1392, which contains a paragraph on the protection of hawks and falcons.

STRUCTURE OF BIRD MIGRATION
Speed and Duration of Sea-Crossings

The smaller passerines appear to travel commonly at air speeds of not more than 40 kmph (about 25 mph). Fast-flying birds like quail, turtledoves, and swifts have been clocked at much higher speeds, and radar observations of such migrants have proved their higher average speed per unit of time (Casement 1966). The speed generated by the bird will be its actual travel speed during calms. Calms were rare, however, when I studied Eleonora's falcon in various parts of the Mediterranean. At Paximada and Mogador strong winds near ground level were very strong on many days (Beaufort scale 3–6). They will accelerate a bird's travel speed maximally if they come from dead astern, and they will decelerate it if they come from dead ahead. During the fall months most winds seem to come from a more or less northerly direction and are therefore likely to increase the travel speed and shorten the total time needed for crossing the water barrier between Europe and Africa. Their considerable force amounted to 20 to 50 kmph. The wind velocity could therefore have added 50 to 100% of a migrant's own travel speed to the effective migration speed if the general migration route were congruent with the wind direction.

The migrant must correct for side winds, causing a loss of travel time compared with a following wind condition. Otherwise they will cause a lateral drift of up to several hundred miles, which could be equivalent to many hours of additional flight.

Most sea-crossings between a southernmost European departure point and a North African arrival point cover some 350 to 480 km. During calms the average migrant (40 kmph) would need 8.8 to 12 hr for such a journey. However, the longer sea-crossings, particularly those over the Ionian Sea, require some 18 to 28 hr of nonstop flight under such conditions (table 8). These flight times are reduced when a moderate to strong breeze from dead astern adds some 20 to 50 kmph to the migrant's own speed. For a crossing from the southwest tip of Greece to Cyrenaica, only 6.7 and 4.4 hr would be needed (instead of 10 hr during a calm). A strong breeze from the north would enable a south-flying migrant to cross the Mediterranean under cover of night except for the Ionian Sea area. In fact, the average migrant would need only some 4 or 5 hr of flight to reach the African coast.

TABLE 8
Crossing the Mediterranean Sea: Distance and Time Factors

Route[a]	Distance (in km)	Direct Crossing Time (hr) during "Calms"[b]	Crossing Time (hr) during Wind (dead astern) of 20 kmph	Crossing Time (hr) during Wind (dead astern) of 50 kmph
Spain, east of the straits, to eastern Morocco	160	4.0	2.7	1.8
South of France to Algeria	640	16.0	10.7	7.1
Sardinia to Tunis	190	4.8	3.2	2.1
Tuscany to Tunis	640	16.0	10.7	7.1
Sicily to Tripoli	430	10.8	7.2	4.8
Malta to Tripoli	350	8.8	5.8	3.9
South Italy ("heel") to Tripoli	960	24.0	16.0	10.7
Albania at 15° east to Gulf of Sirte	1,130	28.3	18.8	12.6
Southwest tip of Greece to Cyrenaica	400	10.0	6.7	4.4
Crete to African coast	350	8.8	5.8	3.9
Rhodes to African coast	480	12.0	8.0	5.3
Cyprus to Delta and Sinai	400	10.0	6.7	4.4

[a]Adapted from Moreau (1961).
[b]Migrant's travel speed estimated at an average 40 kmph.

To the west of Gibraltar, sea-crossings increase in distance with flight routes that run to the west of south. From Cape Saint Vincent, the southwest tip of Portugal, it is some 620 km to the Isles of Mogador. With the help of a strong breeze a migrant would complete this journey in less than 7 hr. Slight following wind support would increase the flight time to over 10 hr, and some 15.5 hr would be required during calms.

The distance from Cape Saint Vincent to the nearest of the Canary Islands amounts to roughly 1,000 km. Given the three conditions listed in table 8, a migrant could cover this distance in 25, 16.7, and 11.1 hr respectively.

During the spring migration season, winds do not blow as often and as regularly from the north as during the fall season. Even so, they are common enough to affect the migration of many migrants. Strong headwinds may double or triple the flight time needed during calm weather conditions. This can turn a 4-hr flight from eastern Morocco to southeastern Spain into a grueling and exhausting 8- to 12-hr journey.

In summary, there is great variation in the distance migrants must cover to cross the Atlantic and the Mediterranean Sea. In many cases, 8 to 12 hr of nonstop flight will be required (sometimes repeatedly, e.g., Italy to Sardinia, Sardinia to Tunis) for the sea-crossing during calm wind conditions. During the fall migration season, northerly winds frequently increase the migration velocity and reduce total flight time to a considerable degree. Even so, some of the longest possible sea-crossings will still require more than 10 hr of nonstop flight by the average migrant.

During the spring migration, winds rarely speed up the migrant's journey. Northerly winds will now decrease the effective travel speed for many migrants.

Migration Height

It was only when radar techniques became sophisticated enough to register very small objects that the true nature of bird migration above land and sea was discovered. Migration height is greatest during calms, great during following wind conditions, and low during headwinds. Adams (1962) measured migration height over Cyprus and found most birds traveling above 1,200 m (4,000 ft), although many were flying above 2,100 m (7,000 ft). Migrants flew higher at night than during daylight hours. Casement's (1966) extensive radar coverage of sea-crossings between Cape Saint Vincent in the west and Crete in the east from a ship-borne radar unit yielded the most valuable information on migration height: "Radar shows that visual observations give a highly misleading picture of the scale of migration across the Mediterranean. The main volume crosses unseen at night at about 3,000–5,000 ft. and it is only when the birds are exhausted by the distance travelled or by head winds that they are forced low and reported by ships." Similar observations have been made in Central Europe, England, Sweden, and more recently near Puerto Rico (Richardson 1974).

I have not come across any data that would show the change in migration height as migrants approach a major coastline after a long sea-crossing. Do they gradually lower their height, or do they continue to fly above 1,000 m until they reach the shore? On the average, I would think, a gradual lowering of the flight altitude will occur.

Migration Direction

For decades it seemed that bird migration was concentrated at the narrowest parts of the sea. Today we know that this holds true only for many of the diurnal migrants like raptors, herons, cranes, and swallows. The huge number of nocturnal migrants, however, cross the sea in a broad front and at a relatively even density. This means that some migrants will pass each of the 4,000 km along the imaginary line extending from Portugal to Lebanon.

Banding records show that each species has a preference for a specific migration route from Europe to Africa. It even appears that individual birds sometimes repeat a nearly identical itinerary for several years, since they have been recaptured in the same trapping location (Moreau 1972). Looking at the cumulative effect of these species-specific migration routes, radar observations have confirmed two major migration directions during the fall season in the Mediterranean basin. In the western and central part, including Italy, almost all migrants hold a course to the west of south. This results in increased numbers and migrant densities in northwest Africa. East of the Ionian Sea, the main direction is south to southeast. Thus, it is the Egyptian coastline over which most migrants will pass in this part of the basin. Radar echoes of small migrants received at high sea by Casement (1966) reflect this general pattern (fig. 18A). These data also confirm the broad front of the migration system between Europe and Africa.

During spring migration a reversal of the fall pattern has been confirmed. Once again there seems to be a certain concentration of the northwest and northeast corners of Africa, primarily due to generally adverse wind conditions in the entire Saharan region. On the other hand, more migrants are visible along the coasts of Tunisia and Algeria at this time. This does not necessarily indicate a higher density of migrants in the central part of the basin. From my own spring observations of weather systems and bird migration in the Sardinian region, I propose to relate the high visibility of spring migrants at the Tunisian coast to the adverse effect of strong headwinds and low pressure systems in the Tyrrhenian Sea. As successive waves of migrants reach the North African coast, they mingle with earlier arrivals waiting for calm and fair weather conditions before they continue their northward migration. Spring data from offshore radar units indicate the specific

RADAR OBSERVATIONS OF FALL MIGRANTS

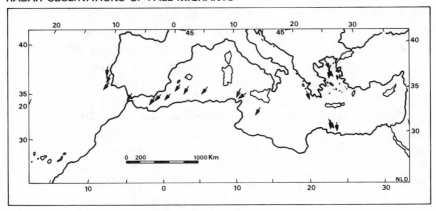

RADAR OBSERVATIONS OF SPRING MIGRANTS

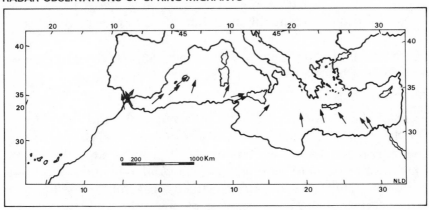

Fig. 18. Flight paths of small bird migrants crossing the sea between Europe and Africa. From original data presented in Casement (1966). Arrows indicate locations where clear and identifiable bird echoes were received by shipborne radar unit.

directions of small migrants: northwest to northeast in the western and central Mediterranean and generally north in the eastern part of the basin (fig. 18B, from various charts in Casement 1966).

The migration course of the nocturnal migrants appears to be genetically fixed; that is, certain navigational information that the bird is able to absorb and "read" from the environment permit it to correct its flight direction in order to reach the species' traditional wintering area. Since many populations have innate mechanisms that cause them to fly toward Africa in a strongly southwesterly direction, an interesting problem arises at the western shores of France and Iberia, which run nearly north to south.

Any migrant passing over this particular coastline and continuing a rigid southwest route for a couple of days will never reach its African winter quarters. Moreau (1961) points out that "on reaching the western part of the Iberian peninsula, a change in direction is the only alternative to a suicidal plunge over the Atlantic." Most of the migrants do not seem to know the extent of the Atlantic Ocean and therefore cannot be aware of the deadly danger of overshooting the western boundary of their normal migration area. To prevent death in the ocean and to remain close to the mainland these southwest migrants must possess a mechanism that produces a change in the flight direction (back to the mainland) after many hours of flight over the open sea. If such a mechanism does not exist, then millions of birds have perished in the Atlantic fall after fall. Moreau (1961) thinks that such an event would over time create a strong selection factor against such offshore migrants. We shall examine this problem in more detail below.

Migration Time

Most of the trans-Saharan migrants fly at night and rest during the day if favorable habitat conditions permit. Everywhere in the Mediterranean basin, migration sets in with a surprising regularity some 45 min after sunset. The radar images of coastal peninsulas and capes appear to actually grow into the sea at this time because of the large number of bird echoes received from migrants moving from the coast over the sea (Casement 1966).

The density of migrants may vary in a spectacular manner from hour to hour. The nature of this "migration pulse" depends mostly on the distance between the observation point and the major source regions of departing migrants. Even lunar disk observations may reveal significant differences in migration density between the hours of a night. A good example are fall observations from the Cyrenaica (ca. 380 km south of Crete) as reported by Kiepenheuer and Linsenmair (1965):

On October 1/2 we observed migration during a perfect calm 600 km E of Sollum, two km from the coast. Here we were able to gain a good idea of migration at the coast. Between 19–21 h migration density amounted to c. 140 birds/mile an hour. Most birds should, however, have departed before this time period. In the following five hours we saw only a single bird at 0:30 h. At 2 a.m. migration from the sea began. It became stronger and stronger and supposedly reached its maximum only after sunrise. It was remarkable that we observed larger birds at first and smaller birds later. Most migrants flew at a rather high altitude. Migration direction and arrival time lead us to conclude that they had departed from Crete.

Such a migration pulse with alternating peak and low densities was convincingly confirmed by radar observations. In the Libyan Sea, Casement (1966) measured a strong migration density throughout the daylight hours. This can be explained only by assuming that migrants had departed from various locations on the Greek mainland during the previous evening. In the northern and central Aegean Sea, however, there were hardly any radar echoes from migrants during the day, a proof for the interruption of migration on islands and the adjacent mainland during the early morning hours. At night, migration reached extremely high values in this area.

These observations indicate a strong correlation between the pulse of bird migration and the geographical factors within the migration region. If we assume that nocturnal migrants find suitable diurnal feeding habitats over most 100-km² areas of southern Europe's coastal and island environments, then we can predict the timing of peak and low migration density for any point in the Mediterranean basin.

If there is no promising day habitat between a departure point A and an observation point B, then the first migrants from A will arrive at B some t hours after takeoff. The flight time t can be calculated as follows:

$$t = \frac{D}{M + W}$$

where D is the distance between A and B, M is the migrant's own speed, and W is the wind-support factor (negative value when headwinds prevail).

A promising day habitat between A and B may complicate this simple distance-time-speed relationship. Suppose B lies on a small cliff some 10 km south of Crete. Throughout the night, various migrant groups will pass over Crete and point B on their way to Africa. From daybreak on, however, most migrants flying over Crete will spot promising day habitats on that large isle and interrupt their migration until about 45 min after sunset the following evening. Thus, most of these migrants will not reach point B on the cliff until they resume their migration after sunset. The large island of Crete casts a "migration shadow" over point B, preventing it from having a significant diurnal migration pulse.

Important diurnal density peaks should, on the other hand, be observed where no such "shadows" exist and where the minimum open water distance between A and B requires some 10 hr of flight. A migrant that has passed over point A some 2 to 4 hr before sunrise is more likely to continue its migration until it reaches point B many hours later than to change its course by 180° and return to point A.

ELEONORA'S FALCON AND THE MIGRATION PULSE

The new, largely radar-acquired knowledge about the nature of nocturnal bird migration above the Mediterranean basin is significant in our attempt to better understand the raptor/prey system that involves both Eleonora's falcon and so many species of migrants. From the falcon's point of view, the migration pulse is of great importance.

Our own observations from the ground complement and confirm the evidence presented above but add the local component that has a decisive impact on the hunting success of a resident falcon population. This evidence, combined with the data presented by Casement (1966) and Moreau (1972), will lead to the development of a general model of the space-time components of migrant-falcon interaction.

Paximada Colony

Migrants attempted to continue a southeast to southeast by east flight course even after having been attacked or chased by falcons above the island. Migrants that had alighted on Paximada during the morning hours had regularly concentrated at its southeast tip at dusk in order to resume migration. Large diurnal migrants such as eagles, hawks, and herons also migrated in a southeast direction across the sea near Paximada. All migrants observed on the island in 1965 are listed in table 32 (Appendix A).

The maximum height of the small migrants above Paximada could not be estimated. The fact that the falcons hunted frequently at the 800 to 1,000 m level must be interpreted with caution: it shows with certainty that more migrants flew at this altitude than at lower ones but says little about the higher altitudes up to 3,000 to 4,000 m. Even the falcons simply disappeared in the sky, to say nothing of the much smaller nocturnal migrants. Radiotelemetry and perhaps radar devices are needed to establish the extreme vertical hunting range of Eleonora's falcon at this colony.

There was a strong correlation between wind force and the number of migrants arriving on Paximada. Two of the most common visitors to the island were the willow warbler (*Phylloscopus trochilus*) and the yellow wagtail (*Motacilla flava*). Strong northwest winds, particularly after a brief calm or a period of light winds, generally caused small invasions. The hunting success of falcons was higher on these days as well. These data indicate that there is a higher migration density at lower altitude with stormlike following winds than with light winds and calms, when birds migrate high. In fact, the rocky habitat of Paximada attracts many migrants during stormy days.

It is possible that more migrants decide to migrate during nights of strong backwinds than at other times, but radar echoes and visual observations do not seem to prove this. Higher hunting success of Eleonora's falcon could indicate such a correlation, but other factors might be responsible as well: strong winds force the birds into lower altitudes, thereby reducing the falcon's hunting distance and time expenditure, and hinder the migrants in their flight ability during escape maneuvers but do not decrease the hunting ability of the falcon.

The hunting period of the Paximada falcons appears to have been optimally adapted to the migration pulse over the island if we take into account the evidence from radar observations in the northern and central Aegean area. During the night—when the Paximada falcons rest—migrants pass over that departed from various large Aegean islands and the eastern coast of Greece some 45 min after sunset. But where is the probable departure point of those migrants that pass through the Paximada airspace during the first two morning hours? There are two possibilities:

1. The migrants originate from the areas mentioned above but do not leave them within an hour after sunset. Rather, they depart later at night. This certainly occurs, but it does not appear to be common.

2. Assuming an average flight speed of 40 kmph and a wind support factor of 20 kmph, the typical nocturnal migrant must have traveled some 10 to 12 hr, or 600 to 720 km, since its departure shortly after sunset.

In the latter case, the migrants' departure points lie somewhere in northern Greece. With no wind support, such migrants would have flown only some 400 to 480 km throughout the entire night before encountering the Paximada falcons in the morning light. This would shift their departure points farther to the south, near Athens, some of the northerly Greek islands, and perhaps even from some coastal areas of western Turkey.

We may also calculate the hypothetical departure points of migrants passing over Paximada at noon or during the early afternoon. The noon arrival of a typical migrant would mean that this bird had flown some 7 hr in a southeast or south direction during full daylight hours in addition to up to 10 hr of prior nocturnal migration. This would maximally project the departure point 680 km (at 40 kmph) to 1,020 km (at 60 kmph effective flight speed) to the north of Paximada, somewhere between Macedonia and Bulgaria. In practice, such a migration history seems rare, since the migrant would have crossed the sea and a number of habitat-rich coastal or island areas during the seven daylight hours. Being a nocturnal migrant, it would surely have interrupted its flight at its earliest opportunity after sunrise and stayed in one of these areas until evening.

In effect, therefore, Paximada's location at the southern edge of the Aegean Sea determines the time period during which a strong migration pulse can be felt. The migration shadow from the Cyclades and the Greek mainland deprives Paximada of significant numbers of daytime migrants except during the early morning hours. The latter time, however, constitutes a prime hunting period because north of Paximada there is a vast expanse of open sea: at least 160 km (ca. 100 miles) separate this isle from the larger islands of the Cyclades. This means that all migrants that are between 10 and about 150 km to the north or northwest of this falcon colony at sunrise find themselves flying over an endless open sea. Radar evidence suggests that these birds continue their southward migration until they reach a habitat-rich area. They constitute the main supply of potential prey for the Paximada falcons. The falcons first encounter those migrants that were already close to Paximada at sunrise. Then—2.5 hr later—there arrive the 60 kmph migrants that had passed over some large and habitat-rich island of the Cyclades within the hour before sunrise. The last arrivals in the Paximada airspace would be slow-flying (40 kmph) birds needing almost 4 hr for the sea-crossing between the Cyclades and Paximada. They would arrive at Paximada about 9:30. This coincides well with the observed period of prey arrivals at the Paximada nest sites (fig. 14): the number of bird prey carried to each nest dropped off sharply after the first three morning hours.

Noon and afternoon hunting activities of Paximada-based falcons are usually directed to the occasional diurnal migrant of small size (swallows, wagtails, waders). At dusk, falcons may chase those few migrants that have spent a day of uneasy rest on Paximada and are now taking off again. The numbers involved are insignificant, however, compared with the mass of broad-front migrants that pass over the island during the night and early morning hours.

Mogador Colony

This falcon colony is situated at a most interesting point of the Iberian–North African migration region. Unfortunately, no direct radar observations have been published so far that would give us an indication of the direction and pulse of nocturnal and diurnal migration. We have to rely on other kinds of evidence.

At Mogador, waders, terns, and other diurnal migrants flew parallel to the African coast in a south-southwest direction. At night, our own moon observations (29 August–1 September 1966) showed a clear preference for the south-southwest and—to a lesser degree—the southwest by west vectors. This indicates a general flight course parallel to the coastline that would keep migrants within contact distance of the land. These flight vectors are an extension of the general southwest trend of migrants in southwestern Europe. They contrast, however, with the visual observations of migrants chased by Eleonora's falcon above and to the north and west of the islands. These migrants were on a south to southeast course heading for the African coast.

The flight altitude of these migrants ranged from wave level to at least 1,000 m. Visual observations indicate that at least the very low flying migrants were much more common than at Paximada. Indirect evidence from the average altitude of hunting flights by Eleonora's falcon also points to a generally lower daytime migrant altitude than at Paximada. It is reasonable to assume that the proximity of the African coast, the tiredness of many migrants, or both are the causes of this relatively low migration height during daylight hours.

Remembering that the Mogador falcons hunt throughout the day and arrive with a large amount of bird prey consisting largely of migrant species classified as nocturnal, we must conclude that it is the nocturnal migrant group that generates a nearly continuous migration pulse during the day. A geographical analysis considering the position of departure areas in their relation to a migrant's flight time clearly establishes the high probability of daylong arrivals at Mogador. Since the southwest tip of Portugal, Cape Saint Vincent, lies half a degree to the east of Mogador, all migrants departing from the southern coast of Iberia would reach Africa north of Mogador if they migrate strictly south or southeast. Mogador arrivals would have to be heading west of south. This latter migration vector has been found to prevail along the entire southern coast of the Iberian peninsula (Wallraff and Kiepenheuer 1962; Casement 1966; fig. 18). If we assume that migrants maintain their west of south vector until they are in visual contact with a habitat-rich land area or are close to being exhausted, the following types of migrants can be expected at Mogador throughout the day:

1. Fast migrants (effective flight speed 60 kmph) need about 10 hr for the sea-crossing between Cape Saint Vincent and Mogador, and slightly longer if they leave Iberia somewhere between the cape and Gibraltar. A bird leaving the cape at 19:00 will arrive within reach of the Mogador falcon colony shortly after 5:00. Migrants with departure points farther inland will arrive there as many hours later as they need in order to first cross over the Iberian coastline at night. For example, a bird migrating from Madrid to Cadiz at the Atlantic seashore would arrive at Cadiz

only about 3:00 and would then still have to fly 10 hr to reach Mogador. It would therefore be expected to arrive there around 13:00. The last migrants on a Mogador course would leave the Iberian coast shortly before sunrise and arrive at Mogador before 16:00. Then no more fast-flying migrants would arrive for another 13 hr until 5:00 the next morning.

2. Slow migrants (effective flight speed 40 kmph) need more time (at least 15 hr) for the sea-crossing in this area. First arrivals can be expected about 10:00, the last ones about 20:00, consisting of migrants that left the Iberian coast at 5:00.

In practice, all kinds of effective flight speeds occur, depending on wind conditions and each bird's flight abilities. Some will be slower and others faster than indicated above. This pattern creates a nearly continuous stream of birds penetrating the Mogador airspace from dawn to beyond dusk. There is no island between the southwest Iberian coastal crossing points and the Moroccan coast that could function as a "migration shadow." The latter exists, however, for all those migrants that cross the latitude of Gibraltar to the east of this famous rock. They will migrate over the African mainland or remain so close to the shores of the continent that they are not likely to be found to the west of the Mogador Isles. At sunrise they will either interrupt their migration at some suitable inland habitat or will continue their migration nonstop above the land, as Moreau (1961) has suggested.

At least theoretically, Eleonora's falcon may also prey on another group of migrants at Mogador. An analysis of Iberian bird migration patterns indicates a strong concentration of migrant numbers in the western (coastal) areas. This concentration can be explained in at least two ways:

1. Inland areas are sun-parched and lack suitable rest habitats for many migrants. Before leaving for Africa, the early waves of migrants stay in the moister, more nutritious coastal provinces for several days or weeks. Their numbers increase from day to day as new migrants arrive but few leave for Africa.

2. Bernis (1962) shows that many migrants cross over the northern and central Portuguese coast at night. At sunrise they can be as far as 400 to 600 km from the Iberian coast. Since Lack (1961) saw migrants crossing the North Sea change their course at dawn for unknown reasons, Bernis suggests that these Atlantic drifters off Portugal will also correct their course to avoid drown-

ing in the ocean. This correction would consist of a movement toward the east, an approximately 90° shift of the original course vector. Such a move would bring the migrant back to the Iberian or African coast, although it might require a considerable number of additional flight hours (fig. 19). Should these migrants have an innate migration vector, they would probably repeat such loops along the Iberian and African coast several times before arriving in West Africa. The total migration speed of such "coast-hopping" migrants would be slower than that of other migrants and contribute to the observed coastal concentration.

Migrants behaving as predicted by the Bernis theory could arrive at Mogador at any time. Their departure points cannot be predicted, since the size of the loop and the point at which a migrant decides it has flown too far off the land are unknown. If such a migration should occur, Eleonora's falcon at Mogador could regularly prey on coast-hopping migrants originating from departure points in Iberia and in Morocco.

The Bernis theory rests essentially on the belief that nocturnal migrants caught over the sea at sunrise will perform an automatic correction: southwest migrants will move to the east, southeast migrants to the west. But since Casement's (1966) radar data show that there is strong uncorrected diurnal migration over the Libyan and western Mediterranean Sea, it is hard to accept that migrants possess such a correction ability. There is a slight chance that southwest migrants can somehow sense that they have strayed too far from their normal course. It is more likely, though, that they continue their flight across the sea as do migrants in the western and eastern Mediterranean Sea. While the latter may eventually reach the African shore, the Atlantic coast "overshooter" will indeed become exhausted and drown in the sea. It will thus accomplish what Moreau (1961) pointed out: the nonsurvival of those genetic factors that cause migrants to fly too far to the west. Since all European migration systems are younger than 15,000 years, perfection cannot be expected at this stage. In addition, there will always be a certain percentage of migrants straying from the "typical" route.

It has been remarked before that on the average the Mogador falcon population spent more time hunting than the Paximada falcons. Most pairs at Mogador also showed strong evidence of capturing enormous numbers of migrants. So many were cap-

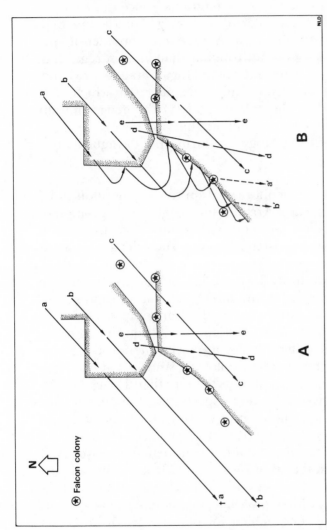

Fig. 19. Principal directions of fall migrants in the Iberian-northwest African region: *A*, Migrants *a* and *b* possess a strong southwest migration vector. If they continue to migrate toward the southwest they will drown. Migrants flying a southerly course (*d* and *e*) or crossing the sea from a more easterly departure point (*c*) will reach northwest Africa. *B*, Modified migration pattern of migrants *a* and *b* in accordance with the Bernis theory (Bernis 1962) and my observations of prey arrivals of Eleonora's falcons at the Mogador colony. Migrants correct their migration vector over the ocean by making a significant, perhaps nearly perpen-dicular (90°) shift toward the southeast that will return them—after several additional hours of flight without rest—to the mainland coast. Because of their innate preference for a southwest vector, such migrants may repeatedly find themselves over the open Atlantic during the same season. They may thus be forced to correct their migration course more than once. Although more exhausting than the migration routes of migrants *c*, *d*, and *e*, such a "coast-hopping" route will permit migrants to reach their West African winter quarters.

tured, in fact, that bird "larders" were common (Vaughan 1961*a*; Walter 1968*a*). The ultimate reason for this phenomenon is the unusual migration pulse at Mogador. The island-free Atlantic between Iberia and this colony site generates a daylong stream of migrants. In addition, millions of migrants concentrate at the southwest tip of Spain and Portugal during August and September. It is quite possible that the average migration density per hour and kilometer is significantly higher than in most regions of the Mediterranean Sea. Thus, falcons at Mogador appear to benefit from (1) a high density of migrants, most of which pass through the airspace of the colony, and (2) the geographically determined time range of migration: the vast majority of sea-crossing migrants arrive at Mogador during the daylight hours.

Conclusions

Crucial for the access of Eleonora's falcon to the migration pulse system between Europe and Africa is the geographical position of a falcon colony in relation to the major migrant departure areas in southern Europe, and any island between such departure areas and a falcon colony.

If the migrants have to fly 10 to 15 hr across open sea before reaching a falcon colony, falcons should be able to capture migrants throughout the entire day. If the minimum sea-crossing distance between a continental coast and the falcon site amounts to only a 5-hr effective flight, we can expect migrant-falcon interaction only during the first 5 hr following sunrise. On the other hand, if the average distance amounts to more than 15 hr, the first migrants will not arrive in falcon airspace until some 5 hr after sunrise. Such a situation might occur at Mogador under calm or lateral wind conditions. An island that lies just a few kilometers south of (or "behind") a large island or continental peninsula will be strongly exposed to that area's "shadow" effect on diurnal bird migration. For instance, a rocky island to the south of Crete— Gavdopoula—is void of Eleonora's falcon although it possesses an excellent and safe breeding habitat for our raptor. However, its distance from Crete amounts to about 35 km. Only a few migrants would pass over Gavdopoula during the day. The vast majority will stay on Crete and continue migration after nightfall. By the time the first migrants reached this small island, it would be too dark for hunting. Characteristically, all confirmed and large falcon colonies near Crete lie to the north and northwest.

Two major colony areas seem to experience an unfavorable migration pulse as the result of the shadow effect: Cyprus and southwest Sardinia. In the Cyprus area, there must be enough migrants that overfly the southern coast at dawn and even during the early morning hours. In September 1977, when I had the opportunity to study the hunting behavior of some Cape Gata falcons, their hunting area, height, and technique varied greatly, sometimes from hour to hour, in response to frequently changing wind directions. Some falcons flew low and far out over sea, others used the standing flight high and low above the coastal bluffs. Migrants were successfully spotted and caught up to several hours before sunset when they attempted to depart from the bluffs in a southerly direction. The diverse and superbly adaptive hunting strategies of this population underline, in my opinion, the existence of the shadow effect as a prey-limiting factor.

A similar hypothesis can be formulated for the classic colonies of Vacca and Toro off the southwest corner of Sardinia. They will be affected strongly by the shadow effect of Sardinia and the two large isles of San Pietro and Sant' Antioco. Again, hunting should concentrate on early morning and (perhaps slightly) dusk. Steinbacher (1971), we recall, also reported here certain nocturnal activities of the falcons. That these activities constitute hunting flights needs to be confirmed, however, although there is undoubtedly a strong migration pulse during the night.

The other Sardinian colony at San Pietro (Mocci Demartis 1973) lies to the west of most of Sardinia. Thus, the falcons can orient themselves northwest and expect a long diurnal migration pulse originating from the French Riviera some 500 to 600 km to the north. Thus, this colony will be only partly affected by the migration shadow of Sardinia.

Figure 20 illustrates the locational and time factors that determine the period during which Eleonora's falcon may interact with the migration pulse. This model is particularly suited for the Aegean Sea, where so many colonies lie on islands. Distance and speed of the migrant populations have been omitted to allow for more variation of the model. Gradually, as the time of sunrise shifts farther to the left (the north), the areas of interaction

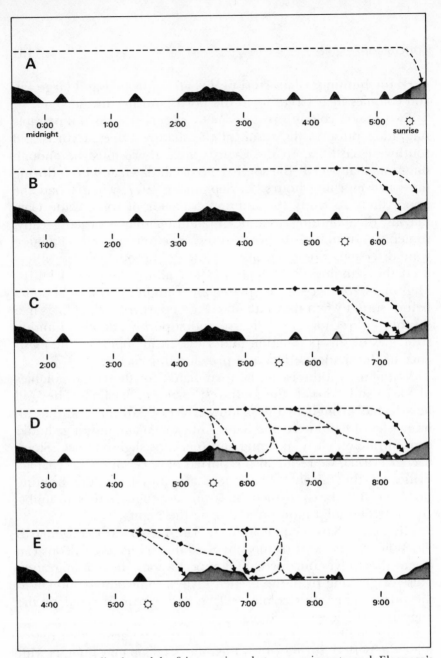

Fig. 20. Generalized model of interactions between migrants and Eleonora's falcons in relation to locational and time factors. Based on normal migration behavior of passerine nocturnal migrants. The latter pass over mainland coastline of southern Europe at night (*extreme left*) then cross over sea interspersed with small and large islands to reach the African mainland (*extreme right*). It is assumed that Eleonora's falcon inhabits all the islands and continental shores. Interaction between raptors and migrants (*rhomboid symbols*) occurs where the latter pass over falcon colonies during daylight.

change, depending on their distance from the departure points and potential rest areas of migrants.

Summing up, the structure of the general flow of bird migration (individual species will be discussed in chap. 7) is strongly influenced by the geography and distance of the land areas of southern Europe and North Africa. The colonies of Eleonora's falcon receive differently timed waves of migration of varying density. The character of the migration pulse can be assessed independently of the hunting behavior of the falcons, but the two appear closely synchronized in a least two major study colonies.

6 A Further Analysis of Raptor/Prey Interactions

In chapter 4 we discussed the hunting of passerine migrants by Eleonora's falcon. The emphasis lay on hunting area, period, and techniques. In chapter 5 we described the nature of bird migration across the Mediterranean basin. Eleonora's falcon must reckon with the direction, height, and speed of migrating birds. Different geographical coordinates of the falcon colonies create a number of different raptor/prey systems in which the raptor is the flexible and adapting part, while the unsuspecting stream of migrating prey appears at first sight to have little if any chance of successful escape. Our understanding of bird migration near the falcon colony can help us probe further into the nature of this interaction between a raptor species and a seemingly anonymous mass of migrants. What is the hunting success of Eleonora's falcon? Does this raptor show any preferences for any particular kind of prey? Do migrants respond to the presence of a colonial raptor in any particular way?

In connection with the bird migration system, we must examine another aspect of raptor/prey interactions. What does Eleonora's falcon feed on *before* the onset of the fall migration? Many falcons have returned from their African winter quarters before the months of May and June. Do they subsist on a nonbird diet during the prebreeding season? If the answer is yes, when and how does Eleonora's falcon switch over to the predominant bird diet that is so characteristic during its young-raising season?

HUNTING SUCCESS

Many small migrant birds passed through the airspace of Paximada and Mogador unharmed. They even managed to survive the flight through the main zone of the falcons forming a broad, high barrier with their standing flight behavior. Unfortunately, I did not collect a great deal of data on hunting success;

often I merely noted that a chase was going on without finding time to follow it and determine the fate of the prey.

Offhand I would say that more than 50% of the pursued birds managed to escape even the onslaught of several falcons. Once they had survived a chase for some 500 to 800 m horizontally and changed altitude to a safer level (where there were few falcons on lookout positions), they were often out of danger.

Although chases involving 11 and 12 different attacks on one migrant were observed, most birds were attacked only 3 to 6 times in all colonies before they were either captured or left in peace. Data from three breeding colonies indicate that only 11% of the observed falcon attacks (4 in 36) are successful. However, repeated attacks by one or several falcon(s) resulted in a high overall capture rate: 22, or 44%, of 50 pursued prey objects were captured (49 birds, 1 dragonfly).

In table 9 I have tried to work out a model situation in which within 60 min 25 migrants are chased in the airspace over a falcon colony frequented by 5 male falcons. Using the same percentages that our data have indicated (11% and 44% respectively), a pattern develops that is similar to our earlier analysis of hunting behavior: within the hour each male pursues between 11 and 17 of the 25 migrants, attacking 16 to 23 times and retrieving 2 or 3 birds. All males together attack 100 times and capture 11 of the 25 migrants chased. These figures can be multiplied for larger groups of falcons and migrants.

The hunting efficiency of most raptors is a little-known field. It appears to vary not only between species but also from one season to another, and between different regions and prey objects. Ospreys (*Pandion haliaëtus*) of northern California had a very high success rate: Ueoka and Koplin (1973) found that 82% of their fishing efforts were successful, with 56% requiring only one dive. In Scotland and Africa, however, Brown (1976) reports a success rate only "averaging about one fish in four attacked" (25%). Collopy (1973) studied the hunting success of American kestrels during the winter months: 46.8% of all dives were successful, but most (85.4%) of the prey items were invertebrates. Only 25% of the "vertebrate dives" were successful compared with 64% of the invertebrate ones.

Balgooyen (1976) studied American kestrels during the breeding season. The success rate was 40% early in the season and up to

TABLE 9
Hunting Success (model)

Migrant Number[b]	Falcon Number[b]					Number of Hunting Falcons	Number of Attacks
	1	2	3	4	5		
1	0	00	0	0	†	4	5
2	0	0	0	0	†	4	4
3	0X	0	0	00	†	4	7
4	†	X	0	0	†	3	3
5	†	†	0	0	†	2	2
6	†	†	0X	—	0	2	3
7	0	†	†	0	00	3	4
8	0	†	†	0	0	3	3
9	00	†	†	000	0	3	6
10	00	0	†	0	X	4	5
11	X	0	†	0	†	3	3
12	†	000	†	—	†	1	3
13	†	0	†	00	†	2	3
14	†	0	0	X	†	3	3
15	†	00X	—	†	†	1	3
16	†	†	0	†	000	2	4
17	0	†	0	†	00	3	4
18	0	†	0	†	X	3	3
19	0000	†	0	†	†	2	5
20	0	†	0	0	†	3	3
21	0	0	00	0	†	4	5
22	—	000	—	—	†	1	3
23	00	0	X	00	0	5	7
24	X	0	†	0	00	4	5
25	†	0	†	0X	0	3	4
Total number of attacks	22	22	17	23	16		100

NOTE: X = successful attack;   0 = unsuccessful attack;
    † = absent from hunting area;   — = present in hunting area.
[b]25 migrants pass through the hunting area of male falcons within ca. 60 min.

90% later on when grasshoppers had appeared, constituting nearly 90% of this raptor's diet.

Other falcons have only occasionally been monitored. An exception is Rudebeck's (1950–51) classic study of the hunting efficiency of migrating and wintering populations in Scandinavia. Their average hunting success appears to have been rather low, perhaps a typical aspect of the prey/predator relationship during the nonbreeding season. Only 19 (7.5%) of 252 attacks of peregrines were successful, while merlins (*Falco columbarius*) caught prey in only 7 of 139 attacks (5%). Brown (1976) is skeptical of these low success rates: "when a peregrine means business it has little difficulty in catching its prey." He prefers to distinguish between "high and low-intensity chases," the latter resulting in low success because the peregrine was not really interested in catching anything at all. Hantge (1968) established a 17–22% success rate for bird-hunting peregrines, and Mebs (1959) found that lanner falcons (*Falco biarmicus*) hunting birds in difficult rocky terrain had a 13% success rate. Clapham (1964) observed sooty falcons on the Dahlac Archipelago (Red Sea) hunting Palearctic migrants in the manner of Eleonora's falcon. He writes: "They [the sooty falcons] were by no means paradigms of efficiency at catching birds, and were seen to fail more often than succeed."

In summary, only the fish prey of California ospreys and the invertebrate prey of American kestrels raised the raptor's hunting success rate above 50%. Where vertebrates, particularly birds, are the intended prey, the hunting success of several, perhaps most or all, falcon species appears to drop well below the 50% success level. Migrating and wintering raptors may have a lower success rate outside their breeding areas than during the breeding season itself, caused by the raptor's unfamiliarity with local terrain and prey ecology.

The effect of group or team hunting on success should not be overlooked. Several solitary species frequently hunt in pairs. Lanner falcons even depend on it in their breeding areas (Mebs 1959), and saker falcons and golden eagles use this strategy to increase their hunting success (Glutz, Bauer, and Bezzel 1971). The sooty falcon hunts "in pairs most often in attacks on high flying birds over the sea" (Clapham 1964). There can be little doubt that the strategy of hunting in pairs and with a coordinated chase pattern is more efficient than solitary hunting in the pursuit of prey that is difficult to catch.

A high success ratio for a group of falcons does not necessarily imply equal success for the individual falcon. The data given above indicate, however, that even the individual has greater hunting success than most of its congeners. The 44% success rate for a group would translate into a 22% individual rate if prey objects were on the average attacked by not more than two falcons. In an average hunting group of four falcons, however, the success rate would drop to 11% per falcon. The average probably lies somewhere between two and four falcons, which would put the individual hunting success rate in the neighborhood of 15%. This value is probably as high as that for other falcons. It seems therefore that the gregarious hunting strategy of Eleonora's falcons accomplishes just about the same hunting efficiency for the individual falcon as solitary and pair-hunting strategies in other species. Since the small and agile migrant prey of Eleonora's constitutes a difficult prey target, selection has probably favored group hunting over other strategies in response to the unusual prey environment. This would also apply to the instances of involuntary or noncooperative group hunting I have described for Eleonora's falcon.

SELECTIVE HUNTING

The shape, size, and color of prey objects is not genetically predetermined in great detail among the genus *Falco*. Individual falcons will modify their prey preferences in accordance with their hunting success. Captive falcons can easily be trained within a few weeks to prefer a new prey species over all others (Brosset 1973). Thus, acquired preferences (as well as avoidances) result in a selection of certain prey species that will be hunted more often than others irrespective of their numbers or population density.

Eleonora's falcon conforms to this general character of its congeneric species, and yet it does not. While no bird appears to be too small for it, birds the size of a turtledove (*Streptopelia turtur*), cuckoo (*Cuculus canorus*), scops owl (*Otus scops*), and the European nightjar (*Caprimulgus europaeus*) constitute its upper limit in prey size. Its frequent coinhabitant of coastal rock habitats, the rock pigeon (*Columba livia*) is a frequent target of pursuits and (mostly playful) attacks but rarely shows up in a list of prey species. This pigeon appears to be too heavy and perhaps also too strong and fast for the average Eleonora's falcon. Quite clearly, this raptor is not well suited to swifts (*Apus* spp.). In the colonies I studied, the three species of swifts (*Apus apus*, *A. pallida*, and the large *A. melba*) proved difficult, usually unattainable game. The swifts' mastery of flight and their incredible speed make them generally superior to a pursuing Eleonora's falcon. More often than not, I observed swifts flying unchallenged through the airspace of a falcon colony. In the San Pietro colony, Alpine swifts (*A. melba*) were standing high above the cliffs in the air side by side with several Eleonora's falcons shortly before sunset (19 July 1974).

Young and inexperienced swifts might offer a better chance of capture. This could explain the high rate of swifts (*A. apus*) taken by Mogador falcons in 1959. Among 250 prey remains there were 54 (21.6%) of swifts (Vaughan 1961*a*). In 1966, out of some 2,328 bird remains (see chap. 7), there were only 34 of swifts (1.6%). Vaughan collected mostly during August, whereas I collected predominantly during September, when most resident swifts had already departed for their winter quarters and even the juvenile birds had become more experienced flyers. My July data from 1969 contain a higher percentage of swift remains: 6 out of 39, or 15%. Four of those clearly were juveniles, since the wing and tail feathers were still blood-filled.

The majority of Palearctic migrants consists of small to medium-sized, slow-flying passerines that live on the ground or in shrubs or trees. When they become discernible to a human observer at a distance of more than 150 m it is usually impossible to distinguish the species or genus. Wagtails and orioles are exceptions. Although equipped with superior sight, Eleonora's falcon also must initially receive only one piece of information: small bird flying at low speed ahead! In effect, most of those passerines appear out of nowhere at a similar speed and in exactly the same hunting habitat. They probably all constitute one prey type to Eleonora's falcon, with complete disregard for species identity. The competitive nature of this raptor's gregarious hunting is an additional factor weighing against selective hunting of this migrant group. A falcon has no time to wait to make out the genus or species, because other falcons take over the potential prey in those few seconds. My hunting observations confirm this hypothesis. Whenever I monitored falcons on hunting flights, they went after any small migrant passing close to their own position, except for swallows and swifts.

The prey remains at the falcons' nest sites (table 33) provide another opportunity to evaluate the existence of selective hunting in Eleonora's falcon. The analysis of more than 5,000 prey remains from Mogador and Paximada colonies (tables 34 and 35) clearly identifies about half a dozen species at each colony that make up the majority of prey items, while many other species each constitute only a few percent of the falcon's diet during the breeding season. This can be interpreted in four ways: (1) selective hunting for a few species out of the large number of other migrant species that are equally abundant in hunting space and time; (2) nonselective hunting of nearly all species—the qualitative and quantitative composition of the prey list corresponds closely to the qualitative and quantitative abundance of prey species in hunting space and time, and a few species are much more abundant than others; (3) greatly differing hunting success even among closely related species; and (4) a combination of some degree of selective hunting and of differing hunting success. The first hypothesis can be discarded. Almost 100 species of birds have been captured by Eleonora's falcon (table 33). Only a handful of small trans-Saharan migrants have not yet been collected from the falcons' nest sites. Generally a species is more common prey in Moroccan colonies if its main migration route is southwest and more common in Aegean colonies if it shows a concentration in the eastern part of the Mediterranean during the fall migration. In addition, the increase and decrease of prey remains among closely related species (warblers or shrikes) parallels the different migration season, corridor, and population size of each species (see Moreau 1972). Thus, we can state as a general rule that Eleonora's falcon captures a small trans-Saharan migrant species more often where the latter passes through in larger numbers.

The other hypotheses cannot be tested by looking at bird pluckings of Eleonora's falcon. The observations reported earlier lead me to suggest that the fourth hypothesis explains the interrelationships best. There is undoubtedly some selection for small, clumsy, or juvenile migrants coupled with and reinforced by some variance in the hunting success of different migrant groups and species. This would mean that falcons that have been unsuccessful in hunting species A but very successful in hunting species B will be more stimulated and determined to chase after the latter species. This selective behavior will, on the whole, be of minor importance, since it is unlikely that the falcons distinguish among many of the about one hundred species. Just a few of them—large, fast, aerial birds—might be recognized as suboptimal prey objects.

An examination of the prey remains of individual pairs provides additional support for this interpretation of the raptor's hunting behavior. From among the prey remains of 20 study nests (Paximada, 1965) I have selected six types of migrants that were frequent prey items and that vary in size, color, breeding habitat, and flight style. They are the hoopoe, short-toed lark, whinchat, whitethroat, and two additional groups represented by several species each—three species of shrike and four warblers of the genus *Phylloscopus*. The warblers are so similar in size, shape, and color that they often pose identification problems to bird watchers. The medium-sized shrikes are of different colors but of nearly identical shape and flight style.

The prey remains were collected from all 20 nests in an identical manner and during the same period. Thus the error of collection should be minimal. Table 31 gives the total number of prey remains collected, the hatching time of the first chick, and the total number of young per nest. Columns A–F list the percentage of prey remains for each of the six prey types. In addition, column R lists the percentage value of all other species collected.

Since the male falcons did most of the hunting in this colony, any particular preference or avoidance of any of the six prey types acquired by one of the 20 males could be expected to clearly identify itself in such a table. This did not happen. There are many differences, but each set of data is not significantly different from the expected values under random conditions (chi-square analysis). Once again, this does not offer any conclusive evidence. Had there been a significant difference, some degree of hunting selection or of different ratios in hunting success among different individuals should have caused it. Instead, all members of the colony appear to have acted in a rather homogeneous way. If they selected and captured prey at different success ratios, then they selected the same prey groups and must have experienced similar hunting success with different migrants. There appears to be no way to gather more evidence on this subject unless we attain a reliable knowledge of the relative abundance of migrant species in the airspace above the colonies.

Killing the Prey

Falcons kill their prey with their beaks by biting and twisting the neck or head. This killing technique appears to be innate and differs from that of other raptors, particularly the hawks of the genus *Accipiter*. The latter kill their prey on impact and with their powerful talons.

Brosset (1973) found that under experimental conditions young kestrels, lanners, and peregrines made the first attempt to attack a potential prey between 22 and 28 (rarely 32) days, grabbing it on the back and killing it with the help of their notched beaks by tearing off the neck and head.

Although this is an innate technique, an older falcon will kill faster and with more skill. The old wild bird performs this work "without the slightest hesitation, with a surgical precision" (Brosset 1973). Adult peregrine falcons forget their killing technique in captivity if they do not use it regularly. Thus, Brosset stipulates a feedback mechanism between an innate ability and an acquired and practiced perfection.

In Eleonora's falcon, observations from the nest site prove that most falcons return with an already killed prey item. It is impossible to observe the killing directly, since it occurs high up in the air or over the sea. Thus the species generally conforms to the behavior pattern characteristic of all members of the genus *Falco*.

A few observations showed, however, that there are exceptions to this rule: a falcon sometimes returns to its nest site with live prey or spends minute after minute plucking feathers off a migrant that is still alive.

16 September 1965 (Paximada)
  6:00   Two falcons are entangled at low altitude above the colony,
         probably a male that wants to deliver prey to his female in the
         air. Suddenly a smaller third bird, an oriole (*Oriolus oriolus*)
         emerges from between the two falcons and flies to the ground
         with no sign of an injury.
1 September 1977 (Mogador)
  7:00   Female 35 returns to her nest site with an Orphean warbler
         (*Sylvia hortensis*) in her talons. The warbler is still alive, beating
         its wings in a desperate attempt to free itself. The falcon does
         not move but stands calmly over her prey for 2 min. Then she
         flies to her young.
 11:00   Male 279 arrives at the nest site with a woodchat (*Lanius senator*)
         that is still alive, rhythmically beating its tail.

Whether the falcons simply forgot to kill their prey right after capturing it or whether other pursuing falcons left them no time to apply the killing technique must remain unanswered. These interesting observations demonstrate convincingly that being held in the talons of Eleonora's falcon need not be deadly or perhaps even injurious for a small to medium-sized passerine.

ANTIRAPTOR BEHAVIOR OF PREY SPECIES

The small migrants that happened to pass over a falcon colony employed a number of flight maneuvers to escape one or several falcons. Sometimes a migrant found an escape by landing at the falcon colony itself. Here on the cliffs, in caves, holes, or in the dry shrubs covering the island, these birds were at least temporarily safe. I watched some of them attempt to take off from this rather inhospitable refuge in broad daylight. Yellow wagtails (*Motacilla flava*) and hoopoes *(Upupa epops)* were among those species. Usually they were captured or driven back to the island by the falcons. In general, once a migrant had landed on Paximada it would remain there until dusk or nightfall, staying in the shrubs near the ground and flying as little as possible.

Some birds were so frightened by the presence of so many falcons that their behavioral response was quite different from their normal antipredator behavior. Once, when walking to my observation post on Paximada, I saw a large red bill protruding from a small cleft. It was an oriole (*Oriolus oriolus*) hiding from the falcons. This bird nests and feeds in the canopy of European forests. To my knowledge it never enters any hole or crevice in its breeding habitat. At Mogador, I saw a hoopoe pressing itself against a vertical cliff of the atoll's inner basin for at least 30 min, moving only its head. This extreme antiraptor response was very functional indeed, since it made the migrants invisible or at least inconspicious. Whenever migrants followed one or several of the above tactics they had an excellent chance of leaving the falcon colony unharmed during the following night.

HUNTING BEHAVIOR FROM APRIL TO JULY

Like other European migrants, Eleonora's falcon returns from its southern winter quarters to the Mediterranean breeding region between March and May. A large proportion of the passerine migrants have crossed the Mediterranean Sea in a northerly direction by the beginning of May. The stream of migrants soon becomes a trickle, and from the last days in May until the beginning of July or August (depending on the geographic position of a breeding colony) there are only a few stragglers passing over the falcon colony sites.

Most of the available evidence suggests that the staple diet of Eleonora's falcon before it is raising young consists of flying insects and other arthropods. Before describing how Eleonora's falcon captures beetles, dragonflies, ants, and cicadas in flight, we must analyze the information concerning additional hunting behaviors before the young-raising period.

The Italian ornithologist di Carlo visited the Tremiti Isles in the Adriatic Sea from 24–28 March 1964. These islands are "departure and resting points for bird migrants of NE direction in spring" from the Italian shore to those of Dalmatia. He observed several specimens of Eleonora's falcon, some wandering around; "others, however, had already more or less selected their nest sites." Once he surprised three Eleonora's falcons resting on the goal bar of the local soccer field. They "descended to the ground from time to time in order to capture grasshoppers and other insects" (di Carlo 1966). Unfortunately, no further observations were made regarding hunting activities.

If Eleonora's falcons return to breeding places in the northern Mediterranean at such an early date, it seems likely that they hunt bird migrants more than anything else; the main difference in this hunting behavior in late summer and fall would be a 180° change of their hunting position. They would wait for the spring migrant arriving from the southwest, south, or southeast. Although the direct hunting of spring migrants by Eleonora's falcon has not as yet been observed, there is some indirect evidence available. Lilford (1875) reported the stomach contents of several Eleonora's falcons shot during May at Vacca and Toro islands off Sardinia: "In one specimen only did we find a leg of some small bird, apparently a Wheatear." Moltoni (1970) shot a male specimen on Lampedusa island on 3 May 1967 "which had fed itself a garden Warbler, *Sylvia borin*."

That the falcons had returned to their breeding sites in late March (a very early date for this species) and that Lilford found them in very large numbers at the end of May (he estimated more than 300 pairs) on Vacca and Toro, which occupy an excellent strategic position for intercepting migrants crossing the open sea between Africa and Sardinia, appears to strengthen the hypothesis that Eleonora's falcon feeds not only on the fall migrants but to some extent also on the spring migrants crossing the seas between Europe and Africa.

Di Carlo's observation of ground-feeding Eleonora's falcons is very interesting for two reasons. First, this species rarely perches on anything but a rock or cliff ledge; the bar of a soccer goal seems as exotic as one of my own observations of this species in Madagascar (see chap. 9). Second, several authors report finding the remains of grasshoppers in falcon pellets. This opens up the possibility that some of them were captured on the ground. In this connection we should mention other items found in falcon pellets (Paximada colony) that could only have been taken from the ground. These include the shells of land snails and the scissorlike extremity of a crab species (Portunidae). Lilford (1875) reports that the falcons were feeding on insects "and, in several instances, small crustaceans." In the next sentences the author writes "but, speaking ignorantly, I should say the falcons feed, or at all events were feeding when we shot them, almost exclusively upon beetles, dragonflies, grasshoppers, and shrimps." Uttendörfer (1952) found two centipedes (*Scolopender*), and Warncke and Wittenberg (1961) found the remains of a sow bug (Oniscidae) in pellets of Eleonora's falcon.

Although I admire the versatility of this falcon's predatory nature, I am not convinced by these data that Eleonora's falcon actually captures live crustaceans and mollusks. Until direct observation proves the contrary, it seems likely that the falcons eat the empty, calcium-rich shells of those organisms for the same reasons they eat the many small white stones (up to 9×5 mm in size) that I found in the insect pellets of Paximada falcons. These hard items may be necessary for crushing and digesting the insect diet.

The findings of lizard remains at falcon nest sites also cannot be regarded as proof of hunting on the ground. The Paximada falcons killed several local lizards (*Lacerta erhardii*) at their nest sites but did not eat them. However, Krüper (1864) found the remains of two lizards in falcon nest sites on Tragonisi. These lizards (*Stellio vulgaris*) "occur on Mikonos," that is, on the nearest large island but not on the breeding cliff, if I interpret Krüper correctly. I myself found the remains of a large Moroccan lizard (*Agama ruderata*) deposited above migrant feathers in a falcon nest site on the atoll isle at Mogador (1966), where no lizard population exists. Those two cases can be explained in two ways. Either the falcons hunted those lizards and flew them to their breeding site, or they forced other raptors (kestrels, hawks) to relinquish their own prey.

The material above demonstrates our ignorance of the daily activities of Eleonora's falcon during the spring and early summer. Many breeding locations appear to be relatively unoccupied by their breeding populations until July. Where are all those falcons and what are their daily hunting activities?

The available evidence suggests that they are spread out over the major islands of the Aegean Sea (Reiser 1905; and see Wettstein 1938 and Makatsch 1969), the Baleares, and possibly the coastal wetlands and fertile valleys of the entire basin of the Mediterranean Sea. During spring and early summer of 1974, I spent many days in the countryside of southwest Sardinia, less than 50 km from the three falcon colonies on Vacca, Toro, and San Pietro. Only once was I able to see a group of Eleonora's falcons.

14 May 1974 (Sardinia)

13:10– Four specimens were chasing insects or other arthropods up
13:25   and down the slopes north of Iglesias near the pass of Genna
        Bogai. Here a steep climb, there a nose-dive attack, sometimes
        far from, other times close to the canopy of the cork oak for-
        ests lining the hills. The nature of their prey was not iden-
        tified. They ate it while gliding across the valley by bending
        the head and bringing the talons forward. The most interest-
        ing part of this observation concerned the climatic factors. The
        falcons were hunting in a small and shifting zone of bright,
        warm sunshine. When clouds and mist suddenly developed all
        around us, the falcon group disappeared. It probably followed
        the area of sunshine moving across the countryside causing
        winged beetles, dragonflies, and others to take to the air.

On Mallorca, von Jordans (1924) observed Eleonora's falcons regularly near the "large swamp area of Albufera" from 23 May onward. He observed 23 birds that day, then "single, several, 5–7, often more than 10 simultaneously". "Particularly early in the morning and toward evening they hunted above the pine forest, very low or also gliding very high, capturing—as I could see with my glasses—some animals and devouring them in flight." One muggy evening, von Jordans was able to determine the food source when the falcons "were dashing forth and back like arrows very low above the pines. There were large swarms of dragonflies out of which they captured their prey" (von Jordans 1924). During the hot noon hours the falcons disappeared. Finally, after long and fruitless searching, he found them "perched in very old, giant pines—the biggest ones that I have seen on Majorca—at the foot of the mountains, as though asleep, seeking protection from the heat."

On 20 May 1934, von Wettstein climbed the highest mountain of Anafi island, Vigla (584 m). "Right at this altitude the falcons were circling. The behavior of the birds was not falconlike but swallowlike. Just like these, they were gliding in a large group, perhaps about 80 falcons, which soon divided into smaller groups, then united again; and while doing this they were moving on all the time over the ridge and summits . . . . Evidently the birds were diligently catching insects; while the total flight was swallowlike, so were the individual movements—for instance, the brief upturn to grab an insect, with subsequent gliding flight downward, or in short turns to the sides." He shot three female falcons, whose stomach contents consisted exclusively of a small species of dung beetle "that apparently was swarming in large numbers on Anafi at that time" (Wettstein 1938).

The same author observed another surprisingly efficient insect-hawking behavior of Eleonora's falcon on the isle of Milos (23 May 1954). A falcon was flying upward along a slope, gliding in such a way as to form several figure-eight loops (fig. 21). At the end point of each loop it captured a "June beetle" (*Amphimallon arianae*), which it dismembered and ate in flight (Wettstein 1959).

Little need be added to those elegant descriptions of hawking Eleonora's falcons. Swarms of flying ants and other winged arthropods have also been reported as hunting targets of Eleonora's falcon during this period (Walker in Vaughan 1961a).

I have seen insect-hawking behavior before and during the breeding season in various places on Crete and also in Morocco.

5 July 1966 (Crete, Potamus Valley)
16:00– Seven times one falcon, twice two falcons, each hawking in-
19:00 sects along the slopes of the valley, covered with vineyards and olive and citrus groves.

9 August 1965 (Crete)
Eleonora's falcons circling over the high plateau east of Sitia during the afternoon hours. One specimen was hunting at one slope for at least 30 min, again and again flying low above a dirt road (looking for cicadas).

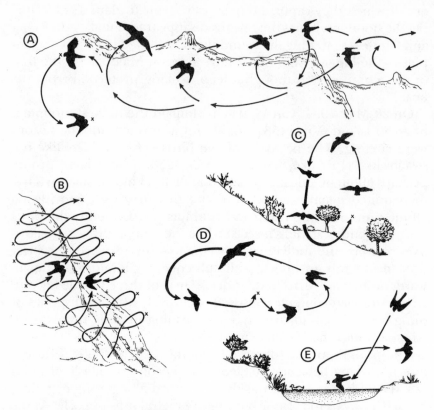

Fig. 21. Insect-hawking: *A*, Gliding and circling above plateaus and hillsides. *B*, Elegant sequence of loops (like a figure 8) on uphill flight, capturing an arthropod at each turning point (see Wettstein 1959). *C*, High-speed chase low above the ground in orchard environment. *D* and *E*, Capture of dragonflies and their consumption during flight.

24 August 1966 (Morocco)

Coast opposite falcon colony in the late morning hours. There are constantly 1–5 Eleonora's falcons hawking dragonflies, perhaps also other insects above the sand dunes and the lake. New specimens are arriving regularly, while the others return to the breeding island.

The main hunting techniques as described above have been summarized in figure 21. Eleonora's falcons have little difficulty capturing flying insects. The latter are simply no match for the great ability of the bird. This holds true even for the largest dragonflies and moths.

10 August 1965 (Paximada)

> A falcon captured a large moth during the early evening
> hours. Although the falcon was some 50 m to the side of
> this insect, it captured it by stooping down upon it even
> though the moth had made a quick zigzag turn.

Rudebeck (1950–51, p. 222) is of the opinion that invertebrates in
general are "not equal to the situation" when hunted by vertebrates. We can therefore assume that whenever flying insects and
ants or termites appear in large numbers, Eleonora's falcon captures many of these small prey items in a short time and with little
effort. Warm, moist locations can be expected to attract considerable numbers of Eleonora's falcons, since they are usually populated by many flying arthropods.

SWITCH FROM INSECT-HAWKING TO BIRD-HUNTING

Eleonora's falcon feeds its chicks almost exclusively with migrant birds. We have seen, however, that the falcon's diet in May,
June, and perhaps even July and parts of August consists largely
or exclusively of invertebrate organisms. When and how do the
falcons switch from the insect diet to the bird diet? We shall investigate this question through an analysis of hunting behaviors in
four major colonies during July and August.

Mogador Colony

As early as 11 July 1969 I observed several male falcons returning
to their nest sites with captured birds in their talons at between
12:00 and 15:00. In addition, rather fresh remains of the European cuckoo (*Cuculus canorus*) and the woodchat (*Lanius senator*)
provided further proof that the falcons had already begun to
hunt migrant birds. Near 10 falcon nest sites between 11 and 20
July I found the remains of 42 birds belonging to 10 different
species (Walter 1971). During the afternoon of 12 July one male
falcon returned with a large moth in his talons.

In spite of the fact that almost the entire population had already
established or reestablished nesting sites and territories, the cliffs
appeared unusually quiet and almost void of falcons during the
first minutes after we landed on 11 July. The reason for the temporary absence of many colony inhabitants became apparent
when we monitored the study population on the submarine cliff

on 12 July. The composition of such a small resident population probably changed constantly as some falcons returned from one or several days of insect-hawking while others were leaving the breeding location for an extensive hunting excursion. Sometimes both partners of a pair were absent at the same time. Whether they were bathing and insect-hawking over the mainland coast or whether one or both specimens were over the sea looking for migrant birds was not determined. Only a dozen falcons were found on the Isles of Mogador in the first days of July 1957 (Contant and de Naurois 1958).

Compared with August and September, bird migration was a trickle in mid-July 1969. However, the falcons regularly captured some migrants and presented them to their mates on 21, 30, and 31 July. The reorientation toward the open sea therefore occurred as early as the second third of July. Observations made by Vaughan and myself indicate, however, that single falcons as well as small and large groups were still leaving the isles en route to the mainland in late August and September.

Mallorca Colonies

Thiollay (1967) reports insect-hawking of Eleonora's falcon on 10 August 1966, when close to sunset he observed 52 falcons circling at an altitude of 80 to 1,100 m above mountains situated 5 km from the sea. They continuously captured small insects. At sunset, their "carousel" broke up, and the birds left one after the other, heading west in direction of the Dragonera colony site, 19 km away. During the following days, however, no falcons were detected in the back country of other Mallorca colonies, although the area was "rather rich in insects." Thiollay wondered: "It would appear impossible that so many falcons feed themselves around such desolate cliffs [of their breeding sites]. The hypothesis remained of hunting at dawn or dusk or at night. To this effect, several trips were conducted at night, particularly around the swamps, but without any success."

From 20 August Thiollay began to monitor the Formentor colony, discovering the massive hunting of migrants over the sea that has already been described.

Frequent observations of falcons leaving for the interior of Mallorca showed that part of the falcon population was regularly capturing insects over the island during the hours when hunting birds over the sea had ceased.

Since we have no July observations from the Mallorca colonies, the exact time when Eleonora's falcon begins to hunt fall migrants cannot be established at present. However, Thiollay's infrequent encounters of falcons hawking insects over the land area of Mallorca seem to point to an early date for the start of the offshore hunting season of fall migrants. His Formentor diary shows both bird- and insect-hunting during the last third of August. Thus, no sudden switch seems to occur; rather, there is a time separation during the course of a day: bird prey during the early morning, then insects in the late morning hours, followed by an extended rest period in the early afternoon. The departure of many falcons after 17:00, observed on 25 August (toward the east) and 26 August (toward the west-southwest) cannot be satisfactorily explained without further observations; they could have been related to insect (and bat) hunting, but also to some bird migrants taking off before darkness.

San Pietro Colony

Observation of a cliff harboring five pairs yielded valuable information with respect to the switch from insect-hawking to bird-hunting. In the late afternoon hours preceding dusk (17:30–20:00 local summer time, equivalent to 15:30–18:00 Greenwich mean time) of 19 July 1974, I witnessed the capture of nonbird prey and watched several hunting flights. Several copulations were also observed at this time.

19 July 1974 (San Pietro)
17:55   Pair 3 returns to nest site, one bird carrying a small prey (not a bird). They are difficult to observe, but are both preening less than 5 min later.
18:09   A dark-phased falcon stands in the air, ca. 200 m high at the cliff top, without beating its wings: it sails in the draft just like five swifts (*Apus apus*) and three large alpine swifts (*Apus melba*) in the same spot. The falcon suddenly chases an alpine swift. The latter swerves away in an elegant move, causing the falcon to terminate its hunting attempt. Two other falcons are now standing in the sky behind and above my observation post.
18:19   No standing flight observed so far. Falcons sail motionless or circle in front and above the cliffs.

19:08   Male 3 returns with a prey item; his female "scrambles" into the nest site area to receive the prey.

19:19   Three falcons in the air. One is chasing something that an alpine swift has also been pursuing. The falcon moves into another position, but two other falcons begin to chase a flying small object (no bird!), followed by a short aerial flight (one falcon may have captured something).

19:54   One falcon stands ca. 200 m high above the sea, then rises gradually to 500 m altitude, facing the wind twice, moving west, then quickly descending and landing on a cliff far to the south at 20:00 (fig. 22*F*), without having given chase to any flying object.

The fading light made it impossible to continue my observations. It appeared as if pairs 2 and 3 and one partner of pairs 4 and 5 were absent at 19:54. During the next hour I still heard one or two falcons flying ca. 500 m inland from the colony.

In summary, the falcon population was observed near and at the breeding site during the late afternoon hours. Two or three falcons were usually found in the air, together with two species of swifts. All three appeared to be after insects or other flying arthropods. The following morning this falcon population exhibited a rather diverse hunting pattern. Some falcons were flying away from the shore, others moved high into the air, remaining close to the shoreline. Most falcons seemed to search for bird migrants, but they sometimes returned without any prey or with some insect in their talons.

20 July 1974 (San Pietro)

6:45   A falcon flies away from the coast toward the northwest; I lose it about 1,000 m from the cape. It flies at about 150 m altitude, alternately gliding and beating its wings, rising and falling in a regular sequence.

6:50–   I follow the flight of a specimen standing above me. It flies
6:57   south, about 150 m high, then moves about 1,000 m west over the sea; it flies lower at about 100 m above the sea, stands relatively motionless against the wind, then makes a few wingbeats, then a circle; it moves farther away, then descends and stoops down upon another falcon, both only about 20 m high now. The two falcons fly together for about 2 min, low and high above the waves, then both—flying low—return to the coast. No chase seen, no prey believed to be held by them (fig. 22*C*).

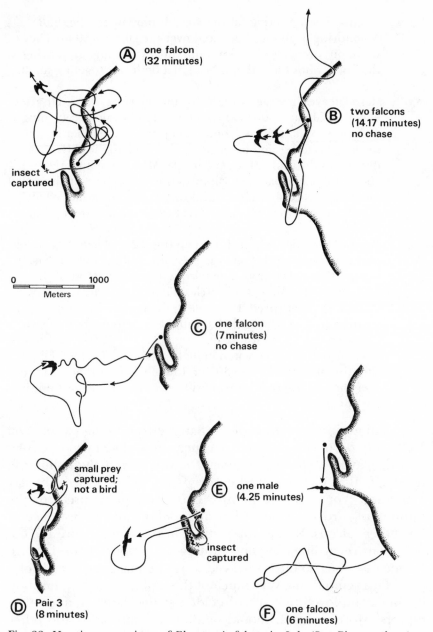

Fig. 22. Hunting excursions of Eleonora's falcon in July (San Pietro colony).

7:45   Followed two hunting falcons for 14 min, 10 sec (fig. 22*B*)
Monitoring begins as they stand over the cliff at 150 m. They
move out over the sea, then south, finally rise higher, moving to
the north until I lose them. Note that both stay together all the
time.

8:09   Male 1 leaves in straight flight for the west (fig. 22*E*). He rises
and after about 1,500 m encounters another falcon returning
with prey. Male 1 turns around and pursues the other one, but
the latter is faster and manages to race back to the cliffs, falling
down into the rocks of the peninsula. Male 1 remains 150 m
above the peninsula, then captures the small object at about 280
m height, probably an insect; falcon swoops down immediately
to deliver prey to the female. Great excitement at the nesting
site.

8:45   Just followed two falcons for 8 min (fig. 22*D*). Flight begins low
over the breeding cliff, goes higher, up to about 400 m, mostly
in a northerly direction. The falcons are gliding most of the
time, also performing back circles. Finally one falcon swoops
down with great speed. It is male 3; the female, his hunting
partner, follows. The male has caught something, but no bird.

9:17   Followed one falcon for 32 min (fig. 22*A*). It catches an insect
after 17 min (which is eaten in flight at 100 m altitude). Flight
altitude varies from 50 to 300 m. I finally lose this falcon far out
over the sea, where it is flying with three other falcons toward
the northwest.

A cautious interpretation of the San Pietro hunting patterns on
19/20 July permits the following conclusions: The falcon population displayed a strong tendency for the search flight hunting
technique that was described earlier from Mallorca (see Thiollay
1967) and from the Salé colony. The technique is used for the
hunting of bird migrants at low altitude and in the presence of
few other falcons. Rather interesting, in my opinion, are the observations regarding the joint hunting excursions of two falcons.
In one case the two birds involved were the male and female of a
pair. This reminds me very much of the well-known joint hunting
methods employed by pairs of golden eagles, lanners, and other
raptors. More research should be done at San Pietro and other
colonies, focusing on the hunting efforts of pairs and and small
falcon troops. This might yield new data on this raptor's hunting
efficiency.

Although a strong wind came from north and northwest on

both days, bird migration appeared to be minimal. Thus, falcons were monitored on very extensive hunting flights that resulted in no sightings of birds and captures of only small insectlike prey items. The presence of flying arthropods offshore and above the coastal cliffs was a surprise. Where did they come from? Their density and number were insufficient, however, to provide the calories needed by the falcon population (the females must have been approaching their egg-laying time). Additional insect food must therefore have supplemented the diet. It may have been caught during the late morning and possibly the evening hours over San Pietro or even the large island mass of Sardinia itself.

The switch from insect-hawking to bird-hunting appears to be gradual. The falcons were already searching for birds on 20 July; they met with little success, rewarded once in a while by insects and a few isolated bird migrants. Male and female falcons were observed hunting together at this time. As the bird migration builds up, the falcons will capture more birds and become less dependent on the insect diet. The female falcon will probably restrict her own hunting excursions as soon as the male can supply her with a sufficient amount of bird prey.

Paximada colony

On 1 and 2 July 1966, only a few Eleonora's falcons were present on Paximada. I arrived at noon and found nearly everything unchanged compared with the previous summer. Walking around the southern half of the isle, I managed to see a maximum of 7 falcons, one of them being immature. Throughout the afternoon hours I was not able to spot any significant arrivals or departures of falcons from or to Crete. The falcons did not assume any particular hunting position. They were gliding and playing in the wind, performing their flight display and territorial calls.

The next morning a few additional falcons appeared to arrive from Crete. I counted a maximum of 11 falcons and estimated a resident population of some 30 specimens for the entire island; that is, only 10% of the breeding population. Some of them were standing very high in the air capturing insects. On the island itself I found a large butterfly.

I concluded at the time that most of the falcons had not yet arrived. It is equally possible, however, that the falcons had already returned to their breeding sites but were temporarily absent from Paximada while on extended insect-hawking excursions over Crete and other islands.

Upon my return on 20 July 1966, I saw from the boat a large mass of falcons above the island. During the early evening hours more than 40 falcons were positioned in 200 to 600 m altitude, forming the typical vertical and horizontal barrier in the Paximada airspace that I had observed in September and October of the previous season. All the falcons were headed into the wind, beating their wings without changing their position. I also observed this standing flight technique the following morning. As early as 4:55, more than 20 falcons were standing high above the island facing a strong northwest wind. Two falcons carried large beetles to their females (at 5:15 and 5:30). Minutes later another falcon returned with a large dragonfly or locust. Three other falcons returned with insect prey between 5:30 and 7:00. A careful search for prey remains yielded only the feathers of one songbird. At the same time, many insect pellets were found.

Bird migration had therefore not yet begun. Even on 10 August 1965, I collected few bird remains on Paximada. Even so, Eleonora's falcon had already adopted the standing flight technique that is so characteristic for the Paximada population. Instead of birds, a considerable number of large beetles and other insects were captured within a short time span. Considering the strong wind coming from the northwest, it seems improbable that they came from Crete. It is more likely that the wind had blown them from the Greek mainland or from the large islands to the northwest across the southern Aegean Sea. The falcons captured them at altitudes of up to 500 m or even higher.

By the middle of August, more and more bird migrants pass through the Paximada airspace. The number of insects should show a gradual decline by September owing to the drought conditions of late summer. But the insects and birds captured over Paximada did not seem sufficient for the needs of the species. A considerable number of falcons were observed repeatedly flying to and from Crete. On 22 August we counted 58 falcons returning from the south (from Crete) and 13 falcons leaving toward the south between 17:00 and 17:50.

The lack of food near the island might also explain the curious fact that we did not see male falcons feeding their incubating female partners during the 1965 season. The Mogador falcons did exhibit such behavior, and the females appeared to be largely or entirely supplied with food by their mates. Thiollay's (1967) study of the Formentor population, however, resulted in several observations of falcons bringing prey to the nesting site followed by the departure of the arriving falcon's partner (25 August 1966).

Although I may have overlooked some Paximada falcons that were constantly supplying their females with food, I am certain that many females were absent from their clutches for several hours each day capturing their own insect diet over Paximada and over the valleys and mountains of Crete. The late beginning of the fall migration of passerine birds would ultimately be the factor responsible for this interesting deviation from typical falcon behavior.

Summing up, the Paximada population was found to be entirely dependent on invertebrate food during July; even in the latter half of August, when bird migration had finally begun, falcons were still observed flying to and from Crete. The standing flight technique was practiced above Paximada as early as July, when beetles and other insects were drifting through the island's airspace. As more and more birds passed through, the falcons captured more of them and gradually changed to a nearly 100% bird diet by the end of August. The late arrival of bird migrants and the isolated geographical position of Paximada appear to force some, perhaps many, female falcons to hunt for their own food during the incubation period.

Conclusion

There is no sudden switch from insect-hawking to bird-hunting in any of the colonies studied so far. In general, as insect-hawking declines gradually during July or August, bird-hunting increases. This brings about a change of the hunting area and the hunting periods from inland to offshore areas and from late morning and afternoon (dusk) hours to early morning hours (in Mogador, also afternoon hours).

The same hunting techniques that were later employed to capture bird migrants were used near the colony site of Paximada a full month before the onset of massive bird migration. High-flying beetles and other arthropods were captured in the same way those falcons captured birds (or vice versa: bird-hunting strongly resembled insect-hawking).

The Mogador population appears to have the shortest insect-hawking season, since the bird diet has already become significant by the middle and end of July, when there is almost no trans-Mediterranean migration in the regions of Sardinia and Crete. As a result, the eastern, and perhaps all, Mediterranean populations of Eleonora's falcons begin to subsist mainly on a bird diet some three to four weeks later than the Mogador population on Morocco's Atlantic coast. Should this difference account for the earlier breeding season of the Mogador falcons? Does the prein-cubation bird diet affect the clutch size in any way? Such questions should be followed up.

7 The Falcon's Prey

Previous chapters have dealt with the modes of hunting birds and insects. This chapter analyzes the quality and quantity of food ingested by Eleonora's falcon during the breeding season. Since Vaughan summarized the older records in 1961, much additional evidence has been collected. But the main emphasis will not be placed on the meticulous recording of every single record of observed or collected ingestion of prey items. Rather, we shall continue to look at the falcon's diverse list of prey items in order to arrive at a better judgment of its present adaptation to its unique locational and temporal relationships—the dependence on bird migration between Europe and Africa at the end of summer.

METHODOLOGY

During our fieldwork on Paximada in 1965, Ristow and I collected as many falcon pellets and prey remains as possible. I myself decided to collect the feather remains of bird prey found in 21 study nests that were easily accessible and were also monitored with respect to natality, mortality, and growth rate of the young. As a rule, all tail feathers and primaries of all bird species were removed from the nest site. In addition, during each collection period I took all those feathers or parts of a bird's body that provided proof that more specimens of that particular species had been captured, killed, and plucked by a falcon (pair) than was evident from wing and tail feathers alone. As an example, the tail feather count and determination (how many central, how many other tail feathers?) indicated that at least 3 hoopoes (*Upupa epops*) had been killed during the past seven days. But there were 4 right wings and 5 bills of hoopoes in the nest. I left behind the large amount of body feathers and smaller wing feathers so as not to disturb the normal thermal and tactile environment at the nest site. In addition, feathers and pellets were collected at many additional nests whenever our limited time permitted.

The well over one hundred thousand feathers carried away from Paximada were compared with study skins and several sets of complete wing and tail feathers that I had begun to assemble on Paximada. The time-consuming determination of *what* species were contained in *how many* specimens in one week's collection was accomplished with the assistance of the always helpful Professor Günther Niethammer and Dr. H. E. Wolters of the Museum Alexander Koenig in Bonn.

In 1966 I made a comparable collection of prey remains at the Mogador colony. Here, I confined myself to collecting tail feathers of small passerine birds, since they had proved easier to identify than the wing feathers. Ristow (pers. comm.) has remarked that counting tail feathers alone gives a lower total number of bird prey than wing feather analysis, since the falcons may tear the tail off a captured prey while still in the air. This may certainly occur, although most prey items I saw falcons bring in still had tails. In any case, the Mogador data communicated below were derived mainly from tail-feather analysis. This means that possibly fewer, but certainly not more, bird specimens were identified with this method than with the wing and tail analysis of the Paximada collection. At Mogador I began to make weekly collections at 17 nests.

In both colonies, the feathers, pellets, and other evidence found in the nest and within the ground territory of a falcon pair were stuffed in an envelope, sealed, and identified by date and nest number.

Unfortunately, the planned methodology was not rigidly executed, owing to unforeseen circumstances: some nests were robbed of their contents (and parent falcons thus ceased to leave normal quantities of prey remains), and logistic problems delayed some collection dates. Thus a comparison of the quantity of prey remains between Paximada and Mogador is possible only if we combine the number of nests from which collections were made with the number of days since the previous collection (nests × days). For example, if 105 bird specimens were identified from remains collected in 5 nests 7 days after the last such effort was made, the falcons had 5 × 7 days to capture those 105 specimens, that is, 35 nest-days. That permits us to calculate the mean rate per nest and per day: 105/35 = 4. On the average, each falcon pair had left behind the remains of at least 4 birds per day during this collection period.

In 1969 I made another collection of prey remains at the Mogador colony (Walter 1971). Because of the massive human-caused intervention in the normal breeding cycle of that season, the data are not representative except for the period before 1 August 1969.

We cannot overlook the large number and percentage of prey items that left no trace or were not found in spite of diligent searching. Thus, all figures in this chapter should always be regarded as absolute *minimum* figures. Later in this chapter I will attempt to clarify how well the prey remains represent the total number of captured organisms. I made a special effort to avoid the repeated counting of the same bird specimens (see below).

Falcon pellets were carefully taken apart and their contents examined and identified if possible, though this often could not be done because the material was deformed and incomplete.

NATURE OF PREY REMAINS

During the breeding season Eleonora's falcon nearly always plucks and prepares its prey at the nest site or at least at specified locations within its ground territory. Insects and sometimes small birds may be totally or partially eaten or plucked in the air. Because of the stormy seasonal winds, remains of prey treated this way will most likely end up in the sea or far away from any falcon nest. But even when the bird is carefully plucked at the nest site many feathers are tossed in the air and carried away. Other remains fall into rock crevices or disappear beneath the vegetation cover (if there is any). The rest form a feather cushion in the immediate nest environs that becomes thicker and higher from day to day while the young are being raised.

Sometimes falcons do not finish a bird meal. They will carefully hide this food somewhere around the nest site (see chap. 8), even if it is only a small part of the bird's body. At Paximada, falcons also occasionally hid complete, untouched birds. Usually, these prey items were consumed by day's end. At Mogador, however, many more such dead but intact birds were found, often mixed

with partly dismembered and decapitated bird carcasses. They
have been described by Vaughan (1961a) as "larders." To avoid the
potential double-counting of specimens that were first discovered
and listed in a meat larder, then eaten by the falcon and retrieved
in the form of feather remains, I carried a special list of such meat
larders. Having convinced myself through clear evidence that falcons at Mogador hardly ever used up any of the birds ending up
in a meat pile (they stank more from week to week where I did not
interfere) I tossed the contents of these piles into the sea. Thus,
prey remains at the next collection day had to come from fresh
captures.

As Vaughan (1961a) has stated, "Most pellets consist in the
main of either bird or insect remains, but a few are mixed. They
vary in length from 25 to 50 mm, and in breadth from 10 to
15 mm." At Paximada I analyzed several hundred pellets in 1965.
They belonged to one of four easily distinguishable pellet types:

1. *Clay-colored small pellets*
Homogeneous, very tightly packed, without recognizable prey
items.

2. *Brown colored and spotted pellets*
Cylinder-shaped and very loose when dried. Dry pellets disinte-
grate when touched. Contain chitinous parts of devoured arthropods and other alien substances (stones).

3. *Dark gray small pellets*
Very small, pointed, shiny pellets, main substance small feathers.

4. *Large gray pellets*
Non-symmetrical, generally large pellets. Usually consist of feathers, but these are rarely undamaged by digestive enzymes and
therefore are not very useful for species identification even if
pellet contains complete feathers. The pellets of falcon chicks
were less well proportioned than those of adult birds. The feather
pellets of Eleonora's falcon serve as principal habitats for the
keratin-feeding larva of a small moth genus, *Trichophaga*. On
Paximada I successfully raised several adult specimens of
Trichophaga abruptella with falcon pellets (Rösler and Walter 1966).
In Sardinia, the congeneric species *T.tapetzella* also developed in
such pellets (Mocci Demartis 1973).

Almost no brown insect pellets were found at Mogador in 1966
owing to the advanced breeding season. In 1969 more of them
were lying around, but no analyses were carried out.

INSECTS AND OTHER NONBIRD FOOD

Before the breeding season, from May to the beginning of July, and in some colonies to the middle of August, the staple food of adult falcons is insects caught in flight.

Insects

In theory, Eleonora's falcon will feed on any insect at least 10 mm long that it can capture with its talons in flight. This excludes from a list of potential insect prey only the flightless, the small, and most of the fast-flying, stinging bees and wasps. Occasionally insects are also captured on the ground.

The evidence from the literature includes the following insect items as summarized by Warncke and Wittenberg (1961).

1. Grasshoppers and locusts (Orthoptera)—sometimes a frequent item
   Poecilemon cretensis
   Stauronotus maroccanus
2. Beetles (Coleoptera)—main component in most pellets
   Carabidae
   Buprestidae
   Curculionidae
3. Dragonflies (Odonata)—regular food item
   Aeshnidae
4. Wasps and ants (Hymenoptera)—rare to occasional
5. Cicadas (Hemiptera)—frequent in pellets
6. Butterflies and moths (Lepidoptera)—occasional

Between 10 and 20 August I examined some 200 brown insect pellets (type 2) at Paximada nest sites. Thereafter, their numbers decreased rapidly as falcons subsisted almost entirely on bird prey. These pellets contained mostly the legs, wings, and thorax parts of medium-sized beetles (subfamily Melolonthinae), grasshoppers (Saltatoria), and cicadas (Hemiptera).

Occasionally Eleonora's falcons captured an insect right above the colony. They were sometimes carried to the nest and fed to the mate or young. Their wings were torn off and were recovered during the feather collection days. I found a total of 6 grasshoppers, 1 cicada, 4 dragonflies, and 3 large moths (*Daphnis nerii, Celerio lineata, Acherontia atropos*).

Among the feathers from the 1966 collection made at Mogador

were remains of grasshoppers or locusts, 8 dragonflies, and 5 butterflies and moths.

Centipedes

Pellets from Theodoros, collected by H. Siewert and B. Mihan in 1942, contained the remains of two centipedes (*Scolopendra*). They can only have been picked up from the ground (Uttendörfer 1948).

Crustaceans

A sow bug (Oniscidae) was found by Warncke and Wittenberg (1961) in a pellet. I observed to my surprise the claws of a crab (Portunidae) in a pellet from Paximada. The crop of one Eleonora's falcon from Vacca and Toro (Sardinia) contained the remains of "small crustaceans" identified as "shrimps" (Lord Lilford 1875).

Snails

Frequently, parts of the shells of two species of snails inhabiting Paximada were found in the falcon pellets. Since damaged and empty snail shells were lying around the entire island in considerable numbers I glued a dozen snail shells to the rock next to nest no. 8 to see whether the falcons would respond. They did not. I believe the falcons merely ingested the already-empty snail shells.

Stones

Small white stones (up to 5 × 9 mm) were also frequently ingested by the falcon and expelled as part of a pellet. They probably helped macerate food particles.

Mammals

A falcon male shot in Liguria in August of 1879 contained the remains of a bat in its stomach (Giglioli 1889–91).

Reptiles

Krüper (1864) found the remains of two Aegean lizards (*Stellio vulgaris*) in two falcon nests on Tragonisi, where this reptile does not occur (K. F. Buchholz, pers. comm., 1965). I found the hindquarters of a Moroccan lizard (*Agama ruderata*) in a falcon nest at Mogador, where it does not seem to exist. Direct field observations are needed to clarify whether the falcons capture these large lizards alive or whether they retrieve them from other predators or raptors.

On Paximada, I found four carcasses of the lizard *Lacerta erhardii* in falcon nests. They were essentially untouched except for head and back injuries. This lizard is extremely abundant on Paximada. It is a true commensal of Eleonora's falcon (and of our own camp on this isle) and will fearlessly enter a falcon's nest site and march around the surprised falcon chicks (Schulze-Westrum 1961; Walter 1967). While R. Lammers was filming at a Paximada nest site in 1969, he saw an Eleonora's falcon kill a lizard but not devour it (pers. comm.). On Paximada, therefore, all available evidence suggests that *Lacerta erhardii* is not a food item of Eleonora's falcon but an occasional nuisance.

Conclusions

Pellets and falcon crops and stomachs provide evidence that insects, particularly beetles, grasshoppers and locusts, flying ants, and dragonflies make up the staple nonbird diet before the falcon's nearly complete switch to a diet of migrant birds. Other insect orders are captured less frequently. Eleonora's falcon searches for insects on the ground, as is evidenced by scolopender and sow-bug remains in pellets and by di Carlo's (1966) observation of ground-feeding Eleonora's falcons on the Tremiti Islands in March 1964.

The remains of crabs, shrimps (?), and snails were probably taken up by the falcons as dead shells (Does some of this material dissolve and augment the falcon's calcium level?). The question of lizard-hunting falcons in my opinion must remain unresolved until further evidence can be provided. Bats are probably taken by Eleonora's falcon more often than the one recorded case indicates.

ANALYSIS OF BIRD REMAINS

The apparently tedious task of going through endless heaps of feathers to determine the kinds and numbers of birds eaten by Eleonora's falcon is in fact very interesting and rewarding. Most of the falcon's bird prey consists of long-distance migrants originating from many European countries. Were it not for the falcon, many of these birds would hardly ever be recovered at this raptor's breeding locations in the Mediterranean and adjacent Atlantic. The longer I saw the falcons bringing down to earth hundreds and hundreds of migrants that were invisible in the unfailingly blue skies over Paximada, the more I began to consider Eleonora's falcon my assistant in the study of the bird migration systems between Europe and Africa. This is not the place to discuss the full relevance of bird remains for bird migration studies, but the more interesting observations will be reported. We are of course first of all interested in the falcon's ability to capitalize on the seemingly abundant supply of bird prey during the fall migration season.

Composition of Species Lists

The first studies of the diet of Eleonora's falcon were made by Krüper (1864) and Reiser (1905) in the region of the Aegean Sea. They identified some of the more colorful and easily recognizable migrants from feather remains, namely, orioles, hoopoes, quail, shrikes, and a few less conspicuous species. When Vaughan (1961a) counted the total number of bird species that "have been reliably recorded among Eleonora's Falcon's prey" he came up with 41 species. In the meantime this figure has risen to at least 90 bird species. It now includes nearly every small-sized European bird species that migrates from the northern to the southern edge of the Mediterranean basin between July and November. I feel quite safe in predicting that the 100th bird species on the prey list of Eleonora's falcon will be added within the next few years (table 33). It has now become a matter of chance when and where to find evidence of new and rare prey species that possess nondistinctive feather characters.

Vaughan felt the need to exclude certain prey species from his list of 41. I have felt obliged to include all available data with the exception of the lists provided by Laferrère (1960), Makatsch (1958), and Contant and de Naurois (1958). In these three cases I also believe that some prey remains of the peregrine may have been counted as being those of Eleonora's falcon. Other questionable evidence relating to seemingly oversized prey items such as domestic pigeons and partridges has been accepted, however, owing to recent positive confirmations of this falcon's preying on those species or to detailed and convincing accounts of the particular prey remains. A glance at the enormous list (table 33) reveals a surprising variety of prey objects. From Cory's shearwater (here I have some doubt but cannot fully deny the possibility of a falcon's capturing this smallest species of the shearwater family) and dwarf bittern to plover, rail, tern, dove, cuckoo, owl, nightjar, swift, kingfisher, wryneck, lark, pipit, shrike, and nearly every possible European warbler, as well as flycatchers, nightingales, thrushes, buntings, sparrows, and orioles, birds from shore, marsh, meadow, hedge, field, and forest habitats alike have been the victims of Eleonora's falcon from the Canary Islands in the west to Cyprus in the east.

Different types of "evenness" can be detected: first, a distributional type. About a dozen species have been found in nearly all major prey analyses. Others have been reported only from the western or eastern part of the range. A third group of species has been recorded only once or twice so far. The second type of evenness looks at the relative abundance of each species among the total number of prey remains. Clearly, the degree of this evenness is small indeed. There are species like *Lanius collurio*, *Lanius senator*, and *Sylvia communis* (woodchat, red-backed shrike, and whitethroat) with several hundreds of specimens and others like *Ixobrychus minutus* (dwarf bittern) with just one certified record.

Some authors apparently only glanced at prey remains during a short visit to a falcon colony. Others collected them once during the breeding season, either at the beginning, in the middle, or near the end of it. In fact, before my systematic attempt to gather feather remains weekly, nobody had made successive collections over most of the young-raising period.

This widespread absence of a methodological basis makes it difficult if not impossible to arrive at any conclusions regarding these prey lists except that a certain number of species had in fact been caught by Eleonora's falcon before the collection date. Quantitative evaluations of dominant prey species, densities, numbers of prey caught per time unit, and so forth, cannot be made with such a data base for a number of reasons.

Feathers of small birds are lighter and disperse and disappear more easily in the wind or into holes and crevices. Thus, collections are likely to find relatively more feathers of larger species. Colorful, bright, and contrasting feathers are more easily found among the scrub or rock surface of the nest site environment.

They will be overrepresented in the feather collection, while inconspicuous feathers will be underrepresented. Feather collections from July and August will contain only specimens of early
trans-Saharan migrants plus some juveniles of local species. Species
whose main migration period falls into September and October
will not appear on the prey list. Feather collections from the very
end of the breeding season (mid-October) contain the late migrants but fall short of representing the specimens that were
caught early in the season. It is difficult to identify such early prey
because insects feed on the feathers, and many feathers are lost or
blown away each day. Several authors give no quantitative breakdown of how many specimens of each species were represented.
Many feathers from a single hoopoe lying around a nest site are
spectacular compared with the remains of 5 to 10 warblers.

Table 10 lists the five most numerous prey species from various
colonies as reported by several authors. The kinds of species represented and their ranking differ strikingly. Only whitethroat
(*Sylvia communis*) and woodchat (*Lanius senator*) are shared by 5
and 3 lists respectively. Is this due to bias, to chance, or to the
nature of bird migration in the Mediterranean region? Most
likely, all three factors have played a role.

In conclusion, the spectrum of bird prey is truly amazing, consisting of nearly every trans-Saharan migrant species and a
number of resident Mediterranean birds. Whereas some species
were found as prey remains in many colonies, others were
confined to a particular region (or show a geographical gradient
of abundance). A few species contributed large percentages of the
total number of prey remains, others only a single record. Thus,
published lists of prey remains show great unevenness. A discussion of factors that may distort the composition of prey lists and
the ranking of prey species on such lists shows that no quantitative
conclusions about the true composition of prey remains can be
made without a proper collection methodology.

PREY REMAINS AT PAXIMADA AND MOGADOR

The results of the systematic feather collections at Paximada
(1965) and Mogador (1966) will bring us nearer to a true list of
these prey remains in specific colonies. Still, my data can only be
compared and taken at face value for the key period during the
breeding season, approximately the first full month of the young

TABLE 10
Birds as Prey of Eleonora's Falcon:
The Five Species Most Frequently Collected in Various Colonies

Atlantic Region		Aegean Region	
1. Canary Islands—Roque del Este (Cott 1931, in Bannerman and Bannerman 1958)		4. Northern Sporades (Warncke and Wittenberg 1961)	
Whitethroat	20	Swift	5
Pied flycatcher	4	Red-backed shrike	2
Redstart	3	Yellow wagtail	2
Woodchat	2	Black tern	2
Melodious warbler	2	Cuckoo	2
2. Mogador (Vaughan 1961a)		5. Crete—Theodoros (Uttendörfer 1948)	
Woodchat	75	Hoopoe	8
Swift	54	Scops owl	2
Whitethroat	29	Whitethroat	2
Nightingale	25	Lesser grey shrike	2
Small warblers	15	Whinchat	2
3. Mogador (Walter 1968a)		6. Crete—Paximada (Walter 1968a)	
Woodchat	424	Small warblers	462
Whitethroat	332	Red-backed shrike	404
Nightingale	301	Whinchat	262
Redstart	295	Whitethroat	249
Orphean warbler	147	Lesser grey shrike	163

falcons' lives. Ideally, the complete list of prey remains should cover the entire breeding period from about 1 July to 1 November. Thus, my data evaluation refers exclusively to the period between 26 August and 23 September 1965 (Paximada) and 26 August and 21 September 1966 (Mogador). These periods offer a nearly complete overlap, although the Mogador falcons were a few days ahead in their breeding schedule (as they usually are), and bird migration patterns may vary considerably from one year to the next owing to macroclimatic factors.

Table 34 lists the total number of specimens identified during the four collection periods at Paximada. A ranking of the 15 species most numerous among the pluckings is given. These alone compose 93.2% of all bird remains. The remaining 56 pluckings belong to at least 21 additional species. In addition, the first "species" on the list, the "small warblers" (*Phylloscopus* spp.) consists of at least four species (listed in table 33, Appendix A). Owing to the difficulty of identifying this group, I have preferred to use the entire genus as a single entry. The willow warbler (*Phylloscopus trochilus*) was by far the most common among the four species.

Another, larger warbler genus (*Hippolais*) and the spotted flycatcher (*Muscicapa striata*) were also grouped together for similar reasons.

At Mogador, 1,124 specimens were identified from at least 30 different species. The list of the first 15 species includes 91% of the prey remains. Again, the genus *Phylloscopus* is composed of more than one species, and *Hippolais* and *Muscicapa* have been grouped together (table 35).

Although a smaller number of nest sites were monitored at Mogador, more bird specimens were recovered. Table 11 compares the values received for both colonies. More than twice as many specimens were found every day at each Mogador nest site (3.06) as at Paximada (1.38). A calculation of weight, using Heinroth's (1926) mean weight data for European birds, indicates that slightly heavier birds are represented in the Paximada lists of the 15 highest-ranked species than in the corresponding list from Mogador. But the latter's daily number of bird prey as documented by feather remains or corpses still weighed twice as much as on Paximada (62 g versus 30 g). Even if we consider all possible error factors that might have influenced the collection process (see above), there remains an undeniable difference between the two colonies. Thus, not only were there more prey remains at Mogador, of which I collected the largest possible part, but there must have been a correspondingly higher number of captures per day and per falcon family in this Atlantic colony. Undoubtedly, fewer birds were plucked in the study nests of Paximada than in the other colony (fig. 23).

We have to search among the 15 highest-ranked prey species to detect those birds that are vital to the diet of Eleonora's falcon. Dominant in terms of numbers (more than 5%) are only 6 species on each of the two lists. These together make up more than 67% of the specimens at Paximada and more than 71% at Mogador.

We may conclude that roughly two-thirds of the prey numbers caught at each colony between 26 August and 21–23 September belong to only 6 species of birds. Only one species, the whitethroat (*Sylvia communis*), appears on both lists as a dominant prey species. In terms of weight (= energy and protein value) the 6 top Mogador prey species represent some 80% of the total weight contribution of the first 15 species; that is, they are worth some 50 g

TABLE 11
Comparison of Prey Numbers and Weights at Study
Nest Sites

	Paximada	Mogador
1. Collection period	8/26–9/23	8/26–9/21
2. Days × nest sites	600	367
3. Number of prey items collected	828	1,124
4. Number of prey items/days × nest sites	1.38	3.06
5. Number of prey items of 15 highest-ranked species	772	1,022
6. Prey items of 15 highest-ranked species compared with total number of prey items	93.2%	91.0%
7. Weight of all individuals of 150 highest-ranked species/days × nest sites	30 g	62

per day and nest in the Mogador colony. Curiously, at Paximada, where the average body weight of a prey specimen is higher than at Mogador, the first six species constitute only 60% of the total weight of the top 15 species. This is so because four heavy bird species occupy rank nos. 7, 9, 12, and 13.

Figure 24 further clarifies the importance of each of the 15 species as a prey item of Eleonora's falcon. At Paximada, the number of specimens per species declines very gradually. Only the top two species stand out. These are the "small warblers" and the red-backed shrike. In terms of weight contribution, however, the "small warblers" represent less than half the cumulative weight of all red-backed shrikes. The hoopoe, ranked no. 9, with only 29 reported specimens, exceeds the "small warblers," as does the short-toed lark (rank no. 5). The capture of one hoopoe (weight 70 g) is worth six captures of a "small warbler" (weight 11 g). At Mogador, the "cascade" of decreasing number of specimens (fig. 24) forms three distinct groups. The first contains the top four species. They are almost even and are separated by a clear gap from the remaining species. The latter are again divided into two groups (rank nos. 5–10, with still respectable figures). In terms of weight, the top five species are in a class by themselves. The woodchat (weight 35 g) not only was the most numerous, but is also the heaviest bird in this group.Thus, woodchats alone contributed an average of 18 g of bird meat to each nest on every day throughout the entire study period; that is, one woodchat every

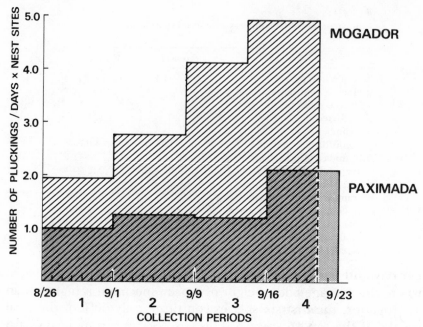

Fig. 23. Number of bird remains collected at Paximada (1965) and Mogador (1966) over four collection periods. The same sampling procedure was used in both colonies.

two days per nest. The cumulative weight of all woodchats was 80% more than that of the nearest value of all nightingales. In fact, 29% of the cumulative weight of the 15 highest-ranked species comes from woodchats alone. The only other remark-markable feature of figure 24 is the importance of quail. These heavy birds (weight 100 g, perhaps more) were still thought by Vaughan (1961a) to be too enormous a prey for this falcon: one quail equals nine "small warblers."

Another comparative perspective (fig. 23) illustrates the availability of prey over a time gradient. This block diagram shows a rather regular stepwise increase in the total number of pluckings/day × nest sites for the Mogador colony for the four collection periods. Curiously, this pattern was not repeated in the Paximada data. The first three periods lie almost on the same "plateau." I have no other explanation for the slight decline during the third period than little hunting success or low migration density over this Aegean island. The contrast between Mogador and Paximada is therefore evident through the four collection periods.

The same approach was used for figure 25, but now each column consists of thick and thin segments representing the top ten species. Each of these is followed through the four collection periods. The Mogador columns indicate an important factor: all of the top ten were still reported at the end of the fourth week, most of them in larger numbers than during the first weekly period. Species no. 4 (redstart), and also nos. 6, 8, and 10 were hardly represented at all in the prey remains of the first period. They increased their share (became proportionately more abundant as falcon prey) from week to week. The redstart became the most numerous prey during the fourth period (27 specimens per 35 nest-days). Such a trend appears parallel the growth rate of the young falcons and their demand for bird food.

The Paximada data show similar trends. Here it is species nos. 3 and 5 (woodchat and short-toed lark) that significantly increase their role as prey species for Eleonora's falcon from the first to the fourth collection period. There is also one species among the first ten, the lesser grey shrike (no. 7), that shows a decline in reported specimens over the total study period. We shall discuss this species in more detail below.

In conclusion, the comparison of prey remains collected at weekly intervals in a limited number of study nests at Paximada and Mogador has yielded the following results:

1. The 15 top species among the prey remains make up more than 90% of the total number of specimens identified.

2. In spite of identical methodology, more prey remains were recovered from the Mogador nest sites. On the average, 3.06 bird specimens were identified at each nest site every day. At Paximada, only 45% of this value was attained (1.38; table 11).

3. The dominant prey species all weighed less than 40 g. On each list of prey remains, 6 species contribute more than two-thirds of all specimens identified. In terms of weight, the top 6 species from the Mogador prey collection represent some 80% of the total weight of the top 15 species. In particular, the woodchat shrike stands out as the key prey of the Mogador falcon population during the study period. Not only was it the most numerous prey found, but the weight of all woodchats identified was some 80% higher than that of the second-ranked species (nightingale).

PAXIMADA

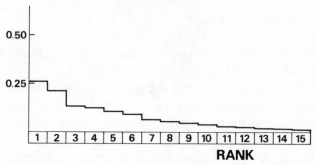

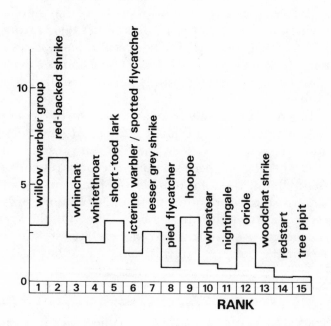

N.L.D.

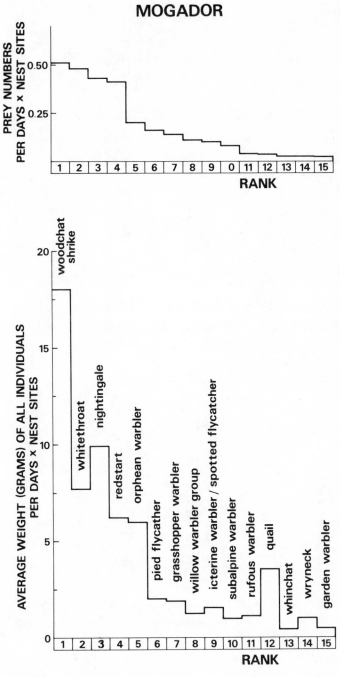

MOGADOR

Fig. 24. Rank order of the 15 most numerous bird species among prey remains of Eleonora's falcon. *Above:* Prey numbers per day × nest sites for each prey species. *Below:* Same ranking order as above, but prey numbers have been multiplied by the mean live weight of each species.

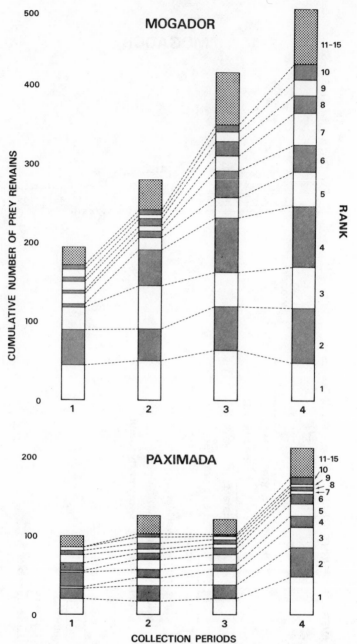

Fig. 25. The fluctuating percentage of prey remains over time. Species with the highest total number of prey remains are at the bottom of each column. Ranking of species same as in fig. 24 (e.g., no. 1 at Paximada: willow warbler group, no. 2 at Mogador: whitethroat). Species nos. 11–15 are grouped together on top of each column.

At Paximada another shrike—the red-backed—also contributed the largest prey contribution in terms of weight. However, in numbers the small warblers, genus *Phylloscopus*, occupy the first spot on the list.

4. There was a stepwise increase in the number of prey remains found at each nest per day in the Mogador colony (figs. 24 and 25). The Paximada pattern, however, does not have such a character. Here rather similar data were obtained during the first three study periods, contrasting with the higher average figure of the fourth collection period.

5. Most of the top 10 prey species were found in higher numbers during the latter collection periods, when the young falcons were between 20 and 30 days old.

PREY BIOMASS AND FALCON ENERGETICS

As in other birds, a falcon's energy exchange with its environment is affected by physical and organismic factors. King (1974) has identified four main physical environmental variables that make up the "climate space" (air temperature, thermal radiation, wind, and humidity) and three main organismic variables (metabolic rate, water loss, and body temperature). Although much progress has been made in recent years with respect to actual measurements of the metabolic rates of birds (Lasiewski and Dawson 1967; Kendeigh 1970; Mosher and Matray 1974), little work has been done with free-ranging birds. This makes it very difficult to assess the energy requirements of raptors under natural conditions. Experience has shown, however, that most birds fall into one of two general categories regarding their metabolic needs: passerines are distinct from the nonpasserine bird species in their energy demands. Several authors have developed equations and curves of the metabolic rate in relation to bird biomass for both categories. In the following I shall attempt to estimate the metabolism of Eleonora's falcon and to relate it to prey biomass and prey numbers. This will permit us to estimate this falcon's impact on the Palearctic-African migration system.

Metabolic Rates and Energy Expenditure

The Basal Metabolic Rate (BMR) of nonpasserine birds has been studied by King (1974) in adult birds that were (a) in muscular and psychic repose, (b) in a thermoneutral environment of some

30°C, and (c) in a postabsorptive state. The BMR can usually be measured in diurnal birds only during their sleep at night. It is strongly weight-dependent and can be expressed as

$$BMR = 3.6\ W^{0.734}, \tag{1}$$

where W is body weight in kilograms and BMR is given in kcal/ hr. The BMR of Eleonora's falcon is 1.67 kcal/hr for males (350 g) and 1.80 kcal/hr for females (390 g). The metabolic rate of resting birds that are not in muscular and psychic repose is slightly higher than the BMR (1.24 × BMR). Very active birds expend much more energy. Tucker has studied the energetics of bird flight. I estimate that the metabolic rate of Eleonora's falcon in flight reaches a normal value for flying birds, 12 × BMR (Tucker 1969; King 1974).

The division of labor that is practiced during the nesting season should have a considerable effect on the energy expenditure of male and female falcons. It seems reasonable to assume that male Eleonora's falcons spend some 3 to 5 hr a day in the air during the breeding season, while their mates use only 1 to 2 hr a day for similar activities of high energy cost. Each sex probably gets some 7 hr sleep during the night and is in an alert but low-energy-demanding state during the remainder of a 24-hr period. Using equation 1 and its multiples, we can compute the total daily energy expenditure for Eleonora's falcon. A male expends energy to sustain 7 hrs of BMR, 12 to 14 hrs of 1.24 × BMR, and 3 to 5 hr of 12 × BMR. This adds up to 100.8–136.7 kcal/day for a male and 69.9–89.3 kcal/day for a female falcon. I think these values are more realistic than those that can be derived from a general nonpasserine notation for the Daily Energy Expenditure (DEE), developed by King (1974):

$$\log DEE = \log 317.7 + 0.7052 \log W, \tag{2}$$

where W is body weight in kilograms and DEE is given in kcal/day. If we insert the weight of Eleonora's falcon into this notation (2), we get DEE values of 151 kcal/day for male falcons and of 164 kcal/day for female falcons. They may be valid during the nonbreeding season when the female has to hunt for herself and when both sexes probably spend more time in the air (hawking for insects) than during the breeding season. King's notation (eq. 2) does not take into account sex-related differences in energy expenditure as they

occur in Eleonora's falcon and even more so in most solitary raptors. The male Eleonora's falcon, although smaller in size and
weight, may indeed expend up to 100% more energy than his
female partner in order to acquire prey for the whole family
during the maximum growth period of their young. At other
times the female may be confronted with slightly higher energy
costs than the male: her gonadal growth period, egg-laying and
more than 50% of the incubation duties require this extra energy.
None of these reaches a magnitude, however, that is equivalent or
even close to the high energy demand of the hunting male falcon
(Ricklefs 1974; Drent 1975).

The male falcon is likely to experience a significantly higher
DEE than the female at the onset of the courtship period. Site
advertising, aerial displays, prey acquisition for "courtship feeding," and so forth, generate a high level of general activity. This is
perhaps not more energy-expensive than many hours of insect-
hawking during the prebreeding season. The female, however,
begins at the same time to reduce her activity radius and to become
oriented to the nest site. This should lead to a significant reduction of her DEE. Lacking any specific data on the seasonal
physiology of raptors, I conclude from the general activity difference between the sexes (see mobility charts, figs. 39 and 40)
that the average Eleonora's falcon male can be expected to have a
50% higher total DEE than his female during the breeding season. I have adopted a mean value of 120 kcal/day for the male and
of 80 kcal/day for the female Eleonora's falcon (or 200 kcal/day
for a breeding pair).

The breeding season spans roughly 90 days between July and
October. If a falcon pair needs some 200 kcal/day, then a total of
18,000 kcal of energy will have to be metabolized from the falcon's
prey. How much prey has to be captured and metabolized to
provide this energy? Ricklefs (1974) has listed the nutritional and
caloric characteristics of various foodstuffs in general terms. The
metabolizable energy contained in 1 g wet weight of insects is 1.18
kcal, while that of birds is given as 1.52 kcal. Ricklefs bases his data
for birds on specimens with an average composition of 69.6%
water, 22.9% protein, and only 5.7% fat. We can expect migrating
birds to contain above-average energy reserves in their fat and
muscle tissues. We are fortunate indeed in having specific data on
this topic. Just to the south of Paximada, on the northwest coast of

Egypt, eleven species of fall migrants were trapped and analyzed by Moreau and Dolp (1970). Their water content had been reduced to below 50%, while the fat content had risen to between 13% and 27% of the live (wet) weight. Using Ricklefs's data on the energy equivalents of fat (9.5 kcal/g) and of protein (5.7 kcal/g), it is possible to calculate the caloric value of these migrant species' combined fat and protein content. On the average, the metabolizable energy value of these birds was 2.5 times higher than the Ricklefs value of 1.52 kcal/g. Thus, I shall use 3.8 kcal/g as the energy equivalent of the average bird migrant captured by Eleonora's falcon. No Mediterranean data are available for the energy values of the falcon's insect food. I suspect, however, that the beetles and dragonflies they catch may also have higher fat and protein content than indicated by Ricklefs (1974).

Like any other bird, Eleonora's falcon cannot metabolize all the captured or even all the ingested food. Lacking detailed data on this point, I must rely on the study of broad-winged hawks (*Buteo platypterus*) by Mosher and Matray (1974). In this hawk, free-ranging birds had a 61% digestive efficiency when feeding on whole prey. This might well be the same in Eleonora's falcon: some 39% of its prey's body mass may be torn off (heads, talons), plucked (feathers), or excreted. Detailed studies on this topic are urgently needed. For this study I have adopted a 61% digestive efficiency. This means that a falcon pair must capture some 328 kcal/day (86.3 g migrant biomass) in order to metabolize the energy resources equivalent to 200 kcal/day.

A pair of falcons at the Paximada colony captures predominantly bird food for approximately 55 days during the bird-hunting season. This equals 328/3.8 × 55 = 4,745 g bird biomass. The entire colony of adult falcons (150 pairs) would require some 712 kg of bird prey for their seasonal DEE.

At Mogador, where the bird-hunting season may exceed 75 days, each pair should feed on 6,474 g of migrants in order to sustain its normal DEE. The entire adult population of 175 pairs (1966) should be able to subsist on some 1,133 kg of bird biomass during this exceptionally long bird-hunting season.

Stresemann (1968) used a different approach for his estimate of the small trans-Saharan migrants that are captured each fall by Eleonora's falcon. He relied on the experiences of falconers with the food requirements of kestrels, peregrines, and goshawks. Cal-

culating their daily food demand/body weight ratio, he postulated
a 20% ratio for Eleonora's falcon, using 400 g as its average body
weight. Our species would then need 80 g of "really utilized food."
A falcon pair would require at least 160 g/day, not counting the
nonutilizable parts of their prey.

In my opinion, Stresemann's assessment is too high, being
based on essentially noncomparable data on other raptors living
in captivity and in different climatic and prey environments. Migrant biomass of 160 g is equivalent to 608 kcal of energy, which is
certainly more than this falcon's energy requirements. Such a
value is about twice as high as the DEE values of King's (1974)
notation (eq. 2) for male and female Eleonora's falcons, and it is
three times as much as my estimate of 200 kcal/day of metabolized
energy.

Two additional facts point to a low energy demand in Eleonora's falcon. First, it appears to be exceptional for these raptors to
capture some 160 g of migrants for their own needs (and
additional prey for their young) in many of the present colonies.
Second, the timing and the Mediterranean region of breeding
point to generally lower energy expenditures compared with
those of many other raptors. In the Aegean Sea, temperatures
do not deviate much from the thermoneutral level of 30°C. During
incubation, falcons appear to have "nest-air temperatures" of
34–35°C (Drent 1975). Since the ambient temperatures are so
close to the required incubating temperature, little energy has to
be transferred from the incubating bird to the eggs. The respective values in the early breeders of northern and temperate
environments should be much higher. Because of the mild night
temperatures of the Mediterranean, the BMR of Eleonora's falcon should be exceptionally low (all other factors being equal).
The Atlantic subpopulation, however, lives in a much cooler "climate space." The falcons of the Canaries and of the Moroccan
Atlantic coast can therefore be expected to require comparatively
more energy for maintenance and production than the falcons of
the Mediterranean. Still, the rather uniform maritime climate of
the Atlantic colonies may require less energy for a raptor of comparable size than the breeding places of peregrines in arid and
temperate continental regions of Europe and North America.

We will now discuss the metabolic rates and energy expenditures of the young falcons. All falcons are semialtricial birds in

which the young hatch covered with down but are unable to leave the nest (Ricklefs 1973). The portion of the metabolic rate expended for maintenance is initially rather low in this group, whereas the portion needed for growth is very high until some 60% of the adult growth has been reached. The total metabolic rate as well as the weight of the young bird at times may exceed that of the adult (Ricklefs 1968, 1974).

A typical growth curve of a young Eleonora's falcon indicates its rapid growth within a period of only 30 days (fig. 26; see also table 7). Some 430 g and more are being added between hatching and fledging. Once again, no detailed analyses of the physiology of young raptors seem to have been published. Stresemann (1968) estimates the food requirements of young Eleonora's falcons on the basis of Heinroth's experiences with young *Accipiter* hawks. The latter found that young goshawks needed about 160 g of pure meat in order to grow some 50 to 60 g per day at the age of about 2 wk; that is, they metabolized one-third of their food for growth. Stresemann concludes that Eleonora's falcon needs some 1,800 g in order to grow some 450 g within 35 days. This corresponds to an average of 2.6 birds of 20 g each per day (or 51 g of bird biomass) and a transfer of one-fourth of their food into production of new body tissues. The young consume 80 g per day between the 35th and 55th days. Each young falcon therefore requires some 3.4 kg during its first 55 days after hatching.

A different approach has been taken by Craighead and Craighead (1956). These authors observed that between hatching and fledging time on the average young raptors consume as much food as an adult bird of the same species. This simple and apparently reliable rule holds up well in the light of modern bird physiology. G. C. Whittow reports in Sturkie (1976) that "the energy cost of protein deposition in chickens is 7.74 kcal of metabolized energy per gram of protein. The deposition of 1 g of fat required 15.64 kcal of metabolized energy." Assuming that the average nestling of Eleonora's falcon reaches a weight of 450 g within 30 days after hatching, we can roughly compute the energy cost of its fat and protein deposition. If the fledgling's biomass consists of about 25% fat, 25% protein (or protein-equivalent tissues like bones), and 50% water, it has added since hatching time (20 g biomass) some 107.5 g each of fat and protein. Their deposition required 2,513 kcal or 84 kcal per day if the energy

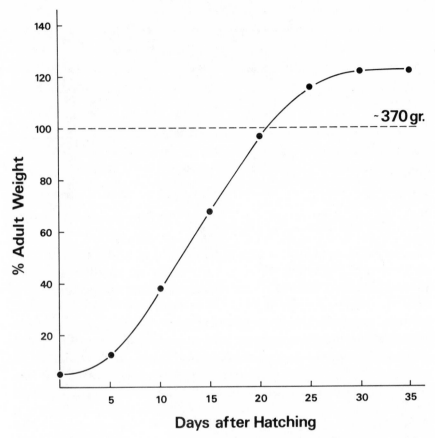

Fig. 26. Mean growth curve of Eleonora's falcon as percentage of adult weight.

cost of deposition was the same as in chickens. This is the production energy required, to which we must add the energy cost of maintenance. The latter is probably much lower than the former during the first 30 days of a falcon's life.

The empirical findings of Craighead and Craighead (1956) stipulate a DEE value of 80–120 kcal/day for a young falcon. I have adopted 100 kcal/day as the mean value; this is equivalent to 26.3 g of metabolized migrant biomass, or 43.1 g of whole prey at the 61% efficiency level. We can assume that the parents feed the young falcons for at least 55 days. This corresponds to 2.37 kg of migrant biomass per young during the bird-hunting season (table 12).

Stresemann's estimate of food requirements is very similar to

TABLE 12
Estimates of Energy Requirements (Migrant Biomass) for Eleonora's Falcon

		Seasonal Needs	
Required by	Daily Needs	Paximada	Mogador
Adult male	51.8 g	2.85 kg	3.89 kg
Adult female	34.5 g	1.90 kg	2.59 kg
Falcon chick	43.1 g	2.37 kg	2.37 kg
Falcon pair	86.3 g	4.57 kg	6.47 kg
Pair with single young	129.4 g	7.12 kg	8.84 kg
Pair with two young	172.6 g	9.49 kg	11.21 kg
Pair with three young	215.7 g	11.86 kg	13.58 kg
Pair with four young	258.8 g	—	15.95 kg
Entire breeding colony	—	1,161 kg (1965)	2,153 kg (1966)

NOTE: Bird-hunting season estimated at 55 days at Paximada colony, 75 days at Mogador colony. The young falcons are fed with birds for about 55 days (both colonies).

the one based on Craighead and Craighead (1956) for the first 30 to 35 days: 51 g/day versus 43.1 g/day. The major difference lies in Stresemann's assumption that the fledgling consumes some 80 g (like an adult) of migrant food between the 35th and 55th days. Such an assumption is even less supported by field evidence than his 80 g/day food requirements of adult Eleonora's. The fledglings of this species are quiet birds that perch on cliffs and rocks for most of the first 20 days after they become airborne. For this reason I prefer to use the lower figure based on Craighead and Craighead (1956) and on the calculated cost of fat and protein deposition (Sturkie 1976).

Since in 1965 Paximada had a low fledging rate of 1.26 young per pair, only some 448 kg of migrant biomass were needed to support the population of young falcons. At Mogador, the high fledging rate of 2.46 (1966) would have required some 1,020 kg of bird biomass had local nest robbers left this colony alone.

The energy expenditure for the production of young falcons during a single bird-hunting season can be added to the energy requirements of the adult breeding population (table 12). At Paximada, adult and young falcons required about 1.16 metric tons of migrant biomass in 1965. The Mogador colony, with a larger population of adults and young, required almost twice as much (2.15 metric tons) bird biomass during the 1966 breeding season.

IMPACT OF ELEONORA'S FALCON ON BIRD MIGRATION

A final set of computations will tell us more about the quantitative impact of Eleonora's falcon on the fall migrants flying from Europe to Africa, a fascinating aspect of our study. The importance of predation for the prey community has been illustrated for many prey/predator systems, but it is usually the predator, not the prey, that is seriously affected by the other's numbers. In our case, Krüper (1864) and Stresemann (1968) "play" with and interpret prey numbers.

Krüper writes: "To maintain the equilibrium among the European migrants, the Eleonora's falcon has been posted as a kind of guard in the Sea of the Cyclades [central Aegean Sea]; it therefore has the purpose of capturing the surplus and weaker specimens of the migrant birds. Since it would not cause a major reduction in the multitude of migrants if left to itself, nature has given it a gregarious character, as well as the instinct to raise its 2 to 3 young during the fall, just when the migrants appear in larger numbers and in a fat condition. These young and the two parents feed daily on at least five birds the size of a shrike, or 150 birds in 30 days. The 7 to 8 falcon pairs of the small breeding islet of Turlonisi will therefore have to capture on Paros some 1,200 birds within a single month of the fall season. The colony on Tragonisi, which may perhaps consist of 80 pairs, has to devour on Tragonisis itself and on Myconos some 12,000 birds a month." This pioneer naturalist of the Aegean then continues: "There is no reason to fear that the European migrant birds will be completely exterminated by these falcons. Nature has set limits to the increase in numbers of this falcon: it has given its young a very fat and tasty meat so that man himself has become the worst enemy of the young falcons." We can easily update Krüper's calculations. The mean weight of migrating red-backed shrikes (*Lanius collurio*) in northwest Egypt was 28.0 g (Moreau and Dolp 1970). If each falcon pair and their two or three young feed on at least five migrants, then the daily consumption is 140 g per family. This would add up to some 1.155 metric tons of bird biomass for the Paximada breeding population of 1965 (assuming a bird-hunting season of 55 days). This updated Krüper (1864) estimate is less than 0.6% lower than my estimate based on metabolic rates, activity observations, and the low fledging rate of 1.26 per pair. In other words, Krüper comes very close to my estimate of metabolic requirements for an Aegean falcon colony.

Krüper's data can also be projected on a larger scale. On the assumption that there are 4,400 breeding pairs of Eleonora's falcon (mean estimate, chap. 2) and that the average bird-hunting season of this world population lasts about 60 days (beginning some 5 days before the eggs hatch), the total impact of Eleonora's falcon on the Palearctic-African bird migration system is 1,265,000 migrants per season (140 g × 4,400 × 55 + 70 g × 4,400 × 5, 35.4 metric tons of migrants at 28 g each).

In Stresemann's (1968) estimate, a world population of only 2,000 breeding pairs (Vaughan 1961a) requires 35 metric tons or 1,750,000 migrants at 20 g each in order to raise two young per pair. This figure escalates to 3,850,000 birds that would be required by a world population of 4,400 pairs. This is more than three times the number of migrants required by Krüper's projection.

My own estimate lies between the two figures, but decidedly closer to Krüper's than to Stresemann's numbers. Since my prey collections bear out the assumption that the average migrant prey weighs more than 20 g, even at Mogador, I have adopted 24 g as the average migrant weight. I have also assumed a general fledging rate of 1.5 per pair, a 60-day bird-hunting season, and daily energy requirements as listed in table 12. The world population of 4,400 falcon pairs needs a minimum of 38.5 metric tons or some 1.6 million bird migrants according to this data base.

The three estimates of the migrant numbers captured by Eleonora's falcon at the daily and seasonal level (table 13) deserve a brief discussion. There can be little doubt that it is quite unlikely that the average family of Eleonora's falcons will normally be able to capture some 14 migrants per day (or even more, since some warbler species weigh less than 10 g). To capture 5 or 6 birds per day, of medium size and with a high fat and protein content, seems possible in most circumstances. My observations of Paximada prey arrivals have shown that most male falcons captured some 3 to 6 birds within their early-morning hunting period. We should also consider that different bird species may offer different energy values (Moreau and Dolp 1970). A few large migrants or even a single large bird may provide energy resources beyond the daily family requirements. How important is this raptor's impact on its bird prey? Stresemann (1968) investigated this question. He refers to Moreau's first estimate of the total number of trans-Saharan migrants (600 million) and concludes: "How close this estimate comes to reality has to remain undecided at this

TABLE 13
Impact of Eleonora's Falcon on Bird Migration:
Estimates of Migrant Prey Numbers per Day and Season

Falcon Population	Krüper (1864)		Stresemann (1968)		This Study	
	Day	Season	Day	Season	Day	Season
1 Pair	4.8	287.6	14.6	875	6.1	364
100 Pairs	479	28,756	1,458	87,500	607	36,444
1,900 Pairs	9,106	546,364	27,708	1,662,500	11,541	692,444
4,400 Pairs	21,076	1,265,000	64,152	3,850,000	26,708	1,603,536
7,300 Pairs	34,986	2,099,156	106,458	6,387,500	44,341	2,660,444

point in time. If we assume that it is correct, then more than one out of 600 migrants" will be caught by Eleonora's falcon. Moreau later (1972) revised his estimate upward to some 5,000 million birds crossing the Mediterranean during the fall season. The falcon's impact therefore needs to be reassessed in the light of larger prey numbers and larger estimates of the falcon's breeding population.

The total daily impact varies from 9,106 to 106,458 migrants, and the seasonal impact over 60 days ranges from a low of 546,356 migrants (Krüper's estimate for a minimum world breeding population of Eleonora's falcon of only 1,900 pairs) to a high of 6,387,500 migrants (Stresemann's estimate for a maximum falcon population of 7,300 breeding pairs). Neither of these extreme values seem realistic. Stresemann's figures appear too high, and the falcon's breeding population is likely to lie around 4,400 pairs. Krüper's and my estimates at this mean population level lie between one and two million migrants. This means that only one out of every 2,500 to 5,000 migrants can be expected to become a prey of Eleonora's falcon (0.02–0.04%).

Conclusion

There can be little doubt that the impact of Eleonora's falcon on bird migration as a whole is negligible. We can probably safely state that the falcons capture on the average fewer than one out of every thousand migrants. Such a predation rate is insignificant compared with the other factors that affect the perilous migration route from Europe to the African winter quarters. We have, however, seen that this falcon preys predominantly on just a few species. The total migration density and number may therefore be much less relevant for our discussion than the numbers of the

dominant prey species. Unfortunately, few if any quantitative estimates exist of the total migration population of shrike and warbler species. The analysis of prey data suggests that shrikes make
up more than 10% of a falcon's bird diet. This would mean that
4,400 pairs of Eleonora's falcon would take well over 100,000
shrikes out of the migration. Such figures may come close to 1% of
the total population of a dominant prey species or subspecies.

At least of equal importance is the effect that changing migration density and, in particular, the population dynamics of dominant prey species may exert on the productive success of
Eleonora's falcon. What if shrikes and warblers became rare all
over Europe as a result of pesticide application and other
environmental alterations? This question will be followed up in
the next section, which investigates in detail some key prey groups
and species.

ARE PREY REMAINS A MIRROR OF MIGRATION DENSITY?

Eleonora's falcon would indeed be the ideal assistant for students
of bird migration in such a difficult area as the open Mediterranean Sea if the quantitative and qualitative composition of all prey
remains (if we could ever collect them all!) accurately reflected the
largely invisible migration over the breeding areas of these falcons. Unfortunately, the prey remains provide only a rather dis-
torted, though still valuable, image.

Several factors contribute to this lack of complete congruence
between migrant birds and prey remains. We do not know for
sure which migrant species are easy prey and which are not. Swifts
and swallows certainly are difficult to catch as adults, but not as
juveniles. Little is known about the relative hunting success ratio
of other species. In general, juveniles are likely to be less agile
because of their incomplete plumage, and they are certainly less
experienced in dealing with predators. Some adults were lacking
certain tail or wing feathers due to molting. I found that between
0.5% and 1% of all prey remains showed incomplete plumage.
The success ratio of the falcon should be higher with such migrants than with experienced adults possessing 100% flight ability.

In general, however, we can assume a constant success ratio,
since most of the migrants are not equipped for quick maneuvers
at high altitude. That the falcon does not capture more of them,

with a higher success ratio, can be explained by its inability to take even this easy prey at the very first opportunity.

We do not know the true migration density above a falcon's breeding area. If a colony captures 1,000 birds in one week and 10,000 in the next, we cannot be sure that ten times more birds passed through the falcons' hunting zone. The falcons could have intensified their predation ten times, or both migration and the predation rate could have increased during the second week. I have already alluded to the basic uncertainty about whether the ratio of the number of captured birds to the number of migrants in the sky remains constant throughout the breeding season.

Figure 27 illustrates the last two points. The number of prey remains over a 5-wk period varies greatly for three species of migrants. Each species' curve is not at all an accurate reflection of the actual increase and decrease in migrant numbers, since the falcons capture from 4% to only 1% of the migrant stream of those three species from week to week. It does not matter, then, whether the migrant density actually varies or whether the falcon's hunting activity is subjected to periodic change.

It must be concluded that the prey remains as a whole cannot provide accurate statistics on migration numbers and density. If a species like the nightingale makes up first 5%, then 10%, of the prey remains, nightingales may actually contribute far more or far less to the total number of Palearctic migrants passing over a particular falcon colony.

ANALYSIS OF PREY MIGRATION PATTERNS

In spite of the existence of so many variables influencing the ratio between prey remains and migration density, rather interesting results can be achieved through comparing the dynamics of prey remains. For instance, the total absence of the dominance of a certain species in prey remains of geographically separated falcon colonies is easily interpreted. Similarly, a sudden or gradual onset of prey remains appears to reflect different migration behaviors of different prey populations.

We shall now examine the diagrams of prey remains for a number of selected species and genera. This will contribute additional information for the final discussion about the adaption of Eleonora's falcon to its niche factors of prey and breeding

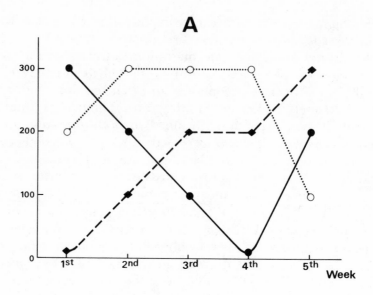

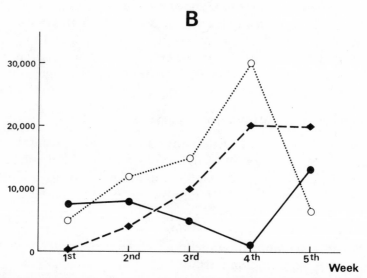

Fig. 27. The relationship between bird migration and the falcon's bird prey. *A*. Three species of migrants have been caught in varying numbers by a falcon colony over a period of 5 wk. *B*. Total number of migrants passing through the airspace of the falcon colony. In this example the falcons have captured 5% of the migrants from each species in the first week, 2.5% in the second, 2% in the third, 1% in the fourth, and 1.5% in the fifth.

season. Figure 28 shows species that either were frequent prey remains in both colonies or were exclusively or at least predominantly found in only one colony.

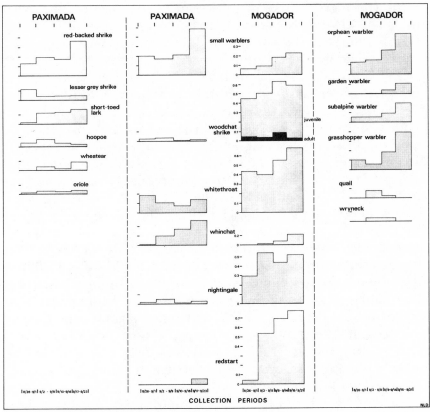

Fig. 28. Frequency of important prey species remains at Paximada (1965) and Mogador (1966). See text for details.

Shrikes (Genus *Lanius*)

The shrike genus pays the highest price to Eleonora's falcon. 18.2% of all prey remains from the study nests at Paximada and Mogador belong to three shrike species. Shrikes are predators themselves but seem to be average or poor flyers when confronted by high-altitude migration and a deadly chase by Eleonora's falcon. In addition, the European shrike species have interesting migration routes. The lesser grey and the red-backed shrike both cross the Mediterranean only at its eastern portion. Thus, even the breeding populations of France and northern Spain travel in a relatively narrow zone across the Aegean Sea toward northeast Africa. This means, of course, that their migration density must be comparatively high in this area.

The lesser grey shrike migrates earlier than most of the prey species of Eleonora's falcon. We know this from bird banding records and visual observations, and the prey remains clearly substantiate such findings. In 1965, lesser grey shrikes were already migrating through the Paximada airspace before our arrival on 10 August. Prey remains peaked at the end of August (fig. 28). However, at least two pluckings were still found after 23 September. In comparison with the red-backed shrike, we can interpret the lesser grey shrike's block diagram in two ways: either the species became rather scarce in the last three periods, or it continued to migrate in good numbers while the numbers of red-backed shrikes vastly increased between the first and the fourth period.

Prey remains of the red-backed shrike (fig. 29) became numerous only after 26 August. The large number of prey remains undoubtedly reflects a strong migration of this species in the Paximada area through September and the first third of October 1965. In this species, adult males look very different from the adult females and the juveniles, which have similar plumage. Of a total of 171 prey remains, only 20 belonged to adult males. If we subtract some 20 prey remains from the remainder and count them as adult females, then we have a ratio of 40:131 for adult/juvenile red-backed shrikes. This means that the falcons caught 3.28 juveniles for each adult shrike.

The woodchat (fig. 29) is a shrike species that migrates predominantly over the western part of the Mediterranean. Still, I found a total of 61 prey remains at Paximada belonging to this attractive bird. (Very few, however, were collected in the study nests.) At Mogador, this is the key prey species during the important first three weeks of the young-raising period. In 1966 migration must have begun very early, since prey remains of this species were predominant at the nest sites on 23 August. In 1969 I found remains of woodchats as early as 11 July (3 adults, 1 juvenile) and again on 20 July (4 adults, 7 juveniles). This indicates that in this species adult and juvenile birds begin the fall migration simultaneously. The happy circumstance that in this shrike the two adult birds have plumage very different from that of the juveniles made it possible to count the prey remains of adults and juveniles separately. In the study nests of Paximada I found the pluckings of 3 adults and 22 juveniles between 11 August and 10 October 1965 (ratio 1:7.3). At Mogador, the respective numbers were 37 adults and 209 juveniles between 23 August and 21 September 1966 (ratio 1:5.6). Since the woodchat's clutch does not contain more than 5 or 6 eggs, this ratio is too high to reflect the true proportion of adults and juveniles in the migration stream (some eggs do not hatch, a good number of young probably do not reach fledgling age). Thus we are once again left with at least two interpretations: adults do not migrate in proportionate numbers where the juveniles are captured by Eleonora's falcon or—and this is much more likely—falcons capture young woodchats more easily than adult and experienced woodchats.

Sylvia Warblers

The whitethroat (fig. 29) is the one species that is a strong dominant at Paximada and Mogador. Moreau (1972) estimates a total Palearctic population of 120 million whitethroats crossing the Mediterranean basin every fall season. The block diagrams (fig. 28) indicate a prolonged migration season. Migration does not appear to begin as early as in the woodchat, however, since I did not find any whitethroats among bird remains at Mogador between 11 and 20 July 1969. Nevertheless, this is another key species for the young falcons. Before 26 August 1965, I found more prey remains of whitethroats than of any other bird. At Mogador it was second only to the woodchat at this time in 1966.

The other *Sylvia* warblers migrate later in the season and display pronounced staircaselike block diagrams (fig. 28). Like the whitethroat, they were either exclusive to or much more common in the Mogador prey collection. Presumably, the onset of migration in these *Sylvia* warblers began in 1966 at Mogador with the whitethroat followed by the Orphean warbler, subalpine warbler, and garden warbler. The migration of these four species continued well beyond the cutoff date of 21 September.

Other Warblers

The willow warbler group was the most common prey found at Paximada in 1965. Because there is considerable intraspecific variation, it was often very difficult to distinguish feathers of the

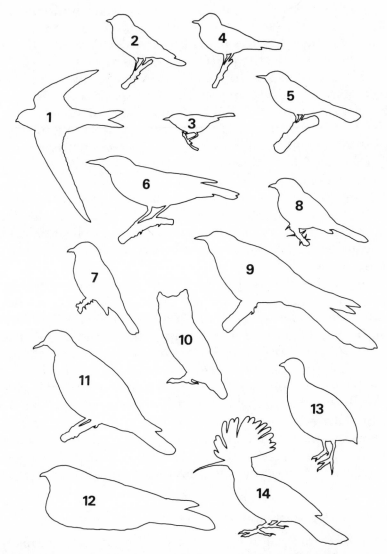

Fig. 29. Characteristic prey species of Eleonora's falcon. The uniform scale of all drawings brings out the difference in size between these trans-Saharan migrants: (1) swift, (2) redstart, (3) willow warbler, (4) whitethroat, (5) nightingale, (6) oriole, (7) red-backed shrike, (8) woodchat shrike, (9) cuckoo, (10) scops owl, (11) turtledove, (12) nightjar, (13) quail, and (14) hoopoe. Original drawing by N. L. Diaz.

four small species concerned. The willow warbler was, however, by far the most numerous prey species of this group. Its small size and inconspicuous feathers made it impossible to collect all prey remains or even as high a percentage as in larger, more colorful bird species. This makes the willow warbler (fig. 29) in particular an even more interesting prey species. The species occupies a vast range in the Palearctic and is a characteristic breeding bird in habitats of the temperate and arctic latitudes. Moreau (1972) estimates that some 900 million willow warblers attempt to cross over to Africa every fall. It is therefore not surprising to find so many willow warblers in the falcon's nests.

At Mogador in 1966, this group was outnumbered by seven other species. It is possible that more of them were caught after 21 September, but that is pure speculation. There can be little doubt that the genus *Phylloscopus* plays only a subordinate role as prey of the Mogador falcon population.

Another rather different warbler is the grasshopper warbler, a secretive species hardly ever seen by bird watchers in its breeding habitats. This is also true for the regions this bird must cross during its fall migration. At least up to 1966, the grasshopper warbler's only records from Morocco and the Canary Islands came exclusively from prey remains of Eleonora's falcon (1 at Roque del Este in 1931, 7 at Mogador in 1959, and 90 at Mogador in 1966). In 1969 the first plucking of this species was found on 20 July. About five weeks later, on 23 August 15 of some 35 fresh bird corpses were grasshopper warblers. These birds almost never fly in their breeding habitats. It is probable that they are rather clumsy when on the wing, making them easy prey for the falcons.

Nightingale, Redstart, and Whinchat

I am aware that nightingales have many a friend among European naturalists, poets, and romantics of all ages. Unfortunately, nightingales (fig. 29) have become rare in many European countries. This is definitely not the fault of Eleonora's falcon, although the nightingale ranks third of all prey species in my 1966 Mogador prey collection. My data indicate that during the first week of September, each falcon pair averaged at least one nightingale every two days. There are millions of nightingales, however, particularly in the Mediterranean countries. It is not the impact of a natural predator like Eleonora's falcon that causes the disappearance of shrub-loving species like the nightingale, but widespread habitat modifications and destruction as a consequence of intensified agricultural practices and urban sprawl. Thus I need not be defensive. It is not the hawk or falcon or quadruped in the breeding habitat that threatens our wildlife. Up to this day it has been unplanned, willful elimination of important wildlife habitats, without regard for ecology, that has diminished our flora and fauna. I like both the nightingale and Eleonora's falcon. Both of them will survive and enrich our biological landscape only if a large part of our society is willing to press for ecological planning that aims at maintaining biological diversity in our humanized landscapes.

Like the nightingale, the redstart (fig. 29) was a much more frequent victim of Eleonora's falcon at Mogador than at Paximada. Redstarts appeared in both colonies quite suddenly in sizable numbers; at Mogador, only 5 prey remains were found during the first period, but 55 were found during the second period (equal number of nest-days). According to Moreau (1972) some 120 million redstarts make the journey from the Palearctic to the African winter quarters.

In both colonies the whinchat exhibits a clear stepwise increase of prey remains from the first to the last period, but it was a much more common prey species at Paximada (3d rank) than at Mogador (13th position). Moreau (1972) provides an estimate of "only" 45 million birds. It is reasonable to conclude from the block diagram that on the average each of 4,500 falcon pairs (mean estimate, see chap. 2) caught some 10 whinchats during the entire breeding season. The actual prey numbers may have been more than twice as high. I shall use the figure of 25 whinchats per pair in each season. That makes 112,500 whinchats out of 45 million, which is exactly 0.0025% of the entire population.

Quail, Wryneck, and Other Migrants

The European quail (fig. 29) is a relatively small bird. Still, it is a heavy prey for Eleonora's falcon. Quail and wrynecks at Mogador distinguished themselves through their unusual migration pattern. Suddenly a number of nests had received a quail, then, quite abruptly, prey remains of these two species failed to show up. This can only mean that during a relatively short period a massive migration passed over the Mogador region.

Figure 28 also shows the block diagrams of the species that were important prey items at Paximada but not at Mogador. The most important of these is the short-toed lark, a Mediterranean species. Again this bird does not have the morphology to be an adept flyer when pursued by several screaming falcons.

The hoopoe must be considered a key species for the Aegean colonies, not so much because of the prey numbers involved (although this has been suggested in much of the falcon literature) but because of weight. In addition, this species has an extended migration period. In 1965 it was available from the very beginning of the young-rearing period. Whether hoopoes are easy targets for Eleonora's falcons is difficult to say. Others and I have seen repeated unsuccessful attacks by Eleonora's falcon on specimens of this extraordinary bird (fig. 29).

Discussion

Prey remains do not mirror migration density and composition. Several of the principal prey species are clumsy flyers and therefore probably are overrepresented, while good flyers like swallows and swifts appear to be underrepresented in the prey collection. Since nobody can tell what portion of the total migration stream is being taken out by a colony of Eleonora's falcons, we cannot compare the absolute prey numbers of one species with those of others. It is possible, however, to detect certain trends regarding migration period and dominance of a prey species. Looking at individual prey species, it appears that shrikes are particularly affected by our raptor. Several warbler species, nightingales, redstarts, whinchats, and short-toed larks also suffer heavy predation. In all these cases, however, we can assume that less than 1/1,000 of the total migration population of the species concerned will be caught by the total breeding population of Eleonora's falcon during one fall season.

With regard to the migration period, a broad spectrum of species seems to be available during the critical young-raising phase of the breeding season of Eleonora's falcon. The data suggest that the migration peaks of several dozen species fall somewhere in the period between mid-August and mid-October.

None of these species can be said to have a strictly fixed migration calendar. Thus, we can expect a species to reach it peak density a week later or earlier, perhaps even two or three weeks, than in the previous year as it is affected by multiple ecological factors during the breeding season before migration. Migration itself is apparently strongly influenced by weather factors like wind, clouds, and moon. This means that Eleonora's falcon is absolutely dependent on a large number of migrant species. Were it otherwise, the falcon would hatch out eggs even though there was a good possibility that its few prey species would not arrive for a week or two, which would of course be fatal for its young. Since the falcons initiate their own breeding season without knowing when the migrants are coming, they must be sure of a sufficient food supply when it is needed. This is accomplished through the fixation of the falcon's breeding season. We have seen before (chap. 2) that there is indeed little variation in hatching dates from year to year within one colony. The slightly earlier breeding season of the Mogador colony can also be correlated with bird migration. My 1969 data (Walter 1971) indicate that at least 10 species were already being captured before 20 July about one month before hatching.

It would be pure speculation to discuss in detail what might happen to this falcon if its few dominant prey species that currently supply more than two-thirds of the prey numbers were to significantly decline in population (habitat removal or biocides might cause such drastic changes). The falcon might suffer from such a major change of the Palearctic-African ecological systems, particularly the populations like Paximada that do not seem to be oversupplied with prey items even today. On the other hand, the decline of some prey species might cause a population increase in other species, thus offsetting the negative impact on Eleonora's falcon. In other words, the falcon not only would have to increase its share of other prey species, but might also find those species more common during the migration period. The worst possibility would be a general decline of all insectivorous birds in the western Palearctic region. That, I submit, would result in a contraction of the breeding range of Eleonora's falcon. Colonies with limited to marginal subsistence potential would be deserted.

The survival of prey species is in no way threatened by Eleonora's falcon, which captures only a small fraction of the total migration stream owing to its low numbers and the hundreds of miles between Portugal and Syria that never see a bird-hunting Eleonora's falcon.

SUMMARY AND GENERAL CONCLUSIONS

This chapter has dealt with the analysis and interpretation of prey remains found at the nest sites of Eleonora's falcon during the breeding season. Since methodological considerations are important when statements are made about dominant prey species, the nature and the type of prey remains have been described and listed. Nonbird items were frequently found during the first third to half of the breeding season, but they became less important during the young-raising phase, when birds made up the diet of adult and young falcons. An updated list of all bird species that have been reported from Eleonora's falcon is given (table 33, App. A). At least 90 species, most of them small songbirds that are trans-Saharan migrants, have been recorded so far. This list therefore includes almost the entire spectrum of small species that make up the bulk of the entire Palearctic-African migration system. More species, particularly larger birds like waders, are likely to be added to this list as more collections are made in the years ahead.

Prey remains collected at the Paximada and Mogador colonies in successive years have been analyzed. A systematic search for all bird remains at weekly intervals revealed which species were the dominant food of falcon families during the critical first three to four weeks of the young-raising stage. The contribution each species makes in terms of prey numbers and weights has been discussed for each colony, and the colonies have been compared. Significantly larger numbers of prey remains were found at Mogador. At this colony the falcons deposit excess food in meat piles.

A subsequent discussion of this raptor's metabolic requirements indicates that for subsistence the average falcon family needs vastly larger numbers and weights of migrant birds than is evidenced by the collected prey remains. Several reasons are given that speak for relatively low energy requirements in Eleonora's falcon, a high energy content in the migrant prey species, and a sexual difference in the daily energy expenditure (DEE) resulting from different activity levels.

The general impact of Eleonora's falcon on bird migration during the fall season is considered negligible, varying between 0.02% and 0.04% of an assumed migration of some 5 billion birds (Moreau 1972), depending on various estimates of the falcon's total population size and its metabolic needs. The actual number of birds caught by Eleonora's falcon during one breeding season were calculated to lie in the region of one to two million migrants.

Prey remains do not mirror the migration density and composition in the sky above and around the falcon colonies. Too many variables exist that prevent an interpretation of migration dynamics based on the changing quantity of prey remains found at weekly intervals. However, the careful analysis of the onset, peak, and decrease of prey remains of any given species over time permits certain conclusions that throw light on the falcon's adaptation and dependence on a fluctuating migration stream consisting of so many different species. A closer look at the principal prey species shows that in few does the bulk of the population pass through the falcons' airspace before the month of September, when nearly all falcon chicks have hatched and attain maximum growth. A considerable number of species, among them dominant prey items such as woodchat, red-backed shrike, whitethroat, and *Phylloscopus* warblers, appear to have a prolonged migration period extending from August to October, which permits the falcon to capture increasing numbers of each of these species between at least the end of August and the end of September—just when the daily weight gains of falcon chicks are increasing from week to week. Finally, some species begin to migrate only in mid-September and even later. Species like nightingale, redstart, and others belonged to this group during the 1965/66 seasons. Because of their large numbers (and perhaps their clumsy flight) they became important prey species during the latter part of the young-raising stage, adding substantial amounts of protein and energy to that provided by the second group (fig. 30).

The sum of the individual species' migration patterns creates a migration flow that is certain to provide sufficient migration density within each young-raising season and also from year to year. Variations of the migration period of individual species from one season to the next are offset by the often independently regulated migration periods of other species. Thus it appears that

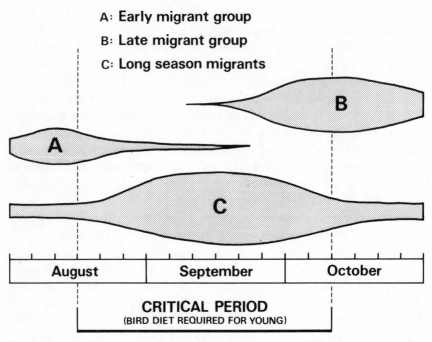

Fig. 30. Synchronization of the falcon's breeding season with the fall migration of Palearctic migrants. During the critical period of her nesting season Eleonora's falcon can prey on early, late, and long-season migrants. The approximate biomass or density of each migrant group along the time gradient is proportional to the width of the stippled area.

Eleonora's falcon has indeed timed its breeding season in an optimal fashion. The falcon's main dietary needs arise at a time when during the average year some species have already passed their peak, others continue to migrate in large numbers for more than a month, and a third group of species begins to pass through in large numbers before the falcon chicks have fledged. Only a substantial general decline of many migrant species could affect the breeding success of Eleonora's falcon.

In conclusion, Eleonora's falcon preys on almost any of the smaller species among the trans-Saharan migrants. Though it does not endanger any of these species through its predation, this raptor itself is not dependent on the population size and migration period of only one or even several migrant species. The falcon's breeding season is synchronized with the general migration flow, assuring the energy needed for raising its brood.

8 Patterns of Falcon Behavior

The gregarious life-style of Eleonora's falcon during the breeding season results in continual interactions between members of the breeding group. These interactions are not confined to the various hunting behaviors that have already been discussed. Since a pair spends most hours of the day at the nesting site, the relationships between mates and neighbors within this fierce and potentially dangerous species deserve to be studied. Although sexual, territorial, and agonistic behaviors actually constitute a rather complex system of intraspecific action-response loops, here I will break them down into separate units so they can be more easily described and interpreted.

This chapter investigates in particular the behavioral attributes that organize the coexistence of many individual falcons in the limited, often seemingly crowded rock and island habitat of the breeding sites. Thus it complements the previous chapters that have focused on the macroenvironment and this raptor's adaptations to bird migration systems of the Palearctic-African regions.

Other more general observations on the ontogenetic development of behavior, family relations, and so forth, will be dealt with only in the context of territorial and agonistic interactions.

STUDY METHODS

Whenever you observe a bird you are witnessing some elements of its behavior in relation to its physical surroundings, its food sources, and its intra- and inter-specific peers or enemies or simply the life forms it encounters. Most of my notes on Eleonora's falcon deal with behavior of some sort.

In 1969 I had planned to devote an entire breeding season to a thorough analysis of the territorial and agonistic behavior of the Mogador colony. My wife Geraldine and I began to monitor the colony on 11 July. Everything went according to plan until 25 July, when our two rowers lost the control of the boat near a somewhat precarious landing point on the Isles of Mogador. The rowers attempted to reach the rocks, against my advice, and the boat capsized within seconds. Photographic equipment, some of my notes on falcon behavior, and six persons went overboard. I mention this terrible situation here only to emphasize how difficult and dangerous work with these falcons can be. Except for my wife, none of the other four passengers could swim, and the heavy, cold surf made it difficult to pull everyone ashore. The current quickly carried the boat and the struggling fishermen farther away. Though I managed to bring three of them ashore, I was unable to save the fourth one, and one of those rescued had to be revived.

This accident dealt a severe blow to my research efforts. We managed to continue, however, with a revised program (see below). Then came another disaster, when two northern Europeans climbed the rocks and collected most of the falcons' eggs. I witnessed the crime from the main island but had no way to reach the egg robbers on the small cliffs. When I shouted at them they fled the rocks and hurried back to the continental shore, where they mailed the eggs to an unknown egg collector.

The loss of my equipment, the confinement of our activities to one isle, and the disruption of the falcons' incubation cycle made me abandon part of the original program and concentrate on the remaining possibilities of monitoring the behaviors of one group of falcons on the submarine cliff. Despite the egg-robbing incident, none of the occupants of this cliff left, thus providing me with an unusual opportunity to study this group before, during, and after a strong disturbance and to watch the behavorial trend gradually return from an abnormal situation to the normal state. The disturbance also served to unleash certain agonistic tendencies that had not been apparent before.

The first week had been spent mapping the isles and the falcons' nest sites and lookout posts as well as selecting four breeding groups whose behavior I planned to study. Each group was to be observed at least once a week for a continuous period of 4 to 6 hr. Twenty elements of the falcon's behavior were monitored in relation to location of the bird and time. Starting from 30 July, the elements were reduced to nine and the observation was confined to the group breeding on the submarine cliff. Two observers, placed 5 to 15 m apart, watched this cliff from a rocky peninsula of the main isle, Ziron; in between were 35 m of foaming water. Observations were noted, sometimes tape-recorded, and often checked with the second observer by walkie-talkie. The falcons did not react to human activity at this place as long as we avoided sudden movements and arm-waving. My study methods corresponded closely to those used by R. W. Nelson in his study of peregrine falcons in British Colombia. Nelson's article on this subject is an excellent introduction to field techniques in general raptor research (Nelson 1973).

All observations of the submarine group took place between 8:00 and 18:00 on 30 and 31 July and 1, 6, 8, 10, 13, 15, 19, and 22 August; preliminary work was done on 12 and 21 July, and late evening and early morning notes were taken during an overnight stay on the rocks on 12–13 July 1969.

SEXUAL BEHAVIOR

Display of the Male Falcon

A male falcon with a potential nest site draws the attention of his fellow falcons and of the human observer by displaying excitement and hectic activity. Such a male rarely stays on his lookout post for longer than 10 to 30 min and will then disappear for some time, returning with a prey in his talons and proudly announcing this with endless loud cries. Again and again he takes off, circles the cliff and lands, crying excitedly. He may start to tear off the feathers of the prey, and even feed on it for a little while, then may hide it somewhere in the rock crevices. A few minutes later, full of excitement he will balance on the uneven rock surface in search of this same piece of prey. I observed this behavior frequently before 20 July among several males of the Smea cliff breeding population.

The male in this stage assumes a conspicuous posture immediately after landing on the cliff: he bends his body down in front, raises the shoulder of his wing and holds his widely fanned tail high over his back. From behind and above, the large surface of the fanned tail—optically enlarged because of the transverse tail bars—covers and hides his body (fig. 31). While doing this the bird utters a roosterlike coarse crow that lasts several seconds. The

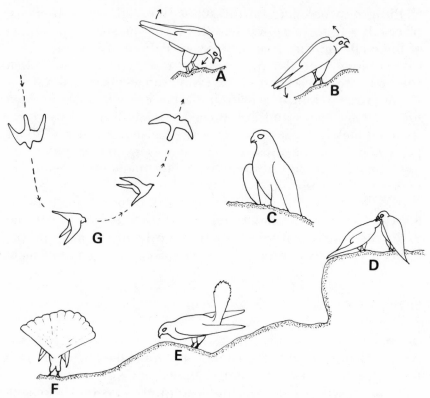

Fig. 31. Falcon behavior. *A* and *B*, "Bowing" of the male as a sign of appeasement or submission. *C*, "Detached wing" posture, often combined with open beak. A threat posture signaling readiness to attack. *D*, "Allopreening" behavior of female *(left)* after copulation. *E* and *F*, "Fanned tail" posture of male in front of a potential nest scrape. *G*, "Nose dive with wing flapping" display above a falcon's ground territory.

fanned-tail posture is also performed when a male falcon is accompanied by a prospective mate. It leads to the nesting-scrape-showing behavior.

This kind of display also serves as a threat to keep other males away from the occupied site. Paired males used this posture when other male falcons stooped down on them, causing the attacking birds to turn upward and away. On 20 July 1966 (Paximada) I observed a falcon being harassed by another that had been sitting 6 m above him on the slope. When the flying bird came close, the falcon sitting in the lower position bent forward and showed his fanned tail. Both falcons were crowing, and they repeated this scene several times. The birds were probably males quarrelling over their chosen nest sites.

Other forms of display are *conspicuous flight maneuvers*. These are not frequent in the Mogador colony, possibly because of unfavorable aerodynamic conditions, but they are characteristic for the Paximada colony. Especially in the minutes before sunset and after sunrise, the falcons put on an artistic show of craftsmanship, flying all kinds of loops near and far off the ground. Directly related to the nest site is a fast smashing flight downward, cushioned just before hitting the ground by two to five noisy wingbeats that send the bird upward again in an almost motionless, elegant manner. I call this the *nose dive with wing-flapping*.

Quite often several falcons pursue each other, stoop down on another falcon flying over the island, or go as far as to "tease" other falcons by scratching their backs with the talons in full flight. It is difficult to assess how important these displays of supreme command of the air are in attracting a mate. Nelson (1970) reports similar behaviors for peregrine falcons during the preincubation phase. He describes the "prominent perching display" (to advertise a falcon's presence to potential intruders), a "cliff-racing display," certain other aerial maneuvers, and the "male-ledge display." The latter includes an element called "horizontal posture and eechip calls," in which the male assumes a horizontal position, and calls excitedly. No mention is made of tail position. This posture is probably a homologue of the fanned-tail posture of Eleonora's falcon.

Courtship

Pair formation seems to take place at the chosen nest site, but many pairs arrive at the breeding area with their former partners. Once a single male has attracted a female to his acquired place, he will pursue three activities. First, he will provide the female with as many prey items as possible, using them as "love bait." Second, he will show her his favorite niches and holes suitable as a nest "cup." Third, he will constantly try to move very close to her and appease her. This is done by a *rhythmic bowing of the head and neck* down to the feet as the male stands in front or beside the female (fig. 31). One bow lasts for less than a second, and bows can be repeated more than 100 times a minute.

During the preincubation period copulation is usually preceded by bowing. More often than not, however, bowing is an end in itself as the female sits quietly watching the male. I found it impossible to predict whether she would show a response to the courtship of her partner. That this frequent and conspicuous bowing behavior indeed originates in the desire of the male to appease the slightly larger female and to counteract her aggressive tendencies is also suggested by other observations of bowing. For instance, the male bows when he wants a share of the prey he has delivered to the female. Males that wish to stay at the side of the female may bow after landing there. This will occasionally be reciprocated by a few bowings of the female. The bowing posture occurs only between two partners of different sexes and is usually not accompanied by any acoustic expressions.

Females that want to be mounted for copulation approach a male with a somewhat extended horizontal body posture and repeated "yeerk, yer, yeerk, . . ." cries. In this case too, a male will respond with moderate to violent bowing and may then mount the female.

Homologous postures and displays have been observed in the peregrine falcon, including the behaviors of bowing, food transfer or "courtship feeding," and nest-scraping (Cade 1960; Fischer 1968; Nelson 1970).

Copulation

At the beginning of this phase the male flies or jumps on the back of the female. The feet lie—with the claws cramped—slightly behind or on the midline between the front and back of the wing. Balancing with the wings, the male moves his tail slowly over the upper tail feathers of the female (noticed only twice). She has assumed a horizontal body position, loosened her feathers—especially the lower tail feathers near the cloaca—and cries with her beak wide open.

After the female has raised her tail the male bends his tail down. Usually—in 90% of more than 60 observed copulations—the act was accomplished from the right side as the female lifted her tail to the left. Balancing on her back the male now pushes his tail and cloaca against her cloaca in a rhythmical movement: the tail keeps relatively still for 1 to 3 sec, then it pushes three to four times within a second. Each copulation lasts between 8 and 12 sec. Many

copulations are incomplete, accomplishing only the mounting of
the female.

Immediately after copulation the male leaves the female, jump-
ing or flying from her back. Sometimes, however, he rests there
for another 10 to 15 sec. If the male takes off he will fly only once
around and then will return to her or to his lookout post. Sometimes the birds sit quietly for several minutes, but in most cases the
male starts preening, soon followed in this by his mate. I observed
several times that at the end of the preening procedure the female
began to nibble at the throat and cheek feathers of the male. The
two birds looked at each other, their bills touching ("billing"). This
may go on for several minutes. This "allopreening" may also accompany the beginning phase of the courtship cycle.

Billing, nibbling, and mutual preening have also been reported
for peregrines (Cade 1960) and several other raptor species.

The falcons copulate most in the morning and evening. The
same pair may have up to at least 5 to 6 copulations within 24 hr,
as is shown from the following data from the records of the second clutch cycle on the submarine cliff in 1969. They do not
differ from those of the normal (first) cycle:

12 August
16:45– 7 copulations and one attempt by pairs no. 1 (2), 8 (1), 9 (2),
19:45 10 (1 try), and 12 (2).
13 August
5:00– 9 copulations and 2 attempts by pairs no. 1 (2), 8 (2), 9 (1), 10
9:00 (1 try), 12 (3 & 1 try), 16 (1), 17 (1).
13 August
9:00– 6 copulations by pairs no. 1 (2), 8 (2), 9 (1), and 12 (1).
14:00

As the breeding season progresses the introductory courtship
behavior is shortened or disappears. Males simply jump suddenly
onto the backs of their mates and attempt copulation. Females
that were apparently asking for copulation were observed approaching their males with their bodies elongated and held horizontally, making long-lasting calls of "yeerk, yer, yeerk..." The
males then responded with moderate to rapid bowing without
always proceeding to copulation itself.

The frequency of copulation resembles that observed in peregrines (Glutz, Bauer, and Bezzel 1971). Kestrels appear to copulate

more often. The American kestrel has been found to copulate 6 to 15 times within a period of only 30 to 40 min (Willoughby and Cade 1964), and 5 times in only 10.5 min (Balgooyen 1976). The European kestrel (*Falco tinnunculus*) may copulate once every few minutes, up to 7 times per hr (Glutz, Bauer, and Bezzel 1971).

Pair Bond and Site Fidelity

Generally speaking, partners stay together for at least one breeding season, but observations from Paximada (1965 and 1966) indicate that the pair bond will often last through at least two seasons:

Four out of 12 pairs returned to their former territories, while 5 other birds (one a female) returned with new partners. Being attached to the same partner and locality certainly reduces the time span needed to establish a population at the breeding grounds (fig. 35, p. 220).

Impressive data on the site fidelity of Eleonora's falcon have been collected by Ristow (1975). Three falcons banded as nestlings on Paximada were found breeding there some four (1) and six years (2) later. Several adults females were recaptured so close to their former nest sites that "we can certainly state that adult females resettle within the colony preferably in their former territory" (Ristow 1975). One female's nest site in 1969 was only 5 m away from her nest site in 1965. Four females occupied nest sites in 1971 at a distance of 5, 10, 30, and 70 m from the ones they held during the 1969 breeding season. Two adult males were found dead some 10 and 40 m from the nest sites they had held four and six seasons earlier.

In one case the pair bond was apparently not strong enough to prevent one partner from seeking relations with a third falcon. At this stage of our knowledge I can only guess the reasons leading to the following conflict situations (see also map of falcon territories, fig. 41).

20 July 1969 (Mogador, Atoll)
Female 6 sits on a ledge 3 m to the right of nest 9; her own nest lies about 13 m higher. She cries, and soon male 15 arrives. I did not see male 15 at his own nest during the minutes preceding this move. He begins to bow while female 6 continues to cry. Male 15 bows a great deal but does not proceed to copulation with female 6. After some minutes male 15 returns to his nest site while female 6 remains at the

site of this meeting for another 15 min. During this scene the respective partners of the two birds are at their nest sites.

When female 6 returns to her nest her mate is eager to show her the nest hole: he walks in and out, sits down in it and turns around. No eggs had been laid at this date.

The same situation is repeated about 45 min later. Female 6 flies down to the place near pair 9; shortly thereafter male 15 lands and starts the bowing procedure. Again there is no copulation. Later male 15 returns to his mate and copulates with her.

This behavior of male 15 explained in a way a situation that had puzzled me on 14 July: Suddenly female 15 was together with a light male (male 15 belongs to the dark phase) that sat in front of nest 15 for several hours. The light male courted her again and again by bowing, but for some reason he hesitated to proceed with the copulation and finally disappeared.

Had male 15 and female 6 been partners before? Had one of them arrived too late, finding its former mate with a new partner? Or were these simply new pairs without a strong pair bond?

The only male that temporarily lured away the female of another male was the bachelor male 14 of the submarine group. His continued courtship of female 12 created some of the most dramatic moments on the cliff. Since sexual ambition was in this case linked with severe agonistic behavior, we shall discuss it in more detail later.

Diurnal raptors are usually monogamous at least during the breeding season. But males with several females each (polygyny) and females with several males each (polyandry) have been reported in at least nine species in five genera (Newton 1976b). In the American kestrel, "copulation is sometimes promiscuous" (Willoughby and Cade 1964). The example of the female Eleonora's falcon's attracting the sexual attention of two males fits well into this general frame.

A considerable amount of tradition regarding nest site and territory has been observed in many a raptor species (Newton 1976b). For the peregrine, it has been proved beyond doubt that certain nest sites have been occupied not only by the same pair (or at least one individual of the pair) over several successive years, but also by a succession of different generations (Fischer 1968). The attraction to a previous nest site may be an important factor in monogamy. A falcon may return to last year's site (philopatry)

and find that last year's mate has done the same. This might lead
to monogamy over several breeding seasons. In the American
kestrel, "if one member of a pair does not return, the remaining
individual leaves the territory; the breeding site acts to facilitate
pairing only when both are present" (Balgooyen 1976). In Eleonora's falcon, Ristow's data (1975) and my own clearly point to a
remarkable degree of philopatry and nest site fidelity within the
falcon colony.

Response to Disturbance

The immediate behavioral response to the egg-robbing incident
of 31 July 1969 was remarkable: the falcons, especially the
females, climbed in and out of their nest holes looking for their
clutches, then settled down for brooding, perhaps in the hope that
the eggs might have been buried beneath the sand and would
reappear after the typical egg-turning movements. The birds
were restless, taking off and landing many times. With the exception of pairs 7 and 9, less than normal incubation time was recorded on 1 August (fig. 32). Unfortunately, I was not able to
inspect the nests on 31 July because of heavy surf and high tides,
and so I do not know whether the egg-robbers took the entire
clutch in each case.

   It seemed quite possible that some or all pairs would leave the
cliff because of this disturbance. Fortunately, this did not happen.

   The incubation period for each pair of the submarine study
population can best be determined by the number and date of
copulations. During the three days 30 and 31 July and 1 August only
one copulation and one such attempt was recorded (pair 4); although that pair had probably not yet started laying eggs, all other
pairs had already entered the incubation period. Some of them,
however, were a week or so ahead of the others. This can be
shown by comparing the sexual behavior of all pairs on 21 July.

   Observations during that day tend to distinguish three groups:
an advanced group consisted of pairs 3, 5, 8, and 9, having no
copulations or only one each, coupled with a strong incubation
trend and the occurrence of regular turns between the mates; a
middle group showed two or three copulations each, being still in
the egg-laying phase; pairs, 1, 10, and 12 belonged to this group.
Then there was the beginner's or late group, in which the pairs
were either still in the phase before egg-laying or had just entered
the egg-laying phase (pairs 2 and 4). Some pairs have not been

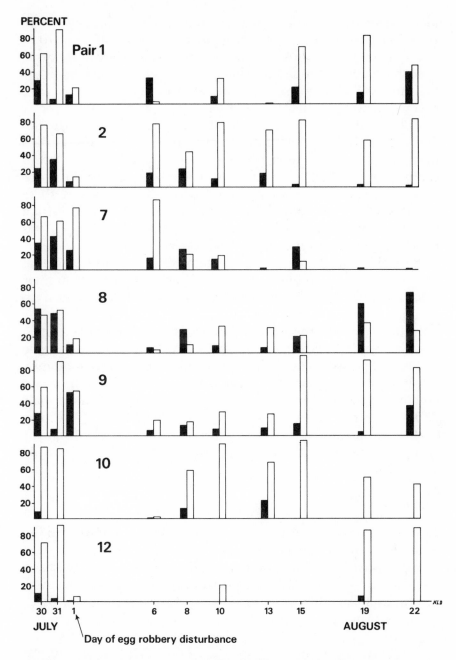

Fig. 32. Incubation time as a percentage of total observation time. Data for males (*black columns*) and females (*white columns*) of 7 study pairs breeding on submarine cliff before, during, and after the disturbance caused by egg robbers. Note the surprisingly active role taken by several male falcons after the disturbance.

mentioned in this context because they are too difficult to see from our observation point on the main isle opposite the cliff.

The falcons that subsequently began a second breeding cycle, probably leading to a second clutch, seem to have come from the first and second groups. This means that when the eggs were stolen they were in their first and second week of incubation after completing the full clutch. The evidence collected during the following weeks indicates that these pairs needed about 7 to 14 days to reach once again the egg-laying phase characterized by 2 or 3 copulations between 9:00 and 17:00. Table 14 contains the records of the observed copulations and figure 33 summarizes these findings. Other pairs continued incubating their empty nests for a long time, as illustrated in figure 32. Worth mentioning in this respect is female 2, which on the average spent 65% of the observation time in incubation. While the females of the three pairs that were later found without any eggs (2, 7, and 10) differed in their behavior, their mates showed a downward trend in regard to incubation time (fig. 34).

Contrary to this, the males of those pairs that had one or two eggs (left behind or from a second clutch) exhibited a rather stable and even upward trend in their incubation periods. It should be emphasized that in pair 8 the male was the force behind the establishment of a second nest (3 m from the first site) and clutch; male 12, on the other hand, did very little to relieve female 12 of her duties, perhaps because of his heavy involvement with bachelor male 14's continuous threat to the territorial integrity and family life of pair 12.

Discussion

The sexual behavior of Eleonora's falcon does not appear to deviate significantly from that of other falcons. Thus, a comparison with the courtship cycle of peregrine falcons (Cade 1960) indicates a similar sequence of display, courtship, and copulation behavior. Eleonora's falcon differs in the almost constant presence of other falcons during all phases of breeding behavior. Whether this tends to intensify a male falcon's display phase in order to increase his visibility in the midst of so many other falcons can only be guessed at this point. In general, as mentioned before, it is rare to observe a falcon without a female at the beginning of the breeding

TABLE 14
Number of Copulations per Pair and Day between 9:00 and 17:00:
Mogador (Submarine Cliff) 1969

Pair Number	July			August							
	21	30	31	1	6	8	10	13	15	19	22
1	2						1	2			
2	2–3						1				
4	1		1 + (1)ᵃ		2				(1)		
5	1										
7	1 + (1)										
8	1				1 + (1)	2	3 + (1)	2	2	1	
9	1					2	1	1			
10	2								1		
11	1								(1)		
12	1–2				(1)	3	2 + (1)	1			
13	1										
15	?					1					
16	?						1		1		
17	?									1	
18	?					1 + (1)	1		(2)		
14					(1)						
Total	14–16 + (1)	0	1 + (1)	(1)	3 + (2)	9 + (1)	10 + (3)	7	4 + (4)	2 + (2)	0

ᵃ ( ) = incomplete copulation.

season. Most already seem to have partners in early July. Are those the old pairs from the previous year (and probably other breeding seasons as well)?

Of great interest could be the observations of the submarine study population before, during, and after the egg-robbing incident. The falcons were terribly excited while it happened and needed several days to settle into a new routine. Subsequent monitoring showed that these falcons are individualistic and that it is impossible to predict their response to such a disturbance.

I found it very interesting that several pairs successfully managed to reset their physiological system and cycles and to start over with the egg-laying phase and the accompanying series of copulation behaviors. This points to a healthy resilience of this population in the face of egg predation.

A second clutch makes sense only if the eggs can be laid and incubated in time for the young falcon(s) to fledge before the falcon population has to leave the breeding area. From this point of view, 31 July seems to be about the last possible date to reactivate the physiological reproduction system and to have some chance of raising the young to fledging stage.

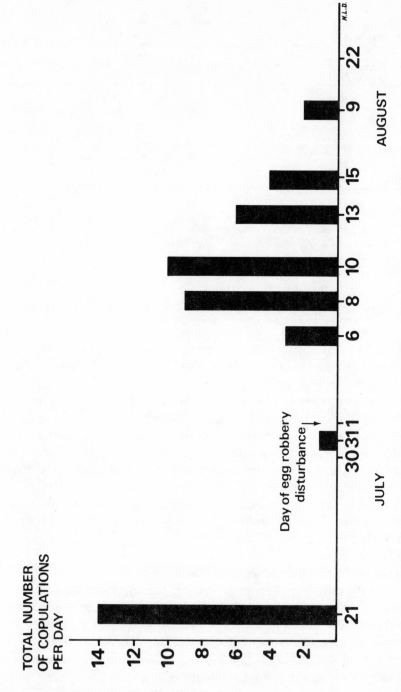

Fig. 33. Number of copulations observed on submarine cliff before and after the egg robbery incident (see text).

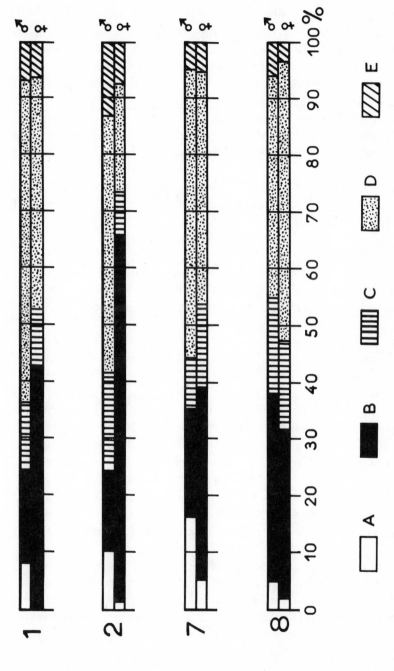

Fig. 34. Activity patterns of individual falcons. Percentage of time spent by 4 pairs in various activities during 3,300 min of observation time (100%) between 9:00 and 17:00. *A*, absent from cliff; *B*, incubating clutch or empty nest scrape; *C*, preening; *D*, resting or watching the surroundings outside nesting site; *E*, other activities (feeding, hiking, sunbathing, etc.).

TERRITORIAL BEHAVIOR

Most pairs and some nonbreeding adult falcons were found to possess a well-defined territory during the breeding season. Initially consisting only of a perch and one or two potential nest scrapes, this territory was often extended throughout the breeding season to cover from 1 to more than 200 m² on the ground and 1 to 10 m of airspace above the ground. The territory is defended against rivals for the *exclusive* use of an individual or a pair. Its shape and size can be determined by recording how and where a falcon makes use of it or defends it.

Territory Size, Shape, and Function

The populations studied showed characteristic differences in the size and role of the territory.

Paximada Colony

The upper slope study population possessed rounded territories with a radius of 5 to 20 m around the nest site. The size varied considerably (60–200 m²). The boundaries were relatively fixed in the latter part of the breeding season. Some no-man's-land (undefended and unused areas) lay in between territories (fig. 35A).

   All activities except flying, hunting, and bathing (in sand) took place in the territory. Thus it served as the area in which the falcons rested, courted, copulated, raised their young, prepared prey, took sunbaths, preened, and kept careful watch on their neighbors and the general cliff environment. In addition, the territory was a virtual sanctuary for the young. The latter often left the nest scrape when they were barely 3 wk old and hiked around, exploring the neighborhood and looking for shaded spots during the hot midday periods. The fledglings were never bothered by other falcons as long as they stayed in their parents' territory. Whenever the young attempted to soar clumsily in the updraft of the hill, they would try to land again in their own territory; failing in this, they would be stooped upon by other adults until they somehow managed to reach their own ground. In 1965 I took a number of banded fledglings and set them free out of sight of their birthplaces, about 100 m away. A few hours later all of them had returned to their original locations. This attests to the excellent memory and acoustic and visual perception of the young birds, and also the importance of staying within one's territory in this colony of raptors.

Perhaps the easiest way to determine the size of the ground territory is to monitor the falcons' food-caching behavior, which is performed by adults and fledglings alike. The Paximada birds had a remarkable memory for the general location of their caches, though they often needed several minutes of intensive search before they actually retrieved a cached prey item. To convey an impression of the frequency of this behavior I include some diary records in summary form (see also Appendix B).

On 30 August 1965 I monitored the upper slope study group from 4:25 to 8:00. During this period the falcon pairs that were in good view captured and "processed" varying numbers of prey items (all of them small birds). Some were plucked and fed to the chicks, some were put in a cache right after the male delivered them to his mate, and the rest were plucked and partially eaten, then cached. The statistics of this morning were:

Pair 16: three prey arrivals, one caching(s).
Pair 19: four prey arrivals, no caching(s).
Pair 21: four prey arrivals, two caching(s).
Pair 23: six prey arrivals, four caching(s).
Pair 24: two prey arrivals, no caching(s).
Pair 52: two prey arrivals, no caching(s).

The retrieval of cached food items may occur at any time of day.

Female 23 was a more active "food-cacher" than many of her neighbors. I monitored her again on 4 September 1965 from 5:10 to 9:45. Her male arrived with prey no. 1 at 5:12, prey no. 2 at 5:35, and prey items nos. 3–5 at 5:52, 5:59, and 6:57. It cannot be excluded that the first feeding had already taken place before 5:10. The female took the first, third, fourth, and fifth birds from her mate and immediately deposited in different places around her nest site. Prey no. 2, a red-backed shrike (*Lanius collurio*), was carried into the nest, plucked, and fed to the falcon chicks. Between 6:00 and 6:40 the female twice hiked toward cache no. 3 but returned to her perch near the nest site before reaching it. At 6:40 she flew behind the area of cache no. 4. She disappeared behind some shrubs, trying to squeeze herself through the stiff branches. She reappeared after some 60 sec (was she looking for an old cache? Did prey no. 4 fall into a deep cleft?). The female perched on a boulder, looked around, then walked toward the *Euphorbia* shrub behind which she had cached her fourth bird. She searched for a while, then walked back to the boulder with prey no. 4 in her beak. She plucked the

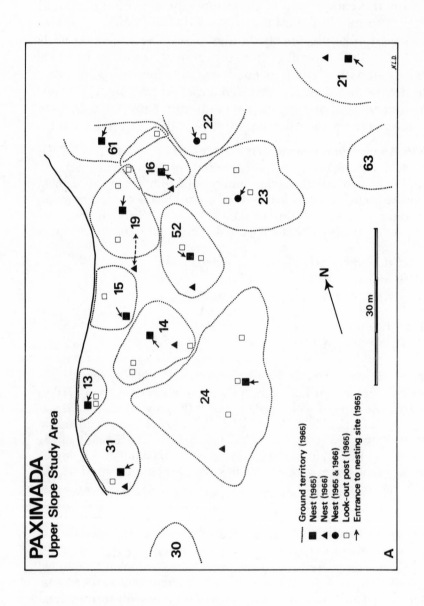

PAXIMADA
Upper Slope Study Area

31
13
15
19
61
16
22
52
23
63
21
14
24
30

N

30 m

Ground territory (1965)
Nest (1965)
Nest (1966)
Nest (1965 & 1966)
Look-out post (1965)
Entrance to nesting site (1965)

A

N.L.D.

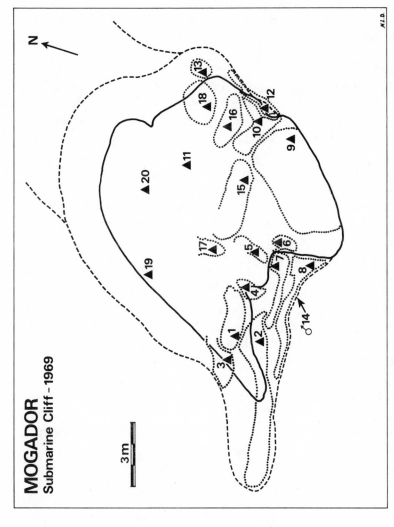

Fig. 35. Territories and nesting sites. *A*, Paximada. Look-out posts, entrance to nesting site, and change of nesting site during the following breeding season are also indicated. *B*, Mogador. Ground plan of submarine cliff with falcon nesting sites and ground territories. Upper plateau (————), shore of cliff at high tide (– – –), and territorial boundaries (. . . .).

bird, first an entire wing, then the primaries of the second wing, the tail, the remainder of the second wing, and the breast feathers, and finally she tore off its head. She then flew into her nest with the corpse. Shortly thereafter male 23 returned with prey no. 5. The female immediately put it in a new cache but retrieved it from there about 50 min later (7:45). Instead of taking it to the nest, she moved it to a new location near one of her perches. At 8:20 she retrieved prey no. 3, plucked it, and took it into her nest.

Mogador Colony

Of the submarine population of 18 pairs (1969), only 7 could be studied regarding their utilization of territorial space (fig. 36). These were situated on the east-facing side of the cliff, the center of which consisted of a projection with sheer walls. Four pairs (nos. 1, 2, 7, 8) lived to the left of it, three pairs (9, 10, 12) to the right of it. The groups were visually but not acoustically isolated from each other and formed distinct "neighborhoods." Social interactions occurred frequently within but rarely between these two neighborhoods. For some time, a single male falcon occupied a small perch and potential nest scrape below the territory of pair 8. This male interacted chiefly with pair no. 12 of the right neighborhood.

Compared with the Crete colony, the territories were small indeed. By 1 August four weeks after the beginning of the reproductive season, the falcons hardly used more than 1 to 3 m² each (fig. 36*A*). Gradually the territories expanded (especially into those areas that had been occupied by gulls) until the maximum size was attained. The territories, averaging 10 m² and very irregular in shape, left few unclaimed areas in the neighborhoods and so constituted a stable network within which most falcon activities were carried out. Despite small territories, these activities remained substantially the same as in the Crete colony.

The initial arrival of the falcons and the establishment or reestablishment of their nest sites and territories were not observed on this cliff and must have taken place before 11 July 1969. This was a surprise, since I had seen only a few Eleonora's falcons at Paximada on 1–2 July 1966, and since Contant and Naurois (1958) had also seen only a few falcons at the Mogador colony before July.

If it proves true that adult falcons returning from their winter quarters take immediate possession of their former territories, then a difficult task looms ahead for falcon enthusiasts: anytime between April and July a falcon pair (or one member of it) may return to its breeding site, claim the accustomed territory or at least some part of it, then stay on the site or leave again for short periods of time. This reasoning would explain two baffling observations: that falcons seem to have a territory in July, but that they are not always present before the egg-laying phase.

Each territory contained a number of key places: the *nest site*, one or more *lookout posts* from which the surroundings were monitored and from which a falcon could instantly take off, *feeding and food-storage areas*, and *sunbathing* sites (fig. 36B). To move from one of these "central places" to another, a falcon flew or hiked over the terrain. Surprisingly often, it hiked. Surveillance and rest periods were frequently interrupted by preening, sunbathing, a brief circular territorial flight in front of the cliff, searching for unfinished prey items, stored away in some cleft or hole, and feeding activities (fig. 36B).

Some of the immediate airspace above the horizontal ground was part of each territory. It is impossible, however, to determine whether that space extended 2, 5, or 10 m into the air. Clearly, the falcons were concerned, and if an unknown or neighbor falcon was hovering in a determined way above a ground territory, its owner quickly chased the intruder away at any height up to 10 m above the ground. Beyond that height gulls, pigeons, and falcons were generally able to use any air corridors above the falcon cliffs.

In 1969 I realized after long observation efforts at Smea and submarine isles that each breeding falcon generally had one or two preferred flight corridors leading to and from its nesting site and principal perches (lookout posts). These flight corridors have been indicated in figures 37A and B to show the importance of individual behavior differences in this species. Falcons perched below a flight corridor were often harassed by the user of the corridor. That falcons are individuals, each with its characteristic traits and routines, became even more evident as I observed their mobility patterns on the ground.

Use of and Mobility within the Territory

The territory of Eleonora's falcon is a private "apartment" and

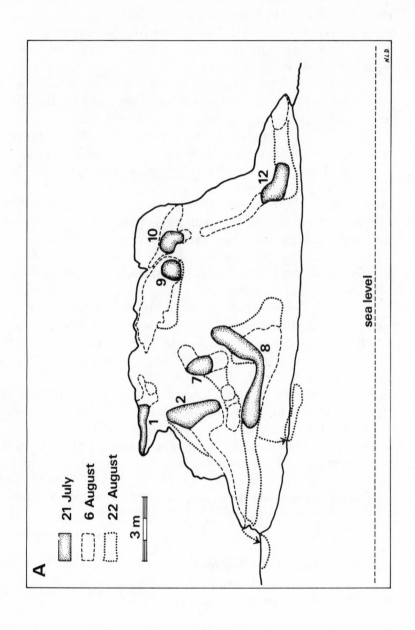

A

- ▓ 21 July
- ☐ 6 August
- ⬚ 22 August

3 m

12

10

9

1

2

7

8

sea level

N.L.D.

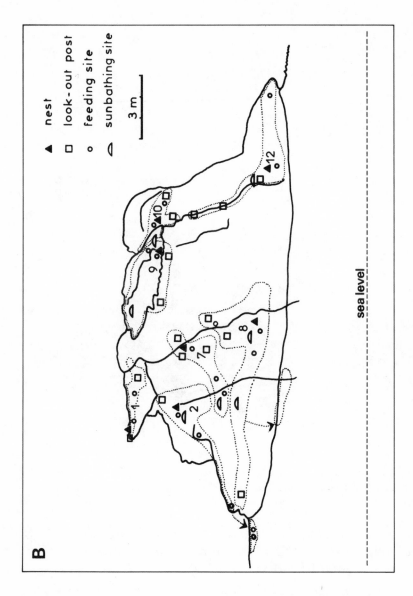

Fig. 36. Territories of study pairs on submarine cliff. *A*, half of the breeding season. *B*, Qualitative use of the Gradual expansion of ground territories during the first ground territories.

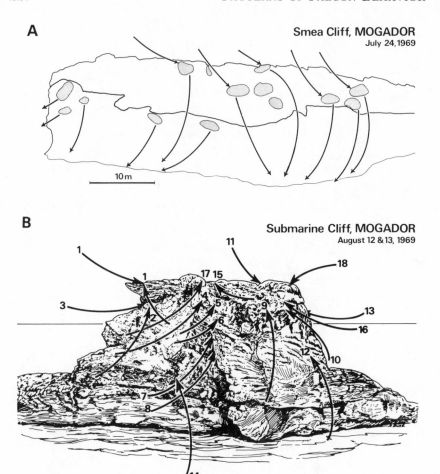

Fig. 37. Major aerial flight corridors used by Eleonora's falcon at the breeding cliff (Mogador 1969). Indicated are the flight headings to and from the ground territories. *A*, Smea cliff; *B*, submarine cliff.

nearly always is completely avoided by all falcon neighbors. I observed only one pair that occasionally shared a corner of its neighbor's ground territory:

6 August 1969 (Mogador, Submarine Cliff)
12:32   Male 9 and female 10 sit very close together at the border of
           their territories, while male 10 sits in front of a deep hole just
           behind the territory of pair 9 and certainly outside its own
           ground. Nothing happens, and after some minutes male 10 flies

back to his nest while male 9 walks to his female, passing the deep hole on the way.

12:49 Female 10 marches to the deep hole and disappears into it; now male 9 leaves his mate, moves to the deep hole, and peeks in, seeming alert but not excited, then disappears into the hole; 30 sec later female 10 climbs out of the hole (without any prey) and male 10 jumps from his territory over to the plateau of pair 9, cries briefly and bows twice. Male 9 leaves the hole and returns to his female; female 10 then flies back to her nest.

13:01 Female 9 goes into the deep hole and female 10 arrives there to look on; by now the dark-phased male 15 walks up to the hole from the back of his territory, until he sits only 1 ft above female 9. He cries and hikes back. Female 10 flies back and sits behind male 10 at border 9/10. Female 9 leaves the deep hole a few minutes later and returns to her mate.

In this case three pairs met at one place near or outside their borders and territories without any aggressive tendencies. Some of the other borders were quite "hot," however, and some males were on a constant alert when their neighbor was at home. More about this can be found in the following section.

After 8 August I was able to delineate the rough shape and size of the various territories and to subdivide each of these into segments that were usually separated by certain physical features such as rock crevices and steep walls. This enabled me to record the movements of each bird within his territory in a more accurate form by gathering data on the qualitative and quantitative use of segments of a territory.

From 10 to 22 August my brother and I monitored the change of place and the period spent on each place by 14 falcons. (This was the same population that had been severely disturbed during the egg-robbing incident of 1 August 1969.) The results indicate that females stayed longer in one segment of their territories than did males (fig. 38). Only female 7 showed the same characteristics as her mate. The segment that was preferred by the females contained the nest. They spent up to 88% (female 2) of the daytime in a small area 1 to 3 m². Although the males show less preference for this segment, it was still the one most used in three cases (males 8, 9, and 12). In one case (male 2) the lookout post was most often used, while other males used several segments with more or less equal frequency. All pairs except one possessed at least two territorial segments of 0 to 5% usage.

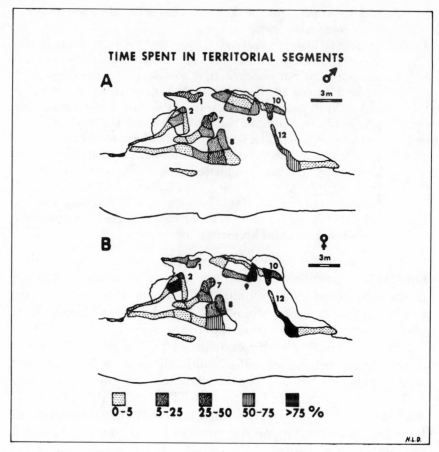

Fig. 38. Time spent in each territorial segment by male and female falcons.

A look at the "traffic" or mobility graphs (figs. 39 and 40) demonstrates that some of the little-used segments were nevertheless regularly visited for short periods of time, as in the cases of females 2 and 7 (also males 2, 7, and 8). These graphs reveal a conspicuous difference in the frequency of changing places within the territory between male and female. The males are more mobile, go to more places, and use a more varied itinerary during their trips from segment to segment. The females, on the other hand, leave their territories much less frequently (females 8 and 9 left only once each during the entire observation period), though some embark on more observation or territorial flights around the

cliff than their male partners (females 1 and 2). Three incubating
females moved much less frequently from segment to segment
than the nonbreeding females (2, 7, and 10). Female 1, however,
was very restless despite an egg in her nest scrape. The wide
"high- and flyways" (figs. 39 and 40) indicate the main connections
between nest, lookout post, and feeding and bathing areas (compare with fig. 36B). This documentation of each falcon's ground
mobility appears to be an excellent way to characterize the different "personalities" among those two falcon neighborhoods.

Other Parts of the Mogador Colony

A number of pairs were breeding in completely inaccessible
pigeonholes in vertical cliffs of the atoll isle. These pairs possessed
little, if any, territory. All activities on the ground were confined to
the sometimes atriumlike entry to the hidden nest scrape. These
falcons could not hike over or on the cliff surface in any way.
They paid more attention to and defended the immediate
airspace in front of their nest entrance. Their young were unable
to move about the rock. The few pairs that were breeding on
open ledges (fig. 41), visible from far away, occupied elongated,
up to 6 m long territories along and above or below their ledge.
One male falcon occupied a couple of square meters of dissected
cliff surface some 15 m away and across an open archway from its
nest hole on the other side.

Salé and San Pietro Colonies

Since both colonies were situated on rather large and mostly
sheer cliffs, territories appeared to be defined less in terms of
private rock surfaces than as exclusive rights of access to the nest
site and unlimited flight maneuverability in the updraft in front of
the cliff. Thus we have here (as on the atoll) a different type of
spatial interest sphere that is difficult to pinpoint in size and shape
but that nevertheless exists.

Discussion

The territory of Eleonora's falcon can be understood as an essential and efficient mechanism or vehicle of individual survival and
reproductive success within the breeding colony. The dispersion
of nest sites (see chap. 3) alone does not provide for a safe and

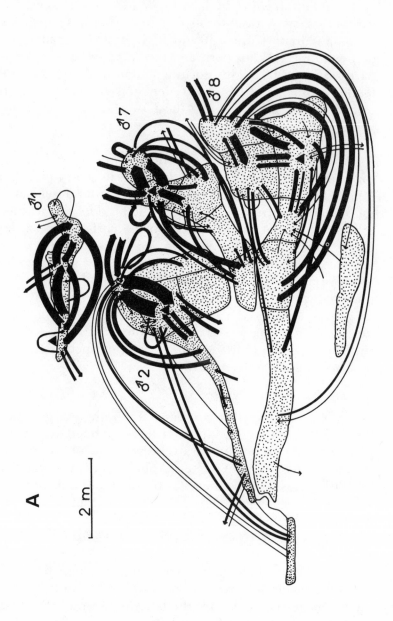

A

2 m

♂1

♂7

♂8

♂2

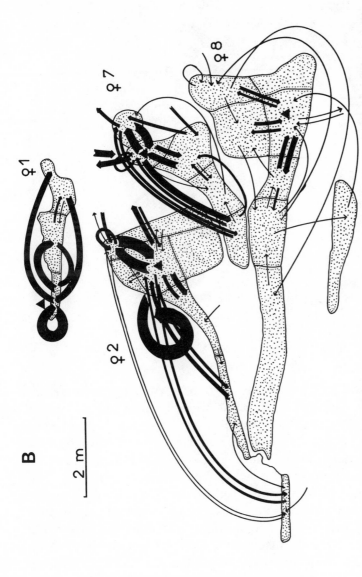

B

2 m

♀1

♀7

♀8

♀2

Fig. 39. Mobility diagrams of four falcon pairs from submarine cliff. Based on data collected during 5 observation days from 9:00 to 17:00. Recorded were all movements resulting in takeoff, arrival, and transfer to another segment. The thinnest lines represent only one flight or hike. Thicker lines indicate several movements (up to a maximum of more than 30). Circular or oval arrows leading back to the takeoff point indicate a falcon's brief reconaissance flights. The lines do not necessarily correspond to actual routes. Nesting sites are indicated by black triangles.

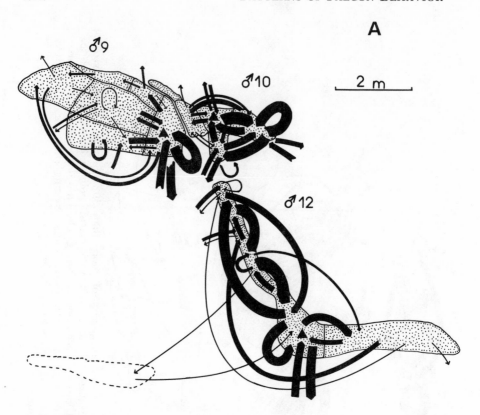

Fig. 40. Mobility diagrams of three falcon pairs from Submarine cliff. See fig. 39 for details.

efficient way of life. As long as anyone, particularly other Eleonora's falcons, can walk or fly right up to the nest site and perch next to it, a falcon, its mate, and its brood face constant danger. But if the nest site is surrounded by a well-defined and exclusive territorial space that must be left alone by others in order to avoid agonistic interaction (see below), it becomes a safe haven. The territory appears to significantly reduce the threat of intraspecific interference and predation in this colonial species. Hole- and cave-breeding Eleonora's falcons do not require such a space when their nest sites are inaccessible except from the air.

It is impossible to judge whether the falcons prefer to settle in areas where a need for territories exists. The fact is that where such territories have been established and maintained on oblique

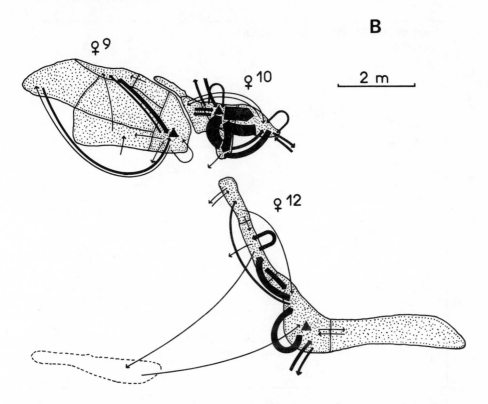

and horizontal surfaces, they are used for additional purposes: sunbathing, storing and hiding or caching prey items (a very elaborate process in the Crete colony), and as a "playground" for the young falcons.

Falcons keep their territory under frequent visual control; it can be surveyed in its entirety from a lookout post. This apparent need for constant monitoring is probably responsible for the strangely shaped territories of the "submarine" populations. More circular or regular shapes of similar size would have included visual barriers like pinnacles and ridges that would make it impossible to have visual command of the whole territory. This leads me to suggest that size and shape are related not only to the general dispersion pattern of a population (if nests are close together, territories must necessarily be small) but also to the visual complexity of the terrain. Rounded and larger territories can be expected on terrain that contains few features obstructing the

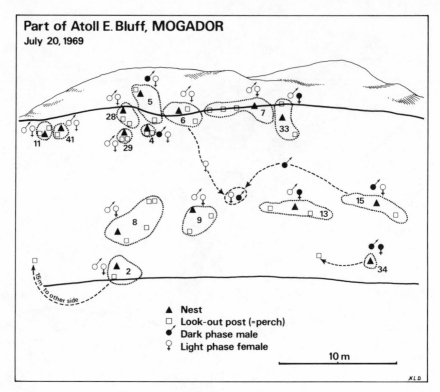

Fig. 41. Territories on the east bluff of the inner walls of atoll isle, Mogador. The meeting place of female 6 and male 15 is also shown (see text).

falcon's view (model A in fig. 42), tiny and irregularly shaped ones in locations where terrain complexity allows for only a small field of vision (model B, fig. 42).

Territorial organization has been described for some noncolonial raptors. Cade (1960) explains the territories of peregrine falcons as a series of circles around nest sites, with only the innermost circle always being defended, while outer circles include rarely defended hunting grounds within the home range. Cavé (1968) showed for the European kestrel that the breeding territories had a maximum radius of 25 to 35 m during all stages of breeding. His observations suggest that "territoriality decreases somewhat during breeding, and that the defended area is possibly slightly extended." His Dutch study population did not defend any individual feeding territories or home ranges during the breeding season.

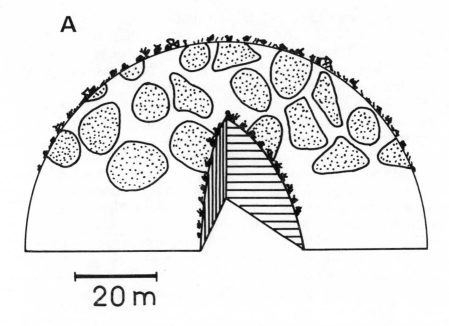

A

20 m

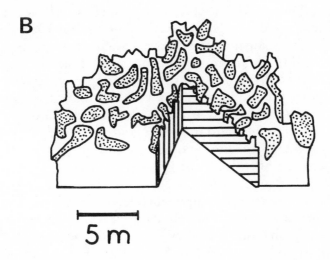

B

5 m

Fig. 42. Model of falcon territories as a function of surface texture. *A*, Large island with relatively smooth terrain: territories are large and of more or less rounded shape. *B*, Small island with rugged terrain: territories are very small and of highly irregular shape.

Other raptors have well-defined home ranges containing the nest sites. A useful study of an entire raptor community contains the maps of home ranges and nest sites of eleven species in the Great Basin of Utah (Smith and Murphy 1973). Research in Africa has yielded similar results from the Ivory Coast (Thiollay 1975) and Kenya (Smeenk 1974). The red-footed falcon is unusual. Here several pairs, breeding in the abandoned tree nests of the rook (*Corvus frugilegus*), will defend a common territory including the feeding area around their occupied rookery against other breeding groups of red-footed falcons (Horváth 1975).

It would be worth while to study other gregarious raptors in terms of their dispersion and territorial systems. Eleonora's falcon resembles many colonial seabirds (Patterson 1965; Bongiorno 1970; Simmons 1970; Manuval 1974) except that the shape and size of its territory show a wider range; in addition, prey storage and hiding have become important attributes not found in most (any?) of the other species. This latter aspect will be discussed in the following section.

The mobility diagrams showing the "traffic density" between the segments of one territory illustrate the importance of the physical microenvironment of the rock surface. Within a few square meters there were many distinct points for each falcon, some vital, others meaningless. To a casual ornithological observer, such a cliff surface consists of sheer cliff, holes, ledges, and crevices. For the falcon, it is a veritable house or apartment with various subunits utilized in specific ways. More than anything else, these diagrams (figs. 39 and 40) bring out the intimate relationships of a breeding falcon to the microlandscape of the breeding colony. They therefore show another kind of adaptation: the interaction between individuals, their peers, and the physical nature of the cliff.

Some falcons were much more active than others. The behavioral contrast between individuals appears to defy a simple mechanistic explanation. Territory size, dominance, and partner choice were in no way correlated. The longer I observed—and I believe this happens to all students of animal behavior—the more I became conscious of the complex personality of each of my falcons.

AGONISTIC BEHAVIOR

If we think of the territory as a "vehicle" essential to a falcon's reproductive success, then agonistic behavior provides the "fuel" or energy necessary to make it work. The establishment, expansion, and daily maintenance of a territory would be impossible without effective behavioral patterns related to threat and appeasement, to offensive and defensive actions. In other words, the rights of "privacy" and "exclusive" territorial space must be gained and confirmed. As in other species, certain agonistic behaviors also serve an important function in sexual relationships.

Constant fighting between falcons would be to the disadvantage of this heavily armed but colonial species. It would inflict heavy losses and create permanent disturbance factors within the breeding population. Instead, a number of acoustic and visual signals are employed to communicate elements of agonistic behavior to other falcons. Such signals often prevent the outbreak of serious conflicts involving physical fighting. They worked so well that to a casual observer the colonies appeared to consist of remarkably (and perhaps disappointingly) peaceful falcon populations. Acute intraspecific conflict situations filled less than 2% of the 3,780 minutes of observation time of the 1969 "submarine cliff" study population. The falcons used a number of vocalizations and body postures to ward off physical confrontations as much as possible. However, with species other than falcons, such signals seldom worked.

Interspecific Agonistic Behavior

Gulls and doves were subjected to continual aggression simply because the falcons appeared annoyed by their presence on the cliff. The falcons used various forms of agonistic actions, as illustrated by the following excerpts from my notebook (submarine cliff, Mogador).

10 August 1969

13:00   Male 8 flew to nest and walked into it when he realized that 4 to 6 doves were sitting in front of the nest entrance; he walked out again, chasing the doves away, and returned to his nest.

30 July 1969

9:15   Male 10 took off, swooped down on immature gulls, which were standing 5 m above the cliff in the air against the wind. Shortly thereafter another falcon pursued a gull in jaegerlike fashion, driving the gull 10 m away from the cliff.

31 July 1969

15:10   An adult gull again tried to land on the cliff. When it had barely alighted, a falcon swooped down on it in five nosedives until the gull took off, still followed by the falcon.

Aggressive acts gradually decreased as the season progressed, mainly because gulls and doves made fewer visits to the cliff (see table 15).

TABLE 15
Agonistic Behavior of Submarine Cliff Study Population, 1969

	Number of Aggressive Actions against Other Species		Number of Aggressive Actions against Other Falcons for			
Date	Doves	Gulls	Food Piracy	Territorial Rivalry	Unknown Reasons	Total
30 July	22	8	1	6	2	39
31 July	26	3	1	2	2	34
1 August	10	2	—	7	2	21
6 August	4	3	—	6	5	18
8 August	10	—	—	3	3	16
10 August	5	—	1	5	3	14
12 August	4	3	—	3	1	11
13 August	8	—	4	13	1	26
15 August	—	1	—	5	2	8
19 August	—	2	—	15	—	17
22 August	1	1	3	16	2	23
Total	90	23	10	81	23	227

Between 30 July and 22 August, 90 aggressive actions against doves were recorded, of which 56 were committed by males, 20 by females, and 14 by falcons of undetermined sex. During the same period 23 attacks were made on herring gulls (three by males, three by females, 17 by birds of unknown sex, mostly flying). No further interspecific aggression was recorded on this cliff.

A more severe response was given when real enemies or potential predators entered the airspace around and above the falcon colonies. At Paximada this included eagles, hawks, herons, and other falcon species. A few, then up to 50 to 80, falcons would literally scramble off the cliffs and quickly climb as high as possible in order to be able to stoop down on the intruder. In all cases the large birds were driven off their course and altitude. The only

real danger for a falcon chick came one day in 1966 when an immature parasitic jaeger (*Stercorarius parasiticus*) suddenly appeared
within meters of the Mogador colony. It was detected and attacked by several falcons until it gave up and flew off over the sea.

Ground predators or intruders like goats, rats, humans, and
presumably also carnivores like foxes are threatened with steep
nose dives and incessant screaming of the alarm call, but this rarely
leads to actual physical interaction (see chap. 3, section on
"Enemies").

In summary, a colony like that of Eleonora's falcon is a bad
place for any diurnal intruder or predator. I noticed not only
individual defense but several unmistakable group defense actions by large numbers of falcons.

Intraspecific Agonistic Behavior

Intraspecific aggression and defense is sparked by disputes over
food, territorial rights, and sexual rivalry. It is a domain of the
male falcons, which were the threatening or attacking birds in 67
of 74 cases (90%). Despite the considerable number of observations that fall under this heading, let me emphasize that all observers were generally impressed by the peaceful (sometimes almost
boringly quiet) behavior of the falcons in different colonies.

Disputes over Food Items (Prey Piracy)

When an Eleonora's falcon returns home after a successful
hunting flight, it is often intercepted by other Eleonora's falcons
before or right at the cliff where its young are eagerly awaiting its
return. This attempted prey piracy creates frequent wild, loud
chases up and down the cliffs. I have observed this in all the
colonies studied. A particularly good place for studying the piracy
and its follow-up is the arenalike inner basin of the atoll island at
Mogador.

Almost every time a falcon flew into the basin with prey in his
talons (which is very difficult for the human observer to detect),
one or more falcons would leave their lookout posts alongside the
steep walls and rigorously pursue the incoming bird. Crying
loudly, this "gang" of falcons flew with astonishing speed around
the arena until one of the pursuers got tangled in the prey. An air
fight followed between the two birds, their claws locked. While

yelling with high-pitched voices, they would cease to fly and would whirl slowly downward, their wings flapping aimlessly.

This "whirling" behavior is usually broken up before the birds reach the ground or sea, and one of the two takes off with the prey. Sometimes the prey is dropped or—even worse—both birds fall into the sea; the latter I observed twice. Once the falcon was so fatigued that it lay motionless on the water with spread wings for 10 sec.

The males participated more in this intraspecific "parasitism." Certain birds, especially those occupying the top ledges of the basin walls, were constantly seen chasing incoming birds.

During the same period the food piracy on the neighboring isle, Smea and submarine, was less conspicuous; I attribute this to the different layout of those isles. Incoming birds were difficult to detect and reached their territories before anyone could intercept them.

In this context it should be mentioned that air fights and chasing in the air are not always related to food piracy. We observed 7 fights in the air involving falcons grappling each other's claws and 16 cases in which one falcon seriously pursued another bird for unknown reasons (submarine cliff). In addition, some male falcons deliver their prey to their females in the air. This latter behavior appears to be less common in this falcon, however, than in congeneric species like hobbies. It is probably too risky a maneuver, considering the presence of many other falcons on the same cliff.

Discussion

Certain falcon populations seem to expend much energy on incessant attempts at food piracy. I cannot see much of a useful component in this behavior. It often appeared to be more of a sport or a game, in which "everyone on the block" participated, hungry or not. The only good can come to weaker, less successful hunters and their mates, who might try to specialize in intraspecific prey piracy. This would allow them to survive using the energy expenditure of the more successful bird hunters. The latter would be "cheated" out of their honestly earned prey but could presumably counteract this by an extra hunting effort. In the case of the atoll population, acts of prey piracy disrupted many normal behavioral sequences of falcon families. They can only be labeled as disturbances.

In the long run, disputes over food might serve to stabilize the breeding density (spacing of nesting sites) on a given cliff. A complex physical terrain offering many visual "niches" (see chap. 2, section on "Dispersion") would encourage a high density with close nest spacings. This would be counteracted by increased interaction, energy loss, and disturbance caused by intraspecific disputes over food. The latter could generally be expected to increase with higher breeding density. Thus, other things equal, we can develop the simple stabilizing model below:

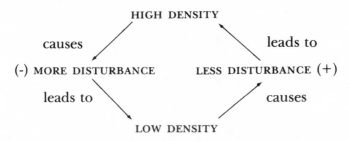

More disturbance would lower reproductive success. After several seasons the density would decline. This would reduce the disturbance factor and improve the breeding record. Eventually, the initial high density would be achieved again.

Territorial Rivalry

The establishment, expansion, and maintenance of a territory is intricately linked with agonistic behavior. Quite often this behavior is almost undetectable to the human observer, since visual and acoustic signals are being used that limit openly aggressive behaviors. From their perches (figs. 35*A*, 36*B*), falcons keep well informed about anything happening within their territories. To achieve an even better control, they frequently take off for brief aerial surveys of the neighborhood. Figure 43 illustrates such flights, which clearly serve an important role in territorial defense: they provide information, and they remind other falcons of a neighbor's vigilance.

Eleonora's falcon possesses a *threat posture*: head bent down, staring at feet, back slightly hunched, tail very horizontal, strong call.

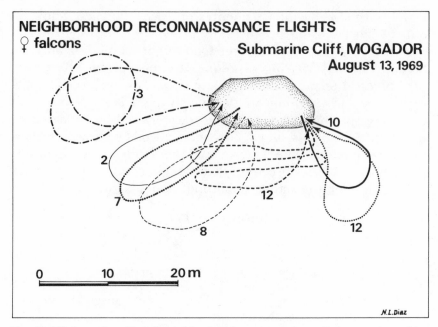

Fig. 43. Flight paths of brief neighborhood reconnaissance flights conducted by female falcons.

This posture may be used by both birds involved in a dispute but may also result in intimidation of one participant, expressed by his bowing.

Another posture with a threatening or intimidating effect was used by falcon males perched above a rival male. Facing the rival below, they stood in an upright position with wings slightly spread and bill half-open.

In most cases a falcon embarked on an air attack without any previous warning. An air attack consists of one or a series of nose dives but may occasionally lead to a more serious confrontation.

Three particularly aggressive interactions will be reported here to illustrate the general nature of these encounters. All three took place on the submarine cliff.

21 July 1969

11:15   Female 7 walked across the steep slope to the left of her nest, probably looking for hidden prey remnants. Male 2, sitting on his lookout post 3 m higher up, watched this and began to crow furiously ("gock-go-gock-go ..."). Then he made at least six nose dives on female 7, which did not defend herself but pressed her body against the slope. Finally male 2 returned to his post, still crying his annoyance, while female 7 hiked slowly back to her nest site. Female 7 never again tried to enter this part of the slope.

22 August 1969

11:40   Female 1 had been harassed by male 3 for almost an hour. Female 1 kept flying around in order to avoid the nose dives of the attacking bird. When female 1 finally landed, a second bird—perhaps male 3—dashed at her with lightning speed. One bird was thrown on its back while the other one managed to hold it down, standing with both feet on its breast. There were violent wing-beatings and high-pitched calls until both took off, followed by males 2 and 7.

19 August 1969

12:40   A nonbreeding, one-year-old Eleonora's falcon visited the submarine cliff. It tried to land on the territory of pair 1, but male 1 shot out of a hole and drove the stranger away. The visitor circled above the cliff and managed, after surveying the location of birds on the cliff, to sit down near the territory of pair 5, both of which were absent. Immediately, however, males 15 and 1 swooped down on it and forced the stranger to leave the cliff in a northerly direction.

The careful monitoring of the submarine study population yielded data on 81 territorial conflicts between colony members at the aerial attack level and above (table 15). Their origin and outcome was related to the dominance that specific falcons had established over their neighbors. Fourteen of these involved the single male 14 that unsuccessfully tried to challenge the "rights" of male 12 to his mate and his territory. Falcons occupying the best lookout posts (protected but with a wide and commanding view) as well as comparatively large territories were found to be dominant, that is, rarely attacked or intimidated by a neighbor. Whether dominance creates the site or the site creates dominance could not be determined.

An analysis of the observed behavior patterns identifies the particularly aggressive pairs. In the left section of the submarine, male 2 was the most aggressive bird, also possessing the largest territory and the best lookout post (sheltered from above and offering an excellent updraft for taking off). His aggressions were

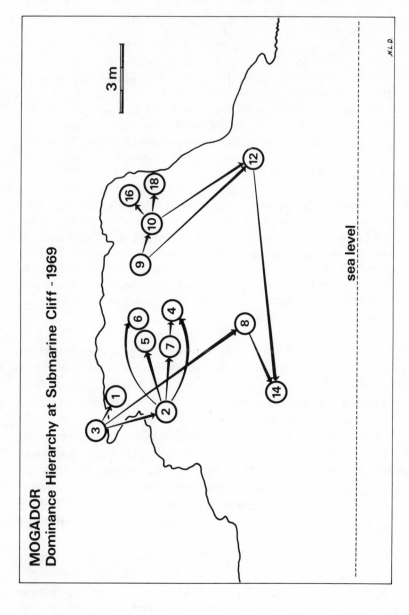

Fig. 44. Dominance patterns of male falcons on submarine cliff. Arrow points identify the falcon(s) dominated by another.

TABLE 16
Number of Physical Conflicts between Falcons on the "Left" Section of Submarine Cliff (Mogador 1969)

Attacking Falcon from Pair Number	Attacked Falcon from Pair Number								
	1	2	3	4	5/6	7	8	Unknown	Total
1								3	3
2		1		2	5	3	2	2	15
3	3	2		1					6
4		1				1			2
5/6					2			1	3
7				4					4
8									1
Unknown	4		1	2					7

mostly directed to his neighbors 4, 5, 6, and 7 which had to fly over his territory to reach their own home grounds. Pair 4 was particularly often attacked, while pair 8 was hardly attacked at all and did not attack other falcons except once (fig. 44, table 16).

It becomes evident then, that some birds were dominant over others, though it is impossible to construct a clear pecking order. Male 3 dominated males 1 and 2; male 2 dominated males 4, 5, 6, 7, and 8, and male 7 dominated male 4. In the right section, male 9 dominated males 10 and 12, while male 10 dominated males 12, 16, and 18. Male 12 fought a long battle with male 14, which it won in the end. Despite this pattern, a tense situation prevailed in this section, since male 12's favorite lookout post was dangerously close to pair 10's post (fig. 36; table 17).

TABLE 17
Number of Physical Conflicts between Falcons on the "Right" Section Of Submarine Cliff (Mogador 1969)

Attacking Falcon from Pair Number	Attacked Falcon from Pair Number								
	9	10	12	13	14[a]	16	18	Unknown	Total
9		5	1				1	5	12
10	1		6			2	1	1	11
12		1			5				6
13		1							1
14[a]			8	1					9
16								1	1
18								3	3
Unknown			1				2		3

[a]Number 14 was the only single male on the submarine cliff.

Since territories 2, 8, and 9 must be regarded as optimal locations from a strategic point of view, the size of a territory and its location above other territories seems to be directly correlated with dominance. In case of the need for defense or attack, it is important for a falcon to be above the adversary from the outset, since this makes the nose dive easier.

In accordance with the foregoing, the single male 14 occupied the lowest position of all males with regard to both social status and location of his territory. Being just a few feet above the spray zone, this male tried in vain to establish a hold on more elevated sites of the submarine cliff.

In the red-footed falcon—the only other gregarious falcon that has been studied in this respect—Horváth (1975) has detected a nearly identical dominance system. He remarks that "the old males ... occupy the most inaccessible nest in a colony, that is the control role in the rookery belongs to that pair where the male is an old bird." This suggests a direct relationship between nest site, dominance, and a falcon's maturity.

Because of our unfortunate accident I was unable to conduct any detailed study of agonistic behavior on the atoll isle and Smea. In 1966, however, and between 11 and 25 July 1969, I observed these falcon populations for a good many hours without noticing any serious fighting over territories. The atoll would offer the most interesting study area. Here many falcons were breeding in typical pigeonholes in 1969, sometimes on overhanging cliffs without ledges or pinnacles. Here territories seemed nonexistent except for the hole entrance. This would make territorial defense quite unnecessary, since a falcon would hardly attempt to land at a pigeonhole already occupied by a watchful falcon. Pigeonhole breeders among Eleonora's falcon could therefore be expected to experience few acts of territorial rivalry. This would favor very dense clusters of breeding pairs wherever the texture of the cliff offered large numbers of suitable nesting holes.

With the Paximada population, which I mostly observed at a later stage of the breeding season than in the submarine study, agonistic behavior most often occurred as a result of intrusion by "obstinate" immature Eleonora's falcons. These young falcons would systematically harass one or two specific falcons, trying to drive them off their "private" lookout posts. The adults would finally take off and chase the immatures over the hill (whence they would promptly return). Only a few acts of territorial aggression, two of them resulting from an experimental situation, were noticed in spite of many long hours of monitoring.

28 August 1965

7:30   Female 24 had hidden a prey item about 33 m from her nest. I took the dead bird and put it directly in front of her nest entrance. She was disturbed and hesitated to return to the nest. Instead, she sat down on a boulder 10 m above her nest, which lies in the middle between nests 24 and 14. Seeing this, male 14 swooped down and attacked the female. Both falcons went to the ground and fought (wing-beating) for 10 sec. Then female 24 retreated closer to her own nest.

25 August 1965

10:30   A stuffed Eleonora's falcon was placed 2 m above nest 23. Immediately after my departure, female 23 landed near the stuffed bird, then jumped on it and began to hit it on the upper back. I interfered at this moment to save the museum specimen from destruction.

8 October 1965

7:30   Male 52 caught a bird above the island. Hard pressed by several pursuing falcons, he missed his own territory when shooting down from a high altitude. He landed not far from nest 24, creating a curious and unique behavior sequence: female 24 was, of course, present at the nest; she did not attack the sudden guest, but started to bow and beg for the prey in his talons. Male 52 hesitated to deliver it, but finally female 24 succeeded in tearing it out of his bill.

Male 52 now began to bow. Female 24 had no intention of giving the prey back to the intruder. She hid it under a bush and began to drive him out of her territory. Since male 52 remained there, she attacked him several times on the ground, pounding her claws into his chest. The fight was accompanied by the most distressing high-pitched cries and continuous wingbeats. After about 10 min of heavy fighting, during which the observer had a hard time refraining from interfering to save a falcon's life, a falcon from nest 13 swooped down and helped female 24 with a number of nose dives to drive male 52 into the direction of his own territory. It appeared later that he had not been seriously injured.

In these cases two of the attacking birds were females. This normally happens when the male is absent and in the latter part of the reproductive season, when the female develops much more defensive spirit than in the initial phases of the season. It should also be noted that males attack females only when the females' partners are absent.

That more territorial rivalry was observed within the submarine group is certainly related to the earlier date of observations and the higher population density. The man-caused interruption of the normal breeding cycle may also have increased the number of aggressive incidents, since two of the pairs without eggs were sitting on the cliff all day with no "work" to do other than watching their neighbors.

A Case Study of Interrelated Sexual and Territorial Behavior

Some of the fiercest aggressive encounters observed during the 1969 monitoring period of the submarine cliff population were caused by the single male 14. In this case, fighting over territorial possession was intricately linked with and melted into rivalry and wooing behavior directed at female 12. Thus, both territorial and sexual elements appear to have constituted one single impact on female 12 that she was not able to resolve by herself. The development and the various stages of this "triangle" among our falcon study population deserve to be fully documented.

Male 14 was the only falcon that had established two possible nest sites, one on the left and one on the right part of the submarine cliff. His main lookout post was situated in one of the lowest cracks running horizontally in the central left section. This was where he landed, spread his tail, crowed, and hid his prey most frequently. Sometimes he flew from there to the far right side, just 1 m below the firmly possessed site of pair 12. Here he hid prey, fed on it and looked at the things pair 12 were pursuing. The two sites were about 12 m apart and out of sight of each other (fig. 36*B*).

Male 14 showed the typical behavior of all falcon bachelors, being excited and noisy about everything and constantly carrying prey from one place to the other. Still, by 31 July he had not yet found a mate, whereas all the other pairs on the cliff had entered the egg-laying stage and many of them even the incubation period.

On 30 July male 14 attacked male 12 from the air five times in a row, and male 12 was seen threatening male 14 when he flew swiftly to his right site after male 12 arrived with prey.

On 1 August 1969, it became clear to the observer that the two males did not quarrel about their territories or prey items, but that male 14 aimed at separating female 12 from her mate and attracting her to his own nest sites. Nobody will ever know if the events of this day were merely a logical consequence of male 14's earlier efforts with regard to female 12 or if they were sparked and facilitated by the great disruption of the colony that took place on 1 August and deprived pair 12 of its eggs. The story of this day can best be told with the help of my diary:

9:40   The egg-robber leaves the submarine cliff.

9:48   Male 12 returns to nest site where his female is sitting.

9:59   Male 14 returns to his left lookout post.

11:15 Male 14 lands at his right lookout post and is attacked by male 12; immediately, male 14 starts swooping down on nest 12, where the pair sits.

11:18 Male 14 flies air attack on nest 12.

12:15 Male 14 has been very restless; he lands and takes off, flies around the cliff, and pursues pigeons.

12:23 Male 14 flies another air attack on nest 12.

13:10 Male 12 goes into the nest hole while female 12 climbs out of it.

13:15 Pair 12 takes off, which leads to an air fight between male 12 and male 14. Female 12 lands at the left potential nest site of male 14. Male 14 lands there too.

13:32 Male 14 has an air encounter with another male (13); during his absence, the site of male 14 is visited by male 12, while female 12 is still there.

14:06 Male 14 is attacked by male 12 on one of his short orientation rounds.

14:12 Female 12 inspects the niches and holes in the crack of the cliff.

14:15 Male 14 and female 12 face each other; male 14 bows eagerly and mounts female 12 for an incomplete copulation of 3 sec; male 14 takes off.

14:28 Male 14 returns while female 12 withdraws into the crack. She then walks forward and drives male 14 off, pursuing him in the air. Afterward she returns to nest 12.

14:32 Male 14 pursues female 12, but male 12 intercepts him and the two falcons chase each other.

15:15 Female 12 sits again with male 14 in the crack at the left side.

15:24 Male 14 lands at a new place—a large hole in the lower center

of the cliff—where female 12 had landed; the male bows continuously for a few minutes, then takes off and lands at the
right site, displaying his tail and crowing like a rooster.

15:32 Female 12 returns to male 12. Male 14 starts feeding on an old
piece of prey and continues doing this until 15:50, when we
interrupt our observations.

Five days later, during our next observation session, male 14
displayed many times at his left lookout post, but we saw only one
air attack on nest 12, followed by male 14's landing at his right
site.

When we arrived at the cliff at 12:00 on 8 August, we found
female 12 sitting with male 14 on his left lookout post. At 12:10
male 14 bowed three times while female 12 was preening. Male 12
sat meanwhile on his lookout post, taking a sunbath. At 12:52
female 12 left male 14 and returned to her nest; 3 min later she
had a very long copulation with male 12 while male 14 looked on
from his nearby right lookout post. At 13:20 we witnessed another
copulation of pair 12. Shortly thereafter male 14 returned to his
left lookout post and remained there quietly, without leaving at all
for his usual rounds before 16:25, when we left the area.

When we returned two days later (10 August), we did not see
male 14 at all but noticed that pair 12 visited the left lookout post
of male 14 for about 40 min. Male 14 had obviously given up his
claim to female 12 and either had been driven away by male 12 or
had left the cliff voluntarily. He was never recorded again, and his
lookout posts were taken over by pairs 8 and 12 (figs. 39 and 40).

Dominance within the Pair Bond

The "reversed" sexual size dimorphism so commonly found in
raptors leads to the question whether a larger female is also dominant over her smaller mate. Willoughby and Cade (1964) experimented with American kestrels of different sizes in an attempt
to relate breeding success to size dimorphism. They did not find
any "consistent or marked indication of dominance-subordin-
ation relationships." Breeding "performance" was nearly identical, and the authors concluded: "size difference between the
mates has no marked effect on social or sexual behavior in captivity."

In Eleonora's falcon, the difference in size between male and
female is hardly noticeable. The male weighs only 10 to 20% less
than the female (Walter 1968a). It has already been indicated that

the female is less aggressive than the male in general, but this must not necessarily be related to the dominance relation between the male and female of a pair. Among the submarine study population, two-thirds of the aggressions were between males, another 24% were directed by males against females, and only 9% were caused by females attacking males. In no case did a male attack his own female.

10 August 1969
15:40   Male 2 was sitting about 1 m above nest in segment 2e when female 2 ran out of her nest and chased him away, pursuing her mate for about 10 m.
19 August 1969
10:27   Male 2 flew down from his lookout post to near the nest; female 2 left the nest, standing close to male 2, which bowed several times. She bit him twice, somewhat carefully, in his wing bow; this caused the male to move 20 cm away from his mate.
19 August 1969
14:32   Male 10 was taking a sunbath on a small plateau close to the border with pair 9 when his female approached him. Possibly owing to the limited space, the female bit her mate strongly in his spread wing. The male immediately folded his wings to make room for his mate.

The frequent bowing of males is a further indication of the submissive attitude that males take in front of their mates. Certainly a male would never succeed in mounting an unknown female without appeasing her first. It seems that the female continues throughout the breeding season to maintain the slight ("unspoken") but stable dominance within the pair bond that she acquires on the very first day of her relationship with a partner. This may also limit the possibility of "extramarital" relationships for these falcons. Remembering the two instances of a female's meeting with two males, we can attempt an explanation for the apparent timidness or reluctance to copulate with the willing but strange female: the male had not (yet) overcome his fear of the larger female. The latter might not have provided all the clues necessary to encourage the male's sexual behavior, particularly her assurance that she would tolerate him. On the other hand, it might have been the female that was not yet ready for this sexual encounter.

Discussion

A necessary component of Eleonora's falcon's adjustment to its ecological niche is the ability to tolerate other Eleonora's falcons at very close range. Compared with other falcons and the *Accipiter* hawks, this species is certainly less aggressive both in a spatial sense and in terms of its threshold for physical aggression. The critical area for triggering intraspecific agonistic behavior is confined to a 20 m radius around its nest scrape, whereas most eagles, hawks, and falcons will attack conspecifics much farther from their eyries. I do not think Eleonora's falcon has lost any of the characteristic attack and defense behaviors or the ritualized threat and submission postures shared by most if not all species of the genus *Falco*. In this case they have simply been adapted to a spatially reduced format, enabling the species to breed in colonies on islands and promontories that are highly advantageous in terms of hunting opportunities.

As in most gull and tern species, the availability and quantity of prey is an independent variable. The prey is passing through irrespective of the existence of falcons and their breeding density. The falcons do not need to defend a food territory against their own kind and other competitors. This important characteristic of Eleonora's niche reduces the need for agonistic behavior to defense of nest sites, perches, prey storage areas, and the family within the small ground territory. In addition, a new form of defense, the group attack against potential enemies like eagles, jaegers, and other large birds, increases the general breeding success and survival of the falcon colony.

Although slightly smaller in size, the falcon male is much more aggressive than the female falcon. The dominating male of the submarine cliff attacked other males and females alike, but females became targets only in the absence of their mates. Females generally did not attack other falcons except if the latter violated the "property rights" of the cliff by intruding into their ground territories.

In the European kestrel, Tinbergen (1940) also observed that the male plays a more active role in defending the territory than the female. Cavé (1968) experimented by placing a stuffed kestrel near the nest boxes of kestrels. The attacks by female kestrels increased greatly during the latter part of the season when nestlings were present: 90% of the attacks at this time were executed by females.

In Eleonora's falcon, Ristow and I observed a similar development at the Paximada colony. The female falcons became more and more alarmed and "annoyed" at our intrusion on their ground territories as their young grew. Their alarm calls became more intense and at times were quite unbearable for my ears.

A rather delicate relationship appears to exist between male and female of a pair. No open hostility has been observed, but the female seems able to push the male aside at will. In my opinion, display and courtship behavior serve to apprise the female of the male's friendly intentions. The submissive bowing of the male and the offerings of "love bait" appear to erode the female's antagonism and independence. During the egg-laying phase, therefore, the male achieves a temporary dominance, culminating in many copulation attempts without any prior courtship behavior. Monneret (1974), studying the agonistic behavior of peregrine falcons in the wild and in captivity, has developed a comprehensive hypothesis that attempts to explain the interspecific agonistic behavior as well as the male's hunting behavior in terms of the changing dominance relationship between the female and male of a pair. According to this hypothesis, the male's submission to a strongly aggressive female at the beginning of the breeding season (February/March) results in displacement behavior on the part of the male: he frequently attacks other birds and begins to accumulate prey items not needed for his own consumption. Hormonal factors during this prenuptial and nuptial phase would be responsible for the highly aggressive state of both birds at this time. Once the female has become used to being fed by the male, the male achieves a short period of dominance. Hormonal modifications during the incubation phase reduce the agonistic factor. Both birds (certainly so in Eleonora's falcon) are oriented toward the clutch and the nesting area, not the outside environment. After hatching, the female regains her high level of aggressivity toward the "exterior" part of the eyrie. This, according to Monneret, explains her more frequent interspecific attacks and her brusque attitude toward her mate. The peregrine male "can in practice hardly reach his eyrie due to being intercepted by his partner which literally assails him in order to get hold of his preys." During the young-raising stage, the male peregrine is dominated by the female and practically excluded from the center of his territory. The abnormal situation activates his agonistic behavior and results in high predation and the "tentative appeasement of the female through the presentation of prey items." The latter is, of course, essential for the survival of the young.

Eleonora's falcon exhibits—as said before—a reduced level of inter- and intraspecific antagonism at all times compared with the sometimes explosively aggressive state of a peregrine falcon. But Monneret's hypothesis fits the behavioral system of Eleonora's falcon well except that the colonial nature of the falcon colony requires the female to tolerate the male falcon near and at the nesting site or hole throughout the breeding period.

Acoustic Behavior of Eleonora's Falcon

Eleonora's falcon is a rather vociferous bird. In July and August—before the young are hatched—the colony is filled with the calls, screams, and echoes of the breeding birds. The repertoire of call notes is rather extensive, probably more so than in other raptors. But research seems to be in the initial stage regarding the comparative aspect and importance of acoustic communication.

Research by Tschanz (1968) on murres (*Uria aalge*) and by Beer (1970) on laughing gulls has shown how important a role acoustic communication plays in the interaction between individual birds. Murres can recognize their young by voice. Beer showed that variations of a specific call made by one gull can still be distinguished from the same call uttered by other individuals. Even rather simple calls can be varied and modified in such a way that the whereabouts and (perhaps) behavior states of individual birds can be accurately communicated to other birds (Jenni, Gambs, and Betts 1974).

M. Konishi (pers. comm.) has advanced the hypothesis that social birds should possess richer and more complex patterns of acoustic communication than solitary species. In 1965 I recorded a large number of calls of Eleonora's falcon at Paximada. The complexity of the sound spectrograms (figs. 45–48) indeed seems to indicate that individual variations and the richness of frequencies used make it easy to differentiate the sounds of individual birds at short distances.

In the following list I have attempted to include all major calls.

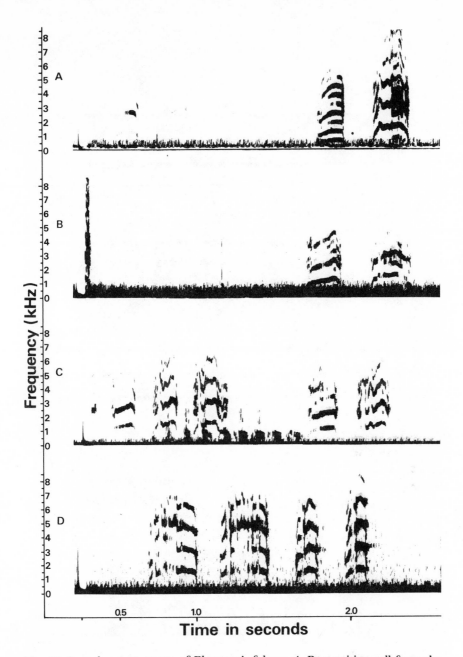

Fig. 45. Sound spectrograms of Eleonora's falcon: *A*, Recognition call from the ground. *B*, Recognition call from the air by the mate of the falcon calling in *A*. The end of call *A* appears on the far left side of spectrogram *B*. *C*, Territorial display call and sound of the "nose dive with wing flapping" aerial display, followed by a two-syllable note. *D*, recognition or territorial call from the air.

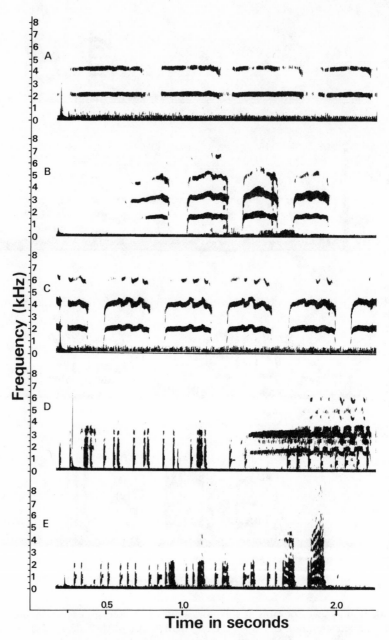

Fig. 46. *A*, "whine" call of female falcon after the loss of her clutch. *B*, Male arrives at nest with his "greeting" call. *C*, "Prey-demand" call of female falcon after arrival of the male. *D*, "Clucking" call of a female from the nest scrape followed by the loud greeting call of the arriving male. *E*, "Greeting" calls inside the nest, a rapid chickenlike clucking.

Notes at and above the Nesting Site

The following calls have a definite meaning and must be considered the principal elements of the acoustic behavior of Eleonora's falcon.

1. Recognition call. "Kyark-krew-it." Uttered in the air and shortly before landing at nesting site. Second syllable higher than first and accented, rising toward the end (fig. 45). This call is probably homologous to "waik, eeway, or wayee" note of the peregrine, described by Nelson (1970) as a recognition or contact call.

2. Territorial call: "Hey-kyerk" or "hey-kirk-kerk," with accent on the last syllable. Tone not rising. Often a very forceful note uttered right above the ground territory or next to the nesting site on steep cliffs. Rarely used when perched near nest. Particularly common as part of the "nose-dive wing-flapping" display: the male calls at the lowest point of the V-shaped trajectory (fig. 45).

3. Display call. An excited crowing "krok-krak-kuuk" of the male falcon, often after uttering the territorial call. In conjunction with fanned-tail display posture. This note seems to be rather different from Nelson's (1970) description of the male peregrine's courtship call, "eechip."

4. Copulation call. A short, repeated high "kirr" during the copulation. Not sure whether it comes from male, female, or both.

5. Greeting call between mates. "Eet-eat-yeet" is the call of the arriving partner at the nesting site. It can be compared with the "treble whine" of the American kestrel (Willoughby and Cade 1964).

6. Prey transfer demand call. Intense, somewhat threatening call of female upon male's arrival with prey. A loud and shrill "ye-err" or "yee-eet" (fig. 46) or "ky-rir-kyrt." Can last for several minutes. Female with back hunched, feathers, ruffled, beak wide open. Rare: two to three syllables, very loud and with maximum emotional pitch. Used to call the mate. This is homologue to the "whine" note in kestrels and peregrines (Willoughby and Cade 1964).

7. Prey arrival call. A soft "dyett-dyett" by the male when he arrives with prey he wants to deliver to the female.

8. Alarm call. Intense, angry-sounding call, "kak, kek, ..." issued many times by the flying bird, mostly the female, above the ground territory when disturbed by an intruding human or animal predator (fig. 47). Also used by the falcon chicks older than 17 days. Very similar to the structure of gull calls and those of jaegers (Anderson 1973, p. 13, fig. 12*e–h*), and other falcons. This is the "klee" note of the American kestrel (Willoughby and Cade 1964) and the "cacking" used by peregrines in an aggressive context (Nelson 1970).

9. Distress call. A repeated "yeert-yeert" call (fig. 46*A*). This is a modified "whine," probably signaling a high state of excitement. Once heard from a female for more than 60 min after the loss of her clutch.

10. Chuckle call. The incubating bird responds to the greeting call (no. 5) of the arriving partner with a long series of low-voiced and very short "uig-uig-uig" notes. Similar to the "clucking" of a chicken. Homologue to the "chuckle" of peregrines when brooding (Nelson 1970). This note can be heard for several minutes. It is often noticeable only within a 10 m radius around the nest. The adults also use this "chuckle" to "talk" with their young and with their eggs when shuffling them around.

Call of Fighting Falcons

Falcons that become entangled in the air during attempted prey piracy (see above) regularly emit a screaming, high-pitched note "tse-eerr." This note can also be heard in the rare event of an attack on another falcon at ground level.

Miscellaneous Flight Calls

The meaning of the following calls remains somewhat unclear. They have been noted many times throughout a breeding season. However, no particular action, response, or interaction took place following each call. In some cases, unusual notes are simply individual variations of a common call. For the time being I will refer

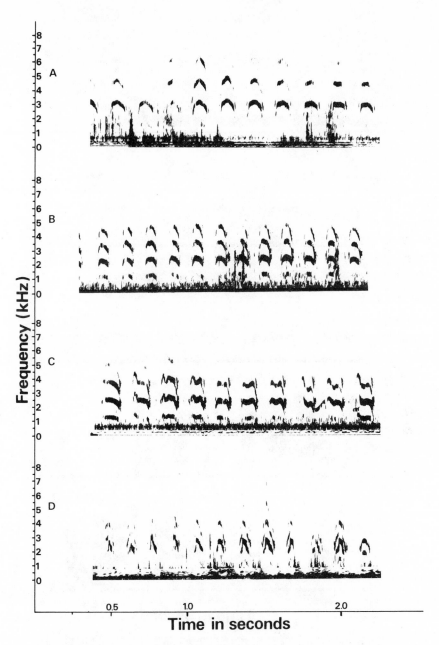

Fig. 47. Alarm calls of four different adult females from the Paximada colony.

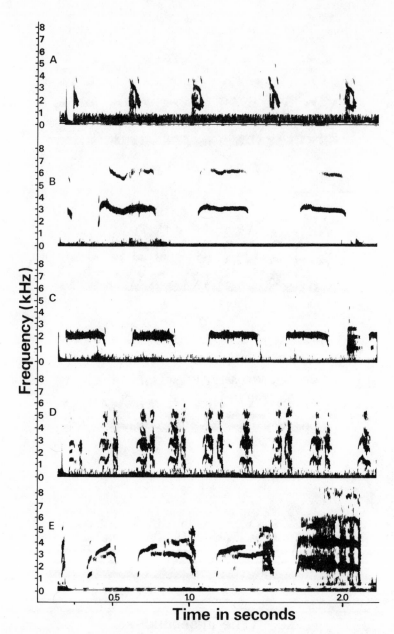

Fig. 48. Call notes of falcon chicks. *A*, Call of discomfort and cold of falcon chick "Sokrates" less than 12 hr *before* hatching occurred. *B*, Begging call of "Sokrates" one day *after* hatching. *C*, Begging call of a 12-day-old chick. *D*, Note of anger of a 13-day-old chick (call no. 21). *E*, Call of excitement of the 24-day-old "Sokrates" when upset about being held for the regular weight check.

to those notes in flight as serving the purposes of contact, identification, and nonagonistic intentions.

11. "Yi-et-yit" (short, metallic note).

12. "Dad-dad-dad ..." (5–10 times, similar to gull calls).

13. "Kyrr" (short, high note, particularly common at dusk).

14. "Dewi" (high, "thin" note like dog whistle).

15. "Tro-et" (cranelike call, rare).

16. "Raerk" (heronlike call, rare).

17. "Yi-et-yit" (short, metallic note).

Special Calls of the Young Falcon

18. "Clicking" of the egg. Up to several days before hatching.

19. Call of discomfort and coldness. "Uip-wuip" from within the
egg and throughout the brooding stage (fig. 48*A*).

20. Begging call I. "Pui-pui" during the first 10 days after hatching.
The chick wants to be fed.

21. Begging call II. "Pyeep-pyeet," long, high call of hungry chicks
older than 10 days (fig. 48).

22. Call of alarm and warning. "Pyep-pep, pyep," a short, loud
note of anger (fig. 48). Heard from chicks between 12 and 17 days
of age. Older chicks use the same alarm call as the adults (no. 8).

23. Call of excitement. "Kyerr-Kyerr" fig. 48). Heard from older
chicks at nesting site.

Discussion

At least 23 different calls have been identified, serving a considerable number of communication needs. Many of these are not
accompanied by any special ritualized posture. Owing to the
difficult acoustic environment of the breeding sites, often only the
calls of a small "neighborhood" population can be heard. Notes of
incubating birds and of the young falcons can be perceived only
for a few meters.

   At the present time, relatively few vocalization studies of raptors have been made. The available evidence certainly supports
M. Konishi's hypothesis. The acoustic behavior system of the gregarious Eleonora's falcon is much more complex than those of the
solitary peregrine (Cade 1960; Nelson 1970) and of the American
kestrel (Willoughby and Cade 1964).

   Quite clearly, a number of notes have evolved that serve (1) the
partner and family only, (2) the falcon "neighborhood" of the

surrounding falcon pairs, and (3) the general colony environment (alarm call, display call). A brief comparison of the sound spectrograms from young and adult birds appear to show a definite relationship between various calls. This might permit tracing the ontogenetic development of the adult calls to the few calls of the falcon chick. The begging call of the chick (no. 20, fig. 48B) is similar to the prey transfer demand call (no. 6, fig. 46D). The alarm call of the adult (no. 8, fig. 47A–D) is certainly an elaboration of the chick's alarm note (no. 21, fig. 48C). There can be little doubt that an in-depth study of the acoustic behavior would vastly increase our understanding of the meaning and importance of acoustic expression in Eleonora's falcon.

BEHAVIORAL DEVELOPMENT OF YOUNG FALCONS

Like other young animals, a falcon chick goes through various developmental stages (ontogeny) that equip it with more and more means of adapting to and controlling its physical and social environment.

Hatching Time

Even before hatching a falcon chick is known to emit a rhythmic "clicking" sound that seems to be the result of respiration (Brosset 1973). Shortly before leaving the eggshell the chick begins to produce the "discomfort" call (no. 18, fig. 48A) as a response to cold and to loss of contact with a warm surface (the brooding adult, the siblings). In Brosset's words (1973), the cause of this note is discomfort (generally feeling cold); therefore the chick appeals for brooding.

The second note is the hunger or begging call "pui-pui" that can be heard within the first 24 hr after hatching. At this stage the chick has a strongly developed head, open eyes, and is able to raise and open its beak just as any small passerine bird would do. The chick can probably distinguish only light and dark objects, but it will react to tactile stimuli.

The young of Eleonora's falcon does not possess an innate image of its parents. Initially and up to about the age of 12 days, a young falcon will beg for food from a human hand or other objects even in a completely natural setting like the Paximada colony. Then it begins to resent the human intruder and show an innate defensive behavior: it moves as far away as possible from the entrance to the nest scrape, throws itself on its back, and points its dangerous talons at the "aggressor." Should the latter try to come close or reach for the chick, it will rapidly push its talons forward, then retract them. This reminded me very much of "bicycling" movements of humans or apes. This very effective defensive behavior is accompanied by a nearly soundless hissing or a loud "pyep-pyep" or "kak-kak-kak" alarm call. The latter is nearly identical to that of the adult birds. During the first two weeks, falcon chicks are protected, sheltered, and frequently brooded by a parent bird. The development of the alarm call seems to be linked to the first occasions of being left alone for extended periods of time.

Spatial Behavior

The ontogeny of Eleonora's falcon does not seem to differ at all from that of the congeneric species—and nearly all of Brosset's (1973) general remarks about the genus *Falco* apply to our species. The young—when resting—prefer the darker corners of the nest environment. Beyond the age of 2 wk they frequently leave the nest scrape and begin their excursions within the ground territory. At Paximada in particular, falcon chicks were often pressed into shady rock crevices and under shrubs up to 2 to 3 m away from the original hatching place.

The behavior of the fledged bird has been mentioned before. It uses the entire ground territory for its still awkward hiking and flight attempts. The ground territory is the only safe haven for the "youngster" in this colony of falcons, and the fledgling has an excellent knowledge of the geographical coordinates of the family's territory.

According to Brosset (1973), young kestrels (*F. tinnunculus*) stay close to their parents' eyrie for exactly 26 days after fledging. Then they disappear. Similar observations were made with black kites (*Milvus migrans*). Brosset postulates the space around the eyrie (in our case the ground territory of Eleonora's falcon) as the "rallying point" or "epicenter" of the fledglings until their final departure. In Eleonora's falcon, I have not been able to study this final and definite date of severing the links to the parental ground space. If it were 26 days after fledging, we would still have most young falcons on the breeding cliffs until 25 October to 1 November of each year, some 10 days later than my own estimate based on the still scant departure data of the literature and my own Paximada observations from 6–10 October 1965. The fledgling stage is much longer in some North American peregrine populations. Nelson (1970) has observed that parents apparently support their fledglings until they "are reasonably or completely capable of fending for themselves. This stage lasts for at least one and one-half months, until the fledglings are at least 90 days of age, and it may continue considerably beyond this time."

Development of Locomotion and Senses

The newly hatched chick is a helpless white cotton ball. But by its second day it is a rather active bird. It grows rapidly and soon begins to assert itself with parents and siblings. Excerpts from my diary of study nest 8 (Paximada, 1965) illustrate some of this development.

8 September 1965
5:43   Female takes off. The chicks (16, 15, and 14 days old) are perched at the entrance to the nest scrape under a boulder, waiting. They are very active, one beating its rudimentary wings, the other two searching the ground with their beaks for food items. One scratches its head. All three bite each others' beaks, heads, and tails: this is a nibbling attempt, not a vicious or aggressive behavior.
5:49   Female returns with the second prey. The young are voracious. Two of them tear at the same piece of meat until one chick loses its balance and falls down.
6:08   Two chicks seem to be full (four birds have been fed to them so far). They move to the back of the hole, into the second line. The local lizards (*Lacerta erhardii*) move around the young to carry away meat bits. This lizard is a true commensal of Eleonora's falcon at Paximada. The falcon chicks watch and follow them closely with their eyes and heads but do not attempt to grab or kill them.
6:15   After the fifth meal the chicks have become sleepy. First one, then the others move their gray skin over their eyes.
7:28   Falcon chicks disappear into the dark corners of the nesting hole.
7:50   Female arrives with prey no. 7 and walks into nest, no chick is waiting. Female feeds herself, then moves deep into the nesting hole, where she feeds at least 1 or 2 chicks.
18 September 1965
4:45   No adult present, chicks are active (26, 25, and 24 days old).

5:20   Young are calling and walk outside nest boulder; all three are beating their wings: heads low, tails high up, only the wingtips vibrating.

5:35   Female arrives with prey (an oriole) and begins feeding the chicks. The youngest chick does not receive anything. It tears at the oriole from below, causing the female that is standing on top of the prey to lose her balance several times. The male arrives with another prey, and the two big chicks start running to him. The female continues feeding; now the youngest chick receives it share.

19 September 1965

5:23   Chicks are standing at nest entrance. They suddenly look up into the sky. Female is landing quietly with prey, begins feeding.

5:35   Oldest chick is preening itself, then vibrating wings. All chicks look up into the sky frequently and follow flying falcons with their head movements.

6:10   First chick lies down, second has difficulty keeping eyes open.

6:26   Young restless, nibble on the many feathers lying around, run out of the nest, then return and do some preening, seeming to yawn repeatedly. They often close their eyes during preening. Eldest chick pulls its primary feathers—even vibrating correctly—nibbling through its beak.

Competition between Siblings

There is a sense of camaraderie among the siblings. They compete with each other, the smallest one often finding it difficult to get enough food in the early morning. However, when the taller and elder siblings retreat into the "second line," the little one remains to be fed by the female falcon. There is some pushing, biting, and scratching between the young but never any kind of vicious fight or attempted or completed cannibalism. This, once again, agrees with Brosset's (1973) observations of kestrels and other falcons.

Conclusion

Within 24 hr after hatching, the chick of Eleonora's falcon has open eyes, crawls about the nest scrape, and wants to be fed. It makes a directional move toward a moving object and uses its begging call. During the first two weeks falcon chicks respond essentially to only two major stimuli: temperature (cold/hot, comfortable or not) and food (very hungry to stuffed with prey bits). Then a third factor begins to be perceived: danger coming from an approaching object not shaped like a falcon (how small can it be?).

If there is more than one chick in a nest, siblings grow up "teasing" each other in a nonviolent manner. Thus, interactions between siblings as well as between chicks and their parents are generally amicable to neutral at the worst.

The older chicks begin to leave the nest scrape, exploring the surrounding space within a 2 to 3 m radius. The fledged birds can be found anywhere within the ground territory. Should several falcon nests (better called "eyrie" in this case) lie above each other on a sheer cliff, the fledged falcons from several nests often congregate in a flock of 4 to 6 birds on top of the cliff. I suspect that they would rather perch near their parents' eyries but find it difficult to alight there owing to their inexperience in negotiating the strong updrafts common along such bluffs.

Some 15 days, perhaps 26 days (Brosset 1973), after fledging, the young falcons leave their parents' breeding site, heading for the winter quarters.

GENERAL DISCUSSION

In spite of the prowess of this raptor, the nature of its social interaction was generally not more or less aggressive or violent than in other gregarious and solitary bird species. This had to be expected, since too much open conflict and fighting would divert energy and attention from the other priorities of the breeding season. Acoustic signals and specific body postures used to communicate and defuse tension and conflict do not differ much from those of solitary falcons (Cade 1960; Monneret 1974; Glutz, Bauer, and Bezzel 1971). This behavioral system functioned well, providing an orderly and protective instrument for the colonies as a whole as well as for each breeding pair.

The not infrequent "intraneighborhood" conflicts on the submarine cliff were probably a combined result of extreme or near maximum breeding density on nonvertical surfaces and of the generally heightened social interaction of those pairs that had lost their entire clutches and failed to replace them (about 50%). Under these conditions the presence of a single male falcon added a stress factor further complicating coexistence on this tiny cliff. However, residents nearly always completely avoided neighboring territories even in the absence of their owners.

Visual stimuli appeared once again as decisive factors in triggering territorial behavior. The proximity of two lookout posts of different males (about 1 m apart, nos. 10 and 12, fig. 36*B*) created constant tension and a higher mobility of these pairs. Had one of them found a perch at the same distance but hidden from the view of the other male, no tension would have occurred. Many such data on the personal relationships between different individuals of the submarine study population indicate that the addition of another single male would have created so many additional "hot spots," with their accompanying agonistic behaviors, that normal breeding activities might have been adversely affected.

The high frequency of disputes over items of prey was typical in most colony segments. The prey resources of this species consist of a passing stream that fluctuates from week to week and sometimes from hour to hour depending on geographic and climatological factors. Falcons are keen to keep food provisions and may accumulate piles of killed migrant birds in their territory. These provisions are an important protein resource in times of reduced hunting success. The careful caching of prey in the Crete colony may be related to the more open terrain, a generally scarcer food supply, and the existence of commensal lizards and rats on the breeding island. This depositing of considerable quantities of captured protein in the falcon's ground territory adds an important defense factor to the territorial behavior of Eleonora's falcon that is absent in gulls and other colonial seabirds but common in social predators like lions (Schaller 1972). The high frequency of the disputes over prey was correlated with high breeding density and good visibility of prey-carrying falcons; it put the inhabitants of the atoll at a disadvantage, since they stood a good chance of being pursued and "tackled" by other cliff residents when they returned from hunting. Low density and poor visibility of incoming falcons, on the other hand, favored the undetected and dispute-free delivery of prey. The two factors, terrain structure and food piracy, should theoretically determine the optimal breeding density of Eleonora's falcon in any given locality.

Then what about this raptor's dual nature of being gregarious and a raptor as well? This species seems to have evolved several adaptive mechanisms that enable it to coexist with other colony members and still preserve its character as a raptor.

The dispersion of nest sites is related to terrain complexity and appears to be the result of an innate or acquired image of the private area needed around a falcon's nest site. This might also be considered the critical distance at which a falcon will tolerate another falcon and nest site. Important in this distance is the "landscape" factor, whose structural complexity determines or codetermines the actual distance between nest sites. If other ecological factors are constant, different physical terrain will result in different breeding densities.

The size and shape of what is essentially a microterritory in comparison with that of other raptors also varies with terrain complexity. Some pairs do not possess a territory at all. They breed in caves and pigeonholes that are inaccessible and offer great privacy; that is, neighbors have little opportunity to participate visually in a falcon's activities during the reproductive season. Thus they are secure both inter- and intraspecifically. Others have small, irregularly shaped territories whose utilization and defense indicate this species' need for visual control. In complex terrain this "landscape" factor will result in predominantly small territories of a very irregular shape, whereas in simpler, more evenly surfaced terrain, effective visual control over large areas results in relatively regular-shaped territories (fig. 42).

The reported observations on agonistic behavior also indicate why dispersion and territorial systems of different colonies are beneficial to individual falcons. Although Eleonora's falcon has a much higher distance tolerance for other members of its species than do other raptors, its raptorial nature has not in any way been suppressed. Individual survival, its possession of a mate, its young, and its stored food resources might be in danger if falcons could monitor each other's activities. Visual privacy appears to be a solution to the problem of how to combine the advantage of a colonial existence with a rather aggressive nature. (Even so, disputes over food items and territorial boundaries do occur.)

The flexible nature of the dispersion mechanism allows falcons to breed in higher densities where more complex terrains supply larger numbers of suitable nest sites. Since such sites are scarce in many parts of the Mediterranean, this might also be seen as an adaptation to maximize breeding wherever possible.

Do different ecological settings affect social interaction in this colonial raptor? The answer must be yes or no and has already been given. The basic and numerous behavior patterns related to agonistic interaction were the same in the principal study sites regardless of their rather different structure and topography.

Characteristic differences were observed in the frequency and strength of many social interactions; they were very particular even to small clusters of nest sites (" neighborhoods") and were determined by multiple factors including slope direction, the nature of the local predator/prey system, the nearest-neighbor distance (see above), the dominance level of individual falcons, and so forth.

In conclusion, the three functionally related mechanisms of dispersion, territory, and agonistic behavior are determinants of a specific optimal density for each type of terrain that is the site of a falcon colony. The term "optimal" means here the spacing out and visual isolation of pairs large enough to minimize predation and disturbance and small enough to maximize the beneficial effects of group defense and other interactions among colony members. The degree to which colony members approximate the optimal density value in practice should, at least in the long run, influence the success of coexistence in Eleonora's falcon

Sexual behavior patterns enter into this system in various ways: (1) it is the larger female that protects the nest scrape and the territory, however extensive it may be; (2) dominance and submission signals are transfered from the sexual into the territorial arena of falcon behavior; (3) the case study of single male 14 shows that it is difficult to attract a female without a suitable territory. Ultimate reproductive success in Eleonora's falcon ties in the sex partner with the factors of prey delivery and territory size and shape, as well as with dominance status in the peer group of falcon neighbors. The young falcons grow up most like solitary falcons. When very young they are well protected in the immediate nest scrape environment by a parent bird. Later they can defend themselves well, but they are usually quite safe in their parents' ground territory. The gregarious reproductive behavior therefore does not appear to have necessitated any modification of those ontogenetic behavior patterns that are commonly found in the genus *Falco*.

9 The Nonbreeding Season

For most of the year, Eleonora's falcon does not reside at its breeding quarters. Much mystery has accompanied the search for the winter range and the migration routes of this raptor, adding still another fascinating perspective to the inquiries into its habits and life cycle. In the following, I will provide some clarification of the species' whereabouts during the nonbreeding season. Still, some of the mystery remains, challenging the student of this falcon's geography and ecology.

Departure from Breeding Areas

About three months after my departure from the Paximada colony I was able to visit it again, on 11 January 1966. My professor at the University of Bonn, Dr. Günther Niethammer, had invited me to accompany him on a brief excursion to Crete. We visited mountain and coastal areas in all parts of the isle, including a visit to the isle of Elasa. There were no Eleonora's falcons anywhere. The same appears to hold true in the entire Mediterranean region. There is no documented proof of this falcon's existence from the beginning of December to March except for two recent records, of a dark-phased Eleonora's falcon at Devejra, Gozo (Maltese Islands), on 26 December 1973 (Gauci 1974), and of two individuals at the isle of San Pietro (Sardinia) on 13 December 1970 (Mocci Demartis 1973). All the other last-of-the-year records from Mogador, Mallorca, Crete, and Cyprus refer to October and November dates (see summaries in Stresemann 1954; Vaughan 1961a; Terrasse 1963).

Sielmann (in Stresemann 1956) observed at the famous Theodoros colony off Crete that on 7 October 1944 the young falcons were fledged and their parents had ceased to utter the chattering alarm calls. About a month later (10 November 1944) no falcons remained on Theodoros. Sielmann saw the last solitary

Eleonora's falcon of the year on 4 November over the man-made lake near the town of Chania (Crete).

Meinertzhagen (1940) found only some 50 falcons, mostly juveniles, at the Mogador colony on 26 October 1939. This observation is of particular interest: assuming a breeding population of at least 150 pairs, and an equal number of fledglings as a minimum estimate, certainly some 80 to 90% had already departed from the breeding sites before the first day of November.

According to Vaughan (1961a), the Cyprus population parallels this behavior: in 1957, "10 were still at one colony on 20 October, but only 3 were there on 3 November, and the last was seen on 7 November (Cyprus Ornithological Society 1957–58). In 1959, Walker tells me, 13 birds were still present on 13 October, but after 31 October "no more were seen save for one on 8 November."

The entire Paximada breeding population seemed to be present from 7 to 10 October 1965. At least all those pairs and their young that I found time to check during those days were registered. There was, however, much more disorder and excitement in the colony. Many falcons took off from the rocks at the slightest disturbance. Throughout most of the last two days, dozens of falcons were circling and spiraling high in the sky for no apparent purpose. I interpreted this at the time as a sign of social behavior while preparing for departure.

Krüper (1864) observed more than one hundred years ago on Tragonisi that the number of falcons became smaller from one day to the next between 2 and 12 October.

In spite of all these observations, some respectable sources have insisted on the year-round presence of Eleonora's falcon in the Mediterranean. These sources include Hartert (1913), Vaurie (1965), and Bezzel (1957) who, I believe, simply summarized data from the last century, that are at best unreliable or refer to species other than Eleonora's falcon.

There are, however, some unconfirmed recent data on winter observations. I myself saw two large falcons hunting starlings (*Sturnus vulgaris*) above their roosting place in the city of Cagliari (Sardinia) on 8 December 1961 at dusk. I still believe they were Eleonora's falcons. Identification was difficult, however, because of the enormous height of the pursuit and the bad light. I should add that I had not yet seen an Eleonora's falcon at that time.

At the Mogador colony I questioned several business people and local administrators. One informant maintained that a good number of falcons remain at Mogador during the winter. I asked him what the falcons would feed on during this period. His answer: "They hunt the starlings that appear in large flocks and roost at and near Mogador."

There is little doubt that millions of wintering starlings could indeed provide a suitable food source for many falcons. Further investigations are needed to determine if, where, and how many Eleonora's falcons are subsisting on such a diet in the Mediterranean during the winter.

At the present state of knowledge we have to conclude that Eleonora's falcon is generally absent from the entire Mediterranean—indeed the northern hemisphere—between December and March. The departure from the breeding colonies begins as soon as many young have reached an age of about 55 to 60 days, perhaps even earlier when breeding pairs have lost their eggs or chicks. Colonies are rapidly thinning out by the middle of October, with few or only solitary birds remaining until November. The two confirmed and the unconfirmed December and winter observations may concern late stragglers or birds on an irregular course. At best they seem to reflect the nonbreeding range of only a tiny percentage of the total world population of Eleonora's falcon.

FALL MIGRATION

Considering that there are more juveniles and adult falcons in October and November than during the rest of the year (mortality will take its regular toll), one must ask a question in need of a praiseworthy answer: Where do some 8,800 adult birds (see mean world population estimate in chap. 2) and some 5,000 to 10,000 juveniles (see productivity data discussed in chap. 3) go? A near to complete ignorance surrounds the first part of the answer: we know nothing about the migration route in the late fall period or about how the falcons migrate.

The only hypothesis that might help explain the total lack of observations comes from raptor specialist Leslie Brown (1970), who provides what I consider very intelligent thoughts relating to the migration behavior of Palearctic falcons in Kenya. He observed a group of hobbies (*F. subbuteo*) and red-footed falcons (*F.

vespertinus) near Lake Naivasha hunting insects in the air and on the ground. Both species "eventually soared to great heights and disappeared into the base of a thundercloud. I estimated that they could have gone out of sight of the naked eye at about 2,000 feet and out of view with ×12 binoculars at well over 20,000 feet. Once into the base of the cloud, they could be carried up to a very great height without effort, as glider pilots know" (p. 128). Later Brown suggests (p. 130) that it seems likely "that all of those birds [red-footed falcon, hobby, Eleonora's and sooty falcons] . . . carry out most of their migration at a great height where they are invisible or unnoticed by humans, coming to ground only to roost, catch a late finch or a bat, or to get a feed of flying termites after a shower."

The hunting behavior of Eleonora's falcon as discussed earlier in this book certainly indicates that our species is capable of such migration at great height. It would also make much sense, since the areas south of the Mediterranean Sea are dried up in late fall and thus are relatively poor in flying insects. Only in the Ethiopian highlands and the West African tropics can falcons expect to meet the amounts of rainfall that bring swarms of termites and other arthropods into the air.

The fact is that there exists only one somewhat unconfirmed observation of Eleonora's falcon in Tanzania's Ruaha National Park, some 250 miles from the coast, during November or December (Brown 1970; A. Forbes-Watson, pers. comm.). All the other records from the fall and winter period come from a somewhat unlikely corner of the world: Madagascar and the Mascarene Islands. To repeat: Eleonora's falcon disappears from the Mediterranean in October and early November; that is, some 14,000 to 29,000 falcons—perhaps even more—vanish from the ornithological record except for the Ruaha observation and a considerable number of late November to April records from islands in the Indian Ocean adjacent to southern Africa.

If for a moment we accept Madagascar as the main winter quarters of Eleonora's falcon and the obvious target of its fall migration, then we have to explain not only the lack of observations (I suggest following Brown's hypothesis of long-distance migration at great height for the time being) on the African continent but also the migration route of the Atlantic breeding population of Eleonora's falcon. How do falcons from Mogador and the

Canary Islands reach Madagascar? There is no doubt that falcons born at Mogador can be found on this minicontinent: Terrasse (1963) reports that a falcon he banded at Mogador on 11 September 1960 was found in Madagascar in the middle of January 1962 (Appendix C). This does not prove beyond a doubt, however, that this particular individual migrated from Mogador to Madagascar in one season. It could have gone to an unknown place during the first winter, then it might conceivably have mingled with a Mediterranean population during the summer of 1961. Subsequently it may have migrated to Madagascar with the Mediterranean population. Vaughan (1961a) states: "It is unlikely that the northwest African population of Eleonora's falcons migrates through the Mediterranean and Red Sea, for this would entail a northeast direction for the first few hundred miles of autumn migration, followed by an easterly flight of over 2,000 miles through the entire length of the Mediterranean, and a further 3,500 miles south down the Red Sea and the east African coast. There are, however, no records yet from the tropical west Africa."

There are still no data from West Africa or from any interior portion of this great continent other than the Ruaha observation. Contrary to Vaughan, I consider it more likely than not for the Atlantic population to winter in Madagascar and to follow exactly the described route northeast to Gibraltar, then east to the Nile, then south-southeast and south along the shores of eastern Africa. My opinion is based on the frequent occurrence of seemingly strange migration routes of bird species. For instance, a small songbird, the wheatear (*Oenanthe oenanthe*), breeds in Europe and Greenland and winters in Africa instead of in Central or South America. The explanation for this bird's voluntarily selecting a longer and perhaps more hazardous migration route is seen in the historical development of its present breeding range. The wheatear gradually colonized first western, then northern Europe, Iceland, and finally Greenland after the end of the last glaciation. Each spring, members of this species retrace this historical and gradual process that may have taken hundreds or even thousands of years. Each fall they take approximately the opposite direction, thus arriving at or near their former "dispersal center" or refuge during the last glaciation, then continuing to tropical winter quarters in Africa.

In Eleonora's falcon, a similar evolution of zoogeography has probably occurred. The initial range of this falcon in the Mediterranean basin at the end of the last glaciation quite certainly was in the Aegean Sea. Gradually, the species expanded its breeding range to the western Mediterranean and finally also to a few outposts in northwest Africa. Each spring, like the wheatear, the Atlantic breeding population retraces within weeks this expansion from the Aegean center. In the fall the populations of Morocco and the Canary Islands first return to this center (perhaps joining other populations there). Subsequently, they begin the migration to the southern hemisphere. Thus they complete a migration route that is unique because it involves a noteworthy northerly vector and points of departure and arrival that lie at opposite ends of the African continent (fig. 49).

Since coastal regions generally are richer in lakes, marshes, and humid valleys full of insects, it is not remarkable that the falcons might choose to follow the coastline rather than attempt to cross the African continent (Morocco to the Nile or Morocco to Mozambique). However, the data are not sufficient to support either hypothesis at present. As to the time span of this long migration route, we do not know when (indeed if) the bulk of the breeding population reaches Madagascar. One excellent result has come from the banding of a falcon chick from the Akrotiri colony in southern Cyprus. It was banded on 22 September 1962 and shot out of a "group of five" near Madagascar's capital city of Tananarive on 30 November 1962 (Terrasse 1963). The fledgling probably did not leave Cyprus until at least 10 October, which would require this juvenile bird to cover almost 6,000 km (straight line) in 50 days or less.

The October observations of Meinertzhagen (1940) at Mogador might indicate that at least some juveniles depart after their parents. The advantage of such a sequential departure is that the juveniles become more capable of flight and finding their own food before they leave the familiar area of the colony. The disadvantage is that the juveniles must find the proper migration route and the winter range without adult guidance. Many small passerine birds that are trans-Saharan migrant (see chap. 7 for *Lanius senator*) show this migration behavior. From the standpoint of population survival it seems indeed that it might be more important that adult birds—having proved their reproductive and

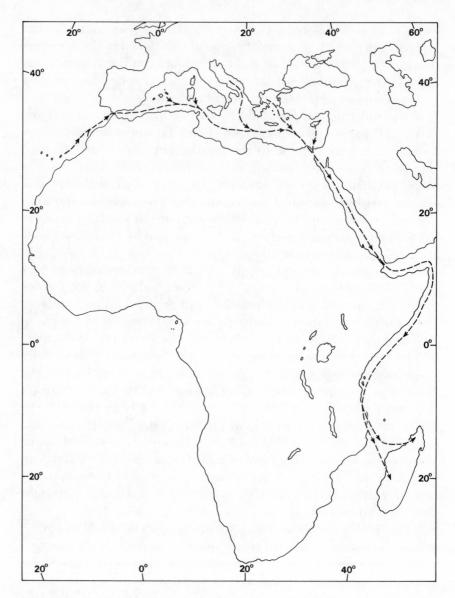

Fig. 49. Probable migration route of Eleonora's falcon after the end of the breeding season.

migration ability at least once before—should have as much time for their migration as possible. Their return is more important to the species than that of still-inexperienced juveniles.

In conclusion, we know nothing definite abou the fall migration of Eleonora's falcon. Considering a number of certified winter data from Madagascar and adjacent islands, the most probable migration route begins in the eastern Mediterranean and follows the coasts of the Red Sea and the Indian Ocean to southern Africa. Occasional excursions into the African hinterland should not be uncommon. The migration may hardly be noticeable owing to the scarcity of observers and its great height and short time period. The Eleonora's falcons that breed in the western Mediterranean and along the Atlantic coast of northwest Africa can be expected to gain the shores of the eastern Mediterranean before their southward migration.

GEOGRAPHY OF THE WINTER RANGE

The winter range of Eleonora's falcon consists of the minicontinent of Madagascar and the comparatively much smaller Mascarene Islands (Mauritius, Réunion, and Rodriguez). The existence of this range has been confirmed in three ways: (1) specimens have been collected and made into study skins that can still be inspected in museum collections; (2) banded birds have been captured or shot and the bands recovered; and (3) birds have been observed in the field. None of the three has so far yielded any data on this falcon's presence during the months of December to March in any other locality of either West, East, or South Africa, not to speak of the arid zones of the Saharan and Arabian deserts. We will therefore assume that Madagascar and the Mascarenes serve as the principal winter quarters for Eleonora's falcon.

Before we discuss the bird's ecology on Madagascar, it seems prudent to introduce the reader to the characteristic environments of this large island and to remove much of the mystique attached to the name "Madagascar" in biogeographical and conservation circles.

Topography of Madagascar

The topography and geographical position greatly affect the climate, and with it the vegetation structure and function. Madagascar lies between latitudes 12° and 25°30' south of the equator and is 400 km from southeast Africa at the narrowest point of the Channel of Mozambique. It has an area of 587,000 km² (240,000 mi²). For a size comparison: California = 158,000, Texas = 206,000, and France = 213,000 mi². There are extensive lowlands along the western coasts, but only a narrow lowland zone exists along the unusually straight east coast. Most of the island consists of hilly and mountainous terrain. Several mountain ranges reach elevations above 2,000 m, the highest mountain surpassing 2,870m (9,468 ft; Mount Tsaratanana). General accounts of the geology, economy, and human settlement structure of Madagascar can be found in Bastian's geographic text (1967), in Rand's (1936) exhaustive introductory remarks to his study "The Distribution and Habits of Madagascar Birds," and in the newer volume 21 of Monographiae Biologicae (Battistini and Richard-Vindard 1972).

Climate of Madagascar

The island's climate is wholly tropical but shows great variations owing to the effect of altitude and geographic location. The January isotherms are 27° to 28°C in the western lowlands and less than 16°C in portions of the central highlands. The July isotherms lie between 18° and 24°C in the coastal belts. At this time (the southern winter season) the mean monthly temperature drops well below 14°C over an extensive zone of the central and southern highlands (Bastian 1967).

Humidity and rainfall vary greatly and are closely related to the prevailing wind systems in the southwest Indian Ocean area. The east coast has no dry season at all, with rainfall varying between 1,529.6 mm at Fort-Dauphin in the south and more than 5,000 mm at Ile Ste. Marie. This is a result of moisture brought to Madagascar by the continually blowing east trade winds. Rainfall decreases over the highest mountain plateaus, varying between 1,000 and 1,900 mm. Here we see a seasonal pulse that is also evident in the western lowlands. There is a near total lack of precipitation during the local winter months May through September. The bulk of the annual rainfall is received from December to March when the northwest trade winds reach the island. The block diagrams of mean monthly rainfall in figure 50 illustrate the extent of the dry and wet seasons for the principal west coast and mountain towns.

The southwest third of Madagascar receives less than 1,000 mm of rainfall. Toward the southwest tip of the island, rainfall diminishes to below 500 and even 350 mm, creating an extensive arid zone that contrasts sharply with the physical environment of the central east coast.

Madagascar Habitats

Madagascar has suffered more from rapid and dangerous soil erosion in recent decades than most other countries. Human modification of the landscape, particularly the destruction of forests, has been the main factor causing this deterioration of an ecologically fragile tropical environment. The reconstruction of the original vegetation communities is not difficult, since (often spectacular) remnants of a former more extensive natural vegetation can be found in many places. Generally, Madagascar was covered by four vegetation types:
1. The dense rain forest of the east coast.
2. The more open rain forests of the central highlands, becoming more impoverished and open with altitude.
3. The dry and deciduous forest of the west coast.
4. The subdesert scrub of the southwest that has largely escaped human destruction "because of the scarcity of combustible material" (Rand 1936).
Just a few hundred or perhaps thousands of years ago, Madagascar is believed to have had a wetter climate, that is, more swamps and lakes (Moreau 1966). That would have created even better conditions for aerial raptors like Eleonora's falcon than exist there today.
During my stay in Madagascar (16 December 1973 to 3 January 1974), I visited the western, central, and southeastern parts of the island. There was heavy rainfall from thunderclouds nearly everywhere at least once a day. The major landscapes encountered were as follows: The highlands were covered with large plantations of exotic American pine and Australian eucalyptus trees. The west coast lowlands were covered with open brush or with baobab-rich savanna. Insects abounded nearly everywhere, but particularly near the west coast lowlands (Majunga and Morondava). There were marshes, lakes, and humid valleys all over the island except in the arid southeast.

FALCON ECOLOGY AND BEHAVIOR

In 1954 Erwin Stresemann published a short article entitled "On the Question of the Migration of Eleonora's Falcon": In this paper Stresemann brought together all available records from the non-breeding season. He counted eight from Madagascar and one from the neighboring isle of Réunion. "The fact that there are only such few [records] cannot weaken my argument that the Madagascar space constitutes the normal winter quarters of the Eleonora's falcon" (Stresemann 1954, p. 183).

Up to the year 1963, a total of ten records comprising eleven different individuals from various parts of Madagascar had been collected. Since then, the number of records has more than dou-bled and the number of falcons observed has more than tripled. The chronological list of all records (Appendix C) contains the data, places, and sources. Figure 50 shows at a glance where Eleonora's falcons have so far been discovered on Madagascar. A concentration of observations in the north and in the central high-lands of the island is apparent. The future will tell us to what an extent population density (causing more shooting of birds) and the higher frequency of ornithologists in certain areas is responsi-ble for this uneven distribution of falcon records over the entire island. More banding efforts in the breeding areas will undoub-tedly result in additional Madagascar records. Ornithological sa-faris will meet this species in the field. At this point my guess is that the species is fairly evenly dispersed over Madagascar except in the arid southwestern environment, where it should be uncommon.

Activities, Feeding, and Behavior

Apart from the geographical locations of the Madagascar record, very little is known about ecology and behavior in the winter habitat. Rand (1936) secured his specimen when "it was perched on a stub in a freshly burned-over area in the forest." Salvan (1970) regularly observed birds of this species "hunting insects and small birds over the lake" (Lake Ambohibao) near Tanana-rive's airport at dusk between 2 March and 3 April 1970. The author does not say how he identified the falcons. A. Forbes-Watson saw only sooty falcons hawking insects over the reed beds of this lake on 16 April 1971 (pers. comm.).

The only other observation and behavioral comment stem

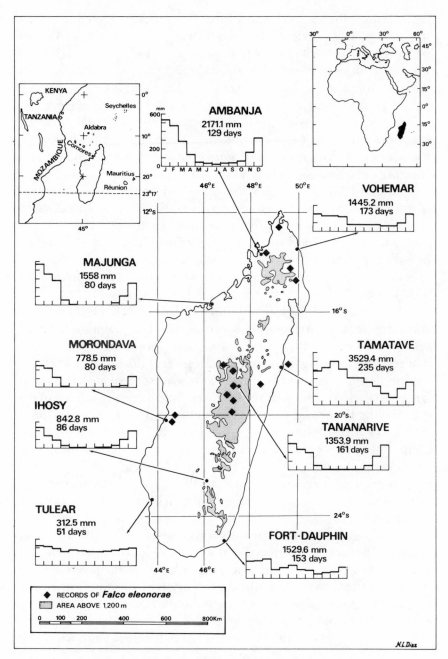

Fig. 50. The wintering area of Eleonora's falcon.

from Milon, Petter, and Randrianasolo (1973): "They hunt often in a group. It is particularly active during the evening, and it may be often observed—like *Falco newtoni* [Madagascar kestrel]— hovering on a spot with a widely spread tail . . . . It hunts in the surroundings and even in the city (of Tananarive) itself, particularly during the evening hours, accompanied by *Falco newtoni*."

This, to my knowledge, is the only record of truly hovering Eleonora's falcons. Considering the all-round nature of this raptor species, it does not sound improbable for it to copy a typical hunting behavior of the kestrel group.

Milon and his co-workers also observed "numerous individuals flying just above the trees in company of *Falco concolor* in order to capture Cetoines [beetles] from the [tree] in florescences." Having summarized the food sources of Eleonora's falcon during the breeding season, the authors conclude with respect to the non-breeding season: "In Madagascar, it seems often to nourish itself with insects."

Between 24 and 26 December 1973 I observed Eleonora's falcon daily in the environs of Morondava. The habitats used for feeding consisted of a mixed and man-modified coastal plain. There were large agricultural areas (several dozen hectares) with dry or flooded rice fields; there were forest clearings not much larger than 1 or 2 ha where the forest had recently been burned out, leaving the major tree trunks standing, and there was a dense secondary forest, often only 5 to 10 m high. Towering high (some 25 to 40 m) above this tall scrub were the truly majestic Madagascar representatives of the baobab tree (*Adansonia*) that is so well known from Africa and Australia. The climate was tropical for this time of the year: hot, muggy, and rich in rainwater pouring down during thunderstorms. These storms began as early as noon and would generally last for only a couple of hours. Blue sky was frequent before and after the numerous cloudbursts. This was only the beginning of that year's wet season. Rain pools already dotted all the unpaved roads, and many had become impassable by car. Irrigation ditches and many fields were also filled.

I observed only a few Eleonora's falcons near Morondava with certainty. Most of the falcons in the baobab forest were wintering sooty falcons (*F. concolor*).

This falcon is a good deal smaller than Eleonora's falcon, but without a direct comparison the two species are not easily distinguished from each other. The adult sooty falcon also comes in two color phases, both of which are darker than the light phase of Eleonora's and lighter than its dark phase. Immature sooty falcons apparently look either like an adult bird, with more or less uniform dark gray or sooty checks, chest, and belly, or very similar to hobby falcons or light-phased Eleonora's falcons. Stresemann (1955) must be given credit for calling attention to this light immature plumage.

The ratio was 10:1 or even higher in favor of this sibling species of Eleonora's falcon. As a result of bad light (rain, dusk, distance) it was often impossible to distinguish the two species at all. Thus, in the following, as much will be said about the sooty falcon as about Eleonora's falcon, if not more. The sooty falcon almost always occurred in small groups. These were rather loose units. Several falcons were perched in the same tree or within about 100 m radius, but they never were closer to each other than some 4 to 6 m. Most groups did not contain any Eleonora's falcons. Eleonora's falcon did not deviate from the normal behavioral patterns of the more numerous species except that it asserted itself as dominant (probably as a result of larger size) over the sooty falcon. It also appeared to be rather solitary, joining groups of sooty falcons for short periods of time.

Falcons were already found hunting shortly after 8:00 in the morning (the earliest I was able to be in the falcon habitat). Others were quietly perched in trees. The sooty falcons clearly preferred to perch on the outer branches, which frequently were leafless stems sticking out of the canopy. If not, they preferred to perch in leafless trees. The highest perches were of course those in the amazingly small crowns of the tall baobab trees. There the falcons were well hidden from view and partly shielded from the sun. Eleonora's falcons used the same perches, certainly a revelation for me, since I had never seen an Eleonora's falcon perched on anything other than a cliff or a sand dune.

Each falcon group was a rather temporary social unit. After some 10 to 15 min some new falcon would join the group or one or more would leave for an insect-hawking excursion. Thus there was constant movement of individuals if the observer remained for a while at the same site.

During periods of moderate to heavy rainfall the falcons remained on their perches. But as soon as the sun broke through

again, or when it had stopped raining, some falcons were back in
the air, swooping up and down, circling high in the sky, or zoom-
ing by at high speed just above the crowns of the baobab forest.
This went on well into the dusk, when photography with normal
film speeds (ASA 64–DIN 18) had become impossible.

I have described the activity pattern in this way because there
was no consistency except for the regular alternation between
periods of resting and flight. Falcon activity appeared to differ
every day of the three days I spent there, owing to the time variations in the frequent tropical cloudbursts. The most interesting
observation of these falcons occurred on 26 December 1973 when
I traveled with my host, Mr. Pieninck, along the road between the
village of Andranomena and the town of Morondava in western
Madagascar. It had just stopped raining, there was no wind, and
the sun's rays broke through the clouds. At 17:50, over a small
clearing, 6 to 8 falcons were hunting diligently at between 20 and
100 m height for some small aerial plankton (certainly no large
dragonflies). The birds also were feeding themselves in the air.
Among them was a light-phased Eleonora's falcon. I gradually
moved out of view with the rest of the group toward the west. But
other falcons arrived from the east, crossing over the road. Soon I
counted more than 25 falcons. All of them were sooty falcons
except the single Eleonora's. Some were molting heavily in their
wings, and many had tapered tails. In general, the sooty falcon's
flight silhouette was more rounded than that of Eleonora's falcon
owing to a shorter and thicker head and a shorter tail.

We drove on, counting another 42 falcons crossing over the
road east to west. We searched another clearing in the forest with
more than 20 falcons swooping around the sky. Once again, all of
them were sooty falcons except a rather reddish light-phased
Eleonora's falcon. I took many photographs, and we gave up
counting. No doubt hundreds of sooty falcons and a few Eleonora's falcons were flying above this rainsoaked open baobab
forest. The ratio of light-phased Eleonora's falcons to all other
falcons was between 1:10 and 1:30.

We continued to see falcons insect-hawking over this habitat at
dusk until we reached the bridge of the Morondava River. To the
west of it, where the large rice fields are situated and where I had
still seen a sooty falcon this morning, there were no falcons at all.

Unfortunately, from the ground I was not able to detect the

food source for this particular concentration of falcons. I suspect it consisted of insects arising from the bush and forest environment, probably from the leaves of tall trees.

This last observation confirmed my assumption about the relative commonness of the two Palearctic falcons in this Morondava sector of Madagascar around Christmastime. From the air, it was evident that this secondary forest covered a rather extensive area. As early as 25 December, I estimated a minimum density of 5 sooty falcons per km², or 500 for a 10 × 10 km area. I crisscrossed at least 1,000 km² of this habitat: could there have been some 5,000 falcons in this area? Why not? If there are 1,900 to 7,300 breeding pairs of Eleonora's falcons on earth (see chap. 2), then there ought to be many more sooty falcons (Moreau 1969), since they have been detected much more frequently than Eleonora's falcon in other parts of Madagascar and on the coast of eastern Africa. Since only a few breeding areas of the sooty falcon have been discovered so far, it appears that many major breeding islands of this raptor remain to be discovered.

There were certainly fewer than 500 light-phased adult individuals of Eleonora's falcon over the 1,000 km² area near Morondava. Some of the light-colored falcons were undoubtedly immature sooty falcons (Stresemann 1955). Since the dark phase of Eleonora's falcon makes up one-fourth of the total population (see chap. 3), we can further calculate that not more than 125 of the dark falcons in the Madagascar sky were the larger dark-phased Eleonora's falcons.

Spring Migration and Return to the Mediterranean Region

It is unlikely that all the Eleonora's falcons leave the wintering area in Madagascar and the Mascarene Islands within a couple of days. More likely is a gradual departure and beginning of the long migration route. The first birds may leave as early as the end of February, the majority probably depart in March, and a few linger on in Madagascar until the middle of April. Four of the 23 records of Eleonora's falcon from Madagascar were made by A. Forbes-Watson (pers. comm.) between 10 and 14 April 1971. So far, nobody has seen this raptor in its winter quarters after mid-April.

Once again, little is known about the spring migration of this falcon. Archer (Archer and Goodman 1937) observed and shot 3 birds on 17 May 1919 and 2 on 5 May 1920 in what was then British Somaliland. Meinertzhagen (1954) added a record from the Gulf of Suez on 12 April 1948.

In the Mediterranean itself, in recent years more and more early spring records of Eleonora's falcon have been obtained in a number of locations. Vaughan (1961a) and Terrasse (1963) list more than a dozen records from various sources. All but two fall into the second half of April. The exceptions are a 7 March record of "a dark Eleonora's falcon near Mandria," Cyprus (Bannermann and Bannerman 1958), and the 6 April 1945 record of a single specimen on the isle of Theodoros off Crete (Stresemann 1954, 1956).

The additional information on the return of Eleonora's falcon is given here beginning with the eastern Mediterranean. On Cyprus in 1972, the first Eleonora's falcons were seen on 25 April (1 ind.) and 26 April (4 ind.) at Akrotiri Cliffs (Cyprus Ornithological Society [C.O.S.] 1973). At another location, Cape Andreas, migrating Eleonora's falcons were seen flying in from the east and northeast, moving to the south and west on 26, 27, and 30 April (C.O.S. 1973).

Ralfs (1961) observed Eleonora's falcon only on 25 and 27 April 1958 "near Rodini and above the city of Rhodos" on Rhodos Island. Kinzelbach and Martens (1965) saw 6 Eleonora's falcons on 29 and 30 March 1963 on Karpathos, 3 of them apparently migrating from the east and from the sea toward the Kyriaki Peninsula.

Di Carlo (1966) saw the first Eleonora's falcon on the Tremiti Isles in the Adriatic Sea on 25 March 1964. On Malta, single falcons were observed in 1973 on 24 April and on 1, 8, and 24 May (Gauci 1974).

In Sardinia, H. Schumann (pers. comm.) saw one falcon each on 25 and 28 April 1961 near Tempio and Alghero respectively. I myself saw a dark-phased Eleonora's falcon at the Sardinian west coast near Tharros on 8 April 1962.

These observations indicate that an advance group of Eleonora's falcons may in some years arrive as early as the end of March and the beginning of April. The most frequently reported arrival date from a large number of locations in the eastern and western Mediterranean appears to be 25 April. I interpret this to mean that by the end of April a sizable number of falcons have not only reached the Mediterranean but dispersed over the eastern, central, and western Mediterranean.

What about the Atlantic population? According to Bannerman (1919), they appear to return in mid-May or perhaps even later at Mogador and the Canary Islands. Such a delay would be consistent with the hypothesis of a longer migration route around northern and eastern Africa for this population of Eleonora's falcon. More observations and a generally increased ornithological activity in the Moroccan/Canary Islands region are needed to confirm this relatively late spring arrival.

Regarding the spring migration, two further observations have to be mentioned. First, Archer (1937) observed in Somalia that the habits of Eleonora's falcon and of the hobby falcon (*F. subbuteo*) are identical during migration. Both species were insect-hawking in mixed groups high in the sky shortly before sunset, particularly after rain had fallen. During the heat of the day, Archer saw several Eleonora's falcons resting in some of the larger thorn trees. He concluded that they fed in Somalia almost exclusively on dusk-loving insects (retranslated into English from Stresemann 1954). This observation fits well into the general picture of the falcon's ecology during the nonbreeding season. It is nearly identical to my own Madagascar observations except that there were baobabs instead of thorn trees on the minicontinent. Archer's observation is very important as a documentation of this species' reliance on invertebrate food during the migration period. It also demonstrates an overlap with the hobby falcon (and probably the red-footed falcon as well) in food resources and hunting behavior.

The second observation was made near Philippeville (today's Skikda, Algeria) on 16 May 1882 by Dixon, who saw close to a hundred Eleonora's falcons passing through the area. This was reported in 1915 by Oustalet, as quoted by Lavauden (1924). The latter—no reasons given—believes that the birds must have been red-footed falcons (*F. vespertinus*). Considering our present knowledge of the existence of Algerian and Atlantic populations of Eleonora's falcon, I find no cause for an argument about Dixon's observation (see also Mayaud's editorial comment in Laferrère 1960). Such a large group of falcons may have been either a local breeding population from the Algerian coast or even a migrating group on its way to the breeding areas in the western

Mediterranean or the Atlantic. Both possibilities are of interest. They would demonstrate the presence of all or most falcons belonging to the local breeding colony in mid-May or the existence of migration in a large group of individuals.

GEOGRAPHICAL DISPERSION OF JUVENILES AND SUBADULTS DURING SPRING AND SUMMER MONTHS

Most Eleonora's falcons probably begin their first breeding season at the end of their second year. The laborious and praiseworthy banding efforts of Terrasse (1963) and Ristow (1975) have provided some answers to the whereabouts of the first- and second-year falcons within the Mediterranean region (fig. 51).

During their first spring and summer as fledged birds, the juveniles—as in many other bird species—do no seem tied to their birthplaces at all. Rather, an exploration of regions far to the north, east, and west has been carried out by those falcons that were recovered within roughly a year after being banded as chicks.

Terrasse (1963) reports that a juvenile from the Mogador colony (banded there on 11 September 1960) was found some 1,150 km northeast of its birthplace at Novaredonda, Central Spain (40°21′ N, 5°08′ W) on 16 September 1961. Ristow and I banded hundreds of young Eleonora's falcons on Paximada during the 1965 breeding season. Three of them were found dead or shot in September 1966 on the island of Khios (Greece), more than 250 km north of Paximada.

Two other recoveries are long-distance dispersals. One falcon, hatched on Paximada near Crete, was found a year later in eastern Corsica, more than 1,600 km to the northwest. Another one, however, moved into the coastal environs of the southwest Black Sea at Ordu, Turkey (41°00′ N, 37°52′ E). This represents the first record of Eleonora's falcon for the entire Black Sea coast except in the immediate area of the Bosphorus. This is some 1,250 km northeast of Paximada.

Two subadult falcons from Paximada were shot in their second summer after birth on Malta in the channel of Sicily, one on 1 May 1973 and the other on 9 September 1971. Since Maltese ornithologists insist the species does not breed on Malta (Ristow 1975 and pers. comm.), these records indicate that at least some

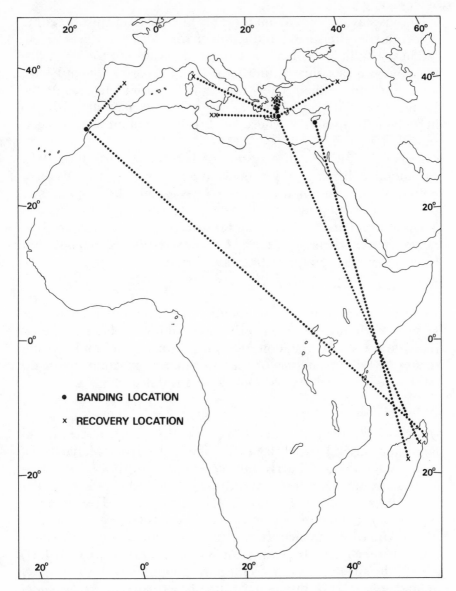

Fig. 51. Dispersion of immature falcons: banding recoveries within first two years of age.

subadults stay far away from their birthplaces (and later breeding areas) during the spring and summer (fig. 51).

These banding records are a surprise because of the large distance between Paximada and the place of recovery. Since I have never seen more than a few nonadult Eleonora's falcons at the Paximada and Mogador cliffs, however, it is not at all surprising to find them in locations where no breeding colonies have been recorded.

In conclusion, the first results of banding efforts indicate a considerable dispersal of juvenile and immature or subadult Eleonora's falcons from their parents' colony during the first and second summers of their postfledgling life. Recoveries in central Spain and northeast Turkey lie far outside the present breeding range of the species. Nothing is known about the ecology and behavior of these nonbreeding populations.

DISCUSSION

In this chapter I have attempted to draw together all that is known—certainly not much at this point in time—about the geography and ecology of Eleonora's falcon during the nonbreeding season. A holistic analysis of the available information opens up several general perspectives on Eleonora's falcon.

Annual Cycle

The available data on departure from the Mediterranean, fall migration, arrival in Madagascar, departure from Madagascar, spring migration, and arrival in the Mediterranean can be translated into a graphic scheme of the time-related whereabouts of the entire population of Eleonora's falcon (fig. 52). The result is somewhat startling, since it shows that there is no clear-cut migration season during which the entire world population of this raptor is neither in the breeding nor in the wintering area. In fact, during the spring, some percentage of the population still lingers in Madagascar while others have already returned to the Mediterranean. At best, shortly before 1 December, there may in general be a few days when all falcons find themselves somewhere along the migration route. Thus, bell-shaped curves seem to best describe the gradual departure and arrival in both wintering and breeding areas. A further extrapolation of the data presented in this chapter suggests that there is only a short period during

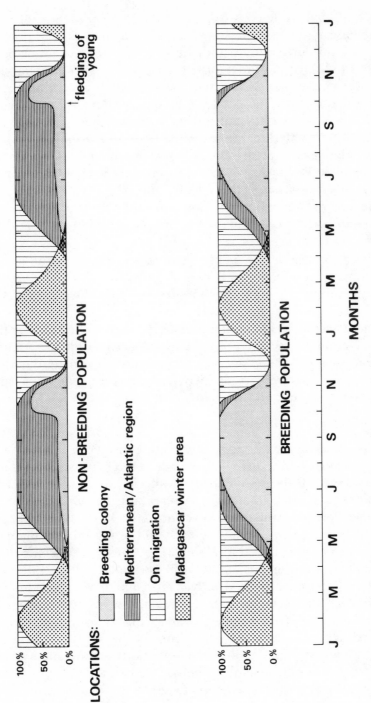

LOCATIONS:

- Breeding colony
- Mediterranean/Atlantic region
- On migration
- Madagascar winter area

NON-BREEDING POPULATION

fledging of young

BREEDING POPULATION

MONTHS

J M M J S N J M M J S N J

Fig. 52. Model of the dispersion of the world population of Eleonora's falcon between breeding, migration, and wintering areas over a period of 24 months. Note the difference between the breeding and nonbreeding populations.

which all mature falcons—100% of the adult population—are in Madagascar (and the Mascarenes). Falcons leaving the breeding colonies no earlier than mid- or late November cannot be expected to arrive in Madagascar before January or February. On the other hand, the early arrivals at the end of March and beginning of April must have left the Madagascar region in February. There remains a tiny chance that some of these late and early records in the Mediterranean come from individuals not wintering in Madagascar at all. This is, however, an entirely hypothetical argument as long as there are no supporting data. The interesting result of the analysis of this falcon's annual cycle is therefore that some part of the total population is always somewhere apart from the main body except during the breeding period from mid-July to mid-October.

Figure 52 also looks at the dynamic geography of the juvenile and immature Eleonora's falcon. Presumably, these birds behave like the adults during the two migrations and the winter period. During the prebreeding and the breeding season, however, most of them are not resident at a breeding colony. They appear to be rather nomadic, not tied to a particular area within the Mediterranean region. When they reach their maturity during their third year (sometimes perhaps as early as the second year) they can be expected to return to the environs of their birthplace.

Falcon Geography in Madagascar

It was certainly rewarding to observe Eleonora's falcon in the few places where I found it. It is equally interesting that I failed to record any of the two Palearctic species in any of the other localities I visited: Majunga, Ankarafantsika, Bongolava, Ankazobe, Perinet, Ambatolampty, and Lake Itasy. Why were they absent? Perhaps it was still too early in the season and many falcons had not yet arrived in Madagascar. More prey seemed to be available in the rain-soaked western lowlands and the Bongolava plateau than in the misty, drizzly, cool Tananarive environment of Ivato Airport. Nevertheless, the falcons seem to frequent the Tananarive environs regularly, since almost everybody has recorded one or both of the two falcon species in the region of the central highlands. More falcon observations and detailed weather records need to be assembled before we can attempt to correlate falcon appearance with climatic factors.

Falcon Population Size in Madagascar

Considering that there are thousands of Eleonora's falcons, should not this species be more common in Madagascar than it was found to be? Not necessarily.

The population estimates (chap. 2) give a figure of 1,900 pairs as the *minimum* breeding population and 7,300 pairs as the estimated *maximum* breeding population. If the entire population of Eleonora's falcon were evenly dispersed over Madagascar, each falcon would theoretically have from 41 to 156 km² for itself. Since the falcons tend to concentrate in certain preferred habitats (lakes), we can indeed expect to find a good deal of land without any Eleonora's falcons. Even considering the maximum possible total population at year's end, including some nonbreeding immature individuals, to boost the total figure to about 20,000 adults and an additional 10,000 juveniles to make a round figure of about 30,000 Eleonora's falcons, each falcon could still "own" some 20 km² without having to share it with conspecifics. Thus the Madagascar minicontinent seems well capable of "swallowing" up large numbers of falcons because of its size and habitat diversity.

Much more research is necessary to determine what, if any, directed and seasonal movements occur within the region of Madagascar. Also, how many falcons move from Madagascar to the Mascarene Islands? It is somewhat perplexing that so many sooty falcons and some Eleonora's falcons have been observed in Madagascar in March and in April when other Eleonora's falcons have already arrived at their breeding cliffs in the Mediterranean.

Falcon Ecology in Madagascar

As expected, the falcons showed the same hunting behavior as known from the prebreeding season in the Mediterranean. The main difference was that the birds regularly rested on trees as lookout posts. There was an abundance of food available, particularly during sunny periods and after the tropical downpours. The hunting of small birds was attempted but probably rarely crowned by success.

Eleonora's falcon may be completely nomadic in the winter range, flying here and there without any particular destination for as long as the food sources support this behavior. Or it may develop a trend toward at least partial "residency" in a particular area, remaining there for days, weeks, or months. Only increased banding efforts will be able to shed light on those aspects of falcon ecology. Sophisticated telemetry could go further still but seems to be out of reach for the moment.

Interspecific Competition

Eleonora's falcon was usually not associated in any obvious way with a group of sooty falcons. Several times I had the impression that a single Eleonora's falcon entered a group of sooty falcons by accident, found it convenient to remain for a short time, then left.

There is no resident bird of prey on Madagascar that feeds on small flying objects. The only other potential competitors for insect food are swallows, swifts, nightjars, and the Madagascar broadbilled roller (*Eurystomus glaucurus*), a large bird that frequently perches on top of a tree, venturing into the air in a falcon-like move in pursuit of a flying insect. None of those, however, were found to be truly competitive. Most of all, swallows and swifts were not nearly as common as one might expect, and Moreau (1966) found the number of swallow species below expectation (only two species). Moreau also suggested that the lack of competition from other raptors might be the main factor making Madagascar the main winter range of sooty falcons and Eleonora's falcons. This appears to be a sound ecological explanation, and I shall contribute additional evidence from the evolutionary past of these two raptors in the next chapter.

10 Evolutionary Ecology

In the preceding chapters we have accompanied Eleonora's falcon to all its geographical locations, through the various seasons of the year, and from the nestling to the adult stage. This chapter and the next summarize, compare, and interpret the data that have been presented in order to arrive at conclusions or hypotheses relevant to modern raptor ecology and the growing field of sociobiology.

In this chapter I shall first contrast the major features of the two study colonies on Paximada and on the Isles of Mogador. This will permit us to separate the specific and local adaptations from the general, specieswide characters of Eleonora's falcon. We shall then discuss the "absence" of Eleonora's or any equivalent raptor in the New World. Finally, I shall make an attempt to probe into the rather misty past of our species looking for relatives and isolating mechanisms.

Comparing Atlantic and Aegean Populations

All Eleonora's falcons occupy the same ecological niche, but each colony has evolved its own specific behavior and strategies to optimize its hunting and reproductive success (to increase its fitness). We have seen that the geographical position of a given colony determines which diurnal periods have low and high bird migration density. Falcons appear to adapt their hunting activities to the migration pulse of their local environment. In addition, hunting altitude and distance from the colony site were shown to be related to the flight behavior of the average trans-Saharan migrant in different locations.

In the following, I will make a brief comparison of the Mogador and Paximada colonies so as to evaluate the importance and cause of the many differences in the reproductive biology and ecology of these two colonies, situated close to the extreme west and east of the range of Eleonora's falcon.

Geography

The Atlantic coast near central Morocco is much cooler than the Aegean Sea environment near Paximada. Fog is frequent at Mogador but is totally absent from Paximada between July and October.

The Atlantic population of Eleonora's falcon is much smaller than the Aegean population. Nevertheless, the Mogador breeding population is certainly not isolated from other populations to the north and west (Canaries).

Population Ecology

There appears to be little difference regarding the phase ratio of the two colonies: the dark phase makes up only about one-fourth of all adults. At Paximada, females of the dark phase had slightly less breeding success than females of the light phase in the same colony: fewer eggs hatched out, and the mean number of fledglings was down (table 30). Mogador data were not available.

Mogador had a much higher clutch size and a larger number of young and fledglings (table 3) than Paximada. This difference appears to be a general characteristic of the Mogador population in contrast to all other colonies of Eleonora's falcon studied so far in the Mediterranean.

The hatching time at Mogador is a few days earlier than at Paximada (table 6). Though there are regularly three to four chicks per pair, the growth rates of Mogador falcon chicks were equal to or better than those of the Paximada colony. The mortality rate of young falcons was higher at Paximada, probably due in part to the large numbers of rats and hole-breeding shearwaters.

Population Behavior

The breeding density at Mogador was much higher than that at Paximada. Ground territories were smaller and of irregular shape at Mogador, larger and circular or oval at Paximada. No differences were found in sexual and agonistic behaviors, but more comprehensive studies might discover such differences. Prey piracy was found to be more common in the atoll part of the Mogador colony than in other parts of this or the Paximada site.

Hunting Behavior and Ecology

The hunting strategies of these two colonies differed considerably (see fig. 17) and were directly related to the nature of the migration pulse at each colony. It seems that the total energy expended by all falcons at each colony optimized the hunting success ratio: except for a few unusual individuals, the large majority of falcons hunted only during periods of high migration density.

Bird hunting began much earlier in Mogador than at Paximada throughout several breeding seasons. In 1969, the Mogador population was preying on bird migrants before the incubation stage in July (Walter, this study), whereas falcons at Paximada were still short of migrant food in the latter part of August (Lammers 1976). Hunting success was higher in this bird than in other raptors as a result of gregarious hunting. Whether the success ratio differs between the two colonies could not be assessed because the prey environments differed.

Prey Composition and Numbers

Twice as many bird prey remains were collected at the study nests of Mogador as at Paximada (table 11). These collected feather remains represented only a small part of the number of birds captured and fed to the young falcons. The principal prey species differed between the two colonies. The migratory habits of these trans-Saharan migrants explain the early beginning of the migration season at Mogador. The concentration of migrants in the southwest Iberian peninsula appears to be largely responsible for high migration density in the Mogador colony. The large distance between the departure point of migrants and their arrival point at Mogador seems to explain the longer daily hunting activity at Mogador.

In the Aegean colony, the falcons used only a brief hunting period during the early morning hours to capture migrants. This also seemed related to source areas and migration distances. The density of migration might be lower over the Aegean Sea than over the Iberian/Moroccan area, but there are no data to substantiate such a hypothesis. Migration, however, begins much later than in the Atlantic region. In addition, the principal prey species are smaller in weight and thus do not contribute as much to the subsistence of Eleonora's falcon as do the prey species at Mogador.

Migration

The migration route of the Mogador population is much longer than that of the Paximada birds, if indeed all Eleonora's falcons migrate to the Madagascar region.

Discussion

When we compare these two colonies, the reproductive statistics, the observations on hunting ecology, the independent information on prey species migration, and the geographical factors of colony location fit together too well to be dismissed as accidental. There can be little doubt that Eleonora's falcon at Paximada (and in nearly all other Aegean colonies as well) has considerably less daily hunting time, a shorter bird-hunting season, and perhaps an overall lower prey density. This colony also shows a rather low overall hunting success. Its clutch size and hatching and fledging rates are far below those of the Atlantic study colony. The latter excels all other colonies in its hunting success ("meat larder" of excess prey items), its hunting periods and season, and its outstanding breeding success (except for human predation).

We can conclude that Eleonora's falcon at Mogador is an extraordinarily successful raptor because of an unusually abundant and accessible prey population. The breeding success is very high under conditions of high breeding density. Paximada, on the other hand, is a normal, perhaps only a marginally successful colony where prey abundance and access to it are limited by geographical factors. As a result, reproductive success is low, and this is further reduced by local predators and human interference. Still, given a very low mortality rate of the adult falcon, even a lower reproductive rate might still enable this raptor to survive and retain its fitness for its unique ecological niche. For instance, another predatory bird, the long-tailed skua or jaeger (*Stercorarius longicaudus*) showed a very low production rate of only 0.53 fledglings per pair per year (Andersson 1976). For this pelagic species the annual adult mortality rate has been estimated as 9 to 16%. It might well be that Eleonora's falcon, which is more of a pelagic raptor than its relatives, might still manage to sustain breeding colonies with an average breeding success of 0.8 to 1.0 fledgling per pair per year. The Paximada data complex appears to be the rule and that of Mogador the extreme or exception to the rule among the 100 or so breeding colonies of Eleonora's falcon. It is quite possible, even likely, that other Atlantic colonies would also show above-normal production rates. They should all benefit from the favorable migration pulse in the Iberian-Moroccan region of the eastern Atlantic.

The differences between Paximada and Mogador accentuate the adaptation of falcon populations to the concrete manifestation of their resource bases. The local modifications of the principal niche factors point once again to the interdependence between the functional properties of the falcons and their niches.

"ABSENT" CARIBBEAN NICHE

The North American continent possesses a richer avifauna than the much smaller European continent. Bird migration in the United States is well known and much appreciated: ornithologists look forward to the seasonal spring and fall migrants, and sport hunters have known the principal migration routes of waterfowl species for many years. Many small passerine species migrate to Central and even to South America. Certain western species migrate over the desert area of Mexico before reaching their tropical winter habitats. In the eastern United States, however, a migration system has evolved that is strikingly similar to the European-African one. The Gulf of Mexico and the Caribbean Sea constitute a wide water barrier between the two New World continents. In between lie a large number of small and large islands: the Bahamas and the Greater and Lesser Antilles. For any bird breeding in New England, Nova Scotia, or Ontario, the shortest flight route to South America leads across the Gulf or the Caribbean Sea or both. Visual and radar observations have shown that considerable numbers of small and large birds leave the eastern and southeastern United States in the fall on a southeast course over the western Atlantic. They have been recorded at Bermuda, the Bahamas, and Puerto Rico. Their winter quarters are known to lie in or south of the West Indies.

The existence of considerable fall migration across the Western Atlantic opens up an interesting possibility. The Caribbean area seems to offer the same food resources that the Mediterranean offers to Eleonora's falcon. In other words, there seems to be an ecological niche available to any raptor capable of exploiting it like Eleonora's falcon. Is there such a raptor? If not, why not?

There is no ecological counterpart of Eleonora's falcon in the western hemisphere. No falcon or other raptor exists in the Caribbean area that exploits bird migration as its major source of protein during the breeding season. Has nature failed to produce the consumer species of this obvious food resource? Is there indeed an "empty" Caribbean niche? Would Eleonora's falcon be able to exist in the New World if it had dispersed across the Atlantic? A closer look at the structure of the migration across the Western Atlantic will provide the answers to these questions.

Considerable research of the inter-American migration system has been carried out with the help of bird banding and moon and radar observations. Richardson (1976) has summarized the current knowledge and added significant observations of fall migration patterns over Puerto Rico:

1. There is good evidence that the normal fall migration route for some or most individuals of nine species of shorebirds "is over the ocean from south-eastern Canada and New England to the West Indies and eastern South America." The blackpoll warbler (*Dendroica striata*) is the only passerine species "for which there is convincing evidence of a predominantly offshore route from New England and Nova Scotia to the West Indies." Other common land bird migrants in the Antilles are other warbler species, as well as bank and barn swallows (*Riparia riparia* and *Hirundo rustica*), bobolinks (*Dolichonyx oryzivorus*), indigo buntings (*Passerina cyanea*), and yellow-billed cuckoos (*Coceyzus americanus*).

Many other species like flycatchers (Tyrannidae), thrushes (Turdidae), vireos (Vireonidae), orioles (Icterus), and tanagers (Thraupidae) appear to take a more westerly course through Mexico or across the Gulf of Mexico.

2. The median altitude of fall migrants over Puerto Rico and other locations in the Antilles was extraordinarily high. The average altitude of passerines was above 2,000 m. Many radar echoes were reported at a height of 4,000 to 5,000 m, higher than reported from any other regular migration route.

3. Wind and weather affect migration speed and direction. Birds usually depart offshore on a southeast course with winds

"that have a westerly component but approach the West Indies with winds that have an easterly component." Weather and wind conditions south of Bermuda cannot be predicted before departure from the United States. Small birds are subject to lateral drift and appear to correct little for it. Birds usually have to fly upwind in the Caribbean region.

4. The coastal alignments of North and South America create very large distances between the two coasts: "non-stop flights of 3000 and probably 4000 km are a regular feature of autumn migration over the Western Atlantic." Even the distance from Georgia to Puerto Rico is 2,100 km, from Nova Scotia, 2,900 km (fig. 53).

5. The principal migration season along the Antilles ranges from late September to mid-November.

The migration system across the western Atlantic is quite different from the Palearctic-African system. The migration season sets in about 30 to 40 days later than in the Mediterranean, and the over-water distances are extremely long in the western Atlantic. The frequent absence of tailwinds creates very exhausting, almost impossible nonstop flight requirements for any passerine species. Flight altitude is extremely high, probably an energy-saving measure of the American migrants. Only some four small land bird species plus a number of American warblers, particularly the blackpoll warbler, regularly migrate from eastern and southeastern North America across the Antilles to eastern South America. Many more species avoid a sea crossing or cross the small water barrier of the Gulf of Mexico by taking a southwest course to Mexico. This crossing of the gulf is very similar to the Mediterranean situation: many potential flight routes would range from 500 to 1,500 km (New Orleans–Vera Cruz in southeast Mexico— some 1,300 km).

In conclusion, only a few passerine species cross the western Atlantic to the east of Florida in order to reach northeast South America. They have to overcome a tremendous distance of inhospitable water. There is hardly a parallel to this migration system in the Palearctic except for nonstop flights from southern Europe across the Mediterranean *and* the Sahara Desert. Most North American land birds that winter in the tropics migrate to or through Mexico.

A falcon with a resource base like that of Eleonora's falcon could

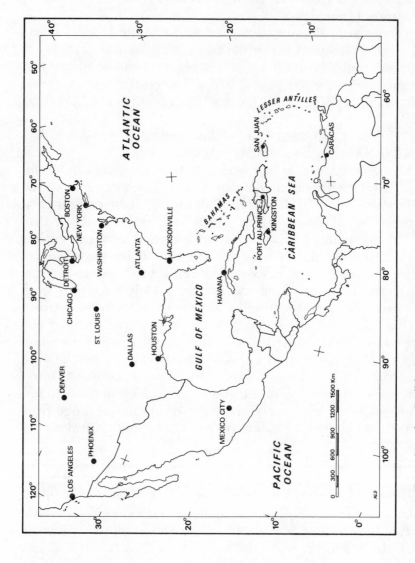

Fig. 53. The Gulf of Mexico, the Caribbean Sea, and the bird migration has been observed in this region, but no islands between North and South America. Considerable raptor resembling Eleonora's falcon is present.

not exist in the Caribbean. The comparatively few species of land birds passing over the islands in the Caribbean Sea represent only a trickle compared with the huge number of Palearctic migrants crossing the Mediterranean. A falcon species would need a huge mass of potential prey, since it has the chance of meeting only a few migrants within its hunting range and of capturing only a small percentage of those attacked. Moreover, dependence on only a few species would be dangerous in the long run: population fluctuations and weather-induced shifts in the migration period might leave a falcon without a substantial amount of bird food during the critical growth period of the falcon chicks. Another unfavorable factor is the extreme flight altitude of migrants over the sea and perhaps even over larger islands. It would require much more energy for the falcon to reach its hunting position in the sky. Thus, the resource base for a raptor similar to Eleonora's falcon would be too small, too variable, and too costly in terms of energy expenditure. We can conclude that there is no counterpart of Eleonora's falcon breeding in the Caribbean region, since an examination of the relevant niche factors has shown that no potential ecological niche exists.

Regarding the apparently much more important migration route across the Gulf of Mexico from the southern coast of the United States to Mexico, it seems quite possible that a falcon would find a sufficiently large and diversified resource base in the many migrating species. However, here we have no islands, or hardly any, at a comfortable distance between departure area and destination. Lack of rocky coast and the presence of ground predators might prevent a falcon from nesting along the eastern mainland coast of Mexico. The average flight altitudes of migrants might still be very high compared with the Mediterranean, where only very few mainland colonies of Eleonora's falcon exist. This region appears to be too different geographically to permit any speculation on a potential niche suitable for such a raptor.

The western Atlantic, unlike the eastern Atlantic and the Mediterranean basin, does not offer the principal niche factors for a falcon exploiting bird migration over the sea: there is no "empty" Caribbean niche because the niche itself does not exist.

ORIGIN OF ELEONORA'S FALCON

Biogeographers have studied the dynamic aspects of the distribution of the European flora and fauna during and after the last glacial advance some 18,000 years ago. This climatic factor has had the most profound impact on the diversity of the avifauna of Europe and the European-African bird migration system. Since the existence of Eleonora's falcon is dependent upon its prey species, we can shed some light on the recent past of our falcon by examining the fluctuating composition and numbers of the flow of migration. We shall then discuss the taxonomic position of Eleonora's falcon and attempt to trace the evolutionary path of this raptor to its ancestors.

Bird migration systems depend greatly on planetary climatic constellations. Glacial advances change the distribution and area of specific vegetation belts, thereby changing the composition of the avifauna. Moreau (1972) estimates that at the height of the last glaciation the vegetation map of Europe showed "virtually no woodland of any sort" north of the Pyrenees, the Alps, and the Caucasus "except for a narrow strip of wooded steppe and wooded tundra . . . across central Russia." All of Scandinavia and most of the British Isles were covered by ice. South of this a large expanse of tundra covered western and eastern Europe. In the south, the lowlands of the entire Mediterranean coast were apparently covered by a steppe with *Artemisia* (wormwood) and chenopods (pigweed family), according to a recent analysis by Wright (1976). Certain mountain areas of the Iberian, Italian, and Balkan peninsulas were covered with mixed or coniferous forests.

The effect of this glaciation on the bird migration systems was phenomenal. Nearly all the species that today are prey items of Eleonora's falcon either could not have maintained themselves in Europe (for example, quail, wryneck, nightingale, lesser grey shrike, and woodchat shrike) or existed in reduced numbers (redstart, whinchat, nightjar, red-backed shrike, and many warblers). Only two of the trans-Saharan migrants of today had the opportunity to be "especially numerous, more so than ever since" (Moreau 1972). These are two birds of open land and cold habitats, the wheatear (*O. oenanthe*) and the red-throated pipit (*Anthus cervinus*). In terms of numbers, Moreau guessed—on the basis of the areas affected by drastic vegetation change—that migration to Africa was reduced "to one tenth of the potential number before and after the glaciation."

Those species that could not maintain themselves in Europe

must have had suitable habitats somewhere to the south and east of the Mediterranean. Wright (1976) proposes the existence of a Mediterranean type of refuge for Mediterranean species in northwest Africa, particularly Morocco. Pollen analysis indicates that hazel and oak forests replaced the steppe vegetation in Spain and Italy about 11,000 years ago (Moreau 1972; Wright 1976). Climatic amelioration—warmer and wetter years—continued until about 7,000 years ago, when world temperatures "ran some 2°C higher than at present. This was the heyday of woodland" (Moreau 1972). At this time almost 90% of Europe was covered by forests. Most of the European woodland bird species dispersed all over this region, and the fall migration to Africa was an estimated ten to twelve times larger than during the height of the glaciation.

Human conversion of Europe's woodlands began soon thereafter. Today, agriculture, human settlements, and other impacts have modified the western Palearctic in such a way that it can accommodate only "one quarter of the former total of woodland migrants" (Moreau 1972).

How do these fluctuations and the recent decrease in the number of migrants affect the food resources of Eleonora's falcon? First, it can be concluded that the human alteration of Europe has reduced the former migration flow of woodland birds by three-quarters. Some 7,000 to 5,000 years ago, some 20 billion birds must have crossed the Mediterranean compared with the estimated 5 billion today. Second, at the height of the last glaciation, bird migration appears to have been less than half what it is today. In addition, a relatively few species dominated the migration flow, and the stable Mediterranean climate did not exist where we find it today. The combination of these factors leads me to suggest that Eleonora's falcon could not have existed in the Mediterranean basin some 18,000 years ago. If the species did not exist there during the glacial period, where did it stay, and how has it moved into its present breeding area?

Taxonomic relationships among the genus *Falco* are not easy to determine, since functional characters often overlie the taxonomic ones. Among the European and African falcon species, Eleonora's falcon has only three close relatives. These are the hobby (*F. subbuteo*), the African hobby (*F. cuvieri*), and the sooty falcon (*F. concolor*). All four share a similar morphology and juvenile plumage. They can all be classified as hobbies—that is,

hunters of aerial insects and small vertebrate prey. This distinguishes them from other falcon groups like kestrels, lanners,
peregrines, and falconets.

The phylogeny of Eleonora's falcon is still a closed book. What I
can suggest about the evolutionary past of this raptor is more
speculation than hypothesis. The "scenario" that is most plausible
to me reads as follows: All hobbies had the same ancestor, a small-
ish but swift falcon adapted to hunting small prey in the open airspace. Ecological and geographic isolation caused speciation into
several genotypes, among them a woodland/savanna form and a
desert/coastal form. The former was the ancestor of today's *subbuteo* and *cuvieri*. Today these two species are allopatric (fig. 54),
one being a tropical African, the other a wide-ranging Palearctic
raptor. Both species are solitary breeders in African or Eurasian
woodland and savanna/steppe habitats. Eleonora's falcon and the
sooty falcon evolved from the other genotype. Both species are
gregarious (but some solitary sooty falcons have been found) and
breed either along the seashore or on islands (both species) or in
the desert (some sooty falcons only). During the nonbreeding season these two species behave very much like hobbies, insect-
hawking along their migration route and in their principal winter
range (Madagascar). They are also allopatric with regard to their
breeding range; the two do not overlap (fig. 54). A third ancestral
genotype may have evolved into hobbylike falcons that live in Asia
and Australia today.

The ancestor of the *eleonorae/concolor* pair probably lived in Africa and the Near East. A likely explanation for its isolation from
the woodland/savanna hobby may have been the desiccation of
entire regions within the general hobby range. Instead of abandoning the arid lands, speciation resulted in new adaptive characters. The new species still hunted insects most of the time but
could not raise its brood with the rather meager flying insect and
bird resources of desert habitats. It then "discovered" and
adapted to an abundant seasonal food resource: the stream of
Palearctic migrants crossing the barren desert lands to reach the
tropical habitats in the south. Once migrant birds had become the
staple food during the reproductive season, the ancestor of our
sooty falcon and Eleonora's falcon could lead the life of a vag-
abond during the remainder of the year, insect-hawking where-
ever possible.

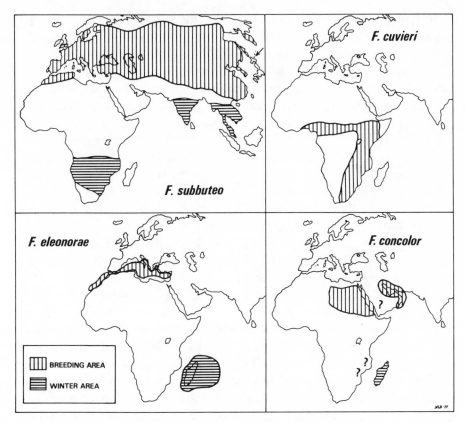

Fig. 54. World distribution of four falcons of the hobby type.

Social habits probably evolved when this species began to breed along coasts and on islands. The strategic position of these breeding sites was so favorable for the falcons that large numbers of breeding pairs could be accommodated without reducing each other's food supply. Group hunting increased the overall hunting success of the individual falcon.

How did the ancestral falcon adapt to the delayed timing of the breeding season? This factor distinguishes the two falcon species from all other Palearctic birds today. In my opinion, no adaptation at all was necessary: in eastern Africa today, many raptors have irregular breeding seasons and some others prefer the period from August to November (often a dry season). Thus, if the ancestors came from African stock that lived in the northeastern part of the continent, it is likely that they either had no fixed

breeding period or had one during the late summer months of
the northern hemisphere. In other words, it is not that Eleonora's
falcon had to shift its breeding season to late summer days, but
that the other European falcons of tropical or subtropical ancestry
had to shift to an early spring or summer breeding schedule.

The ancestral falcon probably migrated south of the equator
during the northern winter with its short daylight hours. Whether
it migrated to Madagascar cannot, of course, be determined. The
absence of *concolor* and *eleonorae* from West and South Africa and
their peculiar concentration in Madagascar today indicate that the
ancestral species must have had a distribution area in eastern and
northeastern Africa or Arabia. It might have gradually used
more and more of the virtually empty aerial raptor niche on
Madagascar. At the same time, other insect-hawking falcons may
have increased in southern Africa, effectively forcing out the
eleonorae/concolor ancestor there.

What could have caused this ancestral population to become
reproductively isolated in two areas of its range? If both *eleonorae*
and *concolor* existed as separate species *before* the end of the last
glacial advance, where did they live? I can find no argument for
their existence in an ecological niche like the one they occupy
today before 20,000 B.C. Eleonora's falcon could not have existed
in the Mediterranean because there were few if any migrants
crossing it during spring and fall. If it lived farther south it would
have had to compete with the sooty falcon unless the latter lived
outside its present breeding range (but where?). It makes good
sense, then, to assume that the evolution of *eleonorae* occurred
between 15,000 B.C. and 5,000 B.C. when the ice retreated to the
north and the annual fall migration of European woodland birds
began to swell rapidly to its maximum of about 20 billion birds
(Moreau 1972). During this time, the ancestral falcon population
began to expand from the Red Sea region into the eastern
Mediterranean, gradually dispersing farther to the west until
finally even the Canaries had been colonized. This Mediterranean/
Atlantic population was subjected to a much cooler and moister
environment, faced a longer migration route, and had to rely
on bird-hunting over the sea. The northern population became
reproductively isolated from the southern population because
of the postglacial woodland belt stretching across the entire width
of North Africa and Arabia (Moreau 1972).

In conclusion, Eleonora's falcon probably has evolved from an ancestral hobby. This species is thought to have been split into two ecologically isolated forms, the solitary open woodland form and the mostly gregarious desert and coastal form. The former gave rise to the African and the Eurasian hobby, the latter began to exploit the abundant food resources of the seasonal fall migration of birds between the Palearctic and the African region south of the barren desert lands. It is hypothesized that Eleonora's falcon evolved from this ancestral falcon as a result of isolation and speciation in the larger form (*eleonorae*) of the relatively cool Mediterranean, and in the smaller form (*concolor*) of the hot deserts and shores of the Arabian seas.

This hypothesis is of course rather speculative. Still, it is intriguing, since it links the evolution of Eleonora's falcon to the increase of bird migration across the Mediterranean that began well after 15,000 B.C. when the giant ice shield lying over northern and central Europe began to recede. If this hypothesis comes close to the real course of falcon evolution, Eleonora's falcon is a rather recent raptor species, with an age of probably less than 15,000 years.

11 Human Impact

Falcons and humans not only have coexisted for thousands of years, they have developed a unique relationship. The power and beauty of falcons so impressed different civilizations all over the earth that falcons became important symbols and acquired significant identities in human thought, culture, and religion. Then came the art of falconry, which bends the falcon's will and energy to the recreational delights of man. In this century people have finally begun to simply enjoy falcons from a distance without killing, capturing, and exhibiting these majestic princes of the air. But this century has also seen a sudden and rapid decline of raptors in many countries. In this section I shall point out the changing interaction between Eleonora's falcon and the human species. Let me begin with a brief essay on the discovery of Eleonora's falcon and the reason this raptor was named after an unusual woman of the late fourteenth century.

DISCOVERY OF ELEONORA'S FALCON

The European falcons were comparatively well known many centuries ago. Their habits, their migrations, and their changing plumage were described in great detail in the literature on the art of falconry. An outstanding example is the famous treatise *De arte venandibus cum avibus*, by Emperor Frederick II of Hohenstaufen. This book is a marvel of keen field observation and critical scientific thought. Frederick discusses and describes nearly all of Europe's falcon species, their color phases, and their juvenile, immature, and adult plummage. Yet he fails to mention Eleonora's falcon. I have read through the English edition (Wood and Fyfe 1961) as well as a German edition (Willemsen 1964) without finding any clues on Eleonora's falcon in this medieval classic. One would expect Frederick to include this species, since he devotes much space to bird migration and its importance for falconry.

The delayed breeding season of Eleonora's falcon, its contrasting color phases, and its hunting habits could have added interesting material to various chapters.

That Eleonora's falcon is not mentioned by Frederick is surprising if not stunning and leaves us with a set of possible explanations. First, Eleonora's falcon may not have been known at the time (thirteenth century A.D.), although it was breeding on islands around Sicily and Italy where Emperor Frederick II had his headquarters. Second, Eleonora's falcon may not have been breeding in the western Mediterranean during the Middle Ages. Third, this species may have been known but confused with another falcon species. I prefer the first explanation. Falconers were perhaps busy with late summer falcon-training and bird-hunting during August and September, thereby precluding contact with the breeding colonies of Eleonora's falcon. Although this might have happened, it is difficult for me to accept such a knowledge gap among falconers, who are usually very well informed.

In a commentary on Frederick's manuscript, Wood and Fyfe (1961) mention that Eleonora's falcon "may well have been utilized in ancient and medieval times as a hunter; but the bird has not been widely employed in Europe" (p. 517). Later on, the same authors declare: "Albertus Magnus ... does, however, recognize a true and important species, also known to Frederick II, viz., the large, dark-colored Eleonora Falcon ..., whose chief habitat is North Africa and the Greek Islands" (p. 552). This statement has to be challenged, since authorities on Albertus Magnus like Lindner (1962) have failed to detect any comment on Eleonora's falcon in his work. I myself have read through several translations of Albertus in medieval German without finding a trace of this species. The translation by Heinrich Münsinger, for example, describes a "black, white, and red falcon." Lindner (1962, 2:201–4) succeeds in identifying them as subspecies of the peregrine falcon. The black falcon is considered to be *F. peregrinus babylonicus*.

Another reference on Eleonora's falcon comes from Schlegel (1844), who states that Artalouche de Alagona, a Sicilian writer of the fifteenth century, mentioned this falcon under the name "sapphire falcon" (p. 18). Considering the confusion about the nature of Mediterranean falcon types that existed during Schlegel's time, it must remain somewhat doubtful whether the "sapphire falcon" was an Eleonora's falcon.

The oldest reliable reference to this species comes from a falconry treatise by Charles d'Arcussia de Capre, published in 1627 (Engelmann 1928; Mayaud 1960). This author mentions hobby-like falcons breeding in August on the "îles d'Or" (today called "Iles d'Hyères") of Provence. These falcons chased birds but failed to capture them. "They are useless and have no courage at all." This latter remark is an outgrowth of the utilitarian attitude of the author: in his opinion, this type of falcon could not be used for any purpose related to falconry.

Knowledge about this late-breeding hobby falcon did not reach the field naturalists and museum scientists of the late seventeenth and eighteenth centuries until the Italian zoologist Guiseppe Gené published a description of Eleonora's falcon in 1839. This date will forever be connected with the entry of this species into modern ornithology.

The Italian naturalist and historian Cavaliere Alberto della Marmora had discovered what he thought was a new species of falcon on the small isle of Toro to the southeast of Sardinia. He shot several specimens and sent them to his friend Gené in Torino. Marmora himself writes (1839) that Gené presented a scientific description of the new species during a session of the Royal Academy of Sciences of Torino on 5 May 1834. This means that Marmora must have discovered the birds on Toro not later than the 1833 breeding season. Gené's official description, however, was not published until 1839.

PRINCESS ELEONORA OF ARBOREA

The new falcon species received the name of one of the few famous women of the fourteenth century, Eleonora of Arborea (ca. 1350–1403), who had distinguished herself as a military leader, as regent, and as a judge (*giudicessa*) of a large part of her native island of Sardinia. Her most important work is an unusually progressive code of laws ("Carta de Logu") published in the Sardinian language in 1392.

Gené named the new falcon after Princess Eleonora for two reasons: the Carta de Logu contains a paragraph providing for the protection of hawks and falcons, and he wanted to honor her for "her admirable wisdom in the century of barbarities in which she reigned to protect the honor, the life and the goods of the people" (Gené 1840). Thus this falcon became the first European bird named after a woman: *Falco eleonorae*.

MEDIEVAL FALCONRY IN SARDINIA

Ever since Gené's publication, Eleonora's falcon has been connected to falconry as practiced at the court of Eleonora of Arborea. Gené himself did not suggest that Eleonora had any specific interest in this species, nor did he imply that she made a specific law to protect this Sardinian falcon.

It was the official discoverer, Alberto della Marmora himself, who used a wording that invites the interpretation that Princess Eleonora made a specific law for the protection of this particular falcon. Without further explanation, Marmora (1839) writes: "Eleonora ... who has forbidden to take this bird out of its nest."

There is no source at all that even indirectly indicates that Eleonora's falcon was used in falconry on Sardinia or anywhere else during the Middle Ages. With the generous assistance of Professor A. Boscolo (University of Cagliari), I was able to examine and "decipher" several medieval documents on Sardinian falcons, none of which referred to a bird like Eleonora's falcon.

The falcons of Sardinia were held in high esteem at European courts and represented an important export of the island. The general term *falcone* is used everywhere. A student of medieval falconry knows that the term "falcon" applies almost exclusively to the peregrine (*F. peregrinus*), then as today the classic object of falconry.

The Carta de Logu of Eleonora deals with raptors in its eighty-eighth paragraph. This is the text from the oldest known manuscript of this famous code of laws: "[Constituimus et] ordinamus que alcuno homine non depiat bogare store dae niu nec falcone et qui l'at bogare siat tenudo su Curadore dae tenellure et dae batirello a sa corte nostra ho a nos sutta pena de pagare su Curadore [libras quimbe]." It prohibits taking the young of hawks (*store* from *astore*, probably referring to the goshawk *Accipiter gentilis*) and falcons (*falcone*) and prescribes that anybody violating this law shall be brought to Eleonora's court by his local authority (prefect) and fined the sum of five pounds.

This law is by no means unique. Similar orders and laws were in force throughout Europe: as mentioned before, their spirit derived not from a modern type of conservationist attitude but from the egotistic perspective of the nobility, who were dependent on a regular supply of young falcons for their prestigious sport.

My excursion into medieval history finally yielded a quote that clearly identifies the kind of falcon the nobility was looking for: "In April of 1428, Luigi Aragoll, commander [*luogotenente*] of the deputy king [*viceré*] in Sardinia, sent various boats to the Red Isle at the Capo di Carbonara and to Toro in order to collect the falcon nests and to deliver them to the king in accordance with custom" (Pillito 1862).

This means that the young falcons were taken from Toro in April. At this time of the year, some Eleonora's falcons are still in Madagascar and others have just arrived in the Mediterranean after a long migration. However, in April the peregrine has young chicks: to recover them for the king was the aim of the boating party.

In conclusion, no reference has been found that would imply any role for Eleonora's falcon in the medieval falconry of Sardinia or of Europe as a whole. The falcons taken from the breeding rocks of Eleonora's falcon were quite certainly young peregrine falcons. It is therefore most improbable that Princess Eleonora ever saw or even heard of Eleonora's falcon. Her falcon protection law was directed at the peregrine resources of Sardinia. It is likely, however, that the general terminology of the law helped to protect other falcon species as well, including Eleonora's falcon. Alberto della Marmora's statement, "Eleonora ... who has forbidden to take this bird out of its nest," is therefore correct although incomplete. He should have written: "to take all falcons out of their nests."

An additional indication of the falconer's lack of interest in our species has, I believe, been provided by an experienced German falconer, Dr. R. Beckers (Cologne). I presented him with a young Eleonora's falcon from the Paximada colony in October 1965, requesting that it receive the proper training for falconry. Dr. Beckers reported after twelve months that he had unusual difficulties with this bird, and that Eleonora's falcon did not compare favorably with the species commonly used in falconry. This experience appears to confirm d'Arcussia's negative statement on the usefulness of Eleonora's falcon (Engelmann 1928).

FISHERMEN AND OTHER PREDATORS

The direct human impact on Eleonora's falcon has traditionally come from local fishermen cruising the coasts and high seas of the Mediterranean and the Atlantic. Observations from many Aegean colonies (Krüper 1864) and from Mogador (Walter, this study) prove that human predation has been very important for several hundred years at least. For the average fisherman the enormous fat layers and the protein of the young falcon's breast constitute an important food resource. We can therefore expect that all accessible colonies within 50 km of human settlements have probably regularly suffered from human predation. The persistence of the species in so many locations where this human impact has existed is probably due to the reproductive capacity of those pairs that had their nests in inaccessible parts of coastal bluffs and islands.

A very recent phenomenon is the bird photographer and bird watcher on an excursion. Both can seriously disrupt the breeding cycles of Eleonora's falcon and other bird species. Colonial species that are rare or unusual are particularly threatened by the interest and affection of these often very dedicated and well-meaning people.

The whole routine of a colony can be disrupted by one person or group. The spread of outboard engines and the increase in recreational and sport boating and fishing in the Mediterranean basin is perhaps the greatest danger to Eleonora's falcon. No cliff, no shore is safe from this group of noisy and frequently ignorant people. They camp on the falcon's breeding isles and walk through the nesting grounds without realizing that they are disrupting the breeding cycle by their presence. According to Parrott (1976), the number of visitors to the Dionisiades island group off Crete reached 28 persons per day in September and October 1974, and 70 persons per day in September 1976. In 1965, hardly any visitors except two or three hunting parties visited these isles.

A traditional threat to raptors comes from the taxidermist. In many countries (Malta, Italy, Spain, and others) it is still popular to exhibit stuffed eagles, falcons, and owls in the living room or on the walls of a restaurant.

If the foregoing sounds ominous, I would like to assure the reader that this combination of direct threats to Eleonora's falcon can hardly be compared with the many tragedies that have afflicted other European birds of prey during the past few centuries. Bijleveld (1974) has written an excellent book on the history of human impact on raptors in this part of the world. The systematic persecution of eagles and other birds of prey began in the sixteenth (Faroe Islands) and seventeenth centuries (Great Britain). Soon raptors became vermin all over Europe. Bounty systems encouraged the decimation or eradication of raptor populations. Even in the 1960s, when a widespread decline of raptors had been recognized, many countries offered no or only partial legal protection to raptors. The "World Conference on Birds of Prey" collected the most recent data on this issue for the Mediterranean countries (Chancellor 1977). A further decline of many raptor species, among them the peregrine, hobby, lesser kestrel, the various eagles, harriers, kites, and most hawks has been observed, although the legal status of raptors has now been improved in several countries (Conder 1977):

1. *No protection*: Malta.

2. *Partial protection*: Italy; no federal law, but many northern regions accord full protection. No protection for all or certain birds of prey in Sicily, Calabria, Puglie, Campania, Lucania, and Abbruzzo. Greece; all raptors are protected except within "breeding, hunting and wildlife reserves," where they are considered to be harmful. (Surely, this must be some of the strangest conservation legislation of all time.)

3. *Full protection*: Portugal, Spain, France, Cyprus, European Turkey. Conder (1977) does not provide any data from the North African countries. Morocco, I believe, accords full protection to all raptors and has imprisoned several Europeans caught taking young falcons from their eyries. Even where full protection is given, enforcement of the law is difficult, if not impossible, particularly in the case of remote islands.

In conclusion, Eleonora's falcon has suffered from human predation for centuries. Today this species is adversely affected by increasing numbers of recreational visitors to its breeding islands. In addition, falcon enthusiasts, photographers, and hunters pose a threat even where full legal protection exists.

INDIRECT EFFECTS OF HUMAN ENDEAVOR

The indirect human impact has probably been more important in the past than it is today. According to Moreau (1972), bird migration has declined since about 5,000 B.C. to one-quarter of its potential maximum, mostly as a result of the human alteration of the European wooded landscape. It is very probable that Eleonora's falcon used to be several times more common in its present breeding area, perhaps nesting on many continental shores and extending farther to the north in the Tyrrhenian, Ligurian, and Adriatic seas.

These former breeding sites were abandoned when the migration flow became too sparse and unpredictable, creating a less than marginal resource base for the falcon. The question must be asked whether some of today's colonies are situated in marginal or submarginal resource areas.

Another indirect impact could result from the habitat alteration in the African region. The current increase in the width of the Sahara and modern land-use practices may seriously affect the suitability of many winter habitats for the trans-Saharan migrants. In addition, Madagascar has changed considerably in less than 1,500 years of human residence. Huge areas have been deforested and drained, which might reduce the average quantity of insect food available to the sooty falcon and Eleonora's falcon during their brief winter stay. Short-term droughts in Africa, as well as cool and wet summers in Europe, may also reduce migrant numbers.

That raptors are bioindicators of environmental quality has become painfully obvious in recent years. First isolated data, (Ratcliffe 1967), then a large number of scientific reports, have pointed to the increasing contamination of our landscapes with biocides and other poisons as an important cause of the decline of raptor populations in Europe and North America. Bijleveld (1974) mentions aldrin, dieldrin, heptachlorine, DDT (and its metabolites DDE and DDD), methylmercury compounds, parathion, and alkylmercury compounds as the key substances that have been detected in high concentrations in bird tissues and eggs. Raptors can accumulate them in lethal or sublethal doses, the latter causing reduced fertility or infertility. The evidence relating these biocides to the high rate of infertility and embryo mortality in certain falcons and eagles is clear and extensive. Biocides disrupt the physiological systems of raptors, particularly in young birds and during the formation of eggs. Eggshell thickness is adversely affected, so that eggs break and the embryos die. Thanks to the many egg collections from the past century and the first three decades of this century, it has been possible to pinpoint the onset of the biocide impact on raptor populations. The eggshell weight of peregrines decreased beginning in

1947 and 1948, shortly after the first small-scale use of DDT in Britain and North America (Ratcliffe 1967; Anderson and Hickey 1972; Peakall 1976). Similar correlations have since been established for various raptors in the Baltic region (Anderson and Hickey 1974; Lindberg 1977) and even in remote and wildernesslike Alaska (Peakall et al. 1975). Here, long-term studies of the raptor community along the Colville River have documented a dramatic decline of local peregrines (White and Cade 1977).

Not all the populations of a species need be affected by biocides. Local food chains and environmental pollution levels vary greatly from country to country, and even between adjacent counties. Hardest hit by biocides have been birds depending either on coastal marine food chains or on seed-eating small vertebrates (many biocides are used for seed dressing and disinfecting). The impact of these human-generated contaminants on the European raptor species has been less obvious than in North America. Other decimating factors (habitat changes, persecution, disturbance, etc.) have also played important roles (Anderson and Hickey 1972; Bijleveld 1974).

Ratcliffe (1967) developed an index for measuring the thickness of the eggshell. Today we have excellent instruments for this purpose, permitting the accurate comparative analysis of eggshell changes through time and between populations and species.

At the end of the nineteenth century, when egg collecting was still a widespread activity, many eggs of Eleonora's falcon were shipped to museums and private collections all over Europe. Nothing, however, has been published concerning the impact of biocides on Eleonora's falcon except for a recent paper by Clark and Peakall (1977). I will therefore present whatever data I have been able to assemble from this and the past century.

In 1965 I weighed and measured a total of 63 live eggs from the Paximada colony. Because of the importance of these data for future analyses, I have listed the individual measurements in table 36 (Appendix A). The pertinent size data are:

Paximada (1965 breeding season): 63 eggs
mean size 41.9 × 33.1 mm
largest egg 45.0 × 36.0 mm
smallest egg 38.5 × 31.5 mm.

All the falcon eggs I have seen and held in eyries of Eleonora's

falcon since 1965 looked normal; they were not visibly deformed
and did not appear to have particularly thin shells.

Other egg data come from various authors. Makatsch (1958)
studied another colony to the north of Crete:

Theodoros (1957 season): 12 eggs
mean size 43.2 × 33.9 mm
eggshell weight 2.02 g.

Reiser (1905) has listed individual measurements from various
Aegean colonies (and perhaps other breeding regions) collected
between 1864 and 1899:

Various colonies (1864–99): 28 eggs
mean size 42.8 × 33.0 mm
largest egg 46.6 × 34.1 mm
smallest egg 38.4 × 31.8 mm.

He has also summarized an analysis of 40 eggs carried out by
Dresser:

Unidentified colonies (before 1900): 40 eggs
mean size 41.7 × 33.2 mm
largest egg 44.25 × 32.5 mm
smallest egg 38.75 × 31.0 mm.

Recently, Wyer (unpublished manuscript written after 1963)
measured a large number of eggs of unknown origin:

Unidentified colonies (dates unknown): 91 eggs
mean size 41.22 × 33.27 mm
largest egg 46.6 × 38.4 mm
smallest egg 35.5 × 29.4 mm
shell weight 1.85 g (range 1.29–2.40 g)
shell thickness 0.23 mm.

Finally, D. W. Anderson has kindly sent me his analysis of 13 eggs
collected between 1863 and 1874 and of 49 eggs collected between
1960 and 1969 (table 37). Anderson concludes that "no differences could be detected. Our failure to find a recent shell
change in *Falco eleonorae* was somewhat blunted by the small
number of historical eggs of this species that we were able to
measure in this study. Feeding as it does on insects and small
migratory birds from mainland Europe, this species offers a clue
to the chemical contamination in ecosystems to the north ....
These results indirectly suggest that DDE residues in certain
European songbirds are probably low" (Anderson, pers. comm.).

Table 37 seems to reflect a small increase in egg volume and thickness index of the post-1959 eggs compared with the pre-1875 eggs. We should not interpret this apparent anomaly as particularly significant for several reasons. First, the sample analyzed was rather small. Second, the pre-1875 eggs may have deteriorated in quality. Third, the pre-1875 eggs are of Aegean origin, whereas most of the post-1959 eggs comes from Morocco. It is not uncommon to find regional differences in the mean eggshell weight and thickness within the same species. It would be advisable for any future analysis to compare large numbers of eggs and eggshells from the same colony or at least from the same breeding region.

Eggshell changes are only one of several indicators of the adverse impact of biocides on bird populations. Of equal importance may be breeding statistics. Clutch size and reproductive success provide valuable insight into long-term population dynamics. Thanks to the pioneering work of Krüper (1864), we have some early data on clutch size and reproductive success of Eleonora's falcon, permitting a comparison between 1862 and the 1960s in the Aegean Sea regions of the total breeding range (see also Reiser 1905 and chap. 3). Krüper writes (1864, p. 13): "The number of eggs in a nest is 2 and 3; so far I have never found 4 or even 5 eggs! Based on my observation, there are as many nests with 3 eggs as with 2. In clutches of 3 eggs, often only 2 have been fertilized; also, where there were 2 eggs I found several times that one had not been fertilized."

The Paximada data (tables 3 and 27) from 1965 and 1969 indicate that the average clutch size may have declined by 10 to 20% since Krüper's times. First of all, Krüper does not mention any clutches of one egg. These are now present, however, even in seemingly undisturbed eyries: 8 out of 85 nests (1965) and 19 out of 79 nests (1969) contained only one egg. In addition, there were 75% (1965) and 100% (1969) more nests with 2 eggs than with 3 eggs. Thus, the 1862 average of Krüper's field observations (2.5) had slipped to 2.24 in 1965 and 2.01 in 1969 (table 2). This is certainly a significant trend that could have serious effects on the long-term population dynamics of this species.

Regarding infertility and hatching ratios, Krüper seems to describe a situation that does not differ from the current one. It seems somewhat curious that during the quite "natural" 1860s a falcon with such a small clutch experienced a considerable amount of infertility that was not related to any biocide impact.

In conclusion, Eleonora's falcon seems to have withstood the impact of modern biocides well. Its eggs do not appear to have become thinner-shelled or otherwise deficient. Its embryo mortality and egg infertility rates have probably not changed over the past hundred years. The average clutch size of certain Aegean falcon populations has declined, however, by 10 to 20% during the same period. The clutch size of these colonies should be carefully monitored to detect further changes, and the causes of change should be investigated. Are biocides responsible, or reduced food resources, or direct and indirect human disturbance? At this point, Eleonora's falcon has not been affected as much by modern technology as have many other raptors. There can be little doubt that its generally remote breeding locations and its diversified diet centered on small insectivorous birds have protected this falcon from the major adverse effects of human activity since 1945.

FUTURE OF ELEONORA'S FALCON

When the Arctic ice shields began to melt away less than 20,000 years ago, climatic conditions gradually caused the return of the wooded landscape to temperate latitudes. With it came the millions and millions of insectivorous songbirds that are so familiar in our suburban and rural landscapes. The annual migration of these birds has provided the staple diet for Eleonora's falcon since it evolved into a Mediterranean hunter of fall migrants in the open airspace over the seas. If my hypothesis on the origin of Eleonora's falcon is correct, then we have here a relatively young species, one that has had only some 6,000 to 12,000 years to gain a firm foothold in the dynamic and competitive world of nature. In its breeding area, Eleonora's falcon is all by itself, since the potential competitors breed earlier in the year. Thus, from nature's point of view, this species has created its own niche in an unchallenged ecological space.

The human factor, however, has had an indirect effect on bird migration numbers for over a thousand years and has become so overwhelming in the past thirty years that the future of Eleonora's falcon—and that of other raptors, for that matter—is uncertain at best. Human population growth, coupled with greater mobility and technology, has begun to affect even the

faraway rocks and cliffs in the most desolate corners of the
Mediterranean Sea. Tourism, yachting, and photography know
no limits, intruding into once-sacred breeding grounds. Nobody
can predict the future interaction between man and falcon, but
one thing seems clear: falcons can coexist with people, even large
numbers of people, as long as the people let them alone. Based on
my own experience and on Krüper's observations in the 1860s, I
am strongly inclined to believe that many major colonies of
Eleonora's falcon have suffered from below-normal breeding success levels for more than a hundred years and that some of them
have ceased to exist as a result of the insufficient production of
young falcons (Gibraltar, Iles d'Hyères). Much of this has been
caused by the exploitation of falcon nests by Mediterranean, particularly Aegean, fishermen. If this perspective is correct, then
protecting the falcon from this predation should not only help to
maintain the current world population of Eleonora's falcon but
should eventually lead to a considerable increase in numbers. This
would then serve as a strong counteracting force to the perhaps
unavoidable increase in mortality and infertility owing to indirect
impacts of human technology.

There remains, however, the almost insurmountable problem
of how to enforce the law. Fishermen and boating parties can
hardly be controlled or monitored, and they will almost certainly
cause a rapid decline and extinction of many colonies of Eleonora's falcon. The first to be affected will be the more accessible
colonies, close to harbors and vacation centers. This trend should,
of course, be opposed as strongly as possible. But the major effort
should be directed at establishing a number of completely protected, regularly patrolled ecological island reserves in the
Mediterranean region. The large breeding colonies of Eleonora's
falcon would certainly qualify for this preservation effort simply
because of the numbers of raptors involved. These islands also
usually harbor other rare bird and mammal species that are in
need of effective preservation.

12 Eleonora's Falcon and Other Birds of Prey: A Comparative Analysis

In previous chapters I have concentrated on the ecology and behavior of Eleonora's falcon itself. Other species, in particular members of the same genus, have been mentioned where it seemed appropriate. In this last chapter, I will relate the research on Eleonora's falcon to raptor studies in general. Eleonora's falcon shares many of its characteristics, particularly behavioral elements, with its congeners, and this must be emphasized in the comparative context. A survey of the mushrooming raptor literature uncovers new research results and concepts of raptor biology related to other species that can also be applied to Eleonora's falcon. A comparative analysis will also settle how different this bird is from other raptors: Is there really anything truly special about Eleonora's falcon? Finally, can the research results of this study contribute new perspectives or new concepts to some of the major problems in raptor sociobiology?

Only a few fields in raptor research will be covered here, but there are many other promising research areas. One area is the similarity of basic cell components in different raptors. Sibley and Ahlquist (1972) found that the starch gel electrophoretic patterns of the egg-white proteins of *F. eleonorae* were very similar to those of *F. subbuteo*. But those of *F. tinnunculus*, *F. naumanni*, and the barn owl (*Tyto alba*) also looked very similar. This analysis is therefore not likely to assist us with the phylogenetic history of Eleonora's falcon. Instead, it poses an interesting general problem of the taxonomic relationship of falcons. The authors comment: "The true falcons differ from the diurnal birds of prey in a number of respects and show some similarity to the owls. Whether the falcons thus form a link between the falconiformes and the strigiforms or merely are convergent to the hawks is not known. This intriguing problem is worthy of intensive investigation." Brown and Amadon (1968) have recognized a suborder of *Falcones* in order to emphasize differences from the Accipitridae. They also list the characters and habits that falcons and owls share: musculature of the head, absence of a nest-building instinct, killing prey by biting and severing the neck vertebrae, holding food in one claw, hissing call of the young, and head-bobbing behavior. As owl behavior becomes better known, perhaps more characters common to both groups will emerge.

ADAPTIVE VALUE AND FUNCTION OF MORPHOLOGICAL CHARACTERS

Falconers and scientists have emphasized for many years the outstanding adaptation of a raptor's body to its function in the pursuit and killing of its prey (Frederick II in Wood and Fyfe 1961; Brüll 1964; Brown and Amadon 1968; Brown 1976). New anatomical (Goslow 1972) and comparative osteometric studies (Bährmann 1974a, b) add further evidence for the species-specific proportions in the size of major body parts that help optimize a raptor's foraging efficiency. We can therefore expect that the body form and structure of Eleonora's falcon is also superbly adapted to its ecological niche as a result of natural selection. Nobody has yet made an osteometric analysis of this species. The relative proportions of Eleonora's falcon and its size have been alluded to in the fourth chapter of this book. One aspect, the reversed dimorphism in size between the sexes, will be dealt with at the end of this chapter, since I consider it one of the most fascinating problems in raptor research.

Raptors vary more than most other bird groups in their intraspecific plumage and color. I refer not only to the age- and sex-specific plumage, but also to the presence of poly- or dichromatic plumage in eagles, hawks, and falcons. Eleonora's falcon is a typical raptor, with more than one adult plumage in both sexes. What is the selective advantage of this intraspecific variability? In two highly stimulating papers, Baumgart (1974, 1975) has developed a well-documented hypothesis on the functional importance of different pattern and color signals in raptors. Many raptors, particularly the small and medium-sized ones, are either streaked or barred below. Baumgart suggests that a *contrast-rich barred underside* serves as a signal expressing intolerance. If worn by a territorial occupant, it has a strong threatening effect on any invading falcon. If the invader should have such a pattern, it will elicit a particularly strong territorial defense. Barred underside patterns are found in raptors that are resident as adults and "permanently

territory-intolerant" like central European goshawks and peregrines.

A second group of species possesses a *contrast-rich streaked underside*. It is less threatening and provokes less territorial defense
behavior. This pattern is found in falcons, (saker, hobby) that are
territorial during the breeding season but nonterritorial, though
solitary and often migratory, in the nonbreeding season. The
juvenile plumage of species with barred underside character in
adults uses a streaked underside pattern to enable them to disperse and search for a territory.

Barred or streaked undersides have disappeared or become
reduced in extent or contrast in territorial species that are gregarious during the nonbreeding season. In this third group there
are also species with variable plumage and with color phases unre-
lated to sex and age. This trend reduces or eliminates any specific
signal functions of the underside in these species.

Baumgart sees the color patterns of raptors as an expression of
their social and migratory behavior. Since the degree of gregariousness is related to the dispersion of food resources (highly dispersed resources lead to large spacing, resource cluster patterns
lead to gregarious behavior and reduced spacing of most sites), it
can be said that "the plumage of birds of prey mirrors their concrete life conditions."

The motivation to develop color phases lies in the need for reduced spacing in temporarily or permanently gregarious species.
This can be accomplished through a "lightening" and a "darken-
ing" strategy. In the former, dark streaks or bars become reduced
or "bleached"; in the latter, the dark spots become enlarged or
merge with a generally dark underside (fig. 55). Selection pressure
should favor such evolutionary trends over the distance-demanding barred and streaked patterns in situations where gregarious
patterns are the optimal response to resource distribution in
space. The extremes, the pattern-free light (leucistic) and the
dark (melanistic) plumage are developed only where a high degree of sociality is advantageous. Which of the two strategies has
been followed "probably depends on selective factors outside the
functional system of intraspecific behavior" (enemies, hunting success, etc.). The preponderance of one phase over the other would
be "proportional to its superiority."

Among other species, Baumgart uses the buzzard (*Buteo buteo*),

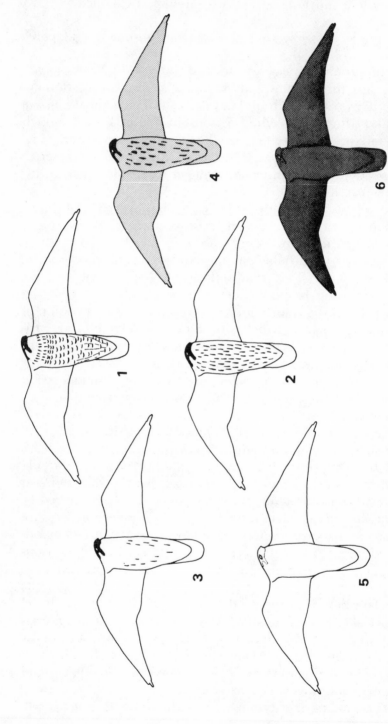

Fig. 55. Signal function of plumage patterns in falcons (after Baumgart 1974). *Type 1*: Strongly barred underside of the highly intolerant, solitary species. *Type 2*: Reduced signal function owing to streaked underside. *Types 3 and 4*: Plumage pattern showing little contrast or greatly reduced.

Types 5 and 6: Underside light or dark without any pattern. Falcons with such a morphology possess reduced territoriality and are likely to be gregarious or at least more sociable than related forms of types 1 or 2.

the gyrfalcon (*F. rusticulus*), and Eleonora's falcon in support of his thesis. Although we talk of a "light phase" and a "dark phase" in Eleonora's falcon, the more common light phase shows a streaked pattern with much buff and brown on the underside. This reduces the contrast and efficiency of the streaked pattern's function. "Individuals of the dark phase appear to be melanistic mutants that have an advantage over the ancestral type birds in real life."

In his discussion of the significance of the color patterns of raptors, Baumgart points out that vocal communication or aerial displays predominate where the signal character of plumage patterns has been reduced. This can be explained in terms of energy. Optical signals like bars and streaks are the most economical. Once they have been developed, they need no care and last for a long time. Acoustic signals are more energy-expensive but are still cheaper than kinematic signals (aerial display, threat postures, etc.), which must be used where the permanent presence of distance-demanding optical plumage patterns is disadvantageous within the sociobiological context (Baumgart 1975).

The Baumgart hypothesis is, I believe, very interesting indeed. It offers a plausible explanation for the existence of the plumage variability in Eleonora's falcon. There is no doubt at all about the need for *distance-reducing signals* in this species. Vocal communication is definitely prominent, and displays in the air and on the ground are frequent (although no comparison has been made of the energy costs of such displays with those of kestrels or peregrines). One might ask, however, why the streaked pattern has persisted in Eleonora's falcon. Would it not be "better" to have only a leucistic or a melanistic plumage pattern? The same question might be asked for other social raptors. It might indeed be that Eleonora's falcon and other species will eventually evolve such uniform, signal-poor plumage. I think it is more likely, however, that considerable plumage variability within a breeding population also has selective advantages. The main advantage would be the easy recognition of individuals within a neighborhood (see chap. 3).

Looking at other social falcons, we find the sooty falcon with an adult plumage that is uniformly sooty and even darker in a rare dark phase. Thus in this species, which appears to be less colonial than Eleonora's falcon (Clapham 1964; Moreau 1969), we have an example of extreme signal reduction. It is possible that the desert habitat of this species has been responsible for this evolution to a near-melanistic state (many birds of hot, tropical environments are dark colored). The latter was probably much more advantageous than the original streaked underside and other intermediate stages. The juveniles of this species still possess a streaked underside.

The typical kestrels (fig. 56) differ from the peregrine, gyrfalcon, and hobby group in that they exhibit sexual dichromatism. The males of *F. sparverius, F. tinnunculus,* and *F. naumanni* have only a few streaks on their breasts and flanks compared with the females and juveniles. If we apply the Baumgart hypothesis to this phenomenon, then the males should exhibit less distance-demanding behavior and more social behavior than the females. This indeed seems to be the case in *F. tinnunculus* and *F. naumanni,* which do not defend an exclusive home range containing their food resources. *F. sparverius,* however, defends a territory including its food resources during the breeding season (Balgooyen 1976) and is not as gregarious during the nonbreeding season as the two European species *F. tinnunculus* and *F. naumanni.*

The male/female patterns therefore appear to agree with the Baumgart hypothesis. But the male American kestrel (*F. sparverius*) does not, since it is highly distance-demanding throughout the year in comparison with the other species.

Another look at the three species made me realize, however, that in kestrels it may be not the underside but the upper back and the shoulders that carry the function of distance-demanding signals (fig. 56). Most other hawks and falcons have uniformly colored upper parts with only a trace of pattern. In the female American kestrel, however, the brown-reddish upper parts are heavily barred. In the male, an unusually contrasting pattern is created, with a small part of the upper back showing a barred pattern framed by bluish shoulders and wings. In the European kestrel, the male has brown-reddish upper-parts with dark streaks and spots and the female looks similar to the male except for her barred upper back. The female of the lesser kestrel is nearly identical, but the male of this species has a pattern-free brown-reddish plumage of back and shoulders. The American kestrel, particularly the male, shows the strongest barred pattern on its back, a signal of threat and of keeping at a distance. In the lesser kestrel

a.

b.

c.

a. American kestrel

b. European kestrel

c. Lesser kestrel

Fig. 56. Three kestrel species. Note the barred upper back in all sexes except in the male of *Falco naumanni*. Drawing by N. L. Diaz.

only the female shows a pattern, while the male has no spots on his upper parts and very few left on his underside. This is, of course, the most social and colonial of the kestrels.

It seems that the hunting style of these kestrels has been responsible for the transfer of those optical signals to the upper parts of the body. Kestrels hover, perch, and fly unusually close to the ground. In this position they are more likely to be encountered by other kestrels or raptors flying above them. The signal function of the back and shoulder plumage can therefore be understood as an adaptation to the hunting habits of the kestrel group.

The most social of the Palearctic falcons is the red-footed falcon (*F. vespertinus*). In this species we have four distinct plumage patterns (see plate in Glutz, Bauer, and Bezzel 1971), one each for immature and adult males and females. The adult male is nearly uniformly dark and does not possess any optical signals of threat or territorial defense. Immature males have a reddish underside with some dark streaks. The adult female has a whitish underside with a few dark streaks, the latter being more pronounced in immature specimens. Little is known about the behavior of this species. The available data (Horváth 1955, 1956, 1975) do not permit any speculation regarding the evolutionary background and relevance of this "quadrichromatic" species.

It might be worthwhile to study the plumage patterns of owls with respect to the Baumgart hypothesis. Here it might be other body parts, perhaps the face and head, that carry optical signals related to territory and agonistic behavior.

Finally, there is good agreement between the optical signal gradient discussed and the reversed size dimorphism in raptors. At least among the North American and Palearctic hawks and falcons, species with a high dimorphism index usually also have a strong and contrasting barred or streaked signal, while those with little or no size difference between male and female possess reduced or variable optical signals or occur in color phases.

DISPERSION, TERRITORIALITY, AND SOCIABILITY

Aristotle observed that "one does not find two pairs of eagles in the same wood" (Brown 1970). This is perhaps the first of many statements on the dispersion and territorial patterns of raptors. Today the factors regulating population numbers and their distribution in space are of the highest interest in raptor research. In addition to the natural limiting factors, man has added a number of potent anthropogenic factors. In their attempt to preserve and rebuild certain raptor populations, researchers need to know the magnitude and direction of each of these limiting factors.

We have discussed at length the dispersion, sociability, and territoriality of Eleonora's falcon. Does this species possess a unique system or pattern of life compared with other raptors? Dispersion is defined as the distribution pattern of a population at a given time. It is usually described in qualitative terms (clustered, regular, random), in terms of density (breeding pairs/study area or km²/pair), or with data on distances between neighboring nest sites. The average breeding density is a valuable index of the interaction of the raptor population with its environment when the latter provides contiguous breeding opportunities. Should the study area, however, contain a substantial area that is completely void of the raptor population, the value loses much of its usefulness. An example for the latter is Eleonora's falcon. Its average breeding density can be estimated (very roughly) as one pair for every 500 km² of a Mediterranean basin land stretching from the Canaries to Lebanon (4,500 × 500 km²). This means very little, since we know about the irregular distribution of nesting habitats on islands and mainland cliffs and realize this species breeds in colonies of variable size. Table 18 contains average *density* data of selected raptors. In most species we can detect a surprising range of values. The highest ones are some 10 to 20 times above the lowest. These values certainly reflect the quality of local resources, habitats, competitors, disturbance, pollution, and so forth. In my opinion they are most valuable when compared with data from the same study area at other times. In addition, the highest densities recorded may come close to the upper limit for a species when intraspecific regulating mechanisms can be expected to become increasingly important.

The spacing pattern can provide additional insight, particularly when we compare the average values with the minimum distance between two nest sites. This distance is likely to reflect the territoriality of a given species or to indicate the dispersion and abundance of food and nesting sites in the study area. Table 38 (Appendix A) contains a large number of data on minimum distance between the nests of 30 European raptors, excluding Eleo-

TABLE 18
Average Breeding Densities of Selected Raptor Species

Species	Density (km²/pair)	Region (year)	Source
Peregrine	12	Saxony (1929/30)	Glutz, Bauer, and Bezzel 1971
	54	Wales	Brown 1976
	76	East central Scotland	Brown 1976
	133	Switzerland (before 1945)	Glutz, Bauer, and Bezzel 1971
	160	Eastern France (1961)	Glutz, Bauer, and Bezzel 1971
	223	West Highlands (Britain)	Brown 1976
Gyrfalcon	130	Iceland	Glutz, Bauer, and Bezzel 1971
	400	Greenland	Glutz, Bauer, and Bezzel 1971
	1727	Southern Alaska	Glutz, Bauer, and Bezzel 1971
Hobby	12	Lorraine (France)	Brown 1976
	10–200	Central Europe	Glutz, Bauer, and Bezzel 1971
	130–260	Britain	Brown 1976
European kestrel	0.8–25	Central Europe	Glutz, Bauer, and Bezzel 1971
	5	Munich, Bavaria (1968)	Glutz, Bauer, and Bezzel 1971
	2.4–7.5	Sussex, England (1968)	Brown 1976
Golden eagle	47–73	Scotland	Glutz, Bauer, and Bezzel 1971
	300	Swiss Alps	Glutz, Bauer, and Bezzel 1971
	225–625	French Alps	Glutz, Bauer, and Bezzel 1971
Goshawk	18.2–77	Central Europe	Glutz, Bauer, and Bezzel 1971
European sparrow hawk	10–125	Central Europe	Glutz, Bauer, and Bezzel 1971

nora's falcon and several of the rarer species. Even if we concede that many of these minimum distances occur only in exceptional circumstances, table 38 is likely to surprise some readers. There is a general belief that most raptors are fiercely territorial and therefore spatially intolerant of each other. The data indicate almost the contrary. In 24 (80%) of those 30 species of falcons, hawks, harriers, kites, eagles, and vultures, the minimum distance between two nests has been found to be less than 1 km. Fifteen species (50%) show a minimum spacing of 100 m or less, and 6 species (20%) have been found to breed 10 m or less from each other. This last group consists of sociable species that have been known to breed in colonies over at least part of their range (*Falco tinnunculus*, *F. naumanni*, *F. vespertinus*, *Circus pygargus*, *Milvus migrans*, *Gyps fulvus*). These are the species that come closest to Eleonora's falcon in minimum distance between adjacent nesting sites. In conclusion, most diurnal raptors have at least once been recorded as breeding within 1 km of a conspecific neighbor's nesting site. Many of these were spaced even closer together. Three falcons, a harrier, a kite, and a vulture species show a minimum distance between nest sites that is comparable to that found in Eleonora's falcon.

In raptors we commonly distinguish between nesting territories, home ranges, winter (seasonal) territories, and day territories. The last can be observed in some migrating and wintering raptors and contain the hunting area of an individual, which is sometimes defended. Nesting territories extend for a certain distance around, above, and below the nesting site. Their measurements have been estimated in only a few species so far (Balgooyen 1976; Cade 1960; Beebe 1960, 1974; Glutz, Bauer, and Bezzel 1971; Newton 1976b). In general, raptors will take any necessary action within the nesting territory to drive away a conspecific intruder, an enemy, certain other bird species (mostly larger ones), or human beings. The intensity of territorial defense and agonistic behavior decreases from the center of the territory (the nesting site, the eyrie) to the periphery. It is difficult to delimit the nesting territory because the agonistic behavior may change significantly in the same individual within the same breeding season. It may also vary between individuals. It is easier to determine what lies outside the nesting territory, defined as any point at which intruders are within visual or acoustic reach of the nesting site without alarming the territorial occupant.

In Eleonora's falcon, the nesting territory is the entire "ground territory." It may be extremely small (radius less than 2 m from the nest), small (radius 5 to 20 m), or perhaps larger in colonies inhabited by widely spaced falcon pairs. In the European kestrel (*F. tinninculus*) the nesting territory was found to have a maximum radius of 35 m in an area where nest boxes were 150 m and 300 m apart (Cavé 1968). The minimum spacing in the lesser kestrel and in the red-footed falcon can only mean that a nesting territory defined as exclusive space of the owner(s) is often not larger than a few cubic centimeters around the nesting site itself. The radius increases as the species become more solitary and reaches distances of several hundred meters in hobby, merlin, peregrine, and gyrfalcon (Glutz, Bauer, and Bezzel 1971). Aggressive encounters are rare among the conspecifics of certain raptors. The golden eagle is a good example. It has one of the more regular spacing patterns (Brown 1976) in Britain; this is achieved without much physical combat or threat. Avoiding other birds' territories is frequent among birds of prey (Balgooyen 1976; Hickey 1969; Ligon 1968). It might therefore be better to define the nesting territory as the "exclusive space" of a pair, containing its nest.

In highly gregarious species like Eleonora's falcon, the nesting territory is not the *only* defended area. Often the general colony space, particularly the vertical space up to hundreds of meters above the colony itself, will be defended against trespassers like large hawks, eagles, or herons. This behavior has also been observed in the red-footed falcon (Horváth 1976). Thus we have here something else, a group or colony nesting territory, also found in gulls and many other colonial species.

The home range is the area where raptors seek and find their prey. Some species defend it (American kestrel), others defend it partially (at certain times or some part of the total area) or not at all. The nesting site and the nesting territory usually lie within the home range. It seems that most Palearctic falcon species do not defend their entire home range against conspecifics, but data are scarce for several of the solitary species. The latter are so widely spaced (tens or hundreds of kilometers) that the conspecific neighbors hardly ever exist (Glutz, Bauer, and Bezzel 1971).

Measuring the actual size of the required home range is rather difficult, particularly under the disturbed conditions of our times, but this is an important aspect of the raptor's ecology. Schoener (1968) has tried to correlate the feeding territories of birds with their body size. In general, larger raptors require larger home ranges. Studies such as those by Brown (1970), Thiollay (1975), and Smeenk (1974) in largely undisturbed areas of Africa tend to confirm this correlation. A similar trend was found in a raptor community in Utah (Smith and Murphy 1973; table 19): the smallest species (kestrel and burrowing owl) had home ranges of 0.80 to 0.93 km², and a pair of golden eagles utilized 23.44 km². But different hunting strategies and prey species seem to offset this general relationship. A prairie falcon pair, for instance, although weighing only 39% of the combined weight of a male and female ferruginous hawk, utilized a larger home range (6.09 km² versus 5.28 km²) than the hawks. Another factor limiting the dispersion of many species is the scarcity of potential nesting sites. Hole-nesting and cliff-nesting species, as well as those that utilize

Table 19
Average Home Ranges of Nesting Raptor Pairs in Utah

Species	Body Size Male/Female (weight in g)[a]	Home Range[b] (area in km²)
Golden eagle[c]	3,739/5,009	23.44
Great horned owl	1,142/1,509	4.87
Ferruginous hawk	1,059/1,231	5.28
Red-tailed hawk	1,028/1,224	5.67
Swainson's hawk	908/1,069	4.74
Prairie falcon	496/801	6.09
Marsh hawk[d]	472/570	4.20
Burrowing owl	159/151	0.93
American kestrel	109/119	0.80

[a] Snyder and Wiley (1976), except for golden eagle and marsh hawk.
[b] Smith and Murphy (1973). All data are from the same breeding season, 1969.
[c] Glutz, Bauer, and Bezzel (1971): weight data refer to the larger European subspecies.
[d] Weight after Craighead and Craighead (1956).

other birds' nests, are absent or occur in extremely low numbers where nesting sites are at a premium. If prey is plentiful and nest sites are not, there is an incentive for the selection of less intolerant genotypes. If one pair has found a good nest site in locality A, it is more likely that there is another one in A than in distant localities B and C. Thus, nest spacing becomes reduced.

The most important ultimate factors in regulating raptor populations, however, are the quality and quantity of food resources (Newton 1976b). If there are no potential prey in the area, no raptor will breed there. Many species fluctuate in a certain synchronic fashion with the population dynamics of their major prey species or show a lower density and smaller home range in areas with unusually low prey densities (Newton 1976b; Brown 1976). On the other hand, some of the best-researched species never reach their theoretically possible breeding density. They seem incapable of increasing their numbers beyond a certain "ceiling" and therefore fail to fully exploit certain opportunities (extremely high prey quality and quantity). This phenomenon leads Ratcliffe (in Hickey 1969, p. 245) to state: "The factor holding numbers down below the 'ceiling' of food supply is evidently of a different kind, an internal regulatory mechanism developed by the species itself, and I believe that it is simply the territorialism that has been inferred above."

The geography of prey availability is as important for raptor dispersion as the geography of nesting sites. If prey is clustered (fishes in a lake, voles in marshes and fields), selection should once again favor the less intolerant raptor genotype in order to permit a somewhat gregarious, or at least clustered, breeding pattern. On the other hand, we could expect evenly dispersed food resources to be complemented by evenly dispersed, solitary raptors if nest site factors and other habitat features are not geographically limiting.

The foregoing should provide us with the basis for an integrative analysis of dispersion, territoriality, and sociability in the genus *Falco*. In figure 57 I have shown generalized distribution and territorial patterns for ten species representing a gradient from extremely solitary to extremely sociable. I am certain that many other diurnal raptors and owls fit the pattern of one of these generalized maps, but there will surely also be some species with an altogether different system of spatial and territorial organization.

The American kestrel (*F. sparverius*) represents the intolerant raptor where nesting territory and home range are the same or almost the same. This hole-nesting falcon is small, its home range is small, and conspecific neighbors are common throughout most of its range.

Model 2 probably represents several falcons besides the merlin (*F. columbarius*), namely, gyrfalcon, lanner, and prairie falcon. These falcons are generally so scarcely distributed over the land that they are not in periodic contact with other breeding pairs. Thus it would be difficult to study their territorial behavior. Whether they will ever show a significant overlap of home ranges between neighbors is an open question. My guess is that they will not.

The peregrine (*F. peregrinus*) has been widely studied, particularly by Cade (1960) and Nelson (1970). Peregrines may become concentrated under unusually favorable prey and habitat conditions (coastlines, islands, river valleys). In those circumstances a certain overlap in the feeding areas of neighbors has been noted. This species is strongly territorial within its nesting territory, however, although overt conflicts are rare because of mutual avoidance (Ratcliffe, in Hickey 1969).

The dispersion pattern observed in the hobby (*F. subbuteo*) indicates another step away from the true solitary falcons (models 1 and 2). In this species, spacing patterns may be reduced to below

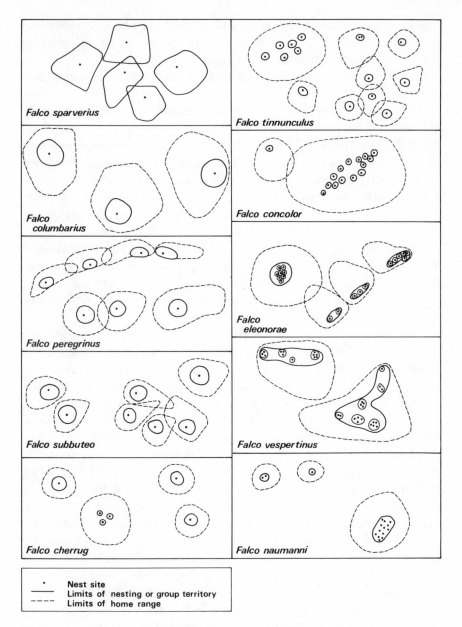

Falco sparverius		Falco tinnunculus
Falco columbarius		Falco concolor
Falco peregrinus		Falco eleonorae
Falco subbuteo		Falco vespertinus
Falco cherrug		Falco naumanni

·	Nest site
——	Limits of nesting or group territory
- - -	Limits of home range

Fig. 57. Model of the territoriality in members of the genus *Falco*.

1 km, and the hunting areas may be shared with breeding hobbies from surrounding areas. This species is also sometimes gregarious while migrating (Brown 1970; Glutz, Bauer, and Bezzel 1971). Individual pairs maintain a sizable nesting territory around their nest sites.

The saker falcon (*F. cherrug*) represents the first real breakdown of the solitary dispersion system. Although it is rare and therefore by necessity is solitary over much of its range, 3 to 4 nest sites have been recorded "here and there" in Southern Russia on areas not larger than 1.2 ha (Karamsin in Dementjew, quoted in Glutz, Bauer, and Bezzel 1971). Qualitative statements indicate that this species is relatively peaceful compared with the falcons of models 1–4 (fig. 57). This means that the saker possesses a reduced level of agonistic behavior near its nest. At the same time, it can breed in close proximity to others, probably as an adaptation to widely dispersed but clustered food resources or to limited nest sites. It is highly probable that a cluster of 3 to 4 saker pairs will show significant overlap in their home ranges.

The other five species represented in figure 57 range from gregarious to colonial. The Eurasian kestrel (*F. tinnunculus*) is often solitary but several or many pairs may breed on the same cliff or building. The feeding areas are not defended in most circumstances. Its well-developed territorial behavior and nesting territory (Cavé 1968) place it in an intermediary position above the saker falcon on the gradient of increasing sociability.

The sooty falcon (*F. concolor*) breeds in loose groups or solitarily on islands and in the extreme desert environment of northeast Africa and Arabia. Clapham (1964) stresses that the falcon is "not a colonial species. Even where breeding sites are abundant, there is always a distance of 40–50 yards between one nest and the next." The same author also states that "there is then a distinct nesting territory, and there is no social reaction towards intruders." This falcon seems to maintain a generally solitary behavioral pattern in very close proximity to a large number of other breeding pairs. Some hunting of migrants apparently occurs within the nesting territory, but a much larger home range that is not defended was utilized on island breeding sites in the Arabian Gulf (Walter, in prep.). The sooty falcon is highly gregarious in its Madagascar winter habitat.

In Eleonora's falcon, the minimum and the average distance

between nest sites is further reduced, and social defense against potential enemies is common. Even here, however, a man walking through a series of nesting territories across an island slope often causes alarm calls and anxiety in only one falcon female at a time. The home range is definitely shared by the entire falcon colony. This species therefore clearly belongs to the colonial falcon type.

The red-footed falcon (*F. vespertinus*) is as gregarious as the lesser kestrel, particularly on migration in Africa. During the breeding season, red-footed falcons feed on arthropods, amphibians, reptiles, and fledged birds. Their food resources are somewhat concentrated in humid valleys. More important, potential nesting sites for this gregarious species often occur in clusters. They are very aggressive toward the occupants of tree nests (magpies, crows) that they want to use as their own nesting sites. They prefer to breed in small and distinct aggregations. In Hungary, not more than 3 to 5 pairs were found to be breeding in the same tree, although the trees contained many additional abandoned nests of the rook (*Corvus frugilegus*). The minimum distance between nests is therefore less than 10 m. Small colonies of 10 to 45 falcon pairs were dispersed over a wooded area of some 0.5 to 1.0 km². The most interesting aspect of this falcon's behavior is its advanced degree of social defense. According to Horváth (1975), "the birds of a colony defend their occupied rookery." There is also some indication of altruistic behavior when one pair attempts to conquer a nest still owned by a crow or magpie. Other falcon pairs "support" the attacking conspecific pair. Glutz, Bauer, and Bezzel (1971) believe that this probably refers only to acoustic support. This falcon also has distinct group feeding territories before, during, and after the breeding season. It is not clear if these territories are defended against other groups, but Horváth distinguishes them from the kestrel (*F. tinnunculus*), which in his opinion has no well-defined feeding territory. Of great interest is Horváth's statement on territoriality in the red-footed falcon: "The numbers of a colony, nevertheless, defend their territory with sound and attack against the birds of another" (Horváth 1975, p. 329).

The red-footed falcon is therefore not only gregarious, it is a sociable bird that has retained a comparatively high level of agonistic behavior. In a breeding colony, the territoriality appears to be channeled into a group or neighborhood effort of communal defense and aggression (even if only through acoustic means). Individual nesting territories may have largely disappeared where several pairs nest in the same tree.

The lesser kestrel (*F. naumanni*) is the least aggressive of all the falcon species occurring in the western Palearctic region. The minimal distances between nesting sites are as small as in Eleonora's falcon. This falcon is extraordinarily peaceful, even fearful of other bird species. Only very few agonistic behaviors have been observed so far—at the nest. Young falcons that move from their own eyrie into another one are fed and adopted by the neighboring pair. I would guess that prey piracy rarely occurs, since the falcon feeds mostly on crickets, grasshoppers, and lizards. It therefore seems that this species has almost ceased to perceive or defend any "exclusive space" of its own along the walls of cliffs, buildings, and so forth, where there may be colonies of 500 pairs or more (Wyer, unpublished manuscript). Even during the breeding season, lesser kestrels frequently hunt in small groups. Occasionally they will defend the colony site against large raptors passing through (Glutz, Bauer, and Bezzel 1971). This species is therefore highly sociable. Its activities and behavior are in my opinion more adapted to nesting in huge colonies than are those of other falcons. Selection in this species has taken the extreme path of combining a raptorial phylogeny and morphology with very low aggressiveness, obviously a successful strategy in areas such as Spain where the small food items of this raptor are abundant (and clustered) but where suitable nesting sites are rather limited.

In conclusion, along the gradient of increasing sociability we have several intolerant, solitary, and nonsociable species at one end and four highly gregarious falcon species at the other end. In between are several intermediary types of generally solitary species showing different degrees of territorial defense, nest-site spacing, and overlap in home range.

Within the gregarious group the sooty falcon appears to be the least sociable species, since its highly agonistic behavior is still centered on nest site and territory even though the latter is rather small (radius probably about 15 to 20 m in a large colony). Eleonora's falcon shows smaller minimum distances between nesting sites and, as discussed in chapter 8, a considerable degree of altruistic behavior in defense of the "status quo" of falcon neighborhoods and in defense of the falcon colony. Its feeding areas are shared by the entire colony. The red-footed falcon (*F. vespertinus*) is not a cliff-breeder and often lives in close proximity with crows, whose nests it uses. This may be one reason why this highly gregarious raptor displays strong agonistic behavior at the breeding sites. This species prefers to breed close to only a few other pairs, a habit that creates distinct family groups or neighborhoods within a colony. These, as well as the colony (and perhaps even the well-defined feeding territory), are defended against conspecifics. The red-footed falcon therefore has the most complex social organization of all the species discussed. The lesser kestrel displays extreme sociability accompanied by almost no agonistic behavior, resulting in a comparatively simple social organization: intraspecific intolerance is minimized, permitting many individuals to share the limited nesting cliffs and to exploit the same feeding territory.

SELECTION AND OCCUPANCY OF NEST SITES

Whether a particular potential nest site is occupied by a falcon pair has been a vexing question for many researchers. Population size and food availability certainly influence the occupancy level of nest sites in a region, but a number of additional factors come into play.

Studying the location and spacing of nest sites within a colony of Eleonora's falcons made me aware of this species' need for safety in the vicinity of the occupied nest. The ground territory usually includes an area large enough to afford "visual privacy" and thus security from intraspecific neighbors. The safety space needed varies with the microtopography within large falcon colonies. At the macroscale, most falcon species, including Eleonora's falcon, are very apt at occupying nest sites that can be defended against conspecifics, mammal and avian predators, and man. This is why so many colonies of Eleonora's falcon, like the ones in Mallorca, lie along inaccessible cliffs. In response to increased disturbance and predation, a falcon population can be expected to give up "vulnerable" nest sites and retreat to safer places. This in itself shows, however, that the new nest sites were not the falcons' first choice, or they would have been occupied long before. Under the conditions of increased disturbance, however, the new sites promise better breeding success. In red-footed falcons, for instance, only some 12 to 13% of the available and largely equal nests in rookeries were occupied by the falcons. Horváth (1955, 1975) has shown that the falcons prefer nests in the highest trees and that dominant adults occupy the most inaccessible nests. This behavior is probably an adaptation to disturbance, predation, and interspecific competition, but it also reflects the social organization (small groups, subcolonies) in this species. Because of the great interest in the recent dramatic decline in peregrine populations (Hickey 1969), more data have become available regarding the breeding of subadult falcons and the role "tradition" may play in the occupancy of certain nest sites (Newton 1976b). It appears that high breeding success leads to higher occupancy rates.

In his stimulating review "Population Limitation in Diurnal Raptors," Newton (1976b) has stated that raptors "appreciate" differences in the quality of nest sites and territories and that in at least two species "they compete more strongly and stick more tenaciously to the good ones."

The knowledgable raptor researcher will develop a "sixth sense" that allows him to predict which of the potential nest sites will be occupied during the coming breeding season. He will also be able to describe the attributes of an optimal nest site that is almost sure to be occupied. This is possible because the researcher has completed a problem-solving exercise in assessing the magnitude and interdependency of the many factors determining nest-site occupancy. We can assume that the raptor population has to solve the same problem. Can we tackle this exercise in a more conscious and systematic manner? With the help of Newton's (1976b) more general data presentation on population regulation, we can discern at least nine factors (table 20) that appear to play a role in nest site occupancy. Confronted with a potential nest site, a falcon (and most other raptors) must decide whether to occupy it largely on the basis of four environmental factors and five population factors. Each factor from one group can be related to each factor in the other group. The factors have been termed in such a way that a "low" or "small" rating, for instance, low quality of nest site or a low level of "absence of disturbance" would make occupancy less probable. "High" or "large" ratings, on the other hand, increase the probability of occupancy.

TABLE 20
Factors Influencing Nest-Site Occupancy in Falcons

Environmental Factors	Population Factors
Food availability near potential nest site	Size of falcon population in study area
Quality of nest site	Degree of sociability
General scarcity of nest sites in study area	Distance from nearest occupied nest site
Absence of disturbance/ predation/interspecific competition for nest sites	Percentage of adult falcons in population
	Breeding success at this nest site in previous seasons

BREEDING BEHAVIOR

The breeding behavior of Eleonora's falcon deserves an intensive effort by students in comparative ethology. Intraspecific interactions of falcons can certainly be observed here more easily than in most congeneric species. In this context it is important that the basic behaviors of courtship, incubation, and parental care are very similar to those of other falcons. The difference lies in the considerable intraspecific tolerance of this raptor and the small physical space in which an individual's social and personal behavior takes place. This probably requires specific behavioral adaptations not found in solitary species. The rather differentiated vocalizations of Eleonora's falcon may serve as an example. The ethology of other gregarious falcons has not been studied in any detail.

The solitary peregrine has only recently become well known (Cade 1960; Nelson 1970). A rather complete index of this falcon's behavior, with excellent data summaries including a large number of behavioral elements identified in ethograms, has now been developed by Nelson (1977). Since much of Nelson's work still awaits publication, I shall save a detailed comparison between Eleonora's falcon and the peregrine until some later date. At this point it is enough to state that most of the peregrine's behavioral elements are duplicated or have homologues in Eleonora's falcon.

Willoughby and Cade (1964) studied the American kestrel, identifying major behavioral sequences and interactions between the sexes. Balgooyen (1976) has further advanced our knowledge of the breeding behavior of this small kestrel. Of particular interest is his "partition of space" model: "Male centripy" exists around a particular potential nesting site at the beginning of the breeding season. This is accompanied by territoriality and a certain promiscuity. Once the pair bond has been established and the male has begun "production feeding" of his mate, "female centripy" develops. The female confines her interest and activities to a small space immediately surrounding her nesting site. This is followed by her maximum centripy of space during egg production, incubation, and brooding of the newly hatched chicks. Finally, "female centrifugy" develops when she resumes hunting and when both parents feed the young. A similar sequence has been described by Cade (1960), Nelson (1970), and Monneret (1974) for the peregrine. These authors were impressed by the apparent strong dominance of the female over the male during a large part of the breeding season. As was described earlier (chap. 8), Monneret (1974) in particular has explained the whole complex of sex roles, division of labor, and the peregrine's prey/predator system as an expression of the fluctuating dominance of the female falcon.

Willoughby and Cade (1964) have tried to test the significance of size difference for the breeding success of American kestrels. The male of this species is usually slightly smaller than his mate. By crossing falcons of different subspecies, pairs were established in which both partners were the same size or the male was slightly larger. The breeding success of these pairs was not significantly different from that of normal pairs (with smaller males).

It would be interesting to study the dominance system in the lesser kestrel. Among this most sociable, nonaggressive falcon there is apparently slight if any division of labor between the sexes (Glutz, Bauer, and Bezzel 1971). If dominance is the force behind the peregrine's pair bond and strong division of labor, it should be less significant or absent in the lesser kestrel. This falcon can also be expected to possess a different "partition of space" for each sex than the American kestrel.

Eleonora's falcon has a strong division of labor between the sexes. The male participates in incubation, however. Individual males may wish to incubate up to half the time, but the females usually prevent them from doing so. This was shown at the submarine cliff (Mogador colony) population after the egg robbery. Several females lost their "centripy" and left the nest site for extended periods. The males stepped in and stayed in the nest scrape for up to several hours at a time. In this raptor the female seems dominant over the male, but this is more subtle than in the peregrine. The same may be true in other large falcons where there are very close and amiable pair relationships including frequent joint hunting of the two partners.

In conclusion, there are good indications that the various members of the genus *Falco* have many behavioral traits in common, but comparative ethology of falcon raptors in general has still to be developed. It will probably distinguish a considerable number of species-specific elements. Only a handful of species have so far been studied in terms of their social behavior. Thus the behavior of Eleonora's falcon, apart from hunting, cannot be compared in detail with that of other species until this raptor's relatives have been studied more extensively. I would also like to emphasize that my studies on Eleonora's falcon did not concentrate on the minute details of its breeding behavior. I am convinced that much more can be learned in carefully planned research efforts.

PREDATOR/PREY RELATIONSHIPS

The timing and sequence of activities throughout the entire breeding season is rather similar among the members of the genus *Falco*. There is really little if anything unusual about the specific activities of Eleonora's falcon except that it delays egg-laying until July. In this it is matched only by the sooty falcon. As we have seen, some colonies of Eleonora's falcon do not seem to subsist on migrant birds until the eggs are about to hatch in mid-August. Clearly, the whole colonial organization of this species is an adaptation to exploit the masses of migrant birds passing by the raptor's breeding sites. Thus the timing of the breeding season is synchronized with the critical period of energy needs in the young falcons, rather than with the period of egg formation in the adult female. The difference in clutch size between the Moroccan Atlantic colonies and the Mediterranean colonies may reflect the different predator/prey systems. In Morocco, migration begins earlier than in the Aegean region. At Mogador, female falcons receive a great deal of "production feeding" (Balgooyen 1976) in the form of birds just before egg-laying. This may permit the development of four-egg clutches, which are not known from the Mediterranean. In the Mediterranean, female falcons depend at least partly on insect food during egg formation.

The timing of the breeding season in Eleonora's falcon appears to be less extreme than in some northern raptor and owl populations. The great horned owl (*Bubo virginianus*), for instance, "begins nesting in late winter when the ground is still covered with snow. Not until weeks later, when the young are well grown and when the female is also hunting, are young prey animals available" (Amadon 1975).

Eleonora's falcon breeds earlier than its nearest relative, the sooty falcon. From the table of nest contents in Clapham (1964) it is evident that hatching in the sooty falcon spans at least the period 17 August to 1 September (the records come from different years), with 7 out of 14 nests visited still containing 1 to 3 eggs between 26 August and 4 September. In the Arabian Gulf region, the young of three nests I inspected in Bahrain on 3 October 1977 were still so small that they must have hatched between 1 and 15 September. Since the sooty falcon's breeding range lies considerably farther south than that of Eleonora's falcon, we would expect its breeding season to lag slightly behind, since the Palearctic migrants will first pass over the Mediterranean region before arriving in the desert belt of the Sahara and Arabia.

It is also interesting that the sooty falcon's "usual clutch is 2–3, but may at times be 4" (Clapham 1964) in the Dahlac Archipelago of the Red Sea. Eleonora's falcon, by comparison, has a maximum clutch size of 3 eggs over the wide Mediterranean range. This is certainly on the low side for most congeneric populations, possibly an adaptation to a fluctuating and unpredictable food source. This may act as a limiting factor, favoring the selection of genotypes with a conservative clutch size of 2 to 3 eggs. The presence of runts in nests with three young points to the validity of this hypothesis.

Perhaps the most spectacular aspect of the ecology of Eleonora's falcon is its ability to exploit the dynamic and short-lived Palearctic-African migration. Other raptors also prey on migrants (peregrines, lanners), but their fates are not linked to the migration stream. It is through a combination of adaptations in physiology (late breeding season), morphology (ability to catch very small birds in the open airspace), behavior (reduced intolerance, high level of sociability for a raptor), and breeding and hunting habitat (islands, coastal cliffs, hunting over the sea) that the ecological niche of Eleonora's falcon is exploited. The sooty falcon depends on a similar migration stream but is less sociable, being highly agonistic near its nesting site, and catches at least some of its bird prey near the ground within its nesting territory (Clapham 1964; Walter, in preparation).

As we saw in the section on falcon energetics, these migrants provide extraordinarily high energy value because of their enormous fat deposits. The biomass is therefore an excellent food resource. It can be compared with the seasonal migration of ungulates in the Serengeti Plains of East Africa and the annual migration of certain fish species. Although bird migration occurs worldwide, Eleonora's falcon and the sooty falcon are the only raptors that manage year after year to exploit it as their principal food resource while raising their brood.

Reversed Sexual Dimorphism in Raptors

Why are the females of raptors and owls larger than the males? This character sets the Falconiformes and Strigiformes (total of some 420 species) apart from thousands of other bird species in which males are larger than or the same size as females. Only the frigate birds (Fregatidae, five species), the skuas and jaegers (Stercorariidae, five species) and a few species from various orders are known to share this reversed sexual dimorphism (RSD) in size.

Frederick II devoted a paragraph to the size dimorphism of raptors, which he found important enough to warrant a complex philosophical statement (Wood and Fyfe 1961). The issue began to stir scientific minds again in this century. Hill (1944) measured thousands· of raptors and clearly considered RSD an unresolved problem in ornithology. Since about 1959 a specialized literature has developed around RSD. Many hypotheses have been proposed (see table 22), but, as Balgooyen (1976) has noted, none has found universal acceptance. Hypotheses of the 1970s are more complex or holistic, often based on extensive documentation or experimentation. The interested reader may explore this issue by reading the original papers: a good sequence would be to start with Hill (1944), then proceed to the introduction in Brown and Amadon (1968), followed by Storer (1966), Earhart and Johnson (1970), Reynolds (1972), Mosher and Matray (1974), Amadon (1975), Balgooyen (1976), and Snyder and Wiley (1976).

Most of the debate, particularly in Storer (1966) and in Snyder and Wiley (1976), has centered on the genera and species showing the strongest RSD in raptors (table 21). In the genus *Accipiter*, for

TABLE 21
Extreme Size Dimorphism in Raptors and Owls (weight in g)

Species	Female	Male	Source
Sharp-shinned hawk	179.0	102.0	Snyder and Wiley 1976
Goshawk	1,095.0	860.0	Snyder and Wiley 1976
Merlin	213.3	157.6	Snyder and Wiley 1976
Prairie falcon	801.0	495.7	Snyder and Wiley 1976
Peregrine	952.0	610.9	Snyder and Wiley 1976
Gyrfalcon	1,752.0	1,170.0	Snyder and Wiley 1976
European sparrow hawk	234.0	137.0	Glutz, Bauer, and Bezzel 1971
Great horned owl	1,509.0	1,141.9	Snyder and Wiley 1976
Great gray owl	1,297.5	935.3	Snyder and Wiley 1976
Boreal owl	139.5	101.6	Snyder and Wiley 1976

instance, some adult females may be twice as heavy as adult males of the same origin and taxonomic unit. In *Accipiter nisus nisus* the osteometric values of certain bones (sternum) of even the largest male do not reach those of the smallest female (Bährmann 1974*b*). There are also bona fide raptors in which RSD is only slight or moderate.

Since the debate on RSD appears to be the nearly exclusive province of North American journals and their contributors, it is not surprising that most attention has been given to North American raptor species. In the following I shall analyze RSD using data on Palearctic species, particularly gregarious species like Eleonora's falcon.

The questions we should ask regarding RSD are simple and straightforward: (1) What is the advantage of dimorphism? (2) Why has RSD become so extreme in the raptor and owl groups? (3) Why don't many more bird families exhibit RSD? Not every paper attempts to answer all three questions. The general approach has been to correlate some observation or finding on sexual differences in behavior, ecology, or physiology with RSD. Some of the early hypotheses have lost most of their value because new research data contradict them. For instance, the long-held belief that male hawks might devour their young were it not for defense by the larger female hawk has not been confirmed in modern behavioral studies. It is true that males of certain species hardly ever visit the nesting site. But if they do, they do not eat their own offspring. Cade (1960) believes the pair bond is more stable when the female is large and dominant. Amadon (1975) adheres to an only slightly rephrased hypothesis, emphasizing the larger female's role in pair formation. Balgooyen (1976) points out that size is only one of several factors affecting dominance and pair bonds. Other factors include age, experience, and territorial ownership. Furthermore, in species like Eleonora's falcon (with a small RSD value) and the burrowing owl (with negative RSD or normal size dimorphism), pair formation and pair bond do not seem to be more difficult to achieve or less stable than in peregrine falcons.

Several hypotheses concern the differential exploitation of resources by the two sexes (table 22). Storer (1966) and others have attempted to prove that each sex in strongly dimorphic raptors feeds on prey of different size-classes. Balgooyen (1976) has applied statistical methods to Storer's original data set. The results showed no significant difference in kind or size of prey between male and female *Accipiter* hawks. European data, however, confirm a remarkable sexual difference in the prey-size spectrum of *Accipiter gentilis* and *A. nisus* (Glutz, Bauer, and Bezzel 1971). Two related hypotheses deal with food specialization (Earhart and Johnson 1970) and with the avoidance of food stress during the latter part of the breeding season (Snyder and Wiley 1976). With the rise of avian energetics have come several analyses of energy requirements, efficiency, and conservation among the sexes

TABLE 22

Major Hypotheses on Reversed Sexual Size Dimorphism in Raptors

A smaller male
1. is no threat to the physical well-being of the female during pair formation (Amadon 1975).
2. is better able to succeed in territorial defense (Schmidt-Bey 1913, cited in Balgooyen 1976).
3. is more agile and better suited for capturing fast prey species (Baumgart 1975).
4. captures smaller prey for the little young (Brüll 1937, cited in Balgooyen 1976).
5. encounters more optimal, accessible prey (Reynolds 1972).
6. conserves more energy (Balgooyen 1976).
7. is a more efficient food provider (Reynolds 1972).
8. requires less energy per gram of weight (Mosher and Matray 1974).

A larger female
9. can protect the young from the male more successfully (Amadon 1959).
10. is more dominant, creating a better pair bond (Cade 1960).

Dimorphism leads to
11. a sex-specific selection of prey requiring a smaller home range (Storer 1966).
12. an increase in the total size range of prey (Earhart and Johnson 1970).
13. less food stress, particularly in bird-hunting raptors, during the late stages of the breeding season (Snyder and Wiley 1976).

(Reynolds 1972; Mosher and Matray 1974; Balgooyen 1976). These studies opened a new door in the RSD debate.

Baumgart (1975) links size with raptors' ability to hunt. He establishes the rule "as small as possible, as large as necessary." More size (weight) means more strength but a loss in agility. Less size increases a raptor's ability to pursue a quick, difficult prey object and is also thought to be an advantage in a male raptor's intraspecific territorial defense (Schmidt-Bey 1913, in Balgooyen 1976). A larger female, on the other hand, is probably well adapted to defend clutch and young at the nest site because of her strength. In addition, very large females may be able to incubate the clutch more efficiently than small females.

These arguments could also be applied to other birds: raven (*Corvus corax*), flycatchers, shrikes, and mockingbirds, for example, seem to benefit from RSD in similar ways. The arguments also imply some knowledge of the direction of natural selection. Did the females become larger, did the males become smaller, or did the two sexes diverge in opposite directions from their initially equal size? This is not known, although Hill (1944) postulates that it was the male that decreased his body size, except for leg and foot. Opposing arguments seem just as valid, however.

Several authors have investigated the life habits of raptors in relation to the dimorphism indexes. They have found a number of interesting correlations that do not constitute a hypothesis, but do indicate a trend or gradient. Earhart and Johnson (1970) noticed that "insectivorous owls are less dimorphic than are the species which feed upon vertebrates." Snyder and Wiley (1976) correlated prey quality with RSD and found the highest and most significant correlation between strong RSD and birds as principal raptor prey. These authors also discuss the low RSD values associated with small-sized prey, with gregarious and colonial raptors, and with ground-breeding species.

A comparative analysis of RSD in the genus *Falco* includes species with very strong and very weak RSD indexes. Since Bährmann (1974*b*) has shown that wing length is a good indicator of the total proportions of the body skeleton of *Accipiter* hawks, we can assume that this measurement will also reflect the minute differences in body proportions among sexes and populations of falcons. Thus, wing length was used to determine the RSD index of the falcon species listed in table 23. From our knowledge of the

European and American falcons we can associate the largest possible numbers of characters with the RSD index of a species. This exercise requires an integration of falcon morphology, anatomy, ecology, behavior, and physiology.

The lesser kestrel has the lowest index of all European falcons (table 23) and is, as we know, the least aggressive, least territorial falcon and also the most sociable. Lesser kestrels feed on innumerable small prey fragments, mostly grasshoppers, crickets, and such. Their breeding behavior is exceptional: the male *does not* feed the female during incubation. Instead, both sexes share incubation and other breeding duties, effectively eliminating the usual division of labor between the sexes. The low RSD index can also be correlated with the plumage of lesser kestrels (fig. 56). In accordance with Baumgart's (1974) hypothesis, the few streaks on the male's underside indicate high tolerance for intraspecific "spatial intruders." In addition, this kestrel's back and shoulders are free of any pattern.

The RSD indexes among the species listed in table 23 generally increase with increasing (1) prey size, (2) time and energy investments for prey location and capture, (3) division of labor between the sexes, (4) size of the nesting territory and defense of a home range, and (5) plumage patterns functioning as optical signals of spatial intolerance. The hunters of small birds (merlin, *F. columbarius*; hobby, *F. subbuteo*; African hobby, *F. cuvieri*) occupy a medium position, with RSD indexes of 6.8 to 9.3. The large falcons have higher indexes, particularly prairie falcon, *F. mexicanus*, and peregrine, *F. peregrinus*. A comparative analysis of their hunting habits (Baumgart 1975) might explain why RSD does not always increase with size of the raptor. The peregrine is much faster than the other falcons, and its hunting techniques require more agility and maneuverability than those of *F. rusticolus*, *F. cherrug*, and *F. biarmicus* (which Baumgart thinks should be considered subspecies of the gyrfalcon). A similar decrease in RSD with increasing body size occurs in the North American and European representatives of *Accipiter*. The smallest species, *A. nisus nisus* in Europe and *A. striatus* in North America, have the highest RSD indexes. In my opinion this can also be correlated with hunting habits and with the greater difficulty the small species have in locating and capturing prey.

There are two exceptions among the species listed in table 23.

TABLE 23
Reversed Sexual Dimorphism: Wing Length (in mm)

Species	Female	Male	Dimorphism Index[a]	Population	Source
F. naumanni	234.8 (11)[b]	233.5 (21)	0.6	European	Glutz, Bauer, and Bezzel 1971
F. vespertinus	245.6 (16)	241.2 (16)	1.8	European	Glutz, Bauer, and Bezzel 1971
F. eleonorae	327 (22)	316 (19)	3.4	Aegean Islands	Reiser 1905
F. tinnunculus	258 (28)	247 (43)	4.4	Swiss and Dutch	Glutz, Bauer, and Bezzel 1971
F. sparverius	193.8 (65)	185.3 (87)	4.5	American	Snyder and Wiley 1976
F. concolor	280 (?)	265 (?)	5.5	Egyptian (?)	F. P. W. Wyer, manucript
F. subbuteo	272 (15)	254 (16)	6.8	Central European	Glutz, Bauer, and Bezzel 1971
F. columbarius	213.6 (51)	197.8 (17)	7.7	Scandinavian	Glutz, Bauer, and Bezzel 1971
F. cuvieri	240.7 (7)	219.4 (17)	9.3	Africa	F. P. W. Wyer, manuscript
F. cherrug	396.8 (29)	361.1 (14)	9.4	European	Glutz, Bauer, and Bezzel 1971
F. rusticolus	395.5 (15)	357.3 (10)	10.1	Scandinavian	Glutz, Bauer, and Bezzel 1971
F. biarmicus	361.7 (9)	321.5 (5)	11.8	Italian	Glutz, Bauer, and Bezzel 1971
F. mexicanus	347.4 (20)	304.3 (20)	13.2	American	Snyder and Wiley 1976
F. peregrinus	348.1 (26)	301.2 (23)	14.4	Central European	Glutz, Bauer, and Bezzel 1971

[a]The dimorphism index is calculated according to the formula given by Storer (1966):

$$D.I. = \frac{\text{Wing length of female} - \text{wing length of male}}{\frac{1}{2} \times (\text{wing length of female} + \text{wing length of male})} \times 100$$

[b]Number in parentheses = N.

One is the American kestrel (*F. sparverius*). This falcon's index is similar to that of the considerably larger European kestrel (*F. tinnunculus*), although the American kestrel is a highly territorial species, has a high division of labor, and has barred patterns on its upper back indicating spatial intolerance. Such species would normally fall into the category of large mammal and bird hunters. Instead, its diet is largely insectivorous, although more vertebrates are taken at the beginning of the breeding season. The explanation seems to lie in this species' unusual habit of nesting in holes. A preference for nesting exclusively in cavities seems to strongly favor no RSD or small RSD values. Other hole-nesting species like the burrowing owl (*Speotyto cunicularia*) and the elf owl (*Micrathene whitneyi*) conform to this rule. Selection can be expected to favor as small an entrance hole as possible so as to reduce access to predators. This view can be supported by experimental data: Balgooyen (1976) enlarged the entrance holes of several American kestrel nests and found that the falcons abandoned the modified nesting sites.

The nonexistent or low RSD of several hole-nesting owls and raptor species can be used to argue against the belief that in evolution the males have become smaller. The need to maintain the near-equal size of hole nesters would indicate that the male maintains his size and the female's remains close to it. In the more open nest scrapes and cups of most raptors, however, the females do not have this constraint. Consequently, they became larger than males (the question remains, Why?). Since cavities are usually available only in limited numbers, they also appear to limit the distribution of hole-nesting owl and falcon species, which may favor territoriality.

The other exception is Eleonora's falcon. When raising its young, this raptor hunts birds almost exclusively. In accordance with the high correlation of RSD with bird prey, this should put this species at least in the medium RSD group. Instead, its RSD index is remarkably low (3.4). Perhaps the prey utilized during the nonbreeding season affects the RSD? Eleonora's falcon then feeds on arthropods, mostly aerial insects (chaps. 5 and 9). These are easy to catch, and Eleonora's catches migrant birds more or less in the same way it grabs insects in the air. Does the high sociability of this species determine the RSD? I have looked at some 20 gregarious raptor species. All of them have low RSD indexes. In raptors, I believe, sociability selects for similar size of the sexes. Gregariousness is, of course, somewhat related to the dispersion of food resources, the dispersion and number of nesting sites, and so on. But it is not always tied to resource dispersion and therefore acts more like an independent variable in its effect on RSD magnitude. Snyder and Wiley (1976) report Hamerstrom's observation on breeding success in hen harriers (*Circus cyaneus*): Large females "appeared to be relatively unsuccessful in reproduction; and thus strongly dimorphic pairs were presumably at a reproductive disadvantage (assuming mates of these females were randomly distributed in size)." The hen harrier reportedly is strongly dimorphic (wing-length RSD index of 11.3) and sometimes semicolonial (Snyder and Wiley 1976). This species is more agile than other harriers in its pursuit of prey, less sociable, and more aggressive in defending its nesting site (Glutz, Bauer, and Bezzel 1971). In conclusion, the low RSD index of Eleonora's falcon can be positively correlated with small prey size, hunting behavior, and sociability. In addition, its plumage patterns have retained little contrast, which reduces their function as optical signals of spatial intolerance.

If we broaden our inquiry to other birds of prey in temperate and tropical regions, we find that RSD is always correlated with a number of variable characters. I have looked at some of the American kite species, African *Accipiter* hawks, and the vultures and eagles of Africa. This comparison has made it clear to me that it is rather simplistic to attempt to correlate differing RSD values with only one of the factors mentioned in this section. I suggest that many variables select for and against a strong manifestation of RSD in raptors and owls. In table 24 I have listed ten such characters (A–J) of RSD that I believe are either independent or dependent variables of a species' ecological niche. Each character has been lined up in five steps against a gradient termed "Probability of Strong Dimorphism." Further quantification is not desireable because a number of the characters usually cannot be quantified. This table represents a model for understanding and predicting the *magnitude* of RSD, but it does not necessarily explain *why* RSD exists in raptors and owls.

The model predicts low or no RSD in a raptor that registers step 1 or 2 along the gradient in most or all A–J characters. In theory,

TABLE 24
Characters Affecting Reversed Sexual Size Dimorphism in Raptors

| Character | Decreasing | | Probability of Strong Dimorphism | Increasing | |
	1	2	3	4	5
A Prey dispersion	Abundant in clusters	Clustered	Patchy	Dispersed	Rare and dispersed
B Prey size (maximum)	Tiny	Small	Medium	Large	Very large
C Prey character	Easy prey (snails, grass-hoppers)	Easy prey (flying insects)	Not easy prey (rodents, fish)	Difficult prey	Very difficult prey
D Residence status	Long-distance migrant	Largely migratory	Partly migratory	Mostly resident year-round	Resident year-round
E Home-range defense	Absent	Weak	Fluctuating or portions only	Strong	Very strong
F Size of nesting territory	Tiny (few m²)	Small	Medium	Large	Very large (several km²)
G Social status	Colonial	Gregarious	Gregarious at times	Mostly solitary	Always solitary
H Nesting sites	Rare	Limited, clustered	Infrequent	Numerous, dispersed	Practically unlimited
I Division of labor	Role of sexes similar	Male regularly relieves female at nest site	Male occasionally relieves female at nest site	Female usually alone at nest site	Role of sexes strongly dissimilar
J Nest type	Cavity only	Prefers cavity	No preference	Nest scrape or cup	Nest cup only

at least, it also predicts an extremely high RSD for species that consistently register at step 5 along the same gradient. Figures 58 and 59 show a number of species curves resulting from the application of this multifactor RSD model (data from Ligon 1968; Thomsen 1971; Glutz, Bauer, and Bezzel 1971; and this study). Figure 58 compares the curves of the four gregarious Palearctic falcons with those of three solitary congeneric species. The latter group has strong to medium RSD, and thus these species' points along the gradient are predominantly on the high side. An exception is the step 1 value for determinant J (cavity only as nest type) in *F. sparverius*. The gregarious group possesses distinctly different curves, since it differs from the solitary group in many ecological and behavioral characters. Figure 59 contains additional gradient points of several owls, two eagles, a hawk, and the bearded vulture (a territorial species with a pronounced RSD index). Analyzing these curves provides some evidence for my opinion that simple correlations do not reflect the reality of the RSD phenomenon in raptors and owls except in the extreme cases of no RSD or very high RSD indexes. In general, prey nature (A–D), sociability (E–G), nesting sites (H), division of labor (I), and nest type (J) of a given species are species-specific components of the ecological niche and result in distinct curves for each species.

This multifactor RSD model does not answer the three questions stated at the beginning. It demonstrates a complex relationship between at least ten ecological and behavioral variables and the magnitude of RSD. Considering the diverse nature of the gradient curves (figs. 58 and 59) and the varied nature of raptor and owl niches on earth, one should ask again: (1) What makes raptors so special as predators that natural selection has evolved and maintained RSD even in many gregarious raptors feeding on nonvertebrates? (2) Is there anything else that makes raptors an exception among birds? I cannot offer a full answer, but I wish to point out another raptor specialty. This will lead to yet another hypothesis on RSD and might bring us closer to the ultimate factor causing RSD. Raptors are different from other birds because in many raptor species most individuals have retained the functional use of two ovaries. The other bird families (with individual exceptions here and there) possess only one functional ovary. A widely used textbook has the following to say about bird ovaries:

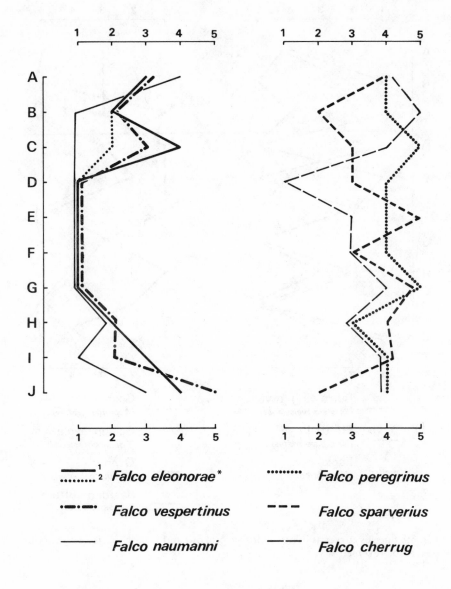

Fig. 58. Species curves of 10 determinants (A–J) along the gradient of dimorphism probability (1–5). See text and table 24 for details. *Left*: Gregarious falcons. *Right*: Solitary falcons.

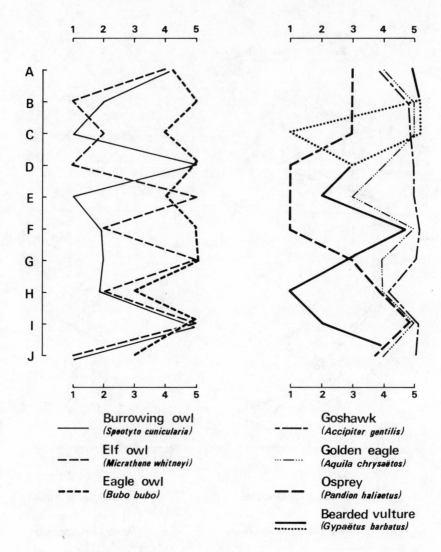

Fig. 59. Species curves as in fig. 58 for several owl and raptor species with varying degree of reversed sexual size dimorphism.

The reduction in ovaries from two to one is in part an adaptation to reduce ballast in a flying machine, but also is an arrangement which protects the developing egg. If birds had paired ovaries and oviducts, a sudden jolt of the body, as in alighting, might crack mature eggs located side by side in the parallel oviducts. Even so, in some birds of prey, especially in the genera *Accipiter, Circus,* and *Falco,* both left and right ovaries persist and function. However, even in these cases it is usually only the left oviduct which develops and carries the eggs. [Welty 1962, p. 136]

These remarks immediately suggest that the predatory life-style of raptors, particularly those that hunt large mammals and birds with powerful strikes, should pose a considerable danger to any egg developing in a bird's oviduct. The impact the raptor suffers when tackling, colliding, or "crashing" into a prey is many times greater than that of "alighting." It would be advantageous for a female raptor (1) not to hunt during egg development and (2) to be specially cushioned against sudden impact. The raptors that undertake the most daring chases probably suffer the greatest impact when hitting their targets. Of equal danger to the female is a defense maneuver by the intended prey. Mammals and birds might strike at the abdomen of the female raptor, destroying a developing egg or damaging the tissues of the ovaries.

It is beyond the scope of this study to fully explore this, but it is in the highly impact-adapted species that RSD is the most developed. The need for special protection of the female's reproductive apparatus (whether one or two functional ovaries) might well be the ultimate factor determining the division of labor among the sexes: it might initially have been confined to courtship feeding but have become extended over much of the breeding season where larger and more difficult prey species were hunted.

Whether a large female can protect her reproductive system better than a smaller one is an open question. If all raptors had larger ovaries than other bird groups of similar size, there would have been a stimulus for selection for RSD. If this train of thought is valid, raptors with no or little RSD should today possess relatively larger ovaries than raptors with strong RSD.

If we assume that raptors had a tendency to have two functional ovaries before they developed RSD, this could also have stimulated the evolution of larger females. During the nonbreeding season ovaries are tiny organs. They enlarge manyfold to reach an enormous extension and weight just before breeding. Lesser kestrels were found to be markedly heavier at such a time because of the weight of their ovaries (Glutz, Bauer, and Bezzel 1971). It can be postulated that the weight of two fully developed ovaries was such a handicap for the females of some raptor species that selection favored an increased body size. Since the relative size and weight of birds' eggs decreases as the birds' size increases, it seems reasonable to assume that the same relationship exists between ovary size and body size. This means that the larger the raptor female, the smaller the relative size of the ovary (as a percentage of body mass).

The debate on RSD will probably continue for some time. Much unknown territory, particularly in the area of avian energetics and physiology (why two ovaries in raptors?), lies ahead. I have tried here to demonstrate the many factors of raptor ecology and behavior that can be correlated with the magnitude of RSD. In my view, it is likely that an integrated research approach taxing our full range of knowledge on raptor biology and ecology will most likely succeed in unraveling the RSD phenomenon.

RAPTOR RESEARCH

This study of Eleonora's falcon has taken a holistic approach to the raptor's ecology and behavior, in particular its adaptations at the micro- and macrolevel to prey, habitat, and falcon "neighbors." Eleonora's falcon has so far been a little-known species. I can only hope that others will feel the fascination for this unusual bird that has inspired my own studies for so many years. Raptor research is a rapidly expanding field, and much basic and advanced work remains to be done. Propelled into the limelight by the sudden demise of peregrine populations in Europe and North America, raptor biologists suddenly had the opportunity to expand their reach. With the help of modern technology, the ancient art of falconry, and the systems approach to environmental management, we have recently acquired a great deal of new knowledge related to population dynamics, food chains, artificial breeding, and other subjects. In the future we hope to learn not only how to keep raptors from becoming extinct but also how to preserve their natural habitats.

Raptor research should be more than breeding rare species and managing raptors within the ecosystem of our anthropogenic landscapes. The advances in sociobiology could provide a base for analyzing raptors as individuals, groups, populations, and communities. There is no lack of poetry and prose written on behalf of raptors. But this appreciation does not overcome our basic lack of facts and evaluation. Some 90% of the world's raptors are poorly understood in their adaptations to prey and habitat.

Raptor research can also contribute to the advance of general sociobiology. The raptor's morphological parameters, its energetic system, its position at the top of most food chains, and its sensitivity to environmental components make raptor populations promising targets for major research projects. Falcons will certainly continue to play an important role in raptor research. Their beauty, their dynamic character, and their high visibility make them ideal study objects. This study of Eleonora's falcon will, I hope, be only the prelude to new questions, new answers, and the determination to preserve this world for people *and* falcons.

APPENDIXES

A. Tables

TABLE 25
Phase Ratios of Adult Eleonora's Falcons

| | Paximada | | | | | | Mogador | | | | | |
| | 1965 | | 1966 | | 1969[a] | | 1959[b] | | 1966 | | 1969 | |
	No.	%	No.	%	No.	%	No.	%	No.	%	No.	%
Individual falcons, total	146	100	19	100	33	100	45	100	136	100	64	100
Light females	66	45	9	47	13	39	—	—	64	47	21	33
Dark females	22	15	1	5	6	18	—	—	18	13	11	17
Light males	34	23	6	32	11	33	—	—	48	35	25	39
Dark males	24	17	3	16	3	9	—	—	6	5	7	11
Dark phase, total	46	32	4	21	9	27	12	27	24	18	18	28
Light phase, total	100	68	15	79	24	73	33	73	112	82	46	72
Pairs, total	58	100	8	100	14	100	25	100	37	100	31	100
Light female and male	22	38	4	50	6	43	—	—	27	73	17	55
Light female, dark male	21	36	3	40	3	21	—	—	3	8	3	9
Dark female, light male	12	21	1	10	5	36	—	—	6	16	7	23
Dark female and male	3	5	—	—	—	—	—	—	1	3	4	13
Dark phase, total	39	34	4	25	8	29	14	28	11	15	18	29
Light phase, total	77	66	12	75	20	71	36	72	63	85	44	71

[a]Data from Ristow (pers. comm.).
[b]Data from Vaughan (1961a).

TABLE 26
Dimensions of Sheltered Nest Sites: Paximada 1965

Nest Code Number	Height (cm)	Depth (cm)	Width (cm)	Entrance (cm²)
5	25	64	34	500
6	24	36	50	1,000
8	26	100	58	750
9	25	25	40	1,000
10	45	50	135	4,000
12	15	50	47	450
14	24	70	50	700
16	21	32	60	1,300
19	25	25	35	400
23	19	50	25	400
24	20	60	50	600
30	20	55	60	700
31	20	24	36	800
40	23	35	42	420
44	20	30	45	800
52	30	45	50	1,000
Mean Value	24	47	51	926

TABLE 27
Paximada: Breeding Success

| | 1965 | | | | | | | | 1969[a] | | | | | | |
| | Clutch Size | | | Total | Average per Pair | % | Average per Pair (corrected)[b] | % | Clutch Size | | | Total | Average per Pair | % | Average per Pair (corrected)[b] | % |
	1	2	3						1	2	3					
Clutches	17	65	29	111	1.00	0	0	0	21	41	20	82	1.00	0	0	0
Eggs	17	130	87	234	2.11	100	0	0	21	82	60	163	1.99	100	0	0
Clutches lost	9	16	1	26	0.23	0	0	0	2	1	0	3	0.04	0	0	0
Eggs lost	9	32	3	44	0.40	19	0	0	2	2	0	4	0.05	2	0	0
Clutches undisturbed	8	49	28	85	0.77	0	1.00	0	19	40	20	79	0.96	0	1.00	0
Eggs undisturbed	8	98	84	190	1.71	81	2.24	100	19	80	60	159	1.94	98	2.01	100
Young hatched	7	82	64	153	1.38	65	1.80	81	17	72	55	144	1.75	88	1.82	91
Young fledged	7	78	55	140	1.26	60	1.65	74	16	71	50	137	1.67	84	1.73	86

[a]Data from D. Ristow (pers. comm.).
[b]Only undisturbed nest sites are included in this computation.

TABLE 28
Mogador: Breeding Success

| | 1966 | | | | | | | | 1959[a] | | | | |
| | Clutch Size | | | | | | | | | | | | |
	1	2	3	4	Total	Average per pair	%	Average per Pair (corrected)[b]	%	Total	Average per Pair	%	Average per Pair (corrected)[b]	%
Clutches	0	5	25	3	33	1.00	0	0	0	20	1.00	0	0	0
Eggs	0	10	75	12	97	2.94	100	0	0	63	3.15	0	0	0
Clutches lost	0	1	1	0	2	0.06	0	0	0	0	0	0	0	0
Eggs lost	0	2	3	0	5	0.15	5	0	0	0	0	0	0	0
Clutches undisturbed	0	4	24	3	31	0.94	0	1.00	0	20	1.00	0	1.00	0
Eggs undisturbed	0	8	72	12	92	2.79	95	2.97	100	63	3.15	100	3.15	100
Young hatched	0	8	66	11	85	2.58	88	2.74	92	57	2.85	90	2.85	90
Young fledged	0	8	63	11	82	2.48	85	2.65	89	52	2.60	83	2.60	83

[a]Data from Vaughan (1961a).
[b]Only undisturbed nest sites are included in this computation.

TABLE 29
Paximada 1965: Reproductive Success of Light and Dark Color Phases in Undisturbed
Nest Sites

Color	Clutches	Eggs	Young	Fledglings
Females				
Light phase	32	68 (2.13)[a]	60 (1.87)	57 (l.78)
Dark phase	14	32 (2.28)	21 (1.50)	18 (1.29)
Total	46	100 (2.17)	81 (1.76)	75 (1.63)
Males				
Light phase	27	56 (2.07)	44 (1.62)	41 (1.51)
Dark phase	19	44 (2.32)	37 (1.95)	34 (1.79)
Total	46	100 (2.17)	81 (1.76)	75 (1.63)
Pairs				
Light male + dark female	11	24 (2.18)	17 (1.54)	14 (1.27)
Dark male + light female	16	36 (2.25)	33 (2.06)	30 (1.88)
Uniformly light phase	16	32 (2.00)	27 (1.69)	27 (1.69)
Uniformly dark phase	3	8 (2.67)	4 (1.33)	4 (1.33)
Total	46	100 (2.17)	81 (1.76)	75 (1.63)
Colony average	85	190 (2.23)	153 (1.80)	140 (1.65)

[a]Number in parentheses is average per pair.

TABLE 30
Paximada 1965: Reproductive Success of Light- and Dark-Phased Females

Color	Clutches	Eggs	Young	Fledglings
Light phase				
Single egg	8	8	6	6
Two eggs	29	58	41	39
Three eggs	19	57	44	38
Total	56	123 (2.20)[a]	91 (1.63)	83 (1.48)
Dark phase				
Single egg	0	0	0	0
Two eggs	15	30	22	20
Three eggs	4	12	6	5
Total	19	42 (2.21)	28 (1.47)	25 (1.32)
Colony average	111	234 (2.11)	153 (1.38)	140 (1.26)

[a]Number in parentheses is average per pair.

TABLE 31
Prey Composition of 20 Falcon Pairs (Paximada 1965)

Pair Code No.	Hatching of First Young	No. of Young	Total No. of Prey Remains	Percentage of Prey Groups[a]						
				A	B	C	D	E	F	R
5	25 Aug.	1	48	21.0	25.0	12.5	10.4	2.0	2.0	27.1
6	26 Aug.	1	38	23.7	18.4	10.5	10.5	5.3	5.3	26.3
8	24 Aug.	3	62	19.4	21.0	6.5	12.9	6.5	3.2	30.6
9	25 Aug.	2	59	11.9	23.7	10.2	13.6	8.5	1.7	30.5
10	1 Sept.	1	50	12.0	8.0	18.0	6.0	8.0	—	48.0
12	28 Aug.	2	76	31.6	15.8	9.2	3.9	3.9	3.9	31.6
14	25 Aug.	2	53	13.2	20.8	5.7	7.5	5.7	7.5	39.6
15	21 Aug.	3	69	20.3	18.8	7.2	7.2	8.7	5.8	31.9
16	19 Aug.	1	68	23.5	29.4	8.8	16.2	—	1.5	20.6
19	19 Aug.	2	77	16.9	20.8	3.9	3.9	9.1	9.1	36.4
21	25 Aug.	2	63	15.9	25.4	11.1	17.5	12.7	—	17.5
22	29 Aug.	2	38	13.2	26.3	13.2	13.2	—	2.6	31.6
23	25 Aug.	2	64	10.9	18.8	10.9	15.6	6.3	4.7	32.8
24	26 Aug.	3	90	13.3	27.8	11.1	10.0	3.3	3.3	31.1
25	29 Aug.	2	59	18.6	28.8	10.2	6.8	5.1	—	30.5
30	26 Aug.	1	23	21.7	8.7	4.3	4.3	13.0	8.7	39.1
31	23 Aug.	1	43	11.6	9.3	4.7	14.0	11.6	—	48.8
40	23 Aug.	2	60	15.0	33.3	6.7	5.0	6.7	1.7	31.7
44	26 Aug.	2	50	24.0	10.0	12.0	6.0	8.0	4.0	36.0
52	25 Aug.	2	75	16.0	22.7	9.3	14.7	9.3	—	28.0
	Mean ($\bar{X}$) per pair			17.7	20.6	9.3	10.0	6.7	3.3	32.5

A = warblers (genus *Phylloscopus*, 4 species); B = shrikes (genus *Lanius*, 3 species); C = whinchat (*Saxicola rubetra*); D = common whitethroat (*Sylvia communis*); E = short-toed lark (*Calandrella brachydactyla*); F = hoopoe (*Upupa epops*); R = all bird species other than A–F.

TABLE 32
List of Bird Migrants observed on Paximada Island
(10 August–10 October 1965)

Name and abundance
Grey heron (*Ardea cinerea*): 1
Squacco heron (*Ardeola ralloides*): 4
Night Heron (*Nycticorax nycticorax*): 2
Short-toed eagle (*Circaetus gallicus*): 5
Marsh harrier (*Circus aeruginosus*): 1
Moorhen (*Gallinula chloropus*): 1
Turnstone (*Arenaria interpres*): 1
Common sandpiper (*Tringa hypoleucos*): 4
Turtledove (*Streptopelia turtur*): 16
Great spotted cuckoo (*Clamator glandarius*): 1
Nightjar (*Caprimulgus europaeus*): 2
Swift (*Apus apus*): 1
Kingfisher (*Alcedo atthis*): 1
Hoopoe (*Upupa epops*): 11
Short-toed lark (*Calandrella brachydactyla*): 2
Barn swallow (*Hirundo rustica*): 7
Golden oriole (*Oriolus oriolus*): 4
Blue rock thrush (*Monticola solitarius*): 5
Wheatear (*Oenanthe oenanthe*): 15
Black-eared wheatear (*Oenanthe hispanica*): 3
Whincat (*Saxicola rubetra*): 11
Common redstart (*Phoenicurus phoenicurus*): 2
Sprosser (*Luscinia luscinia*): 1?
Grasshopper warbler (*Locustella naevia*): 1
Common whitethroat (*Sylvia communis*): 1
Willow warbler (*Phylloscopus trochilus*): ca. 270
Spotted flycatcher (*Muscicapa striata*): 5
Tawny pipit (*Anthus campestris*): 4
Tree pipit (*Anthus trivialis*): 15
Pipits, unidentified (*Anthus*, spp.): 3
Yellow wagtail (*Motacilla flava*): ca. 250
White wagtail (*Motacilla alba*): 4
Spanish sparrow (*Passer hispaniolensis*): ca. 370

TABLE 33
List of Bird Remains from Nest Sites of Eleonora's Falcon

Prey Species	Mogador		Canary Islands		Sardinia	
	Walter (1968a)	Vaughan (1961a)	Lovegrove (1971)	Bannerman (1931)	Steinbacher (1971)	Mocci Demartis (1973)
Puffinus puffinus						
Ixobrychus minutus						
Alectoris chukar						
Coturnix coturnix	24					
Porzana porzana					X	
Porzana parva						
Crex crex						
Charadrius alexandrinus						
Charadrius hiaticula	2					
Tringa hypoleucos	3		1			
Tringa ochropus						
Chlidonias niger						
Chlidonias leucopterus						
Columba livia						
Streptopelia turtur	3				1	
Clamator glandarius						
Cuculus canorus	6		"frequent"		X	
Otus scops						
Caprimulgus europaeus						
Apus apus	34	54	X			X
Apus affinis		< 10				
Apus melba						
Merops apiaster			X			
Coracias garrulus						
Alcedo atthis						
Upupa epops	16	< 10	X			X
Jynx torquilla	18					X
Calandrella brachydactyla	17					
Calandrella rufescens						

Crete (Theodoros)		Crete (Paximada)		Other Locations and Authors		
Stresemann (1956)	Uttendörfer (1948)	Walter (1968a)	Ristow (unpubl.)	Island or Area	No.	Source
				Northern Sporades	1	Warncke and Wittenberg 1961
		1				
				Dragonisi	X	Reiser 1905
				Lemnos	1	Lynes 1912
				Aegean Sea area	X	Krüper 1864
		2		Aegean Sea area	X	Reiser 1905
		1		?	X	Vaughan 1961a
			X			
				Cyprus	1	Vaughan 1961a
			X			
	1					
	1			Northern Sporades	2	Warncke and Wittenberg 1961
			X			
			X (4)	Aegean Sea area	X	Krüper 1864
				Aegean Sea area	X	Reiser 1905
	1	20		Aegean Sea area	X	Reiser 1905
			X			
	1	16	X			
	2	3				
		8		Iles Habibas	X	Mayaud 1960
	1	9				
	1	1	X			
	1	1	X			
			X	Lemnos	1	Lynes 1912
		1				
X	8	151	X	Aegean Sea area	X	Krüper 1864
				Aegean Sea area	X	Reiser 1905
				Iles Habibas	X	Mayaud 1960
X		30				
	1	152				
				?	X	Vaughan 1961a

(continued)

TABLE 33—continued

Prey Species	Mogador		Canary Islands		Sardinia	
	Walter (1968a)	Vaughan (1961a)	Lovegrove (1971)	Bannerman (1931)	Steinbacher (1971)	Mocci Demartis (1973)
Hirundo rustica	1					
Riparia riparia						
Delichon urbica						
Anthus trivialis	4					
Anthus pratensis						
Anthus spinoletta						
Anthus campestris	3					
Anthus bertholeti						
Motacilla flava	5					
Lanius minor						
Lanius nubicus						
Lanius senator	424	75	X	2		
Lanius collurio						
Lanius spp.						
Locustella naevia	90	< 10	X	1		
Locustella fluviatilis						
Locustella spp.						
Acrocephalus palustris						
Acrocephalus scirpaceus	3					
Acrocephalus paludicola	3			1		
Acrocephalus schoenobaenus	10					
Acrocephalus spp.						
Hippolais olivetorum						
Hippolais icterina						
Hippolais polyglotta	69*	< 10	X	2		
Hippolais pallida	16*					
Sylvia conspicillata	1					
Sylvia communis	332	29		720	X	
Sylvia curruca					X	
Sylvia borin	11					
Sylvia nisoria						
Sylvia cantillans	53					
Sylvia spp.						
Phylloscopus trochilus	7					
Phylloscopus collybita				2		
Phylloscopus sibilatrix						
Phylloscopus bonelli	3					
Phylloscopus spp.	77	15			X	X
Muscicapa striata	17*					
Cercotrichas galactotes	35	< 10				

Crete (Theodoros)		Crete (Paximada)		Other Locations and Authors		
Stresemann (1956)	Uttendörfer (1948)	Walter (1968a)	Ristow (unpubl.)	Island or Area	No.	Source
		14		?	X	Vaughan 1961a
		28				
			X			
		49		Mallorca	X	Thiollay 1967
			X			
			X			
	1	15				
				Canary Islands	X	Vaughan 1961a
		31		Mallorca	X	Thiollay 1967
	2	163				
			X			
		61		Aegean Sea area	X	Krüper 1864
X	1	404		Aegean Sea area	X	Krüper 1864
		1				
		10				
		1				
		3				
		} 8		Mogador (1969)	1	Walter, unpubl.
		2				
		3		Mogador (1969)	1	Walter, unpubl.
		2				
			X			
		117*				
			X			
X	2	249				
			X			
		3				
		1				
		7				
X	1	> 130				
	1	> 13				
		> 41				
		> 14				
		> 264				
	1	43*		Aegean Sea area	X	Krüper 1864

(continued)

TABLE 33—*continued*

	Mogador		Canary Islands		Sardinia	
Prey Species	Walter (1968a)	Vaughan (1961a)	Lovegrove (1971)	Bannerman (1931)	Steinbacher (1971)	Mocci Demartis (1973)
Ficedula hypoleuca	128	< 10		4		
Ficedula albicollis						
Ficedula parva						
Saxicola rubetra	33			1		
Monticola solitarius						
Monticola saxatilis						
Oenanthe oenanthe	5					X
Oenanthe hispanica	?					
(Oenanthe spp.)					X	
Phoenicurus ochruros						X
Phoenicurus phoenicurus	295	< 10		3	X	X
Erithacus rubecula						X
Luscinia svecica	17					
Luscinia luscinia						
Luscinia megarhynchos	301	25		2		X
Turdus philomelos						X
Turdus pilaris						
Turdus iliacus						X
Turdus merula						
Parus spp.						
Regulus spp.						
Emberiza caesia						
Emberiza hortulana						
Emberiza melanocephala						
Emberiza spp.						
Fringilla coelebs						
Acanthis cannabina						
Passer hispaniolensis						
Oriolus oriolus	2					X
Aves spp.	101					

Crete (Theodoros)		Crete (Paximada)		Other Locations and Authors		
Stresemann (1956)	Uttendörfer (1948)	Walter (1968a)	Ristow (ünpubl.)	Island or Area	No.	Source
		76		Mallorca	X	Thiollay 1967
			X			
	1		X			
	2	262				
	1	1				
			X			
X	1	100				
		14				
			X			
X		82		Îles Habibas	X	Mayaud 1960
			X			
		2				
	1?	62				
				Northern Sporades	1	Warncke and Wittenberg 1961
X						
				Northern Sporades	1	Warncke and Wittenberg 1961
			X	Northern Sporades	1	Warncke and Wittenberg 1961
		} 7	?	Lemnos	1	Lynes 1912
		9	X			
		2				
			X			
			X			
		6				
X	1	52		Aegean Sea area	X	Krüper 1864
				Dragonisi	X	Reiser 1905
		56				

*It was difficult to separate the feathers of *Hippolais* and of *Muscicapa*. Species listed were identified with certainty but the numbers of prey remains listed above represent only approximate values.

TABLE 34

Bird Pluckings Collected at the Study Nest Sites of the Paximada Colony
(26 August–23 September 1965)

Collection periods	8/26–9/1	9/2–9/9	9/10–9/16	9/17–9/23	
Days/period	7	8	7	7	
No. of nest sites	21	21	21	20	
Days × nest sites	147	168	145[a]	140	
Species		No. of Pluckings			Total
1. *Phylloscopus* spp.	30	29	31	68	158
2. *Lanius collurio*	19	33	25	51	128
3. *Saxicola rubetra*	2	17	25	37	81
4. *Sylvia communis*	27	18	11	20	76
5. *Calandrella brachydactyla*	3	20	18	22	63
6. *Hippolais* spp. +					
Muscicapa striata	14	14	12	15	55
7. *Lanius minor*	17	8	7	7	39
8. *Ficedula hypoleuca*	7	13	8	7	35
9. *Upupa epops*	6	13	6	4	29
10. *Oenanthe oenanthe*	—	7	3	13	23
11. *Luscinia megarhynchos*	3	9	2	4	18
12. *Oriolus oriolus*	2	5	4	5	16
13. *Lanius senator*	4	6	1	2	13
14. *Phoenicurus phoenicurus*	1	1	1	8	11
15. *Anthus trivialis*	—	—	3	6	9
All other species	10	19	18	27	74
Total	145	212	175	296	828

[a]Lower figure is due to desertion of a nest site.

TABLE 35

Bird Pluckings Collected at the Study Nest Sites of the Mogador Colony
(26 August–21 September 1966)

Collection periods	8/26–9/1	9/2–9/8	9/9–9/14	9/15–9/21	
Days/period	7	7	6	7	
No. of nest sites	17	17	16	5	
Days × nest sites	119	119	94[a]	35	
Species		No. of Pluckings			Total
1. *Lanius senator* juv.	48	56	51	16	171
Lanius senator ad.	5	4	8	1	18
2. *Sylvia communis*	52	48	52	24	176
3. *Luscinia megarhynchos*	35	64	41	18	158
4. *Phoenicurus phoenicurus*	5	55	65	27	152
5. *Sylvia hortensis*	16	18	24	15	73
6. *Ficedula hypoleuca*	4	10	31	12	57
7. *Locustella naevia*	13	8	18	14	53
8. *Phylloscopus* spp.	7	10	17	8	42
9. *Hippolais* spp. +					
Muscicapa striata	12	6	11	7	36
10. *Sylvia cantillans*	7	7	9	7	30
11. *Cercotrichas galactotes*	3	6	4	1	14
12. *Coturnix coturnix*	—	10	3	—	13
13. *Saxicola rubetra*	—	2	4	4	10
14. *Jynx torquilla*	1	5	4	—	10
15. *Sylvia borin*	—	1	4	4	9
All other species	23	21	43	15	102
Total	231	331	389	173	1,124

[a]Lower figure is due to desertion of a nest site.

Table 36
Falcon Eggs (Paximada 1965)

Nest Code Number	Date	Weight (g)	Length (mm)	Width (mm)
36	13 Aug.	25.7	41.0	33.0
36	13 Aug.	27.5	42.0	34.0
36	13 Aug.	25.5	42.0	33.0
39	13 Aug.	20.5	42.0	30.0
39	13 Aug.	24.5	41.0	31.0
39	13 Aug.	25.0	41.0	32.0
9	19 Aug.	26.0	38.5	31.5
9	19 Aug.	27.0	39.0	33.0
10	19 Aug.	25.5	43.0	34.0
10	19 Aug.	24.5	43.0	33.5
44	19 Aug.	23.5	40.0	33.0
44	19 Aug.	23.5	40.5	33.5
44	19 Aug.	22.0	40.0	32.0
30	19 Aug.	—	42.0	33.0
30	19 Aug.	25.0	43.0	33.0
30	19 Aug.	24.0	40.5	31.0
31	19 Aug.	27.5	44.0	34.8
40	19 Aug.	28.0	44.5	34.5
40	19 Aug.	25.5	42.5	35.0
12	19 Aug.	28.0	44.5	35.0
12	19 Aug.	28.5	44.0	35.5
13	19 Aug.	25.5	42.2	34.0
13	19 Aug.	23.0	39.0	33.5
13	19 Aug.	25.0	43.1	33.2
24	19 Aug.	24.5	41.5	33.0
24	19 Aug.	27.0	42.2	34.3
24	19 Aug.	27.2	42.5	34.7
52	19 Aug.	23.0	40.0	31.5
52	19 Aug.	23.4	41.0	32.0
23	19 Aug.	24.5	44.0	32.5
23	19 Aug.	25.0	45.0	33.2
14	19 Aug.	23.3	40.5	33.0
14	19 Aug.	23.8	41.5	33.0
15	19 Aug.	22.0	40.8	33.0
15	19 Aug.	23.0	42.0	33.7
15	19 Aug.	22.5	40.0	32.4
19	19 Aug.	22.3	43.0	35.0
19	19 Aug.	25.0	43.0	34.2
5	20 Aug.	22.5	40.0	33.0
5	20 Aug.	19.5	41.0	31.5
34	20 Aug.	19.5	41.0	32.0
34	20 Aug.	24.0	41.3	33.0
34	20 Aug.	25.0	42.4	33.5
4	20 Aug.	23.0	44.2	32.0
4	20 Aug.	22.3	40.4	32.0
26	20 Aug.	29.5	45.0	36.0

(continued)

TABLE 36—*continued*

Nest Code Number	Date	Weight (g)	Length (mm)	Width (mm)
26	20 Aug.	22.3	39.6	33.0
26	20 Aug.	25.0	43.0	34.2
1	20 Aug.	23.0	42.5	32.8
1	20 Aug.	22.0	42.0	32.1
48	20 Aug.	22.1	45.1	31.0
48	20 Aug.	22.0	44.8	31.0
37	20 Aug.	24.8	42.5	33.2
37	20 Aug.	24.0	41.5	33.0
6	20 Aug.	26.0	41.5	34.6
6	20 Aug.	22.0	40.0	32.3
8	20 Aug.	22.0	40.0	32.0
8	20 Aug.	23.0	42.0	32.5
8	20 Aug.	24.0	42.7	33.0
25	20 Aug.	—	42.0	33.0
25	20 Aug.	—	42.0	34.0
54	20 Aug.	23.0	40.0	33.0
54	20 Aug.	25.4	41.5	33.5

TABLE 37

Measurements of Early and Recent Eggshells of *Falco eleonorae*

Variable	No.[b]	*Means ± 95% Confidence Limits for Time Period* 1863–74	No.[c]	1960–69
Eggshell weight (g)	13	1.93 ± 0.13	49	2.11 ± 0.06
Thickness index[a]	13	1.33 ± 0.07	49	1.41 ± 0.03
Thickness (mm)	12	0.27 ± 0.01	33	0.28 ± 0.01
Length/breadth	13	1.27 ± 0.04	49	1.27 ± 0.02
Volume (cm³)	13	24.58 ± 1.14	49	25.72 ± 0.67

SOURCE: Data from D. W. Anderson, personal communication (18 April 1977).
[a] Ratcliffe (1967).
[b] Six females from the Cyclades, Greece.
[c] Sixteen females, most of them from the western Mediterranean and from Mogador (Morocco).

TABLE 38
Minimum Distances between Raptor Nests (in km)

Species	Region	Remarks
Falco peregrinus	West Germany	Neckar and Main rivers: 1.5, 2.0, 2.5, (3 ×), 3.5, and 4.5; Bavaria: 3–7
	Switzerland	3–4.5
	Great Britain	Coastal populations: 2.6–8.4; inland populations: 4.8–10.5
	France	Average 5.0 km, smallest 1.0
Falco rusticolus	Iceland	20–25;
	Alaska	Several km, once only 0.4
Falco cherrug	Russia	3 to 4 eyries on 1.2 ha
	Hungary	Danube River: 4–6; Danube island 5 km long contained several pairs
Falco subbuteo	Central Europe	Berlin: 0.37; Bonn: 0.5
	West Siberia	Often only 0.1
Falco columbarius	British Isles	In exceptional cases below 2.0
	Soviet Union	1.5
Falco vespertinus	Hungary	Several meters only
Falco naumanni	Austria	Less than 2 m
Falco tinnunculus	Central Europe	Occasionally several meters only; 5 to 7 pairs on an 8 ha cemetery
Hieraaëtus pennatus	France	Three pairs within 1.25
	Russia	0.1–0.2
Hieraaëtus fasciatus	France	4.12, once only 2.2
Aquila chrysaetos	Swiss Alps	4.0
	British Isles	1.2
Aquila heliaca	Balkan	0.3; 1.0–1.5 not rare
Buteo lagopus	Soviet Union	10–1.5
Buteo buteo	Central Europe	0.09, 0.1, 0.2–0.25, 0.4, 0.5
Accipiter gentilis	Central Europe	0.6, 0.9, 1.1, and 1.4
Accipiter nisus	Central Europe	0.2, 0.35 (2×); 3 nests within 0.8
Accipiter brevipes	Southeastern Europe	0.1
Circus pygargus	Northwestern Germany	0.06, even 10 m (0.001)
Circus cyaneus	Orkney Islands	In exceptional cases only 15–20 m
	Central Europe	0.05 to less than 0.5
Circus aeruginosus	Western Europe	0.05–0.3; exceptionally 0.02; 6 pairs along a lakeshore of 850 m
Circaëtus gallicus	Southern France	Usually 2–10; shortest one 1.1
Pandion haliaëtus	Central Europe	4 occupied nests within area of 120 × 200 m
	North America	300 pairs within about 1,200 ha on Gardiner's Island
Pernis apivorus	Central Europe	In exceptional cases only several hundred meters; highest density estimated at 1 pair per 16.5 km²

(continued)

TABLE 38—*continued*

Species	Region	Remarks
Milvus migrans	Switzerland	0.008 (22 pairs/1.9 km², 30 pairs/1.8 km², 31 pairs/1.8km² in this area)
	West Germany	2 pairs/km²; 1 pair/8 km²
Milvus milvus	Central Europe	Several hundred meters
Haliaeëtus albicilla	Austria	0.4
	Siberia	5 pairs along 80 km of the Jenissej valley
Gypaëtus barbatus	Africa	One pair needs 140–200 km²: minimum distance probably everywhere at least several km
	Southern France	One pair controls some 300 km²
Neophron percnopterus	Southern France	1.4–1.5
	Bulgaria	2.0–2.5
	Turkestan	12–15
	Turkey	May breed in colonies (minimum distance probably below 100 m)
Gyps fulvus	Southern France	In colonies 2–4 m
Aegypius monachus	Spain	0.1–0.4, 0.2–1.0

SOURCE: All data were extracted from paragraphs describing population density and social behavior of each species in Glutz, Bauer, and Bezzel (1971).

B. Hunting, Feeding, and Food-caching Behavior

Observations from "upper slope" population of Paximada 30 August 4:30–8:30. Takeoffs of falcons were generally not recorded; "arrives with prey" means in all cases that a migrant bird has been caught and is now being delivered to the female, which will pluck it and feed it to the chicks or hide it.

4:25   Falcons begin to call.

4:30   Arrival at observation post.

5:09   First feeding of the day: male 23 arrives with bird prey and delivers it to the female.
       Male 15 arrives with bird prey; female yells and takes it. A common sandpiper (*Tringa hypoleucos*) calls from the shore.

5:13   Pair 13 present, some prey is being delivered (fresh)?
       Male 19 arrives with bird prey; Female takes it.
       Female 16, female 14 are sitting (literally on their belly feathers in front of their nests. Female 23 is hiding prey remains in a scrub.

5:18   Male 52 takes off, flies two circles above slope, returns to its nest.

5:23   Male 52 arrives with bird prey and delivers it. For the last 20 min, a light-colored and immature falcon has been sitting behind territory 16; it takes off now and then, harassing particularly pairs 16 and 52.

5:29   Male 16 arrives with bird prey; so do male 23 (female hides prey right away), and male 19.

5:33   Male 14 arrives with bird prey; takes it, and begins to feed the young.

5:40   In the air above are numerous falcons on their lookout positions.
       One tries to catch a large dragonfly but misses it.
       Male 21 arrives with bird prey and delivers it.
       Male 14 arrives with another freshly killed bird.
       (The red fireball of the sun now stands one finger-width above the horizon.)

5:50   Male 24 arrives with bird prey and delivers it.

5:53   Male 23 arrives with its third bird prey of the day; female 23 takes it to the young.

5:59   Male 19 arrives with prey; his mate sits nearby all the time under the boulder, probably covering her little chicks, while females 16 and 14 (with their larger chicks) perch beside the boulders under which their young sit.

6:05   Males 13, 14, 16, and 23 arrive with bird prey; females 16 and 23 hike around to hide the new prey.

6:15   Male 52 arrives with bird prey.

6:23   Male 21 arrives with bird prey that female attempts to hide.

6:25   A number of falcons chase over the sea after a small bird.

6:30   Male 16 arrives with a very small bird, female 16 takes it into the nest.

6:37   Male 21 arrives with a bird prey, female 21 hides it again.

6:40   Male 19 arrives with bird prey.

6:42   Male 24 arrives with bird prey; female 24 leaves the nest and takes it.

6:50   Male 23 arrives with bird prey in a smashing nose dive directly in front of the nest entrance. Female 23 enters nest with the new prey.

6:53   Male 21 arrives with bird prey; the light-phased immature single bird harasses female 21. She pursues it, calling in flight "ho-det-ded-ded-ded-...."

7:02   Female 23 flies out of nest exit, begins to hide prey remains.

7:07   Male 14 arrives with prey in the upper slope area, sweeps once with
       extreme speed over the slope, turns, calls three times "yeet"; female 14
       begins to call; male 14 lands.
7:45   Male 23 brings yet another bird to his mate. Female 23 "walks" into nest
       with it.
7:55   Male 15 arrives with bird prey.
8:00   End of observation.

C. RECORDS OF *Falco eleonorae* FROM MADAGASCAR, RÉUNION, and
MAURITIUS

Madagascar
   1. An immature male over the sea, some 15 mi off Tamatave (east coast),
end of November 1861 (Stresemann 1954).
   2. One specimen, near Savary, 15 January 1878, collected by Audebert.
Museum of Leiden (Stresemann 1954).
   3. One specimen, in 1878; collected by Audebert, Madagscar (but where?).
Zool. Mus. Berlin, no. 24596 (Stresemann 1955).
   4. One specimen, not later than 1880, collected by Audebert. Zool. Mus. Berlin, no. 24597 (Stresemann 1954).
   ` 5. One individual, near Ankafina, March 1881; collected by J. M. Hildebrandt.
Zool. Mus. Berlin, no. 27771 (Stresemann 1954). Date changed to "March 1880"
in Stresemann (1955).
   6. Two specimens sent to Fring from east Imerina (east central Madagascar)
about 1896 by Rev. Wills (Stresemann 1954).
   7. One male "in the Sambirano at Bezona" (northern Madagascar), 29
November 1930 (Rand 1936).
   8. A banded juvenile from the Akrotiri colony of Cyprus (banded 22 September 1962) was killed at Ankazobe, about 80 km north-northwest of Tananarive on 30 November 1962. Malzy, *L'Oiseau et R.F.O.* 33 (1963): 60.
   9. A banded juvenile (11 September 1960) from the Mogador colony
(Morocco) was taken at Andapahely (14°39′S, 49°40′E) in northern Madagascar
in mid-January, 1962 (Terrasse 1963).
   10. Female, dark phase, Moramanga (eastern Madagascar), 28 March 1963:
obtained for O.R.S.T.O.M. collection at Tananarive (Salvan 1970).
   11. "Regularly observed" at Ambohibao (central Madagascar) from 2 March to
3 April 1970 (Salvan 1970).
   12. Near Moramanga (eastern Madagascar), observed in October and
November by N. S. Malcom (Milon, Petter, and Randrianasolo 1973).
   13. Around Tananarive from time to time between October and the beginning
of April. Hunts even within the city limits; observed by N. S. Malcom after Milon,
Petter, and Randrianasolo (1973).
   14. "Numerous individuals" on the Montage d'Ambre (northern Madagascar)
in January (Milon, Petter, and Randrianasolo 1973).
   15. Four individuals, Manjakatompo (Mount Ankaratra), 10 April 1971
(Forbes-Watson, pers. comm.).
   16. One individual, Mount Ankaratra at 6,700 ft, 11 April 1971 (Forbes-Watson,
pers. comm.).
   17. One individual, Tsarafidy forest (central Madagascar), 12 April 1971
(Forbes-Watson, pers. comm.).

18. One individual, near Ambahimasoa (near Tananarive), 14 April 1971 (Forbes-Watson, pers. comm.).

19. An individual, banded as a chick by D. Ristow on Paximada (Greece) on 29 September 1971, was captured near Andapa (14° 40'S, 49°39'E), apparently just days before 2 January 1973 (Ristow 1975).

20. An adult, dark phase, seen 3 km east of Morondava (western Madagascar), 24 December 1973, hunting dragonflies. Observed by H. Walter and Mr. Pieninck.

21. *a*. One individual, light, phase, 2 km southeast of Bemanonga (western Madagascar), 25 December 1973. Observed by H. Walter.

b. One individual, light phase, near Morondava bridge (western Madagascar), 25 December 1973. Observed by H. Walter.

22. Several falcons near Andranomena (Morondava region) seen hunting insects, termites, and "aerial plankton" in the company of dozens of sooty falcons (*F. concolor*), 26 December 1973. Observed by H. Walter.

Réunion

1. A falcon collected on Réunion, before 1869. No details given (Stresemann 1954).

Mauritius

1. A falcon obtained by Mr. Edward Newton after stormy weather in December (year?). Published by J. H. Gurney in 1882 (Vaughan 1961a; Terrasse 1963).

D. Genetic Base of Color Dimorphism

During the Seventeenth International Ornithological Congress (4–11 June 1978, Berlin) a poster paper entitled "Genetical Aspects of Dimorphism in Eleonora's Falcon (*Falco Eleonorae*)" was presented by M. Wink, D. Ristow, and C. Wink.

The authors investigated phase distribution on Paximada during the 1975 and 1977 breeding seasons. Some 45–51% of the breeding pairs consisted of a light- and a dark-phased falcon, although the dark phase constituted only 25–31% of the surveyed breeding population. The fledgings of the dark phase were distinguished from those of the light phase when the authors discovered that the former possess striped (barred) undertail coverts while the latter do not. This character permitted the examination of the genetic base of the phase distribution.

A total of 18 light-light pairs had 29 light-phased and no dark-phased nestlings. 23 light-dark pairs had 17 dark and 23 light young. Finally, 5 dark-dark pairs had 6 dark and 2 light-phased offspring. Statistical tests confirmed that "'dark' is the dominant gene and 'light' is recessive." The authors conclude: "The homozygote dark phase is represented at 3.4%, the heterozygote dark phase at 30.1% and the recessive light morph at 66.5%."

It is not unusual for dominant genes to be less frequent in a population than recessive ones. The dark phase may be the result of a recent mutation or may be less well adapted to the current niche of Eleonora's falcon than the light phase.

References

Adams, D. W. H. 1962. Radar observations of bird migration in Cyprus. *Ibis* 104:133–46.

Amadon, D. 1959. The significance of sexual differences in size among birds. *Proc. Amer. Phil. Soc.* 103:531–36.

———. 1975. Why are female birds of prey larger than males? *Rapt. Res.* 9(1/2): 1–11.

Anderson, D. W., and Hickey, J. J. 1972. Eggshell changes in certain North American birds. *Proc. XVth Int. Orn. Cong., The Hague 1970*, pp. 514–40.

———. 1974. Eggshell changes in raptors from the Baltic region. *Oikos* 25:395–401.

Andersson, M. 1973. Behaviour of the pomarine skua *Stercorarius pomarinus* Temm. with comparative remarks on *Stercoraiinae*. *Ornis Scand.* 4:1–16.

———. 1976. Predation and kleptoparasitism by skuas in a Shetland seabird colony. *Ibis* 118:208–18.

Archer, G. F., and Goodman, E. M. 1937. *The birds of British Somaliland and the Gulf of Aden*, vol. 1. London.

Arrigoni degli Oddi, E. 1904. *Manuale di ornitologia Italiana*. Part 2. Milan.

Attenborough, D. 1961. *Bridge to the past: Animals and people of Madagascar*. New York.

Bährmann, U. 1974a. Der Sexualdimorphismus beim Habicht (*Accipiter gentilis*) (*Aves, Accipitridae*). *Zool. Abh.* 33 (1): 1–7.

———. 1974b. Vergleichende osteometrische Untersuchungen an Rumpfskeletteilen und Extremitäten von einigen Tagraubvögeln aus den Familien *Accipitridae, Pandionidae* und *Falconidae*. *Zool. Abh.* 33 (3): 33–62.

Balfour, E. 1962. The nest and eggs of the hen harrier in Orkney. *Bird Study* 30:69–73, 145–52.

Balgooyen, T. G. 1976. Behavior and ecology of the American kestrel (*Falco sparverius* L.) in the Sierra Nevada of California. *Univ. Calif. Publ. Zool.* 103:1–88.

Bannerman, D. A. 1914. An ornithological expedition to the eastern Canary Islands. *Ibis* (10) 2:38–90, 228–93.

————. 1919. List of the birds of the Canary Islands, with detailed reference to the migratory species and the accidental visitors. Part III. *Ibis* (11) 1:457–95.

————. 1931. [Report on some birds collected on the East Rock, Lanzerote, by Dr. H. B. Cott.] *Bull. Brit. Orn. Cl.* 52:52–55.

————. 1963. *Birds of the Atlantic Islands*. I. *A history of the birds of the Canary Islands and of the Salvages*. Edinburgh and London.

Bannerman, D. A., and Bannerman, W. M. 1958. *Birds of Cyprus*. Edinburgh and London.

————. 1971. *Handbook of the birds of Cyprus and migrants of the Middle East*. Edinburgh.

Banzhaf, W. 1937. Ein Beitrag zur Avifauna Ost-Thessaliens und der nördlichen Sporaden (Griechenland). *Verh. Orn. Ges. Bay.* 21:123–36.

Bastian, G. 1967. *Madagascar: Etude géographique et économique*. Paris.

Bate, D. M. A. 1928. Excavation of a Mousterian rock-shelter at Devil's Tower, Gibralter. *J. Roy. Anthrop. Inst. London* 58:92–113.

Bateson, P. P. G., and Nisbet, J. C. T. 1961. Autumn migration in Greece. *Ibis* 103a:503–14.

Battistini, R., and Richard-Vindard, G., eds. 1972. *Biogeography and ecology in Madagascar*. Monographiae Biologicae 21. The Hague. Pp. 1–765.

Baumgart, W. 1974. Über die Ausbildung heller und dunkler Phasen bei Greifvögeln. *Falke* 26:376–85.

————. 1975. Die Bedeutung funktioneller Kriterien für die Beurteilung der taxonomischen Stellung paläarktischer Grossfalken. *Zool. Abh.* 33:303–15.

Beebe, F. L. 1960. The marine peregrines of the Northwest Pacific Coast. *Condor* 62:145–89.

————. 1974. Field studies of the *Falconiformes* (vultures, eagles, hawks, and falcons) of British Colombia. *Occ. Pap. Brit. Col. Prov. Museum*, no. 17, pp. 1–163.

Beer, C. G. 1970. Individual recognition of voice in the social behavior of birds. *Ad. Study Beh.* 3:27–74.

Benson, S. V. 1970. *Birds of Lebanon and the Jordan area*. London and New York.

Berndt, R., and Winkel, W. 1974. Ökoschema, Rivalität und Dismigration als öko-ethologische Dispersionsfaktoren. *J. Orn.* 115:398–417.

Bernis, F. 1962. Sobre migración de nuestros *Passeriformes* Transsaharianos. *Ardeola* 8:41–119.

————. 1966. *Migración en Aves*. Madrid.

Bezzel, E. 1957. Beiträge zur Kenntnis der Vogelwelt Sardiniens. *Anz. Orn. Ges. Bay.* 4:589–707.

Bezzel, E.; Obst, J.; and Wickl, K.-H. 1976. Zur Ernährung und Nahrungswahl des Uhus (*Bubo bubo*). *J. Orn.* 117:210–38.

Bijleveld, M. 1974. *Birds of prey in Europe*. London.

Bird, C. G. 1935. A visit to the Cyclades. *Ibis* (13) 5:336–55.

Böhr, H. J. 1962. Zur Kenntnis der Vogelwelt von Korfu. *Bonn. Zool. Beitr.* 13:50–114.

Bongiorno, S. F. 1970. Nest-site selection by adult laughing gulls (*Larus atricilla*). *Anim. Behav.* 18:434–44.

Bonomi, P. 1911. Notizie di Sardegna. *Riv. Ital. Orn.* 1:90.

Booth, B. D. McD. 1961. Breeding of the sooty falcon in the Libyan desert. *Ibis* 103a:129–30.

Bourne, W. R. P. 1960. Migration through Cyprus. *Proc. XII Int. Orn. Congr., Helsinki 1958*, pp. 127–32.

Brisbin, I. L., Jr. 1968. A determination of the caloric density and major body components of large birds. *Ecology* 49:792–94.

——. 1969. Bioenergetics of the breeding cycle of the ring dove. *Auk* 86:54–74.

Brooke, A. B. 1973. Notes on the ornithology of Sardinia. *Ibis* (3) 3:143–55.

Brosset, A. 1973. Etude comparative de l'ontogenèse des comportements chez les rapaces Accipitridés et Falconidés. *Z. Tierpsychol.* 32:386–417.

Brown, J. L. 1964. The evolution of diversity in avian territorial systems. *Wilson Bull.* 76:160–69.

——. 1969. Territorial behavior and population regulation in birds. *Wilson Bull.* 81:293–329.

Brown, J. L., and Orians, G. H. 1970. Spacing patterns in mobile animals. *Ann. Rev. Ecol. Syst.* 1:239–62.

Brown, L. 1970. *African birds of prey*. London.

——. 1976. *British birds of prey: A study of Britain's 24 diurnal raptors*. London.

Brown, L. H., and Amadon, D. 1968. *Eagles, hawks and falcons of the world*. 2 vols. New York.

Brown, L. H., and Watson, A. 1964. The golden eagle in relation to its food supply. *Ibis* 106:78–100.

Brüll, H. 1964. *Das Leben deutscher Greifvögel*. Stuttgart.

C——, H. L. 1946. The Eleonora falcon (*Falco eleonorae*). *Ool. Rec.* 20:27–32.

Cade, T. J. 1960. Ecology of the peregrine and gyrfalcon populations in Alaska. *Univ. Calif. Publ. Zool.* 63 (3): 151–290.

Cade, T. J., and Fyfe, R. 1970. The North American peregrine survey, 1970. *Can. Field-Nat.* 84:231–45.

Carlo, E. A. di. 1966. Saggio sul passo primaverile ed estivo-autunnale nelle Isole Tremiti (Mare Adriatico). *Riv. Ital. Ornit.* 36:324–44.

Casement, M. B. 1966. Migration across the Mediterranean observed by radar. *Ibis* 108:461–91.

Cavé, A. J. 1968. The breeding of the kestrel, *Falco tinnunculus* L., in the reclaimed area Oostelijk Flevoland. *Neth. J. Zool.* 18:313–407.

Cetti, F. 1776. *Gli uccelli di Sardegna*. Sassari.

Chancellor, R. D. 1977. World conference on birds of prey, Vienna,

1–3 October 1975. *Report of Proceedings.* London: *Intern. Council for Bird Preserv.*, pp. 1–442.

Clancey, P. A. 1969. The sooty falcon as a south African bird. *Bokmakierie* 21 (3): 50–51.

———. 1970. A further sooty falcon record for South Africa. *Ostrich* 41:261–62.

Clapham, C. S. 1964. The birds of the Dahlac Archipelago. *Ibis* 106:376–88.

Clark, A. L., and Peakall, D. B. 1977. Organochlorine residues in Eleonora's falcon *Falco eleonorae*, its eggs and its prey. *Ibis* 119:353–58.

Cody, M. L. 1974. *Competition and the structure of bird communities.* Monographs in Population Biology 7. Princeton, N.J.

Collopy, M. W. 1973. Predatory efficiency of American kestrels wintering in northwestern California. *Rapt. Res.* 7 (2): 25–31.

Conder, P. 1977. Legal status of birds of prey and owls in Europe. In *World conference on birds of prey,* ed. R. D. Chancellor, pp. 189–93. London.

Contant, M., and Naurois, R. de. 1958. Observations sur les espèces nicheuses des Iles de Mogador faucon d'Eléonore (*Falco eleonorae*), pigeons Bisets (*Columba livia*), Goëlands argentés (*Larus argentatus*). *Alauda* 26:196–98.

Cott, H. B. 1956. *Zoological photography in practice.* London.

Craighead, J. J., and Craighead, F. C. 1956. *Hawks, owls and wildlife.* Harrisburg, Penn.

Crook, J. H. 1965. The adaptive significance of avian social organizations. *Symp. Zool. Soc. Lond.* 14:181–218.

Cyprus Ornithological Society. 1971. *First bird report 1970.* Nicosia.

———. 1972. *Second bird report 1971.* Nicosia.

———. 1973. *Third bird report 1972.* Nicosia.

Deutscher Bund für Vogelschutz e. V. (DBV) 1975. *3. Denkschrift zur Situation des Wanderfalken in der Bendesrepublik Deutschland.* Stuttgart.

Drent, R. 1975. Incubation. In *Avian biology,* ed. D. S. Farner and J. R. King, 5:333–420. New York.

Dresser, H. E. 1873. *A history of the birds of Europe.* London.

———. 1903. *A manual of Palaearctic birds.* London.

Earhart, C. M., and Johnson, N. K. 1970. Size dimorphism and food habits of North American owls. *Condor* 72:251–64.

Eleonora of Arborea 1392. *Carta de Logu.* Manuscript no. 211. Cagliari: Library of the University.

Emlen, S. T., and Demong, N. J. 1975. Adaptive significance of synchronized breeding in a colonial bird: A new hypothesis. *Science* 188:1029–31.

Engelmann, F. 1928. *Die Raubvögel Europas.* Neudamm.

Etchécopar, R. D., and Hüe, F. 1960. Evolution récente de l'avifaune des Canaries. *Proc. XII Int. Orn. Congr., Helsinki 1958,* pp. 193–96.

———. 1964. Les oiseaux du nord de l'Afrique. Paris.

Farner, D. S., and King, J. R., eds. 1975. *Avian biology.* Vol. 5. New York.

Farquhar, A. M. 1902. Letter to the editor on *Falco eleonorae*. *Ibis* (8) 2:166–68.

Fiedler, K. 1964. Die Inseln der grauen Falken. *Vogel-Kosmos* 1:2–3.

Fischer, W. 1968. *Der Wanderfalk (Falco peregrinus und F. pelegrinoides)*. Wittenberg Lutherstadt.

Foschi, F. 1968. Monografia sugli uccelli dell'Isola di Pantelleria. *Riv. Ital. Orn.* 38:1–44.

Fretwell, S. D., and Lucas, H. L., Jr. 1969. On territorial behavior and other factors influencing habitat distribution in birds. I. Theoretical development. *Acta Biotheor.* 19:16–36.

Fry, C. H. 1961. Movements at sea between southwest Iberia and northwest Africa. *Ibis* 103:291–93.

Fyfe, R. W.; Temple, S. A.; and Cade, T. J. 1976. The 1975 North American Peregrine Falcon Survey. *Can. Field-Nat.* 90:228–73.

Gauci, C., ed. 1974. Ringing group report for 1973. *Il-Merrill, Bull. Malta Orn. Soc.*, no. 14.

Gené, G. 1840. Descrizione di un nuovo falcone di Sardegna (*Falco eleonorae*). *Mem. Reale Accad. Scienze di Torino*, 2d ser., 2:41–48.

Giglioli, E. H. 1889–91. *Primo resoconto dei risultati della inchiesta ornitologica in Italia*. Parts 1 and 3. Florence.

———. 1907. *Avifauna Italica*. Florence.

Glutz von Blotzheim, U. N.; Bauer, K. M.; and Bezzel, E. 1971. *Handbuch der Vögel Mitteleuropas*. Vol. 4. *Falconiformes*. Frankfurt am Main.

Goslow, G., Jr. 1972. Adaptive mechanisms of the raptor pelvic limb. *Auk* 89:47–64.

Gould, J. 1837. *The birds of Europe*. Vol. 1. *Raptores*. London.

Gouttenoire, G. 1955. Inventaire des oiseaux de Tunisie. *Alauda* 23:1–64, 217–18.

Green, J. 1964. The numbers and distribution of the African fish eagle *Haliaëtus vocifer* on the eastern shores of Lake Albert. *Ibis* 106:125–28.

Grossman, M. L., and Hamlet, J. 1964. *Birds of prey of the world*. New York.

Guerra, M. 1960. Note sull'ornitofauna di Montecristo. *Riv. Ital. Orn.* 30:123–37.

Hantge, E. 1968. Zum Beuteerwerb unserer Wanderfalken. *Orn. Mitt.* 20:211–17.

Hartert, E. 1913. *Die Vögel der paläarktischen Fauna*. Vol. 2. Berlin.

Hartert, E., and Jourdain, F. C. R. 1923. The hitherto known birds of Morocco. *Novit. Zool.* 30:91–152.

Hartlaub, G. 1877. *Die Vögel Madagascars und der Mascarenen, ein Beitrag zur Zoologie der aethiopischen Region*. Halle.

Hassler, K. D., ed. 1863. *Heinrich Mynsinger: Von den Falken, Pferden und Hunden*. Stuttgart.

Hatch, J. J. 1975. Piracy by laughing gulls *Larus atricilla*: An example of a selfish group. *Ibis* 117:357–65.

Heim de Balsac, H., and Mayaud, N. 1962. *Les oiseaux du nord-ouest de l'Afrique*. Paris.

Heinroth, O. 1899. Über die Kleider des Eleonorenfalken (*Falco eleonorae* Gené). *Ornith. Monatsber.* 7:19–23.

Herbert, R. A., and Herbert, K. G. S. 1965. Behavior of peregrine falcons in the New York City region. *Auk* 82:62–94.

Heuglin, Th. 1850. Ueber *Falco arcadicus*, Lindermayer, *F. eleonorae*, Géné, und *F. concolor*, Temminck. *Naumannia* 1:31–36.

Hickey, J. J., ed. 1969. *Peregrine falcon populations: Their biology and decline.* Madison, Milwaukee, and London.

Hill, N. P. 1944. Sexual dimorphism in the *Falconiformes. Auk* 61: 228–34.

Hinde, R. A. 1956. The biological significance of territories in birds. *Ibis* 98:340–69.

Hooker, T. 1958. Birds seen on the eastern Canary Island of Fuerteventura. *Ibis* 100:446–49.

Horn, H. S. 1968. The adaptive significance of colonial nesting in the Brewer's blackbird (*Euphagus cyanocephalus*). *Ecology* 49:682–94.

Horváth, L. 1955. Redfooted falcons on Ohat-woods, near Hortobágy. *Acta Zool. Acad. Scient. Hungar.* 1:245–87.

———. 1956. The life of the red-legged falcon in the Ohat forest. *Proc. XI. Int. Orn. Congr.,* Basel 1954, pp. 583–87.

———. 1975. Social pattern and behavior between two *Falco* species (*Aves*). *Ann. Historico-Naturales Musei Nationalis Hungarici* 67:327–31.

Hunt, W. G.; Rogers, R. R.; and Slowe, D. J. 1975. Migratory and foraging behavior of peregrine falcons on the Texas coast. *Can. Field-Nat.* 89 (2): 111–23.

Immelmann, K. 1963. Tierische Jahresperiodik in ökologischer Sicht. *Zool. Jahrb. Syst.* 91:91–200.

———. 1971. Ecological aspects of periodic reproduction. In *Avian biology*, ed. D. S. Farner and J. R. King, 1:341–89. New York.

———. 1973. Role of the environment in reproduction as a source of predictive information. In *Breeding biology of birds*, ed. D. S. Farner, pp. 121–47. Washington D.C.: National Academy of Sciences.

Jany, E. 1960. An Brutplätzen des Lannerfalken (*Falco biarmicus erlangeri* Kleinschmidt) in einer Kieswüste der inneren Sahara (Nordrand des Srir Tibesti) zur Zeit des Frühjahrszuges. *Proc. XII Intern. Orn. Congr., Helsinki 1958,* pp. 343–52.

Javanović, V. 1970. New observations of Eleonora's falcon, *Falco eleonorae* on Adriatic islands. *Larus* 24 (Eng. ed. 1974): 147–48.

Jenkins, D. 1961. Social behavior in the partridge *Perdix perdix. Ibis* 103a:155–88.

Jenni, D. A.; Gambs, R. D.; and Betts, B. J. 1974. Acoustic behavior of the northern jacana. *Liv. Bird* 13:193–210.

Johnson, C. 1964. The evolution of territoriality in the *Odonata. Evolution* 18:89–92.

Johnston, C. S; Campbell, D. H.; and Rolwegan, M. R. 1967. Summer observations on Lanzarote, an eastern island in the Canary archipelago. *Ibis* 109:276–77.

Jordans, A. von. 1924. Die Ergebnisse meiner zweiten Reise nach Mallorca: Ergänzungen zu meiner "Vogelfauna Mallorcas." *J. Orn.* 72:518–36.

Jourdain, F. C. R. 1912. Notes on the ornithology of Corsica. *Ibis* (9) 6:63–82, 314–32.

Kendeigh, S. C. 1970. Energy requirements for existence in relation to size of bird. *Condor* 72:60–65.

Kiepenheuer, J., and Linsenmair, K. E. 1965. Vogelzug an der nordafrikanischen Küste von Tunesien bis Rotes Meer. *Vogelwarte* 23:80–94.

Kiester, A. R.; Gorman, G. C.; and Arroyo, D. C. 1975. Habitat selection behavior of three species of Anolis lizards. *Ecology* 56:220–25.

King, J. A. 1973. The ecology of aggressive behavior. *Annual Review Ecol. Syst.* 4:117–38.

———. 1974. Seasonal allocation of time and energy resources in birds. In *Avian energetics*, ed. R. A. Paynter, Jr. Pp. 4–85. Publ. Nutt. Orn. Club, no. 15, 1–335.

Kinzelbach, R., and Martens, J. 1965. Zur Kenntnis der Vögel von Karpathos (Südliche Ägäis). *Bonn. Zool. Beitr.* 16:50–91.

Konishi, M. 1970. Evolution of design features in the coding of species-specificity. *Amer. Zool.* 10:67–72.

Koplin, J. R. 1973. Differential habitat use by sexes of American kestrels wintering in northern California. *Rapt. Res.* 7 (2): 39–42.

Krpan, M. 1967–68. Some data on the avifauna of the Island of Lastavo. *Larus* 21–22 (Eng. ed. 1970): 65–82.

Krüper, Th. 1862. Ornithologische Notizen über Griechenland. *J. Orn.* 435–48.

———. 1864. Beitrag zur Naturgeschichte des Eleonoren-Falken, *Falco Eleonorae* Géné. *J. Orn.* 12:1–23.

Lack, D. 1961. Migration across the southern North Sea studied by radar, part V. *Ibis* 105:461–92.

Laferrère, M. 1960. Le faucon d'Eléonore *Falco eleonorae* Gené nicheur en Algérie. *Alauda* 28:68–69.

Lammers. R. 1976. Date with death. In Lorne Greene's television show "Last of the Wild." Los Angeles, Station KTTV, 26 September.

Lasiewski, R. C., and Dawson, W. R. 1967. A re-examination of the relation between standard metabolic rate and body weight in birds. *Condor* 69 (1): 13–23.

Lavauden, L. 1924. *Voyage de M. Guy Babault en Tunisie. Résultats scientifiques: Oiseaux.* Paris (?).

Ligon, J. D. 1968. The biology of the elf owl, *Micrathene whitneyi. Univ. Michigan Mus. Zool., Misc. Publ.* 136:1–70.

Lilford, Lord. 1875. Cruise of the "Zara," R.Y.S. in the Mediterranean. *Ibis* (3) 5:1–35.

———. 1889. A list of the birds of Cyprus. *Ibis* (6) 1:305–50.

Lindberg, P. 1977. The peregrine falcon in Sweden. In *World conference on birds of prey*, ed. R. D. Chancellor, pp. 329–38. London.

Lindner, K., ed. 1962. *Von Falken, Hunden und Pferden*. Deutsche Albertus-Magnus-Übersetzungen aus der ersten Hälfte des 15. Jahrhunderts. 2 parts. Berlin.

Lintia, D. 1954. *Pasarile diu R.P.R.* [The birds of Romania]. Vol. 2. Bucharest.

Lofts, B., and Murton, R. K. 1968. Photoperiodic and physiological adaptations regulating avian breeding cycles and their ecological significance. *J. Zool., Lond.* 155:327–94.

Lovegrove, R. 1971. B.O.U. supported expedition to Northeast Canary Islands: July-August 1970. *Ibis* 113:269–72.

Lowerey, G. H. 1951. A quantitative study of the nocturnal migration of birds. *Univ. Kansas Publ. Mus. Nat. Hist.* 3:361–472.

Lucca, C. de. 1950. Contributo all'ornitologica delle Isole Maltesi. *Riv. Ital. Orn.* (20) 2:33–44.

Lynes, H. 1912. Field-notes on a collection of birds from the Mediterranean: With September notes by H. F. Witherby. *Ibis* (9) 6:121–87.

McGahan, J. 1968. Ecology of the golden eagle. *Auk* 85:1–12.

McInvaille, W. B., Jr., and Keith, L. B. 1974. Predator-prey relations and breeding biology of the great horned owl and red-tailed hawk in central Alberta. *Can. Field-Nat.* 88:1–20.

Makatsch, W. 1958. Beobachtungen an einem Brutplatz des Eleonorenfalken. *Vogelwelt* 79:40–47.

———. 1969. Ornithologische Beobachtungen in Griechenland. Part 2. *Zool. Abh. Staatl. Mus. Tierk. Dresden* 30:1–56.

Manuval, D. A. 1974. Effects of territoriality on breeding in a population of Cassin's auklet. *Ecology* 55:1399–1406.

Marmora, A. della. 1839. *Viaggio in Sardegna*. Part 1, p. 143. Paris and Torino.

Martorelli, G. 1895. *Monografia illustrata degli uccelli di rapina d'Italia*. Milan.

Mayaud, N. 1960. Le faucon d'Eléonore *Falco eleonorae* Gené nicheur aux Iles Habibas (Oran): Sa distribution en Méditerranée occidentale. *Alauda* 28:149–50.

Mebs, T. 1959. Beitrag zur Biologie des Feldeggsfalken (*Falco biarmicus feldeggi*). *Vogelwelt* 80:142–49.

———. 1964. *Greifvögel Europas und die Grundzüge der Falknerei*. Stuttgart.

Meinertzhagen, R. 1921. A note on the breeding birds of Crete. *Ibis* (11) 3:126–39.

———. 1940. Autumn in central Morocco. *Ibis* (14) 4:106–36, 187–234.

———. 1954. *Birds of Arabia*. London.

Meng, H. K. 1951. The Cooper's hawk. Ph.D. diss., Cornell University.

Mertz, D. B. 1971. The mathematical demography of the California condor population. *Amer. Nat.* 105:437–53.

Mills, G. S. 1976. American kestrel sex ratios and habitat separation. *Auk* 93:740–48.

Milon, P.; Petter, J.-J.; and Randrianasolo, G. 1973. *Faune de Madagascar*. Vol. 35. *Oiseaux*. Tananarive and Paris.

Mocci Demartis, A. 1973. Récensement de la colonie de faucon d'Eléonore *Falco eleonorae* de l'Ile de San Pietro (Sardaigne). *Alauda* 41:385–402.

Mohr, H. 1960. Über die Entwicklung einiger Verhaltensweisen bei handaufgezogenen Sperbern (*Accipiter n. nisus*) und Baumfalken (*Falco s. subbuteo* L.). *Zeitschr. Tierpsychol*. 17:700–27.

Moltoni, E. 1954. Gli uccelli fino ad oggi notificati per l'Isole di Montecristo (Arcipelago Toscano). *Riv. Ital. Orn*. 24:36–50.

———. 1970. Gli uccelli ad oggi riscontrati nelle Isole Linosa, Lampedusa e Lampione (Isole Pelagie, Canale di Sicilia, Mediterraneo). *Riv. Ital. Orn*. 40:77–283.

———. 1971. Gli uccelli ad oggi riscontrati nelle isole di Tavolara, Molara e Molarotto (Sardegna nord-orientale). *Riv. Ital. Orn*. 41:223–372.

Monneret, R. J. 1973. Techniques de chasse du faucon pélerin *Falco peregrinus* dans une region de moyenne montagne. *Alauda* 41:403–12.

———. 1974. Repertoire comportemental du faucon pélerin *Falco peregrinus*: Hypothèse explicative des manifestations adversives. *Alauda* 42:407–28.

Moore, N. W. 1964. Intra- and interspecific competition among dragonflies (*Odonata*). *J. Anim. Ecol*. 33:49–71.

Moreau, R. E. 1961. Problems of Mediterranean-Saharan migration. *Ibis* 103a:373–472, 580–623.

———. 1966. *The bird faunas of Africa and its islands*. New York and London.

———. 1969. The sooty falcon *Falco concolor* Temminck. *Bull. Brit. Orn. Club* 89:62–67.

———. 1972. *The Palearctic-African bird migration systems*. London and New York.

Moreau, R. E., and Dolp, R. M. 1970. Fat, water, weights and wing-lengths of autumn migrants in transit on the northwest coast of Egypt. *Ibis* 112:209–28.

Moreau, R. E., and Moreau, W. M. 1954. Notas otonales sobre aves de Levante e Islas Pityusas. *Ardeola* 1:86–115.

Mosher, J. A. 1973. The energetics of size dimorphism. *Rapt. Res*. 7 (2): 62–63.

Mosher, J. A., and Henry, C. J. 1976. Thermal adaptiveness of plumage color in screech owls. *Auk* 93:614–19.

Mosher, J. A., and Matray, P. F. 1974. Size dimorphism: A factor in energy savings for broad-winged hawks. *Auk* 91 (2): 525–41.

Mosher, J. A., and White, C. M. 1976. Directional exposure of golden eagle nests. *Can. Field-Nat*. 90 (3): 356–59.

Mueller, H. C. 1973. The relationship of hunger to predatory behavior in hawks *Falco sparverius* and *Buteo platypterus*. *Anim. Behav*. 21 (3): 513–20.

Mühle, H. Graf von der. 1844. *Beitraege zur Ornithologie Griechenlands*. Leipzig.

Munn, P. W. 1925. Eleonora's falcon in Majorca. *Ibis* (12) 1:532–33.

Murdoch, W. W. 1971. The developmental response of predators to changes in prey density. *Ecology* 52:132–37.

Murphy, R. R. 1926. A cruise to Mallorca. *J. Amer. Mus. Nat. Hist.* 26:552–59.

Nelson, R. W. 1970*a*. Some aspects of the breeding behavior of peregrine falcons on Langara Island, B.C. M.S. thesis, University of Calgary.

———. 1970*b*. Observations on the decline and survival of the peregrine falcon. *Can. Field-Nat.* 84:313–19.

———. 1972. The incubation period in Peale's falcons. *Rapt. Res.* 6 (1): 11–15.

———. 1973. Field techniques in a study of the behavior of peregrine falcons. *Rapt. Res.* 7 (3/4): 78–96.

———. 1976. Behavioral aspects of egg breakage in peregrine falcons. *Can. Field-Nat.* 90 (3): 320–29.

———. 1977. Behavioral ecology of coastal peregrines (*Falco peregrinus pealei*). Ph.D. diss., University of Calgary.

Newton, I. 1976*a*. Raptor research and conservation during the last five years. *Can. Field-Nat.* 90 (3): 225–27.

———. 1976*b*. Population limitation in diurnal raptors. *Can. Field-Nat.* 90 (3): 274–300.

Niethammer, G. 1943. Über die Vogelwelt Kretas. *Ann. Naturhist. Mus. Wien* 53 (2): 5–59.

O'Connor, R. J. 1977. Differential growth and body composition in altricial passerines. *Ibis* 119:147–66.

Olendorff, R. R. 1968. A contribution to the breeding behavior of the American kestrel in captivity. *Rapt. Res. News* 2 (4): 77–92.

Oliphant, L. W., and Thompson, W. J. P. 1976. Food caching behavior in Richardson's merlin. *Can. Field-Nat.* 90 (3): 364–65.

Opdam, P.; Thissen, J.; Verschuren, P.; and Müskens, G. 1977, Feeding ecology of a population of Goshawk *Accipiter gentilis. J. Orn.* 118:35–51.

Orians, G. H. and Willson, M. F. 1964. Interspecific territories of birds. *Ecology* 45:736–45.

Ornithological Society of Turkey. 1969. *Bird report no. 1, 1966–1967.* London.

———. 1971. *Check list of the birds of Turkey.* London.

———. 1972. *Bird report no. 2, 1968–1969.* London.

Parrot, J. R. 1976. A report on the status of Eleonora's falcon *Falco eleonorae* at a Cretan colony, Paximada in 1976. Unpub. manuscript, pp. 1–15.

Pateff, P. 1950. *The birds of Bulgaria* (Original in Russian). Sofia.

Patterson, I. J. 1965. Timing and spacing of broods in the black-headed gull (*Larus ridibundus*). *Ibis* 107:433–59.

Paynter, R. A., Jr., ed. 1974. *Avian energetics.* Publ. Nuttall Orn. Club, no. 15. Cambridge, Mass.

Peakall, D. B. 1976. The peregrine falcon (*Falco peregrinus*) and pesticides. *Can. Field-Nat.* 90 (3): 301–7.

Peakall, D. B. ; Cade, T. J.; White, C. M.; and Haugh, J. R. 1975. Organochlorine residues in Alaskan peregrines. *Pestic. Monit. J.* 8:255–60.

Perrins, C. M. 1970. The timing of birds' breeding seasons. *Ibis* 112:242–55.

Pillito, J. 1862. *Memorie tratte dal Regio Archivio di Stato di Cagliari*, p. 37, n. 1. Cagliari.

Pineau, J., and Giraud-Audine, M. 1974. Notes sur les migrateurs traversant l'extrême nord-ouest du Maroc. *Alauda* 42:159–88.

Polatzek, J. 1908. Die Vögel der Canaren. *Orn. Jahrb.* 19:81–119, 161–97.

Porter, R., and Willis, I. 1968. The autumn migration of soaring birds at the Bosphorus. *Ibis* 110:520–36.

Porter, R. D., and White, C. M. 1973. The peregrine falcon in Utah, emphasizing ecology and competition with the prairie falcon. *Brigham Young Univ. Sci. Bull. Biol. Ser.* 18 (1): 1–74.

Preston, D. A. 1956–57. A summer holiday in Mallorca. *Balearica* 1:89–93.

Ralfs, G. 1961. Ornithologische Frühjahrsbeobachtungen auf Rhodos. *Abh. Verh. Naturwiss. Vereins Hamburg* 6:7–18.

Rand, A. L. 1936. The distribution and habits of Madagascar birds: A summary of the field notes of the Mission Zoologique Franco-Anglo-Américaine à Madagascar. *Bull. Amer. Mus. Nat. Hist.* 72:143–499.

Ratcliffe, D. A. 1967. Decrease in eggshell weight in certain birds of prey. *Nature* 215 (5097): 208–10.

———. 1972. The peregrine population of Great Britain in 1971. *Bird Study* 19:117–56.

Reese, J. G. 1970. Reproduction in a Chesapeake Bay osprey population. *Auk* 87:747–59.

Reiser, O. 1905. *Materialien zu einer Ornis Balcanica*. III. *Griechenland und die Griechischen Inseln (mit Ausnahme von Kreta)*. Vienna.

Reynolds, R. T. 1972. Sexual dimorphism in accipiter hawks: A new hypothesis. *Condor* 74:191–97.

Richardson, W. J. 1974. Spring migration over Puerto Rico and the western Atlantic: A radar study. *Ibis* 116:172–93.

———. 1976. Autumn migration over Puerto Rico and the Western Atlantic: A radar study. *Ibis* 118:309–32.

Ricklefs, R. E. 1968. Weight recession in nestling birds. *Auk* 85:30–35.

———. 1973. Patterns of growth in birds. II. Growth rate and mode of development. *Ibis* 115 (2): 177–201.

———. 1974. Energetics of reproduction in birds. In *Avian energetics*, ed. R. A. Paynter, Jr., pp. 86–151. Publ. Nutt. Orn. Club, no. 15, pp. 1–335.

Riggenbach, P. W. 1903. Reise nach dem Rio-de-Oro Juni bis August 1902. *Nov. Zool.* 10:286–94.

Ristow, D. 1975. Neue Ringfunde vom Eleonorenfalken (*Falco eleonorae*). *Vogelwarte* 28:150–53.

Roberts, E. L. 1954. *The birds of Malta*. Malta.

Rockenbauch, D. 1968. Zur Brutbiologie ds Turmfalken (*Falco tinnunculus* L.). *Anz. Orn. Ges. Bayern* 8 (3): 267–76.

Rösler, U., and Walter, H. 1966. Der Falter *Trichophaga abruptella* (Woll. 1858) (Tineidae) und seine Abhängigkeit vom Eleonorenfalken. *Bonn. Zool. Beitr.* 17:135–40.

Rudebeck, G. 1950–51. The choice of prey and modes of hunting of predatory birds, with special reference to their selective effect. *Oikos* 2:65–88, 3:200–31.

Rusch, D. H.; Meslow, E. C., Doerr, P. D., and Keith, L. B. 1972. Response of great horned owl populations to changing prey densities. *J. Wildl. Management* 36:282–96.

Salvan, J. 1970. Remarques sur l'évolution de l'avifaune Malgache depuis 1945. *Alauda* 38:191–203.

Saunders, H. 1871. A list of the birds of southern Spain. *Ibis* (3) 1:54–68.

Schaller, G. B. 1972. *The Serengeti lion: A study of predator-prey relations*. Chicago.

Schlegel, H. 1844. *Kritische Übersicht der europäischen Vögel: Revue Critique des oiseaux d'Europe*. Vol. 2. Leiden.

Schmalfuss, H. 1972. Notizen zum Bestand des Eleonorenfalken (*Falco eleonorae*) in der Südägäis. *J. Orn.* 113:336–37.

Schoener, T. W. 1968. Sizes of feeding territories among birds. *Ecology* 49:123–41.

—————. 1969. Models of optimal size for solitary predators. *Amer. Nat.* 103:277–313.

—————. 1971. Theory of feeding strategies. *Ann. Rev. Ecol. and Systematics* 2:369–404.

Schultze-Westrum, T. 1961. Beobachtungen am Eleonorenfalken. *Anz. Orn. Ges. Bay.* 6:84–86.

Sclater, P. L. 1868. [Report on two Eleonora's falcons presented to the society by Capt. T. Waite.]*Proc. Zool. Soc. Lond.* 1868: 567.

Serventy, D. L. 1971. Biology of desert birds. In *Avian biology*, ed. D. S. Farner and J. R. King, 1:287–339. New York.

Sibley, C. G., and Ahlquist, J. E. 1972. A comparative study of the egg white proteins of non-passerine birds. *Bull. Peabody Mus. Nat. Hist., Yale Univ.* 39:1–276.

Simmons, K. E. L. 1970. Ecological determinants of breeding adaptations and social behavior in two fish-eating birds. In *Social behaviour in birds and mammals: Essays on the social ethology of animals and man*, ed. J. H. Crook, pp. 37–77. London and New York.

Smeenk, C. 1974. *Comparative-ecological studies of some East African birds of prey*. Ph.D. diss., University of Amsterdam.

Smith, D. G., and Murphy, J. R. 1973. Breeding ecology of raptors in the eastern Great Basin of Utah. *Brigham Young Univ. Sci. Bull.* 18 (3): 1–76.

Smith, D. G.; Wilson, C. R.; and Frost, H. H. 1972. The biology of the American kestrel in central Utah. *Southwestern Nat.* 17:73–83.

Smith, K. D. 1965. On the birds of Morocco. *Ibis* 107:493–526.

Snyder, N. F. R. 1974. Breeding biology of swallow-tailed kites in Florida. *Liv. Bird* 13:73–97.

Snyder, N. F. R., and Wiley, J. W. 1976. Sexual size dimorphism in hawks and owls of North America. *Orn. Monogr.* 20:1–96.

Southern, H. N. 1970. The natural control of a population of tawny owls (*Strix aluco*). *J. Zool.* 162 (2): 197–285

Sparks, J. H. 1965. Clumping and allopreening in the red-thighed falconet *Microhierax caerulescens burmanicus. Ibis* 107:247–48.

Steinbacher, J., 1971. Am Brutplatz der Eleonorenfalken. *Gefied. Welt* 95:16–17, 34–36, 53–56.

Storer, R. W. 1966. Sexual dimorphism and food habits in three North American accipiters. *Auk* 83:423–36.

Stresemann, E. 1954. Zur Frage der Wanderungen des Eleonorenfalken. *Vogelwarte* 17:182–83.

———. 1955. Das Jugendkleid von *Falco concolor* Temminck. *J. Orn.* 96:122–23.

———. 1956. Bausteine zu einer Ornithologie von Kreta: Den Tagebüchern von Heinz Sielmann (1944/45) und anderen Stellen entnommen. *J. Orn.* 97:44–71.

———. 1968, Der Eingriff der Eleonorenfalken in den herbstlichen Vogelzug. *J. Orn.* 109:472–74.

Sturkie, P. D., ed. 1976. *Avian physiology* 3d ed. New York.

Swann, H. K., and Wetmore, A. 1935. *A monograph of the birds of prey* (order *Accipitres*). Part 13. London.

Temminck, J. C. 1840. *Manuel d'ornithologie.* 2d ed., part 4. Paris.

Terrasse, J. F. 1963. A propos de deux reprises de *Falco eleonorae. L'oiseau et R.F.O.* 33:56–60.

———. 1969. Essai de recensement de la population française de Faucon pélerin *Falcon peregrinus* en 1968. *Nos Oiseaux* 30:149–55.

———. 1970. Techniques de chasse du Faucon pélerin (*Falco peregrinus*) et éducation des jeunes. *Alauda* 38:186–90.

Thiollay, J. M. 1967. Observations sur le faucon d'Eléonore *Falco eleonorae* et quelques autres rapaces des Baléares. *Nos Oiseaux* 29:29–40.

———. 1975. Les rapaces d'une zone de contact savane-forêt en Côted'Ivoire: Denisté, dynamique et structure du peuplement. *Alauda* 43:387–416.

Thomsen, L. 1971. Behavior and ecology of burrowing owls on the Oakland Municipal Airport. *Condor* 73:177–92.

Ticehurst, C. B., and Whistler, H. 1930. A spring tour in Eastern Spain and the Pityusae Islands. *Ibis* (12) 6:638–77.

Tinbergen, L. 1940. Beobachtungen über die Arbeitsteilung des Turmfalken (*Falco tinnunculus* L.) während der Fortpflanzungszeit. *Ardea* 29:63–98.

Tinbergen, N. 1957. The functions of territory. *Bird Study* 4:14–27.

———. 1967. Adaptive features of the black-headed gull *Larus ridibundus* L. *Proc. XIV Int. Orn. Congr., Oxford 1966*, pp. 43–59.

Toschi, A. 1953. Note sui vertebrati dell' Isola di Montecristo. *Ricerche Zool. Applic. alla Caccia* 23:1–52.

———. 1969. *Avifauna Italiana*. Florence.

Toso, S. 1972. Osservazioni di rapaci diurni in Sardegna. *Riv. Ital. Orn.* 42:435–44.

Trettau, W. 1968. Beitrag zur Vogelwelt der Insel Capraia. *Beihefte der Vogelwelt* 2:85–87.

———. 1971. Ornithologische Beobachtungen auf der Insel Giglio und Ergänzungen zur Vogelwelt der Insel Elba und Capraia. *Orn. Mitt.* 23:101–4.

Tristram, H. B. 1884. *The survey of western Palestine: The Fauna and Flora of Palestine*. London.

Tschanz, B. 1968. *Trottellummen*. Z. Tierpsychol. Suppl. 4.

Tucker, V. A. 1969. The energetics of bird flight. *Sci. Amer.* 220 (5): 70–78.

Tucker, V. A., and Schmidt-Koenig, K. 1971. Flight speeds of birds in relation to energetics and wind directions. *Auk* 88:97–107.

Ueoka, M. L., and Koplin, J. R. 1973. Foraging behavior of ospreys in northwestern California. *Rapt. Res.* 7:32–38.

Uttendörfer, O. 1948. Zur Ernährung des Eleonorenfalken. *Orn. Ber.* 1:242–43.

———. 1952. *Neue Ergebnisse über die Ernährung der Greifvögel und Eulen*. Stuttgart.

Vaglianos, C. M. 1977. Changes in bird population due to the effects of an extensive campaign of aerial spraying against the "Olive fruit fly" (*Dacus oleae*) in the plain of Messara, Crete. *Nature Newsletter Hell. Soc. Prot. Nature*, no. 10/11 (1977).

Vancamp, L. F., and Henry, C. J. 1975. The screech owl: Its life history and population ecology in northern Ohio. *N. Amer. Fauna* no. 71, pp.1–76.

Van Tyne, J., and Berger, A. J. 1976. *Fundamentals of ornithology*. 2d ed. New York.

Vaughan, R. 1961*a*. *Falco eleonorae*. *Ibis* 103*a*:114–28.

———. 1961*b*. Studies of less familiar birds. III. Eleonora's falcon. *Brit. Birds* 54:235–38.

———. 1977. Birds of an Aegean island. *Country Life*, 5 May.

Vaurie, C. 1965. *The birds of the Palearctic fauna: Non-passeriformes*. London.

Voous, K. H. 1963. *Die Vogelwelt Europas und ihre Verbreitung*. Hamburg and Berlin.

Wallraff, H. G., and Kiepenheuer, J. 1962. Migracion y orientacion en Aves: Observaciones en otono en el Sur-Oeste de Europa. *Ardeola* 8:20–40.

Walter, H. 1965. Ergebnisse ornithologischer Beobachtungen auf Sardinien im Winter 1961/62. *J. Orn.* 106:81–105.

———. 1967. Zur Lebensweise von *Lacerta erhardii. Bonn. Zool. Beitr.* 18:216–20.

———. 1968a. Zur Abhängigkeit des Eleonorenfalken (*Falco eleonorae*) vom mediterranen Vogelzug. *J. Orn.* 109:323–65.

———. 1968b. Falcons of a princess. *Pacific Discovery* 21 (3): 2–9.

———. 1970. Zum Badeverhalten von *Falco eleonorae. J. Orn.* 111:242–43.

———. 1971. Juli-Zugbelege aus Marokko in Rupfungen von *Falco eleonorae. Vogelwarte* 26:142.

———. 1978a. Determinants of coexistence in a colonial raptor. *National Geographic Society Research Reports, 1969,* Projects 10:593–620.

———. 1978b. *Breeding locations of Falco eleonorae: A world directory.* Los Angeles (private publication). Pp.1–54.

———. In preparation. Ecology of the sooty falcon (*Falco concolor*) in its breeding and wintering habitats.

Walter, H., and Deetjen, H. 1967. Une nouvelle colonie du faucon d'Eléonore (*Falco eleonorae*) au Maroc. *Alauda* 35:106–7.

Walter, H., and Foers, R. In preparation. Census of *Falco eleonorae* on Cyprus.

Warncke, K., and Wittenberg, J. 1961. Beobachtungen am Eleonorenfalken auf den Nördlichen Sporaden. *Vogelwelt* 82:48–54.

Wattel, J. 1973. *Geographical differentiation in the genus* Accipiter. Pub. Nuttall Orn. Club, no. 13:1–231.

Welty, J. C. 1962. *The life of birds.* Philadelphia.

———. 1975. *The life of birds.* 2d ed. Philadelphia.

Westernhagen, W. von. 1958. Sobre algunas aves de Mallorca durante los ultomos cien anos. *Ardeola* 4:157–68.

Wettstein, O. von. 1938. Die Vogelwelt der Ägäis. *J. Orn.* 86:9–53.

———. 1959. Jagdflug von *Falco eleonorae. J. Orn.* 100:105.

White, C. M., and Cade, T. J. 1971. Cliff-nesting raptors and ravens along the Colville River in arctic Alaska. *Living Bird* 10:107–50.

———. 1977. Long term trends of peregrine populations in Alaska. In *World conference on birds of prey,* ed. R. D. Chancellor, pp. 63–72. London.

White, C. M.; Emison, W. B.; and Williamson, F. S. L. 1971. Dynamics of raptor populations on Amchitka Island, Alaska. *BioScience* 21 (12): 623–27.

White, C. M., and Weeden, R. B. 1966. Hunting methods of gyrfalcons and behavior of their prey (ptarmigan). *Condor* 68 (5): 517–19.

Willemsen, C. A., ed. 1964. Friedrich II. *Über die Kunst mit Vögeln zu jagen.* Frankfurt am Main.

Willoughby, E. J., and Cade, T. J. 1964. Breeding behavior of the

American kestrel (sparrow hawk). *Living Bird* 3:75–96.

Wilson, E. O. 1975. *Sociobiology: The new synthesis.* Cambridge, Mass.

Wood, C. A., and Fyfe, F. M., ed. and transl. 1961. *The art of falconry, being the DE ARTE VENANDI CUM AVIBUS of Frederick II of Hohenstaufen.* Stanford, Calif.

Wright, H. E., Jr. 1976. The environmental setting for plant domestication in the Near East. *Science* 194 (4263): 385–89.

Wyer, F. P. W. Unpublished manuscript on falcons. Library of the Western Foundation of Vertebrate Zoology. Brentwood, Calif.

Wyrwoll, T. 1977. Die Jagdbereitschaft des Habichts (*Accipiter gentilis*) in Beziehung zum Horstort. *J. Orn.* 118:21–34.

Yapp, W. B. 1970. *The life and organization of birds.* London.

Young, E. C. 1972. Territory establishment and stability in McCormick's skua. *Ibis* 114:234–44.

Zink, G. 1973. *Der Zug europäischer Singvögel, ein Atlas der Wiederfunde beringter Vögel.* I. *Vogelwarte Radolfzell.* Möggingen.

Index

Acanthis cannabina, 374
Accidents, 79
Accipiter, 141, 182, 252, 347, 350, 351, 354, 359
Accipiter brevipes, 380
Accipiter gentilis, 313, 349, 358, 380. *See also* Goshawk
Accipiter nisus, 349
Accipiter nisus nisus, 348, 351, 380
Accipiter striatus, 351
Acherontia atropos,163
Acoustic behavior, 254–62, 266, 317
Acrocephalus arundinaceus, 372
Acrocephalus paludicola, 372
Acrocephalus palustris, 372
Acrocephalus schoenobaenus, 372
Acrocephalus scirpaceus, 372
Acrocephalus spp., 372
Activity patterns, 214, 217, 223–33
Adansonia spp., 282
Adaptation: to bird migration pulse, 123; to surface texture, 236
Adaptive value: of breeding season, 201–2, 343, 346; of clutch size, 346; of hunting strategies, 110, 131; of morphological characters, 324–30
Aegean Sea, 296, 297; as distribution center, 30
Aegypius monachus, 381
Aeshnidae, 163
African hobby, 305, 351
Agama ruderata, 145, 164
Aggression, 237, 242. *See also* Agonistic behavior
Agonistic behavior, 237–54; discussion of, 252, 266–69; and dominance, 245–46, 250–51; interspecific, 237–39; intraspecific, 239–54, 266; territorial conflicts, 242–48; territorial rivalry, 241–48

Alcedo atthis, 369, 370
Alectoris chukar, 370
Alpine swift, 138, 151
American kestrel, 89, 210, 257, 258, 328, 329, 357; breeding behavior, 343, 344; home range, 334–35; territoriality, 336–37
Amphimallon arianae, 147
Annual cycle, 290–92
Antagonistic behavior. *See* Agonistic behavior
Anthus bertholeti, 372
Anthus campestris, 369, 372
Anthus pratensis, 372
Anthus spinoletta, 372
Anthus spp., 369
Anthus trivialis, 369, 372, 376
Antiraptor behavior of prey species, 143
Apus affinis, 370
Apus apus, 138, 151, 369, 370
Apus melba, 138, 151, 370
Apus pallidus, 138
Apus spp., 21, 138
Aquila chrysaëtos, 358, 380. *See also* Golden eagle
Aquila heliaca, 380
Ardea cinerea, 369
Ardeola ralloides, 369
Arenaria interpres, 369
Artemisia, 304
Asio otus, 48
Audouin's gull, 18

Bank Swallow (Sand martin), 65, 300
Baobab trees, 282, 283
Barn owl, 323
Barn swallow, 300, 369
Bats as prey, 164, 165
Bearded vulture, 356, 358

Biocides, 317–21

Bird larders, 130, 162, 298

Bird migration, 113–33; in America, 299–303; broad-front migrants, 125; density, 113, 120, 130, 133, 297; departure points, 124; direction, 118, 300, 301; dynamics, 346–47; fall (autumn) migration, 115–22; in Gulf of Mexico, 301; height, 117, 123, 300, 301; in major study areas, 122–30; number of migrants, 113, 123; observation methods, 114; pulse, 120–21, 122, 130, 131, 133, 295, 299; sea-crossings, 115–16, 301; "shadow," 122, 124, 127, 130, 131; south of Iberian peninsula, 120, 127–29, 297; spring migration, 118; structure, 115–17, 133, 300; systems, 299–303, 304, 346–47; time, 120; visible from ground, 369; in Western Atlantic, 299–303; wind force and migrant numbers, 123

Black-eared wheatear, 369

Black kite, 263

Blackpoll warbler, 300

Black rat, 18, 19, 80, 83, 239

Black tern, 169

Blue rock thrush, 369

Bobolink, 300

Boreal owl, 348

Breeding: behavior, 343–45 (see also Sexual behavior); colonies, 16–36; density, 40–42, 331–33, 335, 380, 381; habitats, 13, 16–23; regions, 28; season, 345; success, 51–59, 65, 214–15, 298, 320, 342, 343

Broad-winged hawk, 180

Bubo bubo, 81, 358

Bubo virginianus, 346

Buntings, 167

Buprestidae, 163

Burrowing owl, 334–35, 349, 358

Buteo buteo, 325, 380

Buteo lagopus, 47, 380

Buteo platypterus, 180

Buzzard, 325

Caching behavior. See Food caching

Calandrella brachydactyla, 368, 369, 370, 376

Calandrella rufescens, 370

Calonectris diomedea (Puffinus kuhlii), 18, 52, 81

Cannibalism, 79

Capra hircus, 19, 80

Caprimulgus europaeus, 138, 369, 370

Carabidae, 163

Caribbean, "absent" niche, 299–303

Celerio lineata, 163

Cercotrichas galactotes, 372, 377

Chalcides, 21

Charadrius alexandrinus, 370

Charadrius hiaticula, 370

Chick mortality, 57–58

Chlidonias leucopterus, 370

Chlidonias niger, 370

Circaëtus gallicus, 369, 380

Circus, 359

Circus aeruginosus, 369, 380

Circus cyaneus, 354, 380

Circus pygargus, 332, 380

Clamator glandarius, 369, 370

Clutch size, 51–57; and breeding success, 65; changes, 320, 321; constancy, 56; of early breeders, 65; and energy needs, 345; second clutch, 51; single-egg clutch, 51, 54, 56, 83, 320

Coceyzus americanus, 300

Coexistence, 266–69

Coleoptera, 163

Colonial species, 42

Color phase: adaptive value, 325–27; and breeding success, 53, 367; genetic base, 384; ratio, 37–40, 364

Columba livia, 18, 21, 22, 138, 370

Common redstart. See Redstart

Common sandpiper, 369, 382

Common whitethroat. See Whitethroat

Competition: interspecific, 294

Copulation, 208–10, 212–16

Coracias garrulus, 370

Corvus corax, 22, 47, 350

Corvus corone cornix, 52

Corvus frugilegus, 87, 236, 339

Cory's shearwater, 18, 52, 81, 83, 167; impact on falcons' breeding success, 52, 81

Coturnix coturnix, 370, 377

Cranes, 118

Crex crex, 370

Cuckoo, 138, 149, 169, 194, 195

Cuculus canorus, 138, 149, 370

Curculionidae, 163
Cyprus (falcon colonies): nestling rate, 55; pulse of bird migration, 131

Daphnis nerii, 163
Delichon urbica, 372
Dendroica striata, 300
Density, 266–69; and disturbance, 241; in winter range, 285. See also Breeding
Development of young, 67–77
Dichromatism, sexual, 328
Dimorphism. See Reversed sexual dimorphism
Discovery, 310–12
Disease, 77
Dispersion, 40–44, 49, 266–69; of juveniles and subadults, 288–90; of prey, 355; of raptor species, 331–33, 335
Distribution, 12; map, 14–15
Disturbance, 241; of breeding colony, 51, 52, 83; of breeding cycle, 212–14; at nest site, 341–43
Division of labor, 84–85, 353, 355, 359
Dolichonyx oryzivorus, 300
Dominance, 245–46, 269; within pair bond, 250–51, 253–54
Dove, 167
Dwarf bittern, 167

Eagle owl, 81, 358
Eagles, 81, 238, 316, 317, 324, 332, 354, 356. See also individual species
Egg-laying, 59–60; synchronization between pairs, 64–65
Eggs: color, 11; lost and abandoned, 52, 54, 55, 59; measurements, 11, 378–79
Eggshell thickness, 317–21, 379; index, 318, 320, 379
Eggshell-thinning, 11, 317–21
Eleonora of Arborea (Eleonora d'Arborea), 312
Elf owl, 358
Emberiza caesia, 374
Emberiza hortulana, 374
Emberiza melanocephala, 374
Emberiza spp., 374
Enemies, 79–83; birds, 81; mammals, 80; man, 79
Energetics. See Falcon energetics

Energy expenditure, 177–84
Erithacus rubecula, 372
Euphorbia dendroides, 17, 44
European hobby. See Hobby
European sparrowhawk, 332, 348
Evolution, 304–9
"Extramarital" relationships, 210, 211, 251

Falco, 138, 142, 252, 263, 269, 305, 336, 345, 350, 359
Falco biarmicus, 351, 352. See also Lanner falcon
Falco cherrug, 338, 351, 352, 380. See also Saker falcon
Falco columbarius, 336, 351, 352, 380. See also Merlin
Falco concolor, 9, 282, 283, 305, 337, 338, 352. See also Sooty falcon
Falco cuvieri, 305, 351, 352
Falco mexicanus, 351, 352. See also Prairie falcon
Falco naumanni, 51, 323, 328, 332, 352, 380. See also Lesser kestrel
Falcon energetics, 177–84, 200, 347
Falcones, 323
Falconets, 306
Falco newtoni, 282
Falconiformes, 347
Falconry, 310–14
Falcons, 323, 324, 328, 332; occupancy of nest sites, 341–43. See also individual species
Falco peregrinus, 2, 5, 9, 21, 313, 336, 337, 351, 352, 357, 380. See also Peregrine falcon
Falco peregrinus babylonicus, 311
Falco peregrinus brookei, 9
Falco rusticolus, 47, 327, 351, 352, 380. See also Gyrfalcon
Falco sparverius, 328, 336, 337, 352, 353, 356, 357. See also American kestrel
Falco subbuteo, 51, 272, 305, 323, 336, 337, 351, 352, 380. See also Hobby
Falco tinnunculus, 51, 263, 323, 328, 332, 333, 338, 339, 352, 353, 380. See also Kestrel
Falco vespertinus, 272, 273, 287, 332, 337, 339, 352, 357, 380. See also Redfooted falcon
Fall migration, 272–77

Feeding, 382–83
Ferruginous hawk, 334, 335
Fertility, 53, 57
Ficedula albicollis, 374
Ficedula hypoleuca, 374,·376, 377
Ficedula parva, 374
Field identification: adults, 5–6; dark
    phase, 5; immatures, 6; juveniles, 6;
    light phase, 5; variable characters,
    6–8
Flight corridors, 223, 226
Flycatchers, 300, 350
Food caching, 219, 233, 267, 382–83
Fox, 239
Frederick II, Emperor, 311
Fregatidae, 347
Frigate birds, 347
Fringilla coelebs, 374

Gallinula chloropus, 369
Garden warbler, 144, 191, 193
Geckos, 21
Glaciation, European, 304, 305
Goats, on island cliffs, 19, 80, 83, 239
Golden eagle, 48, 137, 332, 333, 334,
    335
Golden oriole, 96, 114, 139, 142, 143,
    166, 167, 174, 191, 194, 195, 265,
    369
Goshawk, 180, 182, 313, 325, 332, 348
Grasshopper warbler, 175, 196, 369
Great grey owl, 348
Great horned owl, 335, 348
Great spotted cuckoo, 369
Gregarious hunting. *See* Group hunt-
    ing; Hunting techniques
Grey heron, 369
Group attack, 239, 252
Group defense, 239, 252, 269
Group hunting, 110, 137, 138, 154,
    155, 297
Growth rate, 67–77, 296; specific his-
    tories, 69–76
Gulls, 81, 223, 237, 238, 252, 258, 334.
    See also individual species
Gypaëtus barbatus, 358, 381. *See also*
    Bearded vulture
Gyrfalcon, 327, 332, 333, 336, 348,
    351

Haliaeëtus albicilla, 381
Hare, on island cliffs, 19

Harriers, 316, 332, 354. *See also indi-
    vidual species*
Hatching time, 59, 61, 296; early
    breeder, 65; mean date, 65
Hawks, 58, 81, 141, 238, 313, 316, 324,
    328, 332, 348, 356. *See also individual
    species*
Hempitera, 163
Hen harrier, 354
Herons, 118, 238
Herring gull, 18, 21, 22, 238; as falcon
    competitor, 102
Hieraaëtus fasciatus, 380
Hieraaëtus pennatus, 380
Hippoboscidae, 78
Hippolais, 170, 376, 377
Hippolais icterina, 372
Hippolais olivetorum, 372
Hippolais pallida, 372
Hippolais polyglotta, 372
Hirundo rustica, 369, 372
History of discovery, 310–12
Hobbies (falcon group), 305–9, 312
Hobby (European hobby), 51, 59, 61,
    82, 272, 287, 305, 316, 325, 332,
    333; territorial model, 336–37
Home range, 333, 334–41, 355
Hooded crow, 57
Hoopoe, 141, 143, 159, 166, 169, 171,
    174, 191, 194, 195, 198, 368, 369
Human impact: biocides, 317–21; bird
    watchers, 315; coexistence, 321;
    establishment of island reserves,
    321; fishermen, 314, 321; hunters,
    316; law enforcement, 321; on
    Europe since last glaciation, 305;
    photographers, 316; prospects for
    future, 321–22; taxidermy, 315;
    tourists, 315
Human predators, 239, 316, 318, 322
Hunting area, 85, 86–87, 97, 103, 105,
    107; in Madagascar, 285
Hunting behavior, 84–112, 133; bird
    prey, 84–112; before breeding sea-
    son, 143–49; division of labor, 84;
    excerpts from diary, 382–83; in
    Madagascar, 283–85; "selfishness,"
    110
Hunting efficiency, 135, 136
Hunting period, 85, 87,.98, 103, 105–
    6, 107, 108, 112, 298
Hunting strategies, 110, 137, 154, 155,

297. *See also* Hunting techniques
Hunting success, 108, 123, 134–38,
    140, 188, 297, 298; model, 136
Hunting techniques: from April to
    July, 143–58; during calm weather,
    96; group or team hunting, 104,
    110, 137–38; height above sea level,
    87, 97, 104, 105; in Madagascar,
    283–85; search flight, 102, 104,
    106, 107, 109; standing flight,
    89–95, 99, 104, 106, 107, 109, 111;
    at wave level, 95, 100, 104
Hymenoptera, 163

Icterine warbler, 174, 175
Icterus, 300
Impact on bird migration, 184–88,
    201; predation rate, 187; seasonal
    impact, 187; total daily impact, 187
Incubation, 59–61, 212–14
Indigo bunting, 300
Individuals, characters of, 223, 229,
    236
Infertility, 320–21. *See also* Fertility
Insect-hawking, 144–49, 150, 152,
    154, 156, 179, 283–85
Invertebrates, 18, 21, 135, 137,
    144–49, 157; ants, 144, 147, 149,
    163, 165; arthropods, 144, 146,
    147, 149, 155; beetles, 21, 144, 147,
    156, 163, 165, 180; butterflies, 96,
    163; centipedes, 145, 164, 165;
    cicadas, 144, 163; crustaceans, 145,
    164, 165; dragonflies, 96, 144, 145,
    146, 148, 156, 163, 165, 180;
    feather lice, 78; grasshoppers, 136,
    144, 145, 163, 165; insects, 96, 102,
    144–49, 156–57, 163, 165, 179; lo-
    custs, 96, 156, 163, 165; louse flies,
    78; moths, 21, 96, 149, 162, 163;
    snails, 145, 164, 165; sow bugs, 145,
    164, 165; termites, 149, 273; ticks,
    78; wasps, 163
Isolating mechanisms, 295, 306–9
Ixobrychus minutus, 167, 370

Jaegers (skuas), 258, 347
Jynx torquilla, 370, 377

Kestrel (common kestrel of Europe),
    57, 59, 61, 81, 89, 141, 180, 210,
    263, 265; territorial behavior, 234,

252, 328, 329; territory, 332, 333,
    338
Kestrels, 306, 328, 329, 330. *See also
    individual species*
Killing the prey, 141–42
Kingfisher, 167
Kites, 316, 332

Lacerta erhardii, 18, 164, 264
"Landscape" factor, 268
Lanius, 368, 372
Lanius collurio, 167, 185, 372, 376
Lanius minor, 372, 376
Lanius nubicus, 372
Lanius senator, 101, 142, 149, 167, 168,
    275, 372, 376, 377
Lanner falcon, 141, 306, 336; hunting
    success, 137
Lark, 167
Larus argentatus, 18, 102. *See also* Her-
    ring gull
Larus atricilla, 49, 110
Larus audouinii, 18
Larus occidentalis, 42
Larus ridibundus, 43
Laughing gull, 110, 254
Lepidoptera, 96
Lesser grey shrike, 169, 173, 174,
    191–92, 304
Lesser kestrel, 57, 59, 61, 316, 333;
    dimorphism index, 351; dominance
    system, 344; morphology, 328–29;
    ovaries, 360; territoriality, 337, 340,
    341
Lizards, 145; density on falcon cliffs,
    19; as commensals of Eleonora's
    falcon, 19
Locustella fluviatilis, 372
Locustella naevia, 369, 372, 377
Locustella spp., 372
Long-tailed jaeger, 298
Lookout posts, 223, 225
Luscinia luscinia, 369, 374
Luscinia megarhynchos, 374, 376, 377
Luscinia svecica, 374

Madagascar, as wintering area, 273–
    80; climate, 278; falcon records,
    383–84; geography, 277, 292;
    habitats, 279; topography, 277
Madagascar broad-billed roller, 294
Madagascar kestrel, 282

Mallophaga, 78
Mallorca colonies: hunting of migrants, 104–7, 111, 112; insect-hawking, 150–51; population census, 36
Mammals as prey, 164
Manx shearwater, 18
Marsh harrier, 369
Marsh hawk, 335
Measurements, 10
Mechanisms of adaptation, 267–69, 295
Melodious warbler, 169
Melolonthinae, 163
Merlin, 136, 333, 336–37, 348, 351
Merops apiaster, 370
Metabolic rate, 177–84; Basal Metabolic Rate (BMR), 177–78, 181; Daily Energy Expenditure (DEE), 178–83; of young birds, 182; of young falcons, 181–83
Micrathene whitneyi, 353, 358
Migration. *See* Bird migration
Milvus migrans, 263, 332, 381
Milvus milvus, 381
Mockingbirds, 350
Mogador (study colony): biotic factors, 21; bird migration pulse, 125–30; bird remains, 168–77, 200, 377; breeding density, 41; breeding success, 51–53, 366; characters of nest sites, 44–47; clutch size, 51–53; color phase ratio, 38, 364; comparative analysis, 295–98; departure from colony, 271; egg-laying time, 60; habitat description, 19–21; hatching period, 63–64; hunting area, 97; hunting period, 98, 112; hunting strategies, 111; hunting techniques, 99–102, 109, 110; incubation, 60–61; insect-hawking, 148, 149, 150; nest sites, 44–47; physical factors, 20–21; spacing of nest sites, 41; territorial behavior, 222–23, 229
Monticola saxatilis, 374
Monticola solitarius, 369, 374
Moorhen, 369
Morphology: adaptive value, 324–30; barred and streaked patterns, 324–30; distance-reducing signals, 327;

function of, 324–30; optical signals, 327
Mortality, 77–83, 296
Motacilla alba, 369
Motacilla flava, 95, 123, 143, 369, 372
Murre, acoustic communication, 254
Muscicapa striata, 170, 369, 372, 376, 377

Neophron percnopterus, 381
Nest scrape, 44
Nest site: character, 44–47; dimensions, 44, 46, 364; exit direction, 48; occupancy, 342–43; quality, 341–43; selection, 44–51, 341; type, 44–46, 355
Niche, structural, 50
Night heron, 369
Nightingale, 167, 169, 173, 174, 175, 191, 194, 195, 196, 197, 198, 304
Nightjar, 138, 167, 194, 195, 294, 369
Nonbreeding season, 270–94; absence from Mediterranean during, 272; activities, 280–84; behavior, 280; departure from breeding area, 270–72; discussion, 290–94; ecology, 293–94; feeding, 280; interspecific competition, 294; population size, 293; records from the Indian Ocean area, 383–84
Nyctycorax nyctycorax, 369

Odonata, 96, 163
Ökoschema. *See* Spatial perception
Oenanthe hispanica, 369, 374
Oenanthe oenanthe, 274, 369, 374, 376
Oenanthe spp., 374
Oniscidae, 145, 164
Ontogeny, 262–66, 269
Oriole. *See* Golden oriole
Orioles (of North America), 300
Oriolus oriolus, 96, 142, 143, 369, 374, 376
Orphean warbler, 142, 169, 175, 191, 193
Orthoptera, 96, 163
Osprey, hunting success, 135, 137
Otus scops, 138, 370
Ovary: and body size, 359–60; and evolution of reversed sexual

dimorphism, 359; retention of two functional ovaries in many raptors, 356

Owls, 58, 167, 324, 330, 356. *See also individual species*

Pair bond, 210–12
Pandion haliaëtus, 135, 380
Parasites, 78
Parasitic jaeger, 81, 239
Partridge, 49
Parus spp., 374
Passer hispaniolensis, 369, 374
Passerina cyanea, 300
Passerines, 113, 115, 139, 142, 143, 157, 275
Paximada (study colony): biotic factors, 17; bird migration pulse, 122–25; bird remains, 168–77, 200, 376; breeding density, 40; breeding success, 51–53, 365; clutch size, 51–52; color phase ratio, 37–38, 48, 364; comparative analysis, 295–98; departure from colony, 271; egg-laying time, 59–60; fauna, 18–19; flora, 17–18; growth rate of young, 69–72; habitat description, 16–18; hatching period, 61–63; hunting area, 86–87; hunting of migrants, 86–96, 111; hunting period, 87, 88, 112; hunting techniques, 89–96; incubation period, 60; insect-hawking, 155–57; nest site, 44; physical factors, 17; population census, 33; spacing of nest sites, 40; territorial behavior, 218–22
Pecking order, 245
Pellets, 161–62, 163, 165
Perches, 223, 225
Perdix perdix, 49
Peregrine falcon, 2, 5, 21, 56, 58, 81, 82, 110, 141, 142, 180, 254, 261, 264, 306, 316, 325, 348; breeding behavior, 343; breeding density, 332; ecological separation on Mallorca, 105; hunting success, 136–37; pair bond and dominance, 253; reversed sexual dimorphism, 351; sexual behavior, 205, 207, 208; similarity to Eleonora's falcon, 9; territory, 234, 333, 336–37; use for

falconry, 311–14; vocalizations, 257, 258
Pernis apivorus, 381
Phalacrocorax aristotelis, 18
Phase ratio, 37–38, 48, 296, 364. *See also* Color phase
Philopatry, 211, 212
Phoenicurus ochruros, 374
Phoenicurus phoenicurus, 374, 376, 377
Phrygana vegetation, 16
Phylloscopus, 141, 169, 170, 177, 196, 201, 368, 372, 376, 377
Phylloscopus bonelli, 372
Phylloscopus collybita, 372
Phylloscopus sibilatrix, 372
Phylloscopus trochilus, 94, 123, 169, 369, 372
Pied flycatcher, 169, 174, 175
Pipits, 167, 369
Plover, 167
Poecilemon cretensis, 163
Population: census problems, 23, 32–33; decline, 31, 36; dynamics, 36–37; number of nonbreeding birds, 29; regional, 28; size in Madagascar, 293; status, 23–31; total breeding, 25; world, 29
Population estimates: maximum, 28; mean, 25; minimum, 25; regional, 28
Portunidae, 145
Porzana parva, 370
Porzana porzana, 370
Prairie falcon, 334–36, 348, 351
Predator/prey relationships, 345–47; and clutch size, 345; and reversed sexual dimorphism, 355; and timing of breeding season, 346
Predators. *See* Enemies
Preening, 223, 225
Prey: biomass, 177–88, 298; composition, 368; dispersion, 355; piracy, 239–41, 267–69; remains, 161–202, 297; size, 355
Production feeding, 345
Productivity, 58–59
Puffinus puffinus, 370

Quail (European), 115, 166, 172, 175, 194, 195, 197, 198

Rabbits, on island cliffs, 21
Raptors, 49, 50, 118, 316, 317, 318, 323, 324, 348, 356; breeding density, 330–33; dimorphism (*see* Reversed sexual dimorphism); morphology 323–24; nest-site quality, 342; occupancy rates, 342–43; research on, 360–61; selection of nest sites, 44–51, 341; territory, 333–41. *See also individual species*
Rattus rattus alexandrinus, 18, 80
Raven, 22, 81, 350
Red-backed shrike, 167, 169, 171, 174, 177, 185, 191, 192, 194, 195, 201, 304
Red-footed falcon, 57, 59, 61, 272, 287; dominance, 246; morphology, 330; nest-site occupancy, 342; territory, 236, 330, 334, 339–41
Redstart, 169, 173, 174, 175, 191, 194, 195, 196, 197, 198, 304, 369
Red-tailed hawk, 335
Red-throated pipit, 304
Regulus spp., 374
Reproductive success. *See* Breeding, success
Reproductive system, and reversed sexual dimorphism, 356, 359, 360
Reptiles: lizards on falcon cliffs, 19; skinks and geckos on falcon cliffs, 21; as falcon prey, 164–65
Residence status, 355
Reversed sexual dimorphism, 9, 10, 250, 324, 330, 347–60; and avian energetics, 349; characters affecting the degree of, 354, 356; correlation with ecology and behavior, 354; debate on, 347–50; dimorphism indexes, 350; extreme examples of, 348; female's size increase, 353; in hole-nesting species, 353; magnitude of, 354; major hypotheses, 349; multifactor model, 356, 357; probability of, 355
Riparia riparia, 65, 372
Rivalry, intraspecific, 241–48, 266–69
Rock dove. *See* Rock pigeon
Rock pigeon, 18, 21, 22, 223, 237
Rook, 87, 236, 339
Rough-legged hawk, 47
Rufous warbler, 175
Runt, growth rate of, 68, 72, 346

Saker falcon, 325, 336; team hunting, 137; territoriality, 337
Salé study colony: breeding density, 41; breeding success, 55; color phase ratio, 39; hatching period, 64; hunting of migrants, 103–4, 111; nest sites, 47; population census, 36; territory, 229
Saltatoria, 163
San Pietro study colony: breeding density, 42; egg-laying time, 60; hunting in July, 151–55; hunting of migrants, 107–8, 111, 112; nest sites, 47; population census, 36; bird migration pulse, 131; territory, 229
"Sapphire falcon," 311
Saxicola rubetra, 368, 369, 374, 376, 377
Scolopendra, 145, 164
Scops owl, 138, 169, 194, 195
Screech owl, 48
Selection, 138. *See also* Adaptation; Evolution
Selective hunting, 138–41
Sexual behavior, 205–17, 269; comparative ethology, 345; copulation, 208–10, 249, 250; courtship, 207–8, 248–50; display of male, 205–7; pair bond, 207; pair formation, 207; postures, 205–7; site fidelity, 210
Shag (common cormorant), 18, 21, 22
Sharp-shinned hawk, 348
Short-toed eagle, 369
Short-toed lark, 141, 173, 191, 198, 368
Shrikes, 114, 140, 141, 166, 167, 185, 188, 191–93, 350, 368. *See also individual species*
Site fidelity, 210, 212
Skinks, 21
Small warblers, 85, 94, 169, 171, 172, 177, 191, 201
Snakes, 58
Sociability, 331, 336; degree of, 343, 353; gradient of, 340; versus sex size, 354, 355
Sociobiology, 295, 323, 361
Sooty falcon, 86; delayed egg-laying, 345, 346; evolution, 305–9; hunting in pairs, 137; hunting success, 137; in Madagascar, 282–85; morphol-

ogy, 327; similarity to Eleonora's falcon, 9; territoriality, 338, 340, 341
Spacing of nest sites. *See* Breeding, density
Spanish sparrow, 369
Sparrows, 167
Spatial perception, 49
Speciation, 305–9
Speotyto cunicularia, 353, 358
Spotted flycatcher, 170, 174, 175, 369
Spring migration, 285, 288
Sprosser, 369
Squacco heron, 369
Standing flight. *See* Hunting techniques
Starlings, 271
Stauronotus maroccanus, 163
Stellio vulgaris, 145, 164
Stercorariidae, 347
Stercorarius parasiticus, 81, 239
Stones in falcon pellets, 164
Streptopelia turtur, 138, 369, 370
Strigiformes, 347
Study methods, 203–5
Sturnus vulgaris, 271
Subalpine warbler, 191, 193
Sunbathing behavior, 223, 225, 233
Swainson's hawk, 335
Swallows, 118, 139, 188, 198, 294
Swift (common swift), 167, 169, 194, 195, 369
Swifts, 21, 138, 139, 151, 188, 198, 294
Switch from insect-hawking to hunting of birds, 149–58; Mallorca colonies, 150–51; Paximada colony, 155; San Pietro colony, 151–55
Sylvia borin, 144, 372, 377
Sylvia cantillans, 372, 377
Sylvia communis, 85, 167, 168, 170, 368, 369, 372, 376, 377
Sylvia conspicillata, 372
Sylvia curruca, 372
Sylvia hortensis, 85, 142, 377
Sylvia nisoria, 372
Sylvia spp., 372
Sylvia warblers, 193

Tanagers, 300
Tawny pipit, 369
Terns, 110, 125, 167, 252
Terrain complexity, 233–35, 267–69

Territorial behavior, 218–36
Territoriality of falcons, 336–37
Territory: "central places," 223; food caching in, 219, 233; micro-, 268; mobility graphs, 228, 230–33, 236; mobility within, 223–33; model, 233–35, 266–69; of other falcon species, 333–41, 355; overlap, 226–27; as playground for young, 233; shape, 218–23; size, 218–23, 229; use of, 223–33
Thraupidae, 300
Threat posture, 241
Thrushes, 167, 300
Trans-Saharan migrants, 138, 202, 295, 297
Tree pipit, 174, 369
Tree spurge, 17
Trichophaga abruptella, 162
Trichophaga tapetzella, 162
Tringa hypoleucos, 369, 370, 382
Tringa ochropus, 370
Turdidae, 300
Turdus iliacus, 374
Turdus merula, 374
Turdus philomelos, 374
Turdus pilaris, 374
Turnstone, 369
Turtle dove, 115, 138, 194, 195, 369
Tyrannidae, 300
Tyto alba, 323

Ultimate factors, 325, 356
Upupa epops, 143, 159, 368, 369, 370, 376
Uria aalge, 254

Vegetation, postglacial changes in, 304–5
Vertebrates as prey, 137
Vireonidae, 300
Visual control, 49
Visual privacy factor, 49, 50, 268–69, 341
Visual stimuli, 266
Vocalizations, 255–62, 343; of adults, 257–62, 266; alarm calls, 260–62; begging calls, 261, 262; recognition call, 257; sound spectrograms, 255, 256, 259, 260; territorial call, 257; of young, 260–62

Vultures, 332, 354. *See also individual species*

Waders, 125, 200
Wagtails, 139
Warblers, 114, 140, 141, 188, 193–94, 198, 300, 304, 368. *See also individual species*
Weight, 9–10
Wheatear (northern), 144, 174, 191, 274, 304, 369
Whinchat, 141, 169, 174, 175, 191, 196, 197, 198, 304, 368, 369
"Whirling" behavior, 240
Whitethroat, 85, 141, 167, 168, 169, 170, 174, 175, 191, 193, 194, 195, 201, 368, 369
White wagtail, 369

Willow warbler, 94, 123, 169, 174, 175, 193, 194, 195, 196, 369
Woodchat shrike, 101, 142, 149, 167, 168, 169, 171, 172, 173, 174, 175, 191–95, 201, 304
Wryneck, 167, 175, 197, 304

Yellow-billed cuckoo, 300
Yellow wagtail, 95, 123, 143, 369
Young: at night, 108; behavioral development, 262–66, 269; behavior at hatching time, 262–63; biomass, 182; competition between siblings, 265; energy expenditure, 183, 184; experimental exchange of, 74, 76; food requirements, 181–84, 185; locomotion and senses, 264–65; spatial behavior, 263–64; typical growth curve, 182, 183